FROM SLAVERY TO

AGRARIAN CAPITALISM

IN THE COTTON

PLANTATION SOUTH

D1457394

The Fred W. Morrison

Series in Southern Studies

FROM
SLAVERY
TO
AGRARIAN
CAPITALISM
IN THE
COTTON
PLANTATION
SOUTH

Central Georgia, 1800–1880

FRANKLIN PIERCE
COLLEGE LIBRARY
RINDGE, N.H. 03461

JOSEPH P. REIDY

THE UNIVERSITY OF NORTH CAROLINA PRESS

CHAPEL HILL AND LONDON

© 1992 The University of North Carolina Press
All rights reserved
Manufactured in the United States of America

The paper in this book meets the guidelines for permanence and
durability of the Committee on Production Guidelines for Book
Longevity of the Council on Library Resources.

99 98 97 96 95   6 5 4 3 2

Library of Congress Cataloging-in-Publication Data
Reidy, Joseph P. (Joseph Patrick), 1948–
From slavery to agrarian capitalism in the cotton plantation South :
central Georgia, 1800–1880 / by Joseph P. Reidy.
p.   cm.—(The Fred W. Morrison series in Southern studies)
Includes bibliographical references and index.
ISBN 0-8078-2061-x (cloth : alk. paper)—
ISBN 0-8078-4552-3 (pbk. : alk. paper)
1. Plantations—Georgia—History—19th century.   2. Agricultural
laborers—Georgia—History—19th century.   3. Afro-Americans—
Georgia—Economic conditions.   4. Agriculture—Economic
aspects—Georgia—History—19th century.   5. Slavery—Georgia—
History—19th century.   6. Capitalism—Georgia—History—19th
century.   I. Title.   II. Series.
HD1471.U52G47   1992
306.3'49—dc20   92-53620
                                                                CIP

Material in chapters 1 through 4 has appeared in slightly different
form as "Obligation and Right: Patterns of Labor, Subsistence, and
Exchange in the Cotton Belt of Georgia, 1790–1860," in *Cultivation
and Culture: Labor and the Shaping of Slave Life in the Americas*, edited
by Ira Berlin and Philip D. Morgan (Charlottesville: University Press
of Virginia, 1993). Reprinted with permission from the
University Press of Virginia.

To my parents,

Isabel D. Reidy and Patrick J. Reidy,

with love

CONTENTS

. . . .

Conclusion
From Slavery to Agrarian Capitalism in Larger Perspective   242

ILLUSTRATIONS

.   .   .   .

MAPS

. . . .

ACKNOWLEDGMENTS

· · · · · · · · ·

THE MANY YEARS this study has been in preparation have sweetened the joy of thanking those who offered assistance along the way. I owe the greatest thanks to my family. In dedicating the book to my parents, I offer back a small fraction of what they have given. I thank my daughters, Rachel and Megan, for their love and patience, and for keeping my feet on the ground while my head was in the clouds. I owe special gratitude to my wife and best friend, Patricia, for tolerating my preoccupation with this project and for not letting me forget that there are other things in life besides books.

Although somewhat easier to measure, my intellectual debts are no less difficult to repay. I owe most to Otto H. Olsen, who encouraged this project through the years and who unselfishly offered friendship along with sage advice. I am similarly grateful to Fred J. Carrier for introducing me to the joys and challenges of studying history and to Herbert Aptheker for first piquing my interest in slavery and emancipation. During my association with the Freedmen and Southern Society Project I had the incomparable good fortune of working with Ira Berlin, Leslie S. Rowland, Barbara J. Fields, Michael K. Honey, Steven Hahn, Thavolia Glymph, Steven F. Miller, Julie Saville, Wayne K. Durrill, Susan Bailey, Lorraine Lee, and Terrie Hruzd. Colleagues and students, especially at Howard University, also contributed innumerable insights for which I am grateful; of these, Adele Logan Alexander bears particular mention.

Special thanks go to those who commented upon various drafts of the manuscript; in addition to persons already mentioned, these include Stanley Engerman, Eric Foner, Eugene D. Genovese, Pierre Gravel, Carl P. Parrini, Lawrence N. Powell, and Alfred F. Young. Thomas Holt made particularly valuable suggestions during the late stages of revision. I benefited immensely from participating in two conferences at which I presented portions of this research: "Power and Authority in Southern History" at the University of California, Irvine, and "Cultivation and Culture" at the University of Maryland. Thanks to

Steven Hahn and Michael P. Johnson and to Ira Berlin and Philip D. Morgan, respectively, for the invitations to take part in these exciting proceedings.

I am also beholden to Nan E. Woodruff, Pete Daniel, and Peter Wallenstein for timely advice at critical junctures. At the University of North Carolina Press, I wish to thank Lewis Bateman for his patience, Pamela Upton for her technical expertise, and Mary Reid for her keen editorial eye.

My debts also extend to the archivists and librarians who provided research assistance. As historians of the Civil War and Reconstruction well understand, the National Archives is a treasure-trove; I am especially grateful to the late Sara D. Jackson and to Michael P. Musick for pointing the way to the gold. Archivists at Atlanta University, Duke University, the Georgia Department of Archives and History, the University of Georgia, and the University of North Carolina at Chapel Hill unselfishly shared their expertise, as did librarians at Northern Illinois University, the University of Delaware, the University of Maryland, and Howard University.

For financial assistance I am indebted to the graduate fellowship program at Northern Illinois University and to the Department of History and the office of the Vice President for Academic Affairs at Howard University.

FROM SLAVERY TO

AGRARIAN CAPITALISM

IN THE COTTON

PLANTATION SOUTH

INTRODUCTION

· · · · · · · · · ·

ON A STILL WINTER'S MORNING four days before Christmas in 1848, two slaves living in Macon, Georgia, set out upon a fateful journey. William Craft, a cabinetmaker, and his wife, Ellen, a house servant, blew out the lights in Ellen's apartment, said a prayer, embraced, and stepped into the yard, locking the door behind them. By separate routes they proceeded to the railway station and enacted a bold plan by which they achieved freedom and assumed a prominent place in the struggle against slavery in the United States.[1]

For months, if not years, before their escape, the Crafts had contended with the nearly "insurmountable difficulties" of crossing approximately 1,000 miles of hostile territory.[2] Both before and after their marriage (apparently around 1845) they formulated a number of plans, abandoning each in turn. But as the holiday season of 1848 approached, they spent four sleepless nights perfecting a foolproof scheme. Representing their intention to visit a sick aunt of Ellen's, the two secured passes from their masters. Under that cover, they headed north, not through dense woods and underbrush after dark, but upon railroad cars and steamships in broad daylight.

With her hair cut short, her head and arm wrapped in poultices, and a pair of green spectacles covering her eyes, Ellen posed as a rheumatic young white man en route to Philadelphia for medical treatment. William played the part of an accompanying servant. They traveled by rail to Savannah, by ship to Charleston (where they spent a night in a hotel) and to Wilmington, North Carolina, then by rail again for the final leg of the journey. On several occasions they faced detection but handled each situation with aplomb. They reached Philadelphia on Christmas day. At the advice of abolitionists with whom they took refuge, they continued on to Boston.

As whispering voices spread the word of the escape, masters either cringed or fumed while slaves prayed for success. After all, both William and Ellen had led relatively privileged lives. Yet slaves commiserated with the innumerable indig-

Ellen Craft in the disguise worn when she escaped from slavery
(Reprinted from [Craft], *Running a Thousand Miles for Freedom*)

nities that even favored slaves endured. William's parents and his brother had been sold away when he was a boy. At age sixteen he was separated from his sister without so much as the privilege of bidding her farewell.[3] Ellen had light skin, after her father who was her master. Her mistress resented Ellen's presence in the household and looked for a way to remove the objectionable child. The wedding of a daughter provided the opportunity, and at age eleven Ellen was given as a present to her half-sister. Prior to the Crafts' bid for freedom, two of Ellen's cousins had gained local notoriety by escaping. Not content with his own freedom, one returned disguised as a white man to liberate two younger siblings. William later remembered "being highly delighted" by those proceedings, as no doubt were slaves throughout central Georgia.[4]

In contrast, masters viewed the episode through the lens of the growing sectional tension following the Mexican War. The escape confirmed widespread fears of abolitionist influence among the slaves. Dispelling such apprehension required northerners to comply strictly with the new fugitive slave law, but the early signs pointed in the wrong direction. When slavecatchers tracked William and Ellen to Boston late in 1850, they failed to persuade the couple to return. Upon learning of the encounter, a crowd of abolitionists unceremoniously ushered the agents out of town. Robert Collins, the husband of Ellen's mistress and a prominent Unionist politician in Macon, thereupon wrote to the attorney general of the United States seeking federal assistance in apprehending the couple.

Collins argued the case on several levels. Retrieving "their Services, or their value" was one objective, Collins wrote, "but it is more important to us as Slaveholders that they Should be brought back as an example to prevent others from doing, or trying to do, as they have done." "[T]he romantic manner of their escape, the incidents of their travel, and their many introductions at abolition meetings" caused considerable embarrassment. Projecting his personal woes on a broader screen, Collins claimed that "the peace and harmony of the Country" required extradition, for "the very salvation of the Union depends upon the proper and faithful execution of the Fugitive Slave law." In sum, the interests of doing "Justice" to the aggrieved slaveholders, maintaining proper subordination among the slaves, and preserving harmony between the sections necessitated federal intervention.[5]

Although the attorney general took no action, the Crafts decided not to press their luck and took refuge in England, where they remained for the next two decades. During that time, they became deeply involved in a wide range of abolitionist activity that kept them in the public eye on both sides of the Atlantic.

Late in 1852, following the publication of stories in the American press that she wished to return to Georgia and slavery, Ellen affirmed that she had "never had the slightest inclination whatever of returning to bondage." "I had much rather starve in England, a free woman," she declared, "than be a slave for the best man that ever breathed upon the American continent." Neither the threats nor enticements of their former masters could persuade the Crafts to forsake their new lives in freedom. Then the Civil War laid the matter to rest.[6]

For William and Ellen Craft, the Union's victory made possible their return home in 1869. By the mid-1870s they had settled on the coast of Georgia, where they established a vocational school for former slaves that survived until the end of the century. William took an active part in Republican party politics, serving as a delegate to the state and national party conventions in 1876.[7] The wartime destruction of slavery marked the dawn of a new era for them, rich with the prospects of individual fulfillment and the collective improvement of the former slaves.

William's former master, a transplanted New Yorker named Ira H. Taylor, drew different lessons from the war and emancipation. Profoundly "depressed" by the Reconstruction Acts and "crushed to despair at the present prospects of his once happy country," he took his own life in May 1867.[8] The end of the old order had destroyed his moorings; a world without slavery was more than he could bear.

THIS STUDY examines a typical South Atlantic cotton region over the course of several generations through the birth and death of slavery and the origins of capitalist agriculture. It describes how the actions of ordinary nineteenth-century Americans, like William and Ellen Craft, not only changed their own lives, but also affected the course of the nation's history. The larger framework is the profound changes through which the United States passed as a result of the maturation of industrial capitalism, first in Western Europe and then in the North. In practical terms, this meant that more and more of the inhabitants of the planet—especially those living in the subtropical and temperate zones— became drawn into producing goods for the expanding world market. Although this process occurred neither evenly nor irreversibly, its dynamic shaped the histories of affected societies and the lives of persons living within them.

From the dawn of the nineteenth century, the spirit of change permeated the Atlantic world. Paced by the Industrial Revolution in England and the political revolutions in the United States and France, merchant capitalism gave way to industrial capitalism.[9] Although the full effects of this transformation were not immediately apparent—and are still unfolding today—the immediate result was a rise in demand for raw materials to be processed into finished goods in the European metropolises. Largely in response to this new demand, European settlers fanned across the globe. Favoring the temperate zones both north and south of the equator, they moved eastward into Eurasia, westward into the interior regions of the Americas, and farther west still to Australia, New Zealand, and the islands of the Pacific. In one degree or another, these movements depended for their success (if not necessarily their initial impetus) upon the world market. If in Russia, Argentina, and Pennsylvania the link was wheat, in India, Mississippi, and Georgia it was cotton.[10]

Much recent scholarly debate has focused upon the extent to which world market forces affect societies whose members produce goods for international trade. At one extreme, partisans of the world-system perspective see the world market enforcing a worldwide division of labor that sorts all humanity into either bourgeoisie or proletariat.[11] Without denying the importance of world-market forces, other scholars have preferred to view the world market as a context within which human actors make the choices that ultimately shape their history. To understand that history thus involves careful analysis of the particular circumstances of any given society as well as knowledge of the opportunities and constraints that are a function of the state of the world market in any historical period. The following analysis of central Georgia operates within the latter framework.

THE STORY BEGINS with the economic and political revolutions of the late eighteenth century that advanced the spread of capitalism in the Atlantic basin.[12] New areas were drawn into the capitalist world economy, and areas that had been incorporated previously underwent additional change. The United States embodied both these tendencies.

In the North, the urban centers of the original colonies witnessed the rise of industrial capitalism and the eclipse of commercial capitalism. Although the process occurred unevenly, with movements backward as well as forward, a wealth of recent scholarship has demonstrated the general process. In short, the world of the craft artisan—centered in household production, social hierarchy, the transmission of skills, and the workers' control over the labor process—gave way to the world of the factory. Even in the rural centers of industry, factory owners consolidated control over production, despite workers' resistance to the development of capitalist relations of production, wherein they lost control over productive resources and had to exchange their labor power for a wage in order to purchase the necessities of life.[13]

Similar changes altered the fabric of farm life in the North. The increasing commercialization of agriculture, coupled with population growth and intensive land use, undermined traditional social relations based upon landed proprietorship, household-centered production, and the mutual exchange of goods and labor. Although rural areas of the original colonies felt these pressures most keenly, newly settled areas west of the Appalachian Mountains did not escape for long.[14]

South of the Mason-Dixon line, planters resisted these changes. They found themselves in no less trying a relationship with the world economy than did their northern counterparts, but they had a vested interest in preserving slavery. Aside from the matter of property, they had a new political stake thanks to the provisions of the federal Constitution. Planters in the Chesapeake region grappled with changing world-market conditions and lingering political effects of the independence struggle. Accordingly, they continued the shift from tobacco to wheat that they had begun during the mid-eighteenth century and emancipated or sold south their excess slaves, even while clinging fiercely to the principle of slavery.[15] But in South Carolina and Georgia, slaveholders found new commercial opportunities supplying raw material to the cotton factories in England, the seedbed of the Industrial Revolution. Settlers to the southern backcountry struggled not against the socially disintegrating effects of commercial agriculture, but rather against the challenging prospect of making the best of new commercial opportunities within the framework of the traditional master-slave relationship.

Like northern free labor, southern slavery provided the institutional foundation for a society divided along class lines. The recognition in law of human property conferred both privilege and power upon the masters that no northern employer even came close to approximating. Moreover, title in slave property also endowed masters with ownership over the natural increase of their chattels and everything that the slaves' labor produced. And slaveholders could demand of government special protection for their property rights, above and beyond those claimed by owners of every other kind of property. For, as Benjamin Franklin reportedly once asked, who ever heard of an insurrection of sheep?

Upon such a foundation, large slaveholders—the planters—established disproportionate economic and political power and social influence.[16] In numerous ways they resembled slaveholders throughout the Americas, though their prominent place within a federal government born of a bourgeois revolution also made them different. Southern planters wielded power at the local, state, regional, and national levels in such bodies as county courts, legislatures, and executive offices. They formed the core of southern agricultural societies and political parties; they served as trustees of churches, schools, and a host of public and fraternal groups and organizations. Their virtual monopoly over international cotton supplies guaranteed them powerful friends in the commercial and financial centers of the North and of Europe.

Notwithstanding this concentrated power, slaveholders could not take their supremacy for granted. Even apart from fluctuations in world market conditions and growing international scrutiny following the American and French revolutions, slave masters faced varying degrees of internal political opposition as well. Nonslaveholding yeomen conceded a large measure of power to the planters in return for shelter from the encroachment of unrestrained market forces. But the yeomen were citizens, every bit as protective of their political rights—rooted in traditional republican virtues—as were the planters of theirs. A democratic polity provided a framework for mediating certain differences, but it neither altered the hierarchical class structure nor eliminated the tensions that resulted from social inequality.[17]

Though unenfranchised, slaves throughout the Americas influenced local, national, and international politics. In central Georgia, as elsewhere in the southern United States, the influence percolated up from cotton fields and slave quarters. The chief arena of struggle was the master-slave relationship itself. Because this connection was ultimately personal, antebellum slavery defies facile generalization. What was general and constant was the slaves' effort not only to survive, but to wrest control over their bodies and their lives from their masters. Prior to the Civil War, comparatively few slaves won this struggle in the absolute sense of escaping their masters. But slaves pressed the quest for autonomous action and self-fulfillment in other, more achievable directions.

Most notably, they fashioned a distinctively African American culture, whose warp consisted of a series of strong institutions that took shape in plantation quarters, the most significant of which were families and religious organizations. The transfer of slaves from one master to another extended this fabric across plantation lines and, indeed, across the South. As the spatial foundation of this cultural renaissance, slave quarters became contested sites over which masters attempted to gain unquestioned control and slaves attempted to create and preserve what was distinctively theirs.[18]

Despite the keen insights that derive from such a perspective on slave communities, slaves at work, not slaves at rest, were the mainspring of the plantation system. Examining the organization and performance of field labor along the lines recently charted by colonial historians promises rich returns.[19] After the Revolution, as plantation agriculture spread beyond its colonial boundaries, masters and slaves struggled for control over field routines in the newly settled areas. Among its various components, this contest addressed such matters as the duration and intensity of labor, implements and techniques of cultivation, supervision, and time off. While producing staples such as cotton was the ultimate aim, considerable labor went into raising foodstuffs, in the interest of keeping slaves constantly occupied as well as supplying edibles. Although most of this production centered around raising grains (particularly corn) in plantation fields, it also encompassed slaves' seeking access to land for gardens and time to cultivate them. In other time that they established as their own, slaves also sought and often gained permission to hunt and to fish and to produce handicrafts; by the same token, they wished to barter or sell such items.

Throughout the Americas slaves produced goods for both home consumption and sale, though the incidence of such production in North America never approximated that characteristic of the Caribbean. In the islands, a slave family's provision grounds might extend to several acres, and in some instances slaves nearly monopolized the distribution of fresh produce through the institution of Sunday markets.[20] In one sense, the enjoyment of such privileges reinforced the slaves' allegiance to the larger system, but other, more subversive, consequences might also follow. Slaves who controlled their labor and its products during the time at their disposal might well wonder why they did not enjoy such control all the time.

Even as those larger issues awaited resolution, North American slaves pressed to transform such privileges granted by individual masters into rights honored by all.[21] The nature of this specific struggle not only varied from plantation to plantation, but also changed with time. Both masters and slaves attempted to take advantage of external and internal circumstances favorable to their objectives. The depression of the 1840s prompted a redefinition of the boundary of control; so, too, did the national political crisis of the 1850s, which occurred amidst an unprecedented cotton boom and an accompanying commercialization of life in the slave South. In each case, the interaction between slaves and masters reverberated beyond the boundaries of individual slaveholdings. When slaves pressed for the privilege of trading corn and chickens, for instance, masters frequently objected lest such authorization encourage theft and the consumption of alcohol. When slaves identified free persons willing to trade surreptitiously, masters understood that keeping slaves subordinate involved larger issues of social control, whose outcome they could not dictate unilaterally or influence by brute force alone. As they railed against the machinations of northern abolitionists, slaveholders understood the threat of homegrown subversives, slave and free. Masters properly sensed that the slaves' incessant and increasingly irresistible requests to take the train on visits to friends and relatives might one day provide cover for the escape of a William and an Ellen Craft.

And the war came. From within the heartland of the Confederacy, masters confidently assumed that slavery would provide the measure of victory against the North. Accordingly, they fashioned a defense based upon the proposition that slaves would labor on the home front, producing the food and fiber required by soldiers and civilians alike. In time, they expanded the slaves' role to include manufacturing the weapons of war, and, by the end of the war, they were willing to arm slaves in the last-ditch struggle for southern independence. Slaves did not mistake the changes that the mobilization wrought upon their lives. They witnessed a new vulnerability on the part of their once-invulnerable masters; the agents of change were Confederate impressment and tax officers, months before William Tecumseh Sherman set foot in Georgia.[22]

In struggling for self-fulfillment, slaves in wartime Georgia hastened their own freedom, the defeat of the rebellion, and the return of peace. But the peace would be no simple status quo ante bellum. Both psychologically and physically, the war destroyed slavery. Still, neither Lincoln nor the congressional Radicals misunderstood the importance of the Thirteenth Amendment to the Constitution of the United States.[23] Constitutional abolition demolished the legal foundation of the social class that had led the South to secession and the nation to war. In time, the Yankees' need to secure the peace necessitated imposition of military rule and passage of stringent legislation and additional constitutional amendments. As Eric Foner has recently demonstrated, Reconstruction in Washington can only be understood in the context of events in the South.[24] And as the growing body of comparative historical studies illustrates, events in the South can only be understood in the larger hemispheric context of slave emancipation.[25]

In the southern United States, the struggle between former masters and former slaves—which took up directly where the struggle between masters and slaves had broken off—fueled those events. With the legal foundation of the antebellum regime shattered, it remained for former masters and former slaves, under the oversight of the War Department's Bureau of Refugees, Freedmen, and Abandoned Lands, to pick up the pieces of the shattered system of slavery.

Two key tasks lay ahead: reconstructing the ravaged economy on the basis of the juridical freedom of the laborers and reincorporating the defeated states into the Union, with adequate provision that rebellion would not recur and that the emancipated slaves would enjoy government protection of their citizenship rights. From the national perspective, these developments largely reflected the Republican party's effort to consolidate power in the central state.[26] But from the perspective of ordinary citizens throughout the South, these changes entailed an extensive—and far from peaceful—process of renegotiating the conventions governing routine social interactions. Emancipation destroyed the old structure, and a new one had to take its place.

Economic reconstruction antedated Appomattox. Planting for 1865 had already begun amidst enormous confusion about the future. Where masters still held sway, they attempted to carry on as usual, but not generally with the full cooperation of their laborers. Too many masters had simply abdicated their responsibility to provide for their slaves, and too many slaves had freed themselves for the old rules to apply without question. Die-hard masters clung desperately to their prerogatives, and when Freedmen's Bureau officers began arriving in the Georgia upcountry (and other parts of the South) during the summer of 1865, they encountered some stubborn pockets of resistance holding out against hope that slavery had not expired with the Confederacy. Yet most former slaves and former masters agreed to terms whereby laborers would be compensated for their efforts, even if only in the traditional form of food, housing, and medical attention.

Bureau officials, from Gen. O. O. Howard at the top to the lowliest lieutenant in the field, placed the highest priority upon reshaping the labor system of the South. But their vision was predicated upon an ideal of free labor that was itself in a rapid state of flux. Recent changes in the North—particularly the growth of the factory system, whose operatives included large numbers of immigrant, female, and child laborers, and the emergence of a permanent class of dependent wage workers—undermined the traditional republican virtues of manly independence rooted in the ownership of productive property. New constellations of values were developing around the laborer's right to the fruits of his toil and the supposed juridical equality between employer and employee. Not all participants in the emerging labor markets shared the same set of ground rules, however.[27]

If the ideal did not fully match reality in the North, it bore even less relationship to conditions in the South. Although many Yankees fervently believed that free markets would spring fully blown from the ashes of slavery, events quickly proved otherwise. Neither former masters nor former slaves were accustomed to interrelating on the basis of compensated labor, much less juridical equality. Both sought to preserve favored elements of the old order while rejecting objectionable features of the new. To most northern observers, both parties required considerable remedial work before free labor could develop a momentum of its own.[28]

The federal program of political reconstruction addressed similar difficulties with similar handicaps. During the Presidential Reconstruction of 1865–66, former slaveholders—led by the self-styled moderates of antebellum Whiggish persuasion—regained much of what they had lost during the Civil War. Specifically, they retained control over the land and made huge strides toward restoring their former political power. Even as they rebuilt the bridges to Washington they had earlier burned, they seized control over the legislative process, masterminding a set of ordinances, quickly dubbed black codes, which aimed to circumscribe as closely as possible the former slaves' rights as laborers and citizens.[29]

In such circumstances, every aspect of the lives of the freedpeople assumed a political dimension that they may not necessarily have welcomed but could not for the life of them escape. How they worked, how they addressed white people, how they comported themselves in public, how they worshipped—all these matters and more became subjects of political contest, as former masters attempted to recapture the discipline and control over the labor force they had enjoyed before the war. More overt signs of independence in the form of schools, quasi-political organizations, and combinations among workers often met violent resistance. Both freedpeople and federal authorities struggled to contain the bloodshed while continuing the battle for the peace. Congress had little choice but to inaugurate Radical Reconstruction, imposing military rule on the South, disfranchising former Confederates, and granting the vote to black men.

As freedpeople fully appropriated these new protections into their struggle for autonomy and self-fulfillment, the resentment of former masters knew no bounds. From mid-1868 through 1871, the Republican party governed Georgia—a comparatively brief span when compared to the neighboring states of Alabama, where Republicans stayed in power until 1874, and Florida and South Carolina, where the party's rule persisted until 1876. Georgia Republicans bequeathed the state a mixed legacy. Despite promising early attempts to attract yeomen, former slaves were the major constituents. Although the new state constitution of 1868 laid the foundation for a liberal-capitalist political economy, state officials became more preoccupied with railroad speculation than with broad economic development, and they compromised the new commitment to state-sponsored social services through a combination of political bungling and fiscal mismanagement. The plea to the yeomen died aborning, and the secessionist coalition of planters and associated commercial interests got a new lease on life.

As northerners grew increasingly weary of the southern political charade, they shelved the notion of remaking the South in their own image, to be used for future reference against Indians of the Great Plains and Philippine "insurrectionists" later in the century. Leading Republicans at the national level chose instead to use the power and authority of the strengthened federal government to promote industrial development in the North and to make the Great Plains and Rocky Mountain regions safe for capital investment and Anglo-American settlement. Beyond insisting upon the jurisdiction of federal law and federal courts in the South, most northern officials and citizens were content to let former masters and former slaves thrash out the boundaries of the new social order on their own.

By 1880, its characteristic form was clear. On the agricultural front, former masters and former slaves had fought to a standstill, subsuming their differences within a system of tenancy. White landowners subdivided their holdings into plots of approximately forty acres, each one of which was worked by a black family. Although some black men (and a smaller number of black women) owned land outright, few could support themselves entirely from the produce of their marginal holdings. Most black agriculturists were tenants or sharecroppers, but at various times wage laborers constituted a relatively large or small segment of the agricultural work force. The proportion of rural whites who were tenants or laborers rather than farmers also grew over the last quarter of the nineteenth century, as a result of the turmoil of war and slave emancipation.[30]

Stereotypes to the contrary notwithstanding, postbellum tenancy demonstrated as much fluidity as rigidity, consistent with its purpose of providing a framework for struggle over the surplus agricultural product. Tenure relations evolved over time, often undergoing dramatic changes in the compass of a restricted space. Hence the decline in the status of sharecroppers was not inevitable.

In their attempt to gain maximum control over the crop, landowners undertook parallel initiatives to minimize the laborers' discretion over field routines and access to subsistence goods. Planter-businessmen aimed to reduce tenants (croppers, especially) into agricultural proletarians, divorced from productive resources and exchanging their labor power for subsistence. Freedpeople resisted subjection to the kind of controls that landowners seemed anxious to enforce. They sought the relative autonomy of rental tenure or, failing that, opted for subsisting themselves through a combination of casual labor (especially during the cotton harvest) and hunting and fishing. They were proletarians who resisted the full implications of proletarianization.

On the other side of the coin, landowners evolved into an agrarian bourgeoisie as part of the same process whereby the laborers became a rural proletariat. Politics both reflected these changes and contributed to their development. A combination of New South agrarians (consisting of antebellum planters and prosperous yeomen-turned-tenants who employed black laborers) and an emerging urban elite of merchants, creditors, and ginners assumed control over governmental affairs. Like local elites elsewhere in the world, they recognized the power of the world market and trimmed their sails accordingly. Though reluctant to toss overboard the ballast of tradition—particularly in the form of a modified paternalism—they ran strong before the winds of capitalist development.

1

. . . .

The World of
the Yeoman Settlers,
1800–1835

WILLIAM FAULKNER might just as believably have situated Yoknapatawpha County in central Georgia as in central Mississippi. In both areas a fairly large Native American population ceded its aboriginal homeland to European American settlers over the first four decades of the nineteenth century. Many of the newcomers brought with them slaves, sizable numbers of whom had been born in Africa. The migrants came largely from the Carolinas and Virginia. Few were slaveholding planters with their sights fixed upon carving cotton plantations from the wild. Many were hunters and trappers, traders, sharpers, or adventurers. Most were yeomen whose subsistence depended upon the cooperative efforts of family members and neighbors. However disparate their means of livelihood, the settlers prized the virtues of independent proprietorship and republican government.

In a comparative blink of an eye, the frontier areas took on the appearance of older settled areas. The hunters and trappers all but disappeared, and the ranks of Native Americans thinned even before their unceremonious removal west. Slaveholders became more numerous and the size of their holdings grew. Yet planters remained a distinct minority, despite the larger-than-life figures they often cut. For the first third of the nineteenth century, smallholding yeomen shaped the upcountry in their own image. They affected settlement patterns, agricultural practices, political and social institutions, and relations between masters and slaves. But to some extent they became victims of their own success. Cotton growers profited handsomely, often increasing their landholdings and slaveholdings. In time, they began to share the values and the worldview of their planter neighbors. Yeomen who wished to avoid commercial entanglements found it harder to maintain the necessary distance. The Thomas Sutpens were coming, with the Will Varners close behind.

FOLLOWING THE American Revolution settlers from all thirteen states headed west. Their motives varied, often reflecting religious and political considerations as well as the desire for fresh land. The sense of ebullience following victory over the British and the birth of the United States clearly played a part, and states both north and south of the Mason and Dixon line boosted this spirit by distributing available land. Westward moved the seeds of commercial agriculture and republican government.

Central Georgia has no definitive geological boundaries, but for present purposes it includes the six-county plantation area surrounding the city of Macon, approximately in the geographical center of the state.[1] The counties form a cluster with Bibb (the home of Macon) at the center, Jones to the northeast, Twiggs to the southeast, Houston to the southwest, Crawford to the west, and Monroe to the northwest. To the east is middle Georgia, an older plantation area wherein lies Milledgeville, the antebellum capital of the state, approximately thirty miles east of Macon. Roughly 100 miles farther to the east on the Savannah River lies Augusta, from colonial times a major upcountry market. Southwest Georgia, situated below Houston County, was the state's cotton frontier by the mid-nineteenth century.

Geographically, central Georgia straddles the fall line, running northeast to southwest, and the Ocmulgee River, flowing northwest to southeast. All of Monroe, most of Jones, and the northern halves of Bibb and Crawford counties lie above the line in the gently rolling hills of the lower Piedmont. There the humus from decaying hardwoods over millennia produced rich deposits of soil. On the flat coastal plain below the line lie Twiggs and Houston counties as well as the southern halves of Bibb and Crawford. Despite scattered areas of relative infertility, such as the sand hills along the fall line and the wire-grass region in eastern Twiggs, rich bottomlands along the Ocmulgee and its numerous tributaries alternated with sandier soils on the uplands. Both formations were ideally suited for agriculture. The freshness of the soil promised abundant yields of food and cash crops, an irresistible lure to occupants of tired lands in older agricultural areas.

Although slavery came late to Georgia, arriving only in the mid-eighteenth century, colonial settlers quickly viewed it as the key to their future prosperity.[2] On the eve of the Revolution, settlers had begun moving to the backcountry in pursuit of commercial gain as well as subsistence. Besides trading furs, livestock,

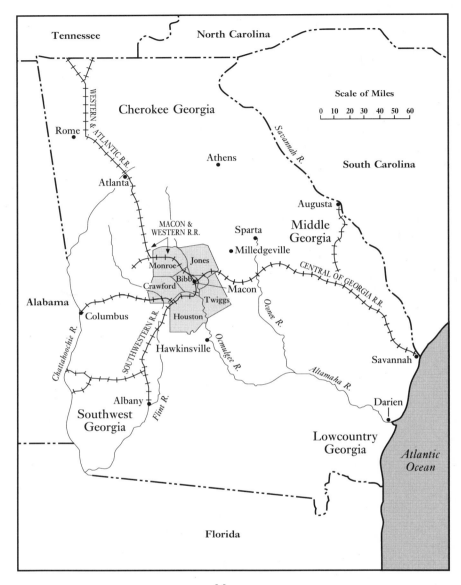

Map 1.
Georgia during the nineteenth century

Map 2.
Central Georgia

and other goods, they also raised tobacco.[3] By the mid-1790s, Eli Whitney's cotton gin inflamed the desire of coastal residents to put slaves to work on fresh soil. Over the next generation, white settlers and black slaves poured into the upcountry.

Like officials in other states, Georgia's lawmakers distributed land by lottery. Each adult male was eligible for 202½ acres (sometimes more) at nominal prices, with preference given to veterans of the Revolutionary War. Under pressure from state and national governments, the Creek Nation relinquished its aboriginal rights in a series of treaties: in 1802 to the land between the Oconee and the Ocmulgee rivers in the central part of the state; in 1821 westward to the Flint

River; and, finally, in 1826 all the way to the Chattahoochee River, Georgia's western boundary. Jones and Twiggs counties, east of the Ocmulgee, were organized in 1807 and 1809 respectively. Bibb, Houston, Monroe, and Crawford counties, west of the river, were organized in 1821 and 1822.[4]

From its founding in 1824, Macon served as the focal point of development in central Georgia, as in fact it had been for generations earlier. By virtue of its place at the fall line of a river that flowed to the sea, Creeks had long traded and held ceremonial gatherings there. The frontier trading outpost of Fort Hawkins was also located there. From the 1830s, as railroads began coursing through the interior, Macon's prominence grew. By the 1850s, it stood as the hub of lines stretching southeast to Savannah (the Central of Georgia), northwest to Atlanta (the Macon and Western) and southwest to Albany (the Southwestern Railroad). This network placed Macon in the center of not only the economic development of the upcountry, but political affairs and social and cultural life as well.

Each county boasted at least one commercial center of its own, though none quite as vibrant as Macon. The respective county seats—Forsyth in Monroe, Clinton in Jones, Marion in Twiggs, Perry in Houston, and Knoxville in Crawford—served as places of business and recreation as well as government service, from earliest days containing merchants' and artisans' shops, churches, and schools as well as the county courthouse. The other rural towns, such as Fort Valley in Houston County, offered comparable amenities.[5]

Through the 1830s, rivers and streams constituted the main commercial arteries. Improved roads (such as they were) generally led to river landings. Every major settlement, including Macon and the other county seats, was located along a waterway. Cotton moved to coastal markets aboard "pole boats," flats guided downriver by slaves using long poles. Until the dawn of the steamboat era in the 1820s, the vagaries of the Ocmulgee and its tributaries hampered the movement of goods back up the river from the coast. Most trade items arrived in central Georgia overland from Augusta, and, accordingly, commercial ties with the Savannah River towns of Augusta and Savannah remained strong. Advances from factors provided upcountry agriculturists with operating expenses during the growing season and capital for purchasing slaves and land. Although the railroads made river transportation obsolete, they reinforced Savannah's place as Macon's chief link to the commercial world.[6]

THE HISTORY OF central Georgia's rise to prominence is the history of King Cotton. In scarcely more than a generation, the area surrounding Macon devel-

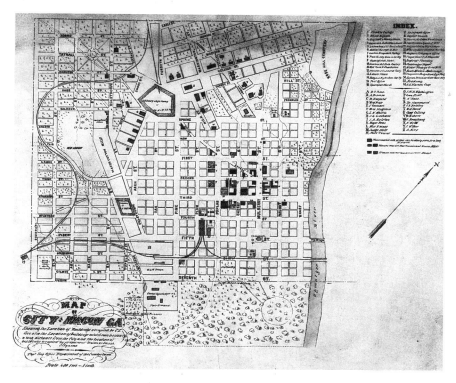

Map 3.
Macon, Georgia, 1865 (National Archives)

oped into the heartland of Georgia's upland cotton kingdom. Cotton grew there as nowhere else in the state, and cotton growers prospered apace. These changes transformed the social landscape as much as the physical one. In the early years of settlement, slaveless yeomen and small slaveholders predominated. Unlike smallholders in Georgia's upper Piedmont, where distance from markets would have made commercial agriculture difficult even had they desired to pursue it, smallholders who settled in central Georgia apparently integrated commercial cotton growing into a flexible and wide-ranging pattern of subsistence agriculture when circumstances permitted. These circumstances depended upon the nature of the soil they farmed, the composition of their immediate family and the strength and endurance of its members, the number and kind of their work stock, and—most important of all—whether or not they owned a slave. For slaveless yeomen, cotton assumed its place alongside corn, wheat, oats, barley, honey, eggs, and butter as items that could be consumed or sold as the household's needs required and local demand for such products allowed. But after crossing the Rubicon into purchasing a slave, there was no turning back: farm produce had to generate cash as well as subsistence. Slaves increased the burden of debt even as they eased the burden of work, and nothing canceled debts like cotton.

The white settlers of central Georgia came from three main directions (often after a stopover of several years or more in middle Georgia): the lowcountry of coastal Georgia and South Carolina, where rice and long-staple cotton sustained a true aristocracy during the colonial period; the tidewater of Virginia, where generations of tobacco monoculture had thrown the plantation order into disarray; and the backcountry stretching from the Carolinas to Pennsylvania, where smallholders from assorted backgrounds (including Scotch-Irish and German Protestant dissidents) pursued religious as well as economic independence. The newcomers sought resources—water supplies as well as soils—similar to those they left behind. In central Georgia the fall line provided a handy line of demarcation: migrants from the Piedmont tended to stay above the fall line; those from the coastal plain remained below it.[7]

Even by the standards of the nineteenth-century South, conditions on the frontier were primitive. Such roads as existed were generally old Indian trails that had been widened but not otherwise improved for wagon traffic. "[S]tumps and roots of fallen trees" were everywhere.[8] Rain turned the roads into quagmires; bridges were ramshackle in every season. Migrants moved most conveniently on foot or horseback.

Homesteaders from elsewhere in Georgia generally settled in two stages. At first only men (the master, his grown sons, and his adult male slaves) made the trip, clearing the land, erecting shelters, and planting a crop of corn. The second phase involved moving the rest of their families and property to the new home.[9] Migrants from greater distances made only one move, but rarely without advice from an advance party. In 1826, for instance, the family of James Rowe Coombs, with all its slaves and belongings, left North Carolina for Twiggs County in company with a group of neighbors. Joining a settlement of "old Carolina friends," they cleared land and began farming. In the settlement process, the web of kinship and friendship that ultimately formed civil society extended southwestward, weaving in new threads and extending old ones that stretched back to eastern Georgia and beyond.[10]

During the first settlement wave between 1800 and 1820, the white population of Jones and Twiggs counties grew from a mere handful to nearly 17,000, and the slave population reached nearly 12,000. During the 1820s, settlement

Log cabin in the forests of Georgia (Library of Congress)

west of the Ocmulgee produced a similar surge in population. Thereafter, in a pattern reminiscent of the older cotton counties in the eastern part of the state, the free white population declined while the slave population continued to grow.[11] In 1830, the white population in the six counties surrounding Macon stood at more than 33,000 and the slave population just under 25,000 (roughly 43 percent of the total).[12] By 1840, the white population declined to 31,000, and slaves achieved numerical parity. Macon and Bibb County had a white majority for the entire antebellum era, but slaves were a majority of the population in Jones County as early as 1830 and in Houston and Monroe counties by 1840 (see Appendix).

As population increased, so did cotton crops. Beginning in 1801, when 20,000 bales were raised in the state of Georgia, the total crop approximately doubled every decade until reaching 326,000 bales by the end of the 1830s. At that time, the six counties immediately surrounding Macon accounted for 50,000 bales, and Macon cleared through its markets nearly one-third of the state's total crop.[13] By 1840, Houston and Monroe counties ranked among the top five cotton-producing counties in the state. Within scarcely a generation, the Macon area had emerged as the heartland of King Cotton's Georgia domain.

Small planters with relatively few slaves accounted for this surge in cotton production. During settlement, as many as two-thirds of the settlers owned no slaves, at least half of the masters owned five or fewer slaves, and two-thirds of the slaves lived on holdings of twenty or less.[14] Surviving inventories of smallholders' estates indicate equally modest holdings of work stock and implements: horses or oxen generally provided animal traction, and plows were of a nondescript variety.[15] Hence the increase in cotton output resulted from the large number of settlers and their slaves applying their energy to the work.

Despite its other symptoms, cotton fever did not blind the early settlers to the need for self-sufficiency in foodstuffs and clothing. Accordingly, farmers' fields contained corn, wheat, oats, barley, potatoes, and even an occasional "Turnip patch"; their homes contained cotton cards, spinning wheels, and looms for making cloth.[16] The natural bounty of the wild provided assorted supplements, ranging from fruits, nuts, and berries (which could be used as cotton dye as well as food) to herbs and game. Like their contemporaries elsewhere throughout North America, yeomen in upcountry Georgia no doubt traded extensively for goods they did not produce. These items included firearms, coffee, gold watches, silverware, and mahogany furniture, some of which had traveled thousands of miles from the point of production, reversing the path traveled by the cotton grown in central Georgia.[17] It is likely that yeomen borrowed blacksmithing and carpentry tools from their more prosperous neighbors, given the scarcity of such items in smallholders' tool kits.[18] And farmers of every description traded labor services with each other, sometimes in collective efforts such as barn raisings, for which no accounts were kept, but also in private exchanges for which compensation in kind was expected.[19] The net result was a combination of market transactions and reciprocal exchanges of goods and services, which preserved a sense of communal mutuality against the unbridled influence of world market forces. During the early nineteenth century, such hybrid systems of labor and trade typified frontier areas in Europe and the Americas as they began producing commercial goods for export.

If at first cotton cultivation meant more work, investing profits in a slave could alleviate that problem. Thus commercial agriculture offered yeomen assorted benefits, including entry into the complex of privileges and values associated with slave ownership. Yet yeomen often found such reward as elusive as the fabled City of Gold. Cotton took time, energy, and resources away from subsistence. Because cash returns followed the harvest, farmers accumulated various debts (for seeds, tools, hardware, powder and shot) before they could settle their accounts. A succession of poor crops or a period of falling prices might entail foreclosure, tarnishing, if not destroying, the yeoman's dream of landed independence.

Slave ownership promised a measure of security from the vagaries of commercial agriculture even while exposing the master to a host of new risks. Slaves provided supplementary labor and an investment whose value appreciated. Yet there were the corresponding drawbacks of death, debilitating disease, accident, flight, or rebellion. In the circumstances, the person with the resources to invest in a single slave disproportionately purchased a woman of childbearing age. Slave women proved a good investment. They generally sold for less than first-class men, and each child born to the slave woman increased the master's capital without additional cost beyond that of support, which could be partially offset by the labor of the mother in field or home. Masters also considered women more tractable than men. Given the general dearth of cash through most of the antebellum period, such a strategy of capital accumulation appealed strongly to slaveless and small slaveholding yeomen.

The technique proved remarkably successful, especially among those whose limited holdings denied them access to regular channels of credit. Statistics of slave ownership patterns in Jones County establish the point. In 1820, 147 masters (not quite 10 percent of the total) held only one slave apiece. Of those, more than 60 percent owned a female under forty-five years, whereas less than 30 percent held a male in that age bracket.[20] Despite the immediate needs for men to break new land, most owners of one slave invested in a woman of childbearing age. This preference for slave women cut across differences in age, sex, occupation, and residence of the owner. It characterized holdings of single slaves throughout central Georgia for the entire antebellum era. The strategy could pay handsomely. In 1857, an insolvent Crawford County planter offered for sale twenty-five slaves, described as tawny-colored, "all the children and grand-children of a half-breed woman," who was included in the lot.[21]

The yeoman character of pioneer society profoundly affected the lives of the slaves. During the first decade of the nineteenth century (which also was the last decade of the legally sanctioned African slave trade), it is likely that more than half of the 3,000 slaves who settled in Jones and Twiggs counties were from Africa. The rest came from the Chesapeake tidewater and the coastal lowcountry.[22] After 1810, as the networks of the interstate slave trade developed, most slaves came from the Upper South or elsewhere in the Carolina and Georgia upcountry. Although field hands predominated, there were also carpenters, tinners, painters, blacksmiths, and well diggers.[23]

The twin curses of sale and migration stamped the experience of slaves during the first third of the nineteenth century, central Georgia's pioneer stage. Here again larger developments in the world market played an important part. During the second half of the eighteenth century, slaves in the Upper South experienced unprecedented access to freedom due to the combined influence of stagnant tobacco prices, rising grain prices, and the ferment of revolution throughout the Atlantic world.[24] But by the early nineteenth century, with the African slave trade abolished and the Industrial Revolution increasing the demand for cotton, slaves from the Upper South satisfied the need for laborers on the frontiers of the Lower South.

Although exact figures are difficult to reconstruct, it is unlikely that even half of the slaves who trekked to the fresh lands of central Georgia did so in company with their masters. When they did, the familiarity might have eased the physical hardships, though probably not the emotional ones. Recognizable faces and voices could not entirely compensate for families, friends, and places left behind. Yet most slaves came not with their masters, but as members of slave coffles assembled in the Upper South. "[L]ate in the even's we stretched the tents and cooked supper and spread out blankets an' slept," recalled Catherine Beale, who traveled in such fashion from Richmond to Macon. "Then after breakfas', bout sunup, we start travelin' again." Sickness and death were constant companions.[25] Opportunities for escape at times presented themselves en route, judging from runaway advertisements. No doubt masters kept a lock and chain, if not also a gun sight, on individual slaves suspected of runaway proclivities; in coffles men were routinely manacled, but women were joined together with ropes rather than irons. Slaves still managed to "stray," some seeking refuge with the Indians, but most doubtless heading back whence they had come.[26]

In short, the settlement of central Georgia, like other cotton areas of the Lower South, disrupted existing social structures and habits, which of necessity had to be reconstructed in the new setting. Even among masters and slaves who had simply moved from one location to another, new circumstances often required modifying customary practices, if not formulating entirely new ground rules governing behavior. This revamping was not a new phenomenon—it had characterized American slavery from the beginning. It took as its starting point the pattern of "reciprocal rights" and responsibilities that masters and slaves had fashioned during the late colonial period.[27]

In upcountry Georgia, the adjustment produced a crazy-quilt pattern of social relations, with masters and slaves settling upon whatever arrangements worked best for them. Given the large proportions of smallholding masters and African-born slaves, habits of domination and submission evolved on the ground, with considerable give and take and no doubt considerable violence. Within the limitations of terrain, material circumstances, and collective skill in the arts of frontier survival, customary distinctions between master and slave might disappear.

Nowhere was this pattern clearer than in the work that pioneering small-holders and their slaves shared. Former slave G. W. Pattillo recalled that in such side-by-side work settings the pace and duration of labor depended as much upon the energy and endurance of the master as that of the slave. This character-ization applied equally well to the women's domestic sphere of cooking, washing, and spinning and weaving as to the men's outdoor sphere of clearing and tilling the land, all of which were physically demanding tasks. The variety of work and the pace of its performance varied from day to day and season to season as well as within any given day. Certain chores may have dictated long days of labor strung end to end, perhaps without even the customary Sabbath break for women or men. But there were slack seasons as well. Sara Crocker remembered that on her master's small farm in Twiggs County "when there was not much work to do" slaves hunted and fished at their pleasure.[28]

Commingled sweat alone did not dissolve social distinctions and the innumer-able prerogatives of mastership. Masters had little reason and less inclination to share dirty or disagreeable chores with their slaves. Slaves of smallholders also had to perform additional chores—spinning and weaving for women, tending animals for men—when the masters rested. Nonetheless, there was simply no comparing labor on the diversified smallholding with that on the cotton planta-tion. If nothing else, the yeomen's aversion to swampy and other malarial lands guaranteed their slaves a healthier environment than that in which plantation slaves often labored.

As they worked, so also did they live. In the estimation of an English traveler to central Georgia during the late 1820s, intimacy between upcountry masters and their slaves resulted in the latter's being better fed, better treated, and more intelligent than slaves along the coast. Astonishing as it was to report, he "more than once" observed slaves seated in the same room as masters, "a thing never dreamt of elsewhere." Other breaches of customary etiquette, such as casual forms of address, grew directly from intimate living arrangements. This famil-iarity surely bred contempt, but what most impressed travelers and upcountry planters was the flagrant violation of accepted canons of proper subordination.[29]

Even short of suspending the conventions of mastership, smallholders had to grant various concessions to their slaves, due not so much to benevolence as to the demography of newly settled areas. Smallholders quickly learned that allow-ing slaves liberal visiting privileges promoted domestic peace, even while provid-ing additional leverage over the slaves' deportment. Yeomen similarly permitted their slaves to take spouses. Slaves often accompanied their masters to commu-nity events such as barn raisings, official events such as sale days and court days, and religious events such as camp meetings so that they might socialize with their fellows.[30]

Perhaps no upcountry institution satisfied the communal impulse of masters and slaves alike as the church did. Settlers brought their religious affiliations with them and quickly established churches in the new areas. Professing slaves often carried letters of separation from their home congregations. Others found religion upon arriving in the upcountry. In any event, as early as the 1820s the names of slaves—mostly women—appear in central Georgia church records, and by the 1830s some congregations had also licensed slaves to preach.[31]

Camp meetings blended religious sensibilities with the pioneers' desire to socialize. Generally held in late summer, during the laying-by season when crops outgrew the need for constant weeding, the gatherings attracted masters and slaves from a wide area. The meetings lasted for days, and the excitement of evangelical religion coupled with the break in the routine of agricultural life invariably created a holiday air. Attendees picnicked and often camped at the meeting site. Both masters and slaves sported their finest garb. "I had my brogan shoes over my shoulder and had my dresses an' my pantalettes tied up with a string to keep 'em from getting dirty in the dust," recalled Catherine Beale, a former slave who lived within walking distance of a meeting ground. "I let my dress an' pantalettes down and put on my shoes when I got in sight of the meetin'."[32]

Whatever their benefits, camp meetings alone could not satisfy the slaves' desire to socialize. Accordingly, masters and slaves had to devise general guidelines governing travel for such purposes: acceptable destinations, conditions of behavior, durations of absence, and the like. However circumscribed, the privilege of traveling enabled slaves individually to develop bonds of kinship and friendship. Mobility also enabled slaves collectively to piece together again the community life that had characterized the Georgia-Carolina lowcountry and the Chesapeake tidewater during the late colonial period. Hence it was worth behaving for.

Not all masters considered traveling privileges negotiable, and their objections were not always frivolous: the dangers to life and limb represented by natural hazards and a host of predators; the temptation to flee; the chance that congregating slaves would perpetrate mischief. Yet smallholders—especially those in isolated areas—well understood that excessive restriction promoted flight more than docility. A slack halter was preferable to an empty one. Slaveholders also realized that visiting privileges could be used to their own advantage. Masters who shelved their reservations and sanctioned mobility did so upon the understanding that slaves would behave as expected or lose not just the privilege, but a pound of flesh as well. As a precaution, masters required passes of traveling slaves.

Some slaves insisted upon their right to move about at their own discretion. "[S]hrewd" slaves such as Daniel learned the rudiments of reading and writing to forge passes and thus cover their unauthorized movements. And even illiterate slaves, such as Jim Darby, had free whites (in his case, an Irish railroad laborer) write a "freepass" for them.[33] In the early days of settlement, slaves seeking escape took advantage of the comparatively thin population, scattered residences, underdeveloped surveillance and retrieval mechanisms, and proximity of Creeks to the west and Spaniards to the south.[34] But by the mid-1830s, as the hope of fleeing to another nation or to the depths of the wilderness faded, overworked and homesick slaves headed east and northeast to rejoin family and friends from whom they had been separated.[35] Although slaves sold to central Georgia from the Upper South faced a formidable task backtracking across hundreds of miles of hostile territory, some braved the odds nonetheless. Particularly daring slaves declared their plans before leaving. Jerry, a slave originally from Maryland, aimed for Baltimore—or Philadelphia, he defiantly added![36]

Slaves deserted their masters for any number of reasons. Although many masters presumed a direct connection between flight and corporal punishment,[37] they typically pleaded ignorance of what caused a given slave to flee or suspected the involvement of a sinister white person. One incredulous master reasoned that his slave Jim must have been enticed away, inasmuch as Jim had not received so much as a reprimand from the overseer in a year. Enticed or not, the slave demonstrated foresight. Having left on the pretext of attending a "negro quilting," he took $30, a watch, and his clothing with him. Other escaped slaves carried musical instruments such as fiddles. One incomparably equipped fugitive was carrying a rifle, shot, and shot molds in addition to a silver watch and some silver coins when apprehended.[38]

Throughout the antebellum period, most runaway slaves made their escape during the summer and fall, when the weather was favorable and field and forest offered sustenance. Given the intensely personal nature of flight, individual slaves took advantage of their masters' inattention whenever such an opportunity presented itself. The numerous distractions of holidays offered premier conditions for escape. The brothers Jo and Sterling ran off at Christmas time, "without any provocation" their master could fathom. Jimmy disappeared over the Fourth of July, perhaps having been enticed by a white person, in his owner's opinion.[39]

Runaway slaves used more ruses than their masters ever thought possible. Susan pretended to be an idiot. Sixteen-year-old Mitchell, "artful, lying and roguish," played upon his youth and small stature to allay suspicion of his intentions. Recognizing what is in a name, fifty-year-old Luke passed himself as a "preacher of the Gospel." The "keen, artful fellow" Harrison circulated false reports of his death to cover his escape. When "foolishly proud" Jack absconded, his master worried that he had fled with a white boy who would try to sell him.[40] Some runaways passed themselves off as free, others as white.[41] The well-known case of Ellen and William Craft has already been noted, as has that of her light-skinned cousin who first escaped and then returned, disguised as a white man, and freed two younger siblings. Nearly a decade after the flight of the Crafts, a master still haunted by their feat suspected that his slave woman and her nearly white daughter might try to pass as mistress and body servant.[42]

Under cover of the relatively fluid state of society during the settlement stage, slaves expressed collective as well as individual dissent. Masters understood their vulnerability, especially as a result of the rapid growth of the black population. From the earliest days of slavery in central Georgia, rumors of slave revolt had repeatedly surfaced. The press usually scouted such reports, on one occasion during the summer of 1827 conceding that "some disturbance appeared to exist among the blacks" but dismissing its significance. Four years later, more serious rumors circulated in the wake of Nat Turner's Virginia rebellion. Early in October 1831, a report reached Macon that slaves in Jones and Baldwin counties contemplated revolt. The problem turned out to be nothing more than an altercation among a small group of slaves. The trouble quickly subsided, but whites formed a cavalry corps for good measure.[43]

During the turbulent 1830s, when rising cotton prices accelerated the pace of social change, the currents of backcountry revivalism, Jacksonian democracy, and abolitionism—each with its own message of equality—swept across the world of the slaves no less than that of the masters. An 1835 insurrection plot in Monroe County illuminates the complex interplay between widespread physical mobility, intensified commercial production, growing political and social tension among free white men, and the spread of egalitarian ideology among the slaves.[44] In the heat of the summer, rumors that abolitionist literature had appeared in the Macon area produced many a sleepless night. Into the fall "the groundless rumors . . . of 'negro insurrections'" persisted, though the *Georgia Messenger* confidently attributed "almost every difficulty" to slave intemperance. Late in October, a group of sober slaves added substance to the rumors.[45]

The conspirators met at a camp meeting where they formulated loose plans to rise on election day, when masters would be preoccupied at the polls and likely under the influence of hard cider. Authorities discovered the plot and captured the "principal instigator," a slave named George, and several of his accomplices before the plan matured. Slaves who testified at George's trial showed no clear conception of what was to transpire. One man credited George with saying that the king of England would give Andrew Jackson money to free the slaves. Another's testimony pitted the "Clark men," one of the state's two political factions, against their rivals, the "Troup men," in an effort "to have the blacks set free."[46] Still another's featured a local white man serving as "a great general" leading the slaves to freedom beyond the Mississippi River. Of course, tales of murdering men, raping women, and enslaving children abounded. Forced confessions tended to produce such discrepancies; still, all witnesses agreed upon the main objective: "to obtain their freedom." Ultimately, George and two accomplices stood trial. One of the latter was acquitted; the other was recommended for mercy and eventually suffered a whipping, branding, and ear cropping. George was hanged.[47] Among other reprisals, slaves in one Baptist congregation had the church building closed to their religious meetings.[48]

The 1835 insurrection symbolized the end of the pioneer phase of central Georgia's history. For the slaves, the westward retreat of the frontier (and the Indians) drastically reduced their prospects of freedom in the wilderness. Accordingly, they turned inward in two important senses. First, they redoubled their efforts to built internal community structures. Second, they sought additional privileges and safeguards within a system of bondage from which they evidently had little hope of escaping.

The defeat of the slaves also coincided with a marked change in circumstances among slaveless yeomen and small slaveholders. Cotton was surely booming, with prices rising steeply between 1830 and 1835. But the attendant prosperity was misleading. To the extent that smallholders committed land and energy to cotton, they compromised their ability to subsist themselves and (however inadvertently) subjected their livelihoods to market fluctuations. And the lure of earning cash to purchase the growing array of consumer goods had long-term consequences. Deteriorating soils cast a pall over the quest for larger cotton crops, and heavy mortgages to purchase slaves created a real threat of foreclosure. The good news was that new lands beckoned to the west. But the bad news was that, once undertaken, the commitment to commercial agriculture was difficult to reverse.

Without doubt, planters benefited most from the passing of the frontier, even as their actions had helped to speed the day. On the certain knowledge that the aborted uprising kindled white inhabitants' deep-seated fears of Haiti, large slaveholders proposed new ground rules governing the relationship between masters and slaves that would minimize the likelihood of future revolt. The plantation would displace the yeoman farm as the context for the new understanding. The ensuing tension between planters, smallholders, and slave laborers proved a powerful force. It profoundly influenced the economic, social, and political history of central Georgia—and, by analogy, of the cotton plantation South generally—for the rest of the slave era and beyond.

2

· · · · · · · ·

The World
of the Planters,
1820s–1850s

DESPITE THE NUMERICAL preponderance of yeomen during the settlement period, planters exerted influence far beyond their modest numbers. This power rested upon command over the premier resource of the southern agricultural economy: slaves. Slaves raised the cotton, the profits of which made possible the purchase of additional laborers, who in turn cleared more land for cultivation, raised more cotton, and generated more profits. When prices fell, the most successful (often the largest) planters expanded their holdings of land and slaves at the expense of their insolvent neighbors, thereby consolidating wealth, power, and influence.[1]

Although they never succeeded in reducing free white men to the subservience of slaves, planters believed implicitly in social hierarchy. Historians remain divided over the extent to which a democratic polity mitigated the planters' power. Numerous recent works, building upon the studies of Frank Owsley and his students, emphasize not only the smallholders' propensity to exercise their political rights, but also the planters' desire to mollify their fellow citizens of humbler means.[2] In yet a broader context, these considerations have sparked a debate over the extent to which southern slaveholders were a pre-capitalist, seigneurial class or merely a special case of capitalist entrepreneurs.[3] This, in turn, is part of still a larger debate over the transforming influence of the world market within societies producing goods for international export. Such an analytical context encompasses not only the nineteenth-century South, but also much of the world over the past five centuries.[4]

Clearly not all slave systems were equal. The social structure and the political system of the antebellum South were not as rigidly hierarchical as those of

Brazil, but that does not invalidate the analysis of the South as a slave society dominated by a planter class.[5] In fact, it was precisely their strength within the international economic and domestic political systems that enabled southern planters to assume pride of place among the plantation aristocracies of the Americas. They were the wealthiest, and they owned the largest number of slaves. They nearly monopolized production of one of the world's most valuable raw materials, and they held founding membership in a republic that by midcentury spanned the North American continent.

Whereas Brazilian planters presided over a society descended in spirit, if not necessarily in blood, from medieval feudalism, and whereas British West Indian planters were largely absentee capitalists with diverse investment portfolios, southern planters were neither. In the absence of strong feudal traditions, they created a system of slavery to take advantage of financial opportunities presented by the growing world market. Once having done so, they prized not just the material benefits, but the power over their fellow men, white as well as black, that accrued from slave ownership. They fought to the death to preserve the system, and when they lost, the slave regimes elsewhere in the Americas quickly collapsed. Southern slaveholders were in the world market, to be sure, but not of it. The depth of their participation and the intensity of their resistance to bourgeois influence combined to make them the bellwether planter class of the Americas.[6] Central Georgia's planters represented a segment of the extended family of planters that stretched from Virginia to Texas.

FROM EARLIEST settlement days, planters stood out from yeoman-settlers by the size of their households. A planter who could command a gang of ten or more working slaves enjoyed numerous advantages. He could lay the groundwork for a homestead—constructing cabins, stables, and other necessary outbuildings, felling trees, clearing fields, and building fences—with greater dispatch than a yeoman working with only his sons and a slave or two. Although the larger household's subsistence needs would have been proportionately larger, its capacity to satisfy them was exponentially greater. And the concerted labor at the planter's disposal permitted production of such inedibles as tobacco and cotton for sale in distant markets.

Planters often gained access to the choicest tracts, frequently through the assistance of speculators. Such men made their moves early, often in advance of the Indians' land cessions, much less the state-sponsored lotteries. The most

enterprising ingratiated themselves to Creek sachems. Thus did James Abing-
don Everett, one of the most prominent early residents of Houston County, build
his empire. After the War of 1812, he opened a trading post and a ferry on the
Flint River southwest of Macon and married an Indian woman from whose
family he gained "a large reserve." He remained a shrewd investor and business
promoter, even after establishing himself as a landed patriarch. He built the
trading post into one of the largest merchandising firms in the upcountry, and he
granted land to create the town of Fort Valley. His strong support for the
Southwestern Railroad won routing through Fort Valley instead of the county
seat of Perry. At his death in 1848, he was the wealthiest man in Houston County
and one of the wealthiest in the state. John ("Flint River Jack") Rushin similarly
engrossed large holdings of choice land. From dealers in land they became
masters of men, rising to elite status in the process.[7]

Most of the early planters in central Georgia were members of established
plantation families. From colonial times, planters had expanded onto fresh land
to accommodate their children's coming of age and the natural growth of their
slave populations. The most successful antebellum families—North Carolina's
Camerons, South Carolina's Hamptons, Georgia's Lamars—spread branches
across the South.[8] Communities of planters often transplanted themselves whole
to new areas. Kinfolk, neighbors, or church members generally formed the core
of such groups. Typically, the prospective migrants sent scouting parties to
survey the terrain, looking at the lay of the land as well as its quality, the
availability of water and timber, and access to transportation. Often they settled
near "old . . . friends." After establishing their new homes, they continued to
shunt slaves and other resources from one site to another as need required.[9]

Within such core communities, social networks developed. Planters routinely
rubbed shoulders with small slaveholders and slaveless yeomen. The calendar of
official events provided regular occasion for men to congregate: sale days occurred monthly; courts met only quarterly but stayed in session for days on end;
the militia mustered semiannually. The cycle concluded with annual election
days. In an era of voice voting, there was no such thing as an individual vote of
conscience. Instead, what Bibb County grand jurors in 1838 denounced as "the
pernicious and demoralizing practice of electioneering," marked "by assemblages for drinking, barbecues, etc.," characterized most election days. Although
ostensibly designed to bring together men of different social standing on a plane
of equality, electioneering subtly but effectively reinforced social hierarchy. After
all, it was the planters who dispensed the treats, carefully noting who accepted

Blount House, Jones County, built in 1847
(Historic American Buildings Survey, Library of Congress)

and who shunned the hospitality and who voted for whom. Voters had to choose their patrons carefully, for in a polity of equals, the big men were more equal than the humble ones.[10]

Men of different stations could also reinforce social ties on innumerable informal occasions, ranging from barn raisings and hunting trips to chance encounters on public roads. They discussed the weather and the crops, the price and control of slaves, and political affairs. Planters' wives strengthened these networks by visiting and by participating in assorted organizations, such as church groups, that made up woman's sphere.[11]

Besides satisfying social needs, these networks strengthened the planters' common interest in property, particularly slave property. Marriage served that purpose quintessentially, laying the foundation for the creation of dynasties. The circle of planter families formed the pool of eligible mates. The rituals of courtship and marriage gave planters control over admission to the elite, enabling them to keep at arm's length wealthy but boorish upstarts and to admit promising outsiders, even an occasional smallholder or overseer.[12] Marriage facilitated the creation of interlocking directorates within the planter class.[13]

Planter families integrated vertically as well as horizontally. Sons routinely entered merchandising or the professions, especially law, medicine, and the ministry. Such a strategy served a number of purposes. It provided planter families with direct access to the specialized expertise upon which their family fortunes and their class interests depended. It also helped ease the pressure of succession from one generation to the next, particularly in cases where individual planters had large numbers of sons.

To facilitate keeping company with each other and with other suitably appointed persons, central Georgia's planters tended to settle in the towns. Macon, which was incorporated in 1828, particularly attracted them for its healthful location as well as its amenities. By the 1850s, the city served as a showcase for ostentatious display of wealth as well as the political, social, and cultural center of the region. The seats of government in the other plantation counties provided similar oases, with the disadvantage of having fewer perquisites, but with the advantage of lying closer to the plantations.[14]

BECAUSE POWER in a slave society ultimately rested upon domination over slaves, from the beginning planters placed high priority upon increasing the size of their slaveholdings. During the first decade of the nineteenth century, imported Africans filled the bill. Thereafter, importations from the Upper South as well as natural increase produced a steady rise in central Georgia's slave population. Not surprisingly, the absolute number of planters increased as did their proportion among slaveholders. In Jones County in 1820, for instance, slightly more than half the household heads owned slaves; one-eighth of those owned twenty or more slaves, but one-half owned five or fewer. In Houston County between 1830 and 1840, the proportion of slave owners among household heads increased from 33 percent to over 50 percent, and the proportion of planters among slaveholders from 9 percent to 22 percent.[15]

Besides revolutionizing the regional demography, central Georgia's growing numbers of planters also set about to reshape the social relations of production. Lured by the prospect of lavish returns on producing cotton for the world market, the early planters in central Georgia grappled with their own and their slaves' relative ignorance with regard to raising short-staple cotton commercially. Planters faced the challenges of the new environment and the new crop with the tools and experience they had gained in other crop cultures, specifically rice and long-staple cotton in the coastal lowcountry and tobacco and grains in the Chesapeake tidewater. Planters from the Upper South played an especially important role in the developing agricultural system. Attributing agricultural stagnation to the improper management of slaves, they studied how to make their laborers more productive. Inspired by George Washington's prescription of working slaves "as much in the 24 hours as their strength without endangering the health, or constitution will allow of," such planters made the workday the length of the solar day and in some instances longer.[16] Although they allowed breaks for rest and meals, they expected steady labor at all other times, with liberal doses of the whip when necessary.

Those most obsessed with cotton viewed raising provisions "as altogether a secondary object" and planted only as much corn "as serves to fill up the intervals" in cotton cultivation.[17] Of course, even the most penny-pinching planters had a vested interest in providing sufficient rations of meat and meal to sustain life. Given the imperfect development of inland markets, planters could not always count on ready supplies of purchasable foodstuffs. But because they did not wish to withhold valuable land from cotton, they shifted much of the responsibility for subsistence onto the slaves. In one popular practice, they permitted slaves to clear new land for gardens and then at the end of each year converted the gardens to general plantation use.[18] There was nothing sentimental in these arrangements. Planters required slaves to grind their corn and prepare their meals after the day's labor in the cotton fields.[19]

Planters who hailed from the lowcountry of Georgia and South Carolina—a small but prosperous segment of the early settlers of central Georgia—preferred working their slaves by the task, with the hoe as the implement of choice. Under this arrangement, each slave was assigned a daily task, following the satisfactory completion of which the slave was entitled to leave the field. Slaves had access to provision grounds, upon which they grew products for their own consumption, for barter with other slaves, or for sale to the public at large. Planters who championed this system contended that it provided not only the best motivation for slaves to work industriously, but also the most humane method of accounting for "the ability of the hand."[20] The "Carolina rule," whereby slaves raised produce on their own account, survived in pockets throughout the upcountry down to the Civil War.[21]

Some planters from the lowcountry mixed the features of gang and task labor. One who had settled in Houston County tasked his hoe hands while employing gangs in all other plantation work. At times when the crop required only a "light" hoeing, "the workers were often out of the field by 12 o'clock."[22] Among small planters, even greater diversity reigned. What with the lay of the land, the owner's experience, and the size and composition of the slave force, a plethora of work routines developed. Variations from the larger patterns reflected solutions to the new challenges devised by individual masters and their slaves. Nonetheless, by the 1830s gang labor had become the norm.

In placing jurisdiction over field operations in the hands of overseers, planters encouraged the liberal use of the lash, the prime mover of slaves working in gangs. Cracking whips constantly punctuated field labor, but slaves suffered more serious whippings—often in the form of "settlements" at the end of the day—for falling short of quotas, losing or damaging tools, and injuring animals. Defiance of plantation rules, such as keeping cabins clean, met the same kind and degree of punishment. Masters restrained runaways with manacles, chains, iron collars, and various noisemaking headgear. Some masters took even more drastic measures, resorting to the oaken "cobbing board," which had holes bored into it that raised blisters on the paddled flesh. Especially sadistic owners followed the cobbing with a whipping, which burst the blisters and caused excruciating pain.[23] Insubordination or threatened violence might bring a slave within a few strokes of death.[24]

Planters devised nearly diabolical punishments to subdue incorrigible slaves and to plant terror in the hearts of everyone else. One such torture machine common in central Georgia was the picket, a kind of gallows from which the victim was hung by the wrists with one heel positioned on a pointed stake driven into the ground below and then whipped. Not everyone survived such treatment; those who did might limp for months afterward.[25] On occasion, individual cases of cruelty attracted public attention.[26] One particularly vicious overseer, described by a contemporary as "very wild in his notions and actions," reportedly fed his dogs the heart of a slave whom he had hanged.[27] In another case, the Crawford County coroner investigated the death of slave boy at his owner's hands. A diarist acknowledged the man's reputation for being "severe upon negros," while denying "that he intended to kill" the boy. "Such an unpleasant occurrence," the commentator hoped, "will teach others to treat their slaves with humanity."[28] But in Georgia, like the other slave states, killing a slave during "moderate" correction was no crime, and there was no such thing as immoderate correction.

The planters' monopoly on force gave them a decisive advantage in molding work routines to their liking. It thus facilitated the spread of the plantation system, which, in turn, made for larger cotton crops, which brought new wealth to the planters and commercial development to the upcountry. In short, the gang system of labor, backed by the lash, proved an excellent mechanism for subordinating large numbers of slaves to the will of a small number of masters.[29]

Planters devised this program of control in part to counter what they perceived

A flogging (Library of Congress)

as an utter absence of discipline on small slaveholdings. Untoward familiarity between yeomen and slaves not only offended polite sensibilities but also promoted insubordination among slaves in general. Having failed by example and gentle persuasion to convince smallholders of the need for proper discipline, planters began taking steps to gain greater influence over the slave population. Assorted tactics served that end, but direct ownership offered the surest strategy for control.

As they increased the size of their slaveholdings, central Georgia's planters entered the second phase of their campaign to reshape the relations of production. Having successfully introduced gang labor to the upcountry, they set about subjecting to its rigors the slaves they were acquiring from insolvent smallholders and from Upper South coffles. "Scientific management"—of seeds, soils, animals, implements, and techniques as well as of laborers—provided the framework.[30] The depression that began at the end of the 1830s speeded this effort forward. In brief, the crisis produced wholesale bankruptcy: of marginal cotton growers who had operated dangerously close to the margin in flush times and of overextended planters whose prior opulence had depended upon advances from factors. In 1840, a Monroe County resident reported "a general failure," with "no cotton made and every body in debt."[31] As creditors pressed for payment, debtors sought relief from their "pecuniary embarrassments" by stretching their meager resources, calling upon kinfolk, or humbling themselves before their solvent neighbors. Slaveholders attempted to hire out their slaves, thereby generating cash while reducing expenses. Railroad construction appeared a good bet: in 1840, the Monroe Railroad advertised for 1,000 slaves. Other lines did the same, offering such attractions as "liberal wages" or "healthy" working conditions. But because slavery had stunted the growth of markets in hired labor, this option offered only limited relief. Moreover, as the depression dragged into the mid-1840s, such opportunities all but disappeared. In 1845, the Monroe line went bankrupt.[32]

Debtors also scrambled for third party loans, particularly from estates in probate. But interest rates soared to usurious levels. When all else failed, debtors sold out, further depressing the value of land, animals, implements, and slaves in the process. The most solvent planters benefited from the adversity, increasing their holdings of land and slaves at the expense of insolvent neighbors. Dramatic demographic change resulted: emigration produced an absolute decrease in the size of the free white population; importation and natural increase produced an absolute increase in the size of the slave population (see Appendix). Consequently, the average slaveholding in Monroe County grew from 7.9 to 12.2 between 1830 and 1850. The proportion of planters among slaveholders increased at the same time. Even in areas of deteriorating soils east of the Ocmulgee River, similar concentration occurred.[33]

The experiences of Houston County's two wealthiest planters, James A. Everett and Joseph Tooke, illustrate this process. Between 1839 and 1848, Everett increased his already substantial landholdings only modestly, from 11,096 to 12,144 acres, but his slaveholdings rose dramatically, from 156 to 242 slaves. Over the same period, Tooke augmented his acreage from 1,780 to 5,012 and his slave force from 61 to 168. Like Everett and Tooke, wealthy planters elsewhere in the Georgia upcountry learned that flush times spread the wealth and depressed times concentrated it.[34]

Depressed cotton prices also exposed the folly of rapacious agricultural practices. According to both contemporary and modern estimates, by 1835 the land east of the Ocmulgee was ravaged, the topsoil gone and deep gullies worn into the underlying red clay.[35] The most solvent planters turned to agricultural improvement. Insofar as they were able, they invested in new machinery, particularly deep-cutting plows with iron shares, seeding drills, and "cultivators, sweeps, shovels, bull tongues, etc." for breaking up soil between rows and for clearing it away from or throwing it toward the roots. One improving planter wondered how the preference for hoe agriculture had survived so long "in this utilitarian and labor-saving age." Another bluntly challenged the view that "the quality of plows" had "no bearing upon the management of negroes." He asked rhetorically, "[I]f a negro has to push his plow in, hold it steady, guide it and the horse, . . . is [he] not a used up negro to all intents and purposes?"[36] Improving planters also systematically replaced horses and oxen with mules during the 1830s and 1840s if they had not done so earlier. In fact, from about 1840 onward, the presence of mules on a plantation almost certainly predicted the use of improved agricultural implements. Only backward farmers plodded along with oxen and wooden plows.[37]

To prevent erosion, reclaim worn fields, and increase soil productivity, the agricultural innovators experimented with new techniques as well as new implements. Houston County planter Hugh Lawson, for instance, laid out his fields "in grade ditches and horizontal rows." To increase soil fertility, they applied manure; to bring fresh land under cultivation, they drained swamps; to conserve time and timber, they adopted new fencing materials and designs. And to disseminate information they formed agricultural societies and subscribed to agricultural journals. They championed agricultural reform as though it were a crusade.[38]

Innovative planters also embraced self-sufficiency as both a political cause and the practical means of dealing with the crisis. By the 1840s, the growth of regional markets for corn, hogs, and other necessities made the option of purchasing foodstuffs viable in the remotest corners of central Georgia.[39] But without the income from cotton, farmers could not purchase such supplies. Accordingly, innovative planters sought products that would satisfy the needs of home consumption as well as commercial gain. Agricultural journals abounded with articles on fruits and vegetables, grains and grasses, cattle and sheep. To the proponents of diversification, the collapse of cotton prices was a blessing in disguise. But rearguard opposition remained. One planter charged that diversification involved so much "dibbling and jobbing" that his slaves had "little to show for their labour by May-day."[40] And few slaves conceded the wisdom of these new techniques. Hence the innovations did not take firm root. As the depression receded in the late 1840s, cotton fever again began to rage, killing off most of this experimentation.

But the campaign to "manage" the slaves—the "starting point" of all proper management—did not disappear.[41] Arguing the superiority of closely supervised gangs, planters sought to root out all surviving remnants of the task system and the lax practices characteristic of small slaveholdings and pioneer days. They had no illusions about the "Herculean task" of "reducing to a system and order the complicated operations of a plantation, where nothing like system or order ever prevailed."[42]

Surviving elements of the task system represented a major variety of such disorder. South Carolina's James Henry Hammond typified the challenges faced by upcountry Carolina and Georgia planters whose slaves held fast to lowcountry ways. Through the 1830s and 1840s, Hammond struggled with only mixed success to disabuse the slaves of their traditional habits. Hammond opposed task labor for its tendency to promote overexertion; he also frowned upon the relative independence slaves enjoyed after completing their tasks. In his view, steady, moderate labor "from sunrise to sundown," with appropriate intervals of rest, accomplished several objectives: it guaranteed good health and greater output, and it reduced the amount of time at the slaves' disposal. Undermining the slaves' subsistence activity made them more dependent upon their master's largess, a vital component of the idealized social order paternalistic planters were attempting to create.[43]

Like South Carolina's Hammond, Georgia's advocates of the gang system aimed to root out every hint of slaves' control over their own labor. One typical critic faulted the "old system" of tasks as neither "reasonable . . . [nor] just" in requiring "the same quantity of work" from all hands. Whereas a "strong young man" could finish by mid-afternoon and then go "home to work in his own field, or enjoy himself in any manner he thinks proper," a "delicate female" only "with difficulty" finished "by sun-down." "The one who least requires it," the observer concluded, "has plenty of leisure and time to rest himself, whilst the other who needs this the most has the least."[44]

Opponents of tasks left no stone unturned. One partisan argued that by dividing the work force into "fast and slow hands," supervised by their respective "foremen," "more work is obtained, every one does in proportion to his ability, and all are insensible of the quantity they actually do beyond the usual task."[45] Another advocate of the change made additional refinements, proposing several gangs, ranging from full hands ("all the strong and active of both sexes") to quarter hands ("all of the young and the old negroes"), with the respective gangs assigned "work suitable to their abilities." "There is always on all plantations," he insisted, "work requiring different degrees of strength to accomplish, which would enable a planter to assign to each gang, its appropriate labour." Such a system would promote "the spirit of emulation . . . which is always highly desirable, and which makes them work with more cheerfulness, and . . . makes them execute the work better."[46]

In practice, this effort to subject slaves to the greatest direct supervision took more than a generation to accomplish, and even then the results were mixed, with each plantation undergoing a somewhat different experience. Large planters contended against their slaves' strength in numbers. As Hammond and others realized, this could be a source of immense frustration. But once the planter gained the upper hand, a large slaveholding could have the opposite effect: in their collective interest, slaves would enforce conformity within their own ranks and help socialize newcomers from local smallholdings or from the Upper South.

Planters on the make confronted similar difficulties to those faced by established planters. When an enterprising smallholder increased his holdings incrementally over time, he could alter the routines and expectations of his slaves gradually. But slaveholders on the make also had little patience—they wanted to seize opportunity before it passed them by. Those who got rich quick had to convince their erstwhile work partners that the old camaraderie was a thing of the past and that the flexible work routines would have to give way to a more structured, hierarchical environment. And to complicate matters, especially prosperous owners might also find themselves adding inexperienced and sullen slaves from the Upper South into this unstable setting. The varying backgrounds, temperaments, and designs of the planters, coupled with the vagaries of individual landholdings and slaveholdings, helped reproduce exactly the kind of confusion that the planters were trying to eliminate.

As BOTH ESTABLISHED and upstart planters imposed greater control over field operations, they pursued a parallel campaign with respect to the nonworking lives of the slaves. The effort began with a reorganization of domestic space, specifically the construction of specially designed quarters. They built sturdy wooden cabins—often containing floors, ceilings, doors, and windows—with fireplaces attached, kitchen gardens adjacent, and fresh water close by.[47] "My servants are not crowded," one such planter boasted, "and each family is separate to itself."[48]

Constructing quarters served several interrelated purposes in the planters' campaign for greater control over slaves and greater influence over free men. At a symbolic level, the size of the plantation village demonstrated to the world the status of the proprietor: large numbers of houses meant large numbers of slaves. But just as important, whether few or many, the cabins themselves stood as monuments to the planters' benevolence, his provision of shelter to his family. The quarters also represented order in their physical layout: cabins neatly arranged in facing rows with the overseer's dwelling situated at the end of the street. Practical benefits accompanied the symbolic value. Improving physical amenities meant healthier slaves, which as a rule meant proportionally fewer deaths and more births. Not without reason, then, did planters expect the quarters to tie their slaves materially, socially, and psychologically to the plantation order.

By promoting family stability and the growth of community, the slave quarters further served the planters' objective of control. Even more so than physical amenities did, stable families facilitated reproduction and promoted strong emotional attachments, which, in turn, encouraged conformity to plantation rules and discouraged flight. To such ends, one Bibb County planter built a church and sanctioned a slave preacher to baptize and marry his slaves.[49] Planters especially intent upon eradicating practices from yeoman-settler days forbade the taking of spouses from beyond the plantation. For one thing, the quarters negated the earlier demographic justification for such accommodations. Moreover, in the view of these masters, slaves moving about to visit wives were subject to mischief. One Houston County planter insisted that his slaves marry "at home" because "they are the most happy who seek their happiness at home." To his "deep regret," he was "not able to furnish a husband for every woman." Yet he prohibited the slaves of other masters from visiting his plantation, just as he prohibited his own slaves from roaming about.[50] Almost routinely, planters contradicted other stated objectives regarding slaves' families as well. Dividing families by sale and otherwise subverting familial relations, for example, produced discord rather than harmony.

Once the quarters were in place and guidelines regarding off-premises visitation and marriage established, planters brooked no deviation from the prescribed rules. One slave who had defied his master's wishes and taken a wife living on another plantation endured a session on the picket.[51] Earlier, such actions reflected the violence of the settlement stage; now, violence became institutionalized as the glue that held together the new plantation order. To the extent that all whites benefited from the greater subordination of slaves, "public opinion" sanctioned the greater use of force to achieve that end, even as it began to react against the more barbaric expressions of wanton cruelty toward slaves.

Planters also employed other means, both material and psychological, to bind their slaves more tightly to the plantation order. In short, they sought to improve the slaves' industry and bolster their loyalty by substituting positive incentives of a material variety for the negative incentive of whipping. This strategy did not signal an abandonment of physical compulsion; virtually every planter persisted in believing that slaves would not work except under threat of corporal punishment. But it did mark the development of a more sophisticated arsenal—paternalism—to defend the bastions of privilege that planters occupied.

Peculiar, often idiosyncratic, patterns resulted from the effort to prohibit objectionable practices from pioneer days. Some planters extended new prerogatives to their slaves even as they and their neighbors were busy revoking others. The planter noted above, for example, who banned marrying and even visiting beyond the plantation, authorized his slaves to keep gardens and raise poultry.[52] Smaller planters often took the cue of their more prosperous counterparts. In Houston County, for instance, where James A. Everett and Joseph Tooke permitted their slaves to keep gardens, raise chickens and pigs, and earn cash through such piecework as cutting railroad ties and shingles, other planters followed suit.[53]

Every planter imposed limits upon the exercise of such privileges to prevent slaves from concluding that they could maneuver their way piecemeal to practical freedom. Planters also discouraged activity they viewed as detrimental to plantation order. Masters who authorized gardens, for instance, normally stopped short of permitting slaves to raise cotton or corn, lest (in the words of one) "temptation" be afforded to "an unscrupulous fellow to mix a little of his master's produce with his own."[54] Most masters viewed market activity itself as a threat to the larger interests of the plantation order; "the possession of too much money," opined one, "is calculated to generate bad habits, and produce disorder, where sobriety, good feeling and happiness should prevail."[55] Planters on the whole had no desire to see their slaves (and their society) ruined by money. Yet some viewed money as a pacifier and had no objection to slaves' earning it on their own account.

The incidence of such privileges, either on individual plantations or over a wider compass, further illuminates the development of planter paternalism. Paternalists understood that the slaves' possession of petty cash was not going to subvert the entire system. The slaves were still property, not free workers capable of selling their services to the highest bidder. Yet even the most confident paternalists wished to curtail the spread of market relations, precisely because they feared the corrosive effects of such developments. They attributed many of the North's ills to runaway commercialism, wherein everything under the sun could be had for a price. While not denying the importance of markets—in land, slaves, cotton and other agricultural products, and everyday household goods, for instance—to the orderly working of society, planters wished to shield slaves from market activity. As a rule, they reasoned that the slaves' primitive nature stunted the otherwise innate desire for material goods, just as their ignorance made them vulnerable to sharp traders. Hence it was necessary for masters to mediate between their dependents and such large, impersonal institutions as commercial markets and governments.[56] Permitting slaves to produce and trade on a small scale did not contradict this reasoning; on the contrary, it strengthened the social order by providing an outlet for slave discontent.

Besides granting slaves a material stake in society, planters also attempted to win over their minds and hearts. Organized religion provided one such line of approach. From the early days, the largest planters of central Georgia were religious men. But before the 1830s, most planters were indifferent toward the religious sensibilities of their slaves. Then, perceiving the need both to foil abolitionist criticism of their own Christianity and to provide an ideological glue to the plantation order, they made a concerted effort to proselytize slaves.

Besides the pulpit, where they stressed the message of slaves' duty to obey their earthly masters, they used church disciplinary boards to influence the ideas and the actions of the slaves. In Baptist congregations especially, boards of deacons reviewed the behavior of black as well as white members and, when warranted, imposed punishment that ranged from censure to dismissal. White Christians held high expectations of their black "brothers and sisters." During the 1820s and 1830s, Baptists in Monroe County passed judgment in disciplinary cases involving failure to attend services, disorderly conduct, dishonesty, theft, and insurrection, and in domestic cases involving "unchristian like conduct . . . in haveing more then one wife," fornication, wife-beating, and quarreling. Of all aspects of the slaves' deportment, marital fidelity caused the most concern, a sentiment mocked by the booming trade in slaves. Even before 1830, congregations with large black memberships had begun to establish separate meetings wherein specially tailored readings and sermons could be directed at the slaves. In this setting planters hoped to bend Christianity into an instrument of social control.[57]

To strengthen the foundation of slave property, planters at times had to suppress their self-interest as individuals. Perhaps nowhere is this clearer than in their ceding certain police and judicial authority over to the state. Even in the face of growing abolitionist criticism of the arbitrary power individual masters enjoyed over their slaves, masters clung to the prerogative of corporal punishment as an unassailable right. But with the passage of time and growing national and worldwide scrutiny of their behavior, respectable masters aimed to make the business of slave control less embarrassing to polite society. At the same time, fears of unrest prompted them to tighten the restraints on all forms of slave activity.

In 1833, the state's penal code consolidated the various laws previously passed regarding slave importations, slave manumission, property rights of free persons of color, and trial and punishment of slaves and free blacks accused of crimes. Courts composed of three justices of the peace decided cases involving noncapital offenses. Those judgments, in turn, could be appealed to the county superior court. Although the 1833 code (and all subsequent revisions) deemed slaves "chattels personal" and affirmed the master's right of correction, the code also protected slaves from excessively cruel treatment by masters and physical correction by anyone other than the master or overseer.[58] At the same time, it forbade black preachers from addressing more than seven slaves at a time. Two years later, supplemental legislation banned more than seven slave men from traveling together unless accompanied by a white man and prohibited free blacks from harboring fugitive slaves.[59]

While planters ceded certain power over to civil government, they demanded in return that it take a more active role in safeguarding the integrity of slave property. Optimally, slave discipline involved a division of labor. Individual masters (or their agents) held responsibility for the overall behavior of their slaves and the enforcement of industrious labor and good order on the plantation or farm. County officers organized patrols within each militia district to provide protection at night and during periods of unrest. Departure from that pattern both compromised the rights inherent in slave proprietorship and corroded the personal link between master and slave.

Slave owners preferred to discipline their own slaves and use the government-authorized functionaries as the disciplinarian of last resort, but by the 1840s the state took full control over capital cases, providing counsel for the accused, hearing evidence, rendering judgment, and passing sentence. Before 1846, special juries consisting of twelve white freeholders judged all capital cases; thereafter, county superior courts assumed that responsibility. Convictions for capital crimes could be appealed only to the governor for pardon until 1845; the newly created state supreme court had jurisdiction thereafter.[60] Although courts effected a modicum of procedural justice and, in crimes against property (including those committed by one slave upon another), at times displayed considerable leniency,[61] they did not trifle with crimes against white persons, particularly when the charge was murder, assault, or rape. Although comparatively few central Georgia slaves were accused of such crimes, few of them escaped with their lives.[62] Antebellum southern legislators and jurists may well have increasingly recognized the humanity of slaves, but their determination to secure the property of the masters and the subordination of the slaves disposed them toward swift, sure, and generally deadly punishment.[63]

Aside from the obvious value as a foil against antislavery propaganda, the planters' concern for procedural due process in the trials of slaves also paid dividends at home. It certified the legitimacy of the state in matters relating to social order, applicable to free white persons as well as slaves. Although the planters never succeeded in resolving the contradictory nature of slaves as persons and property, slave trials provided a forum for articulating values to be imbibed by every member of society. In the words of Henry G. Lamar, one of the state's most prominent jurists, such proceedings should "teach one important lesson to the slave—that while he has secured to him by law an impartial trial in case of its violation, yet, he is and must of necessity be subordinate to the white man." This subordination "is a necessity, not a choice—and obedience in all cases results to the benefit of the slave." It "costs him nothing," but "it secures him safety and protection." With those words, Lamar pronounced the death sentence upon a slave who had killed a member of the slave patrol at a Bibb County camp meeting, but he spoke to planters and yeomen, artisans and laborers, as well as slaves.[64]

MORE THAN simply an end in itself, establishing control over the slaves also served as a means to another important objective of the planters, that is, power and influence among free men. Even before the age of Jackson, Georgia had a vibrant tradition of democratic politics that planters could ill afford to ignore. Whether they liked it or not, they had to abide by the principle of one man, one vote. But a democratic polity did not prevent planters from exerting disproportionate influence. Believing the plantation to be an ideal model for society rather than simply a structure for managing slaves, they strove to translate that vision into reality.

Planters built and maintained a host of institutions to reinforce and disseminate their worldview. Churches stood at the center, both literally and figuratively, of their communities. Professing planters supported churches as repositories of fundamental social values. By the 1840s, established planter families included a minister or two in their ranks.[65] In the same spirit, they also built academies to educate their children (especially daughters). The more famous of these in Macon, in Hayneville (Houston County), and in Forsyth (Monroe County) drew students from across the South.[66]

In addition to founding such institutions, the most successful planters came to understand how they might harness the visual symbolism conveyed by building structures to propagate the plantation ideal. Accordingly, logs and wooden frames gave way to bricks and stones in churches, academies, courthouses. But

Crawford County Courthouse, built in 1851
(Historic American Buildings Survey, Library of Congress)

whereas individual wealth or private subscription underwrote most such projects, when planters wanted to build new courthouses (or refurbish old ones) they relied upon public support. Small planters and yeomen did not uniformly favor such apparent extravagance, especially at the cost of higher taxes. Yet beginning in the 1830s, planters won public approval for new courthouses, which, when completed, stood both as safe repositories for property records and as symbols of power.[67]

In the same spirit, successful planters also built elaborate dwellings, both on their home plantations and in nearby towns. They spent lavishly on household furnishings, clothing, and the finer things in life such as Madeira wine and other exotic products imported from the four corners of the earth. In 1857, for example, William B. Johnston, a Macon merchant, undertook construction of a mansion whose initial estimate of cost was $70,000. Three years later, as the structure neared completion, the figure had nearly doubled—and did not include the imported furniture from Paris. In short, planters projected an aura of permanency, of commitment to place, and of class distinction.[68]

The upper crust of planters fully expected that their influence would permeate society, but political reality required subtlety rather than brute force. Accord-

William Blackstone Johnston House, Macon, completed in 1860
(Courtesy of Georgia Department of Archives and History)

ingly, planters established bonds of reciprocity and paternalism with white citizens of lesser means. The provision of credit illustrates the case. Although cotton growers might well have benefited from impersonal financial markets to facilitate their business transactions, planters preferred the personal touch. This preference largely reflected opposition to the growth of capitalist institutions—a sentiment not unknown to many of their northern contemporaries. Prior to the 1830s, few banks functioned in central Georgia, and those that did were located in Macon and connected with one or another railroad project. Only three survived the depression that followed the panic of 1837.[69] Factors and merchants provided credit until harvest for a wide variety of essentials and luxury items.[70] But the true medium of exchange was the note from one party to another. Generally due one year from date of issue with moderate interest, the notes were often endorsed by holders and then exchanged as currency. Creditors often overlooked due dates, permitting debts to ride for years.[71]

Such loans obligated the debtor socially and politically as well as financially. Through the selected dispensation of their largess, planters created strong, and at times extensive, client networks. At the time of his death in 1848, for instance, James A. Everett held outstanding notes in the names of hundreds of persons. And during the time that his estate was in probate, the executors perpetuated the clientage, renting land and slaves and selling provisions to neighbors.[72] When the chips came due, planters accepted repayment in cash or kind, or in labor services or votes. In times of illness, bad crops, or similar misfortune, small-holders could count on an extension after a suitable demonstration of humility. When debtors became insolvent—especially upon the death of a household head—planters upheld the traditional custom that necessities for survival be exempted from sale by the sheriff. In addition to bedding and eating utensils, such articles often included animals and tools as well. However much planters may have increased their holdings of land and slaves at such sales, they scrupulously avoided violating the canons of neighborliness.[73] When they overstepped the bounds, humble folk communicated the message.[74]

Grudgingly or not, most slaveless yeomen and small slaveholders of central Georgia accommodated to the view that the plantation order offered the greatest good to the greatest number of people. Conceding the creek bottoms and the oak and hickory lands to the planters, they retreated to the sand hills and scrub pine areas less suited to cotton cultivation. Some sections—northern Houston and eastern Twiggs counties, for instance—were yeoman strongholds throughout the slave era. Denizens of these areas raised cereals and hogs, hunted and fished, and worked for nearby planters carpentering, hauling, or performing general farm labor. It is also likely that they disposed of surplus foodstuffs to planters, thereby reinforcing their mutual interdependence.[75]

Central Georgia's planters also increased their influence over the free population through an increasingly sophisticated use of the political process. This connection is nowhere more clearly evident than at the level of local government. By state law, five-member inferior courts functioned as executive, legislative, and judicial bodies in the respective counties, controlling revenues (both taxes and expenditures), dispensing poor relief, and overseeing the construction and maintenance of roads, bridges, and public buildings. In short, these bodies represented unvarnished concentrations of power. In the plantation belt surrounding Macon, planters dominated the inferior courts, calling them into existence during settlement days and furnishing the overwhelming majority of justices for the rest of the antebellum period.[76] The inferior courts became political battlegrounds, due both to larger social divisions and to emerging partisan divisions within the planter class.

The apportionment of public funds on behalf of county roads illustrates how local politics balanced the specific needs of particular planters against the "public convenience" or "utility to the community," but with a thumb on the planters' side of the scale. Inferior courts appointed road and bridge inspectors who obligingly noted the deplorable condition of those public facilities. Taxpayers were reminded of their obligation to perform road duty (or offer the services of their slaves). Special contracts were awarded to make repairs or undertake new construction. Overall, however, the system tended to work to the advantage of large planters, who viewed their ease of access to markets as synonymous with the general good. As a result, the best-maintained roads ran from individual planters' cotton gins to the nearest river landings, and even they were in their best condition at the start of the harvest. Heavy use quickly rutted them again, and thus they remained until summer.[77]

Men with a penchant for higher public office generally set their sights upon the state legislature. Meeting once annually after the harvest for a several-week session, the legislature provided the combination of prestige and influence over public policy attractive to planters. On occasion, particular planter-legislators served their constituents for decades, but most reentered private life after a relatively brief stint in public office.[78] Although every planter was a politician, few pursued politics as a career. The power and the glory were in planting.

The rebirth of partisan politics in the 1830s exacerbated broadly social divisions between commercial and subsistence areas of the state and provided a new context for factionalism within the planter class. What eventually emerged as substantial fault lines began as hairline cracks that did not follow clearly discernible patterns. In some cases, partisan positions seemed to reverse over time. The Whigs, for instance, who originated in the states' rights opposition against the perceived nationalism of the Jacksonian Democrats, soon became proponents of Henry Clay's American System and its implications of broad governmental powers when exercised on behalf of the common good. As is well known, Whiggish planters and urban merchants favored improvements in the transportation network to ease the shipment of cotton to market and believed that subsistence-oriented yeomen had little use for railroads. The influence of the largest planters within the party gave it a paternalistic cast, which Democrats dubbed "elitism" to considerable political effect.[79]

For their part, the Democrats appealed strongly to the common man on the basis of opposition to concentrated power, whether in government or in private special interests such as corporations. Yet not even Democrats objected to governmental actions on behalf of Indian removal or protecting the rights of slave owners. A residual unionism characterized Democratic yeomen in non-plantation areas, even as black-belt Democrats pressed the issue of states' rights against perceived encroachments of federal power. As part of these larger developments, politics also began to reflect the growing demand of smallholders for government protection of their rights and for the extension of selected government services. Both state legislators and county-court justices sought a formula for satisfying those demands, lest they foment unrest among yeomen, but without raising taxes, lest they foment unrest among planters. To that end, they devised a program of funding internal improvements and a measure of social welfare spending through tax-free sources: disbursements from the federal treasury and profits from a state-owned railroad.[80]

Planters became interested in railroads as an alternative to unreliable river transport during the 1820s and sought government assistance. In the 1830s and 1840s, with backing from the state and money from the federal treasury, they supported a number of railroad schemes in the upcountry. The Central of Georgia linked Macon with Savannah; the Macon and Western (which joined the Western and Atlantic) headed northwesterly from Macon through Forsyth to Atlanta and beyond; and the Southwestern funneled the magnificent cotton crops from the southwest frontier of the state through Macon. Houston County's James A. Everett invested $50,000 in the Southwestern Railroad, and large planters in other counties did likewise.[81]

Both supporters and critics desired that the railroads not become agents of social change. The state-owned Western and Atlantic road, for instance, was intended to link the grain- and livestock-producing areas of the Tennessee Valley with the plantations of Georgia's black belt and not to commercialize the yeoman-farming areas that it crossed. Planters did not object to financing railroad construction with tax revenues—of which they paid the bulk—provided they reaped the major benefit. In return for not having to pay for the railroads, yeomen would largely be shielded from unwanted commercial development. As it turned out, planters had less success protecting the black belt itself from rampant commercialization.

Comparatively few planters aspired to national political office, although Georgia's men in Washington established an impressive record, as the antebellum triumvirate of Howell Cobb, Alexander H. Stephens, and Robert Toombs vividly attests. Service in Washington almost always entailed sacrifices that only selected planters were willing or able to make. A term of office in the federal legislative or executive branch required long absences from home. Not every officeholder had at his disposal the expert services of a brother-in-law to manage family affairs, as Howell Cobb, scion of a planter family and Democratic politician who spent years in various offices in Washington, did in the person of John B. Lamar, scion of another prominent family who managed both their properties from his headquarters in Macon. As a result, most planters forsook federal positions.

In the pursuit of still larger class interests, planters mastered political theory as well as political practice. They studied the classics of Western political thought.[82] And they touted the benefits of plantation slavery to slaves, masters, and nonslaveholders alike. Drawing upon biblical lessons, the histories of ancient Greece and Rome, and studies of poverty in England and the North, proslavery ideologues pronounced slavery the best means of mobilizing labor ever devised by human society. American slaves, they argued, "are the healthiest and happiest of any class of labourers on the face of the earth."[83]

Planters anchored their defense of slavery, as South Carolina's James Henry Hammond explained, on " 'the rock of ages'—the Bible."[84] The Old Testament provided any number of references to slavery, the most common being the curse upon the descendants of Ham. The wealthy planter Howell Cobb of Houston County (whose nephew and namesake was the prominent Democratic politician) flatly asserted that *"African slavery is a punishment, inflicted upon the enslaved, for their wickedness."* But masters served as the instruments of God's beneficence as well as his wrath. Slavery was a school, wherein the purported heathenism, childishness, laziness, improvidence, and promiscuity of the children of Africa— where tropical abundance had reinforced presumed natural inclinations—were to be corrected.[85] Cobb proclaimed American slavery *"the Providentially-arranged means whereby Africa is to be lifted from her deep degredation, to a state of civil and religious liberty."*[86]

As the critics of slavery marshaled secular evidence to support their case, proslavery apologists fired back in kind. Both sides battled fiercely over the lessons of history.[87] In the slaveholders' view, abolitionist notions of human equality and individual rights were mere fads, thoroughly lacking in historical substance. Involuntary servitude, argued T. R. R. Cobb (brother of the younger Howell Cobb and codifier of Georgia's antebellum statute law), had "at some time, been incorporated into the social system of every nation whose history has been deemed worthy of record."[88] Georgia planters aimed to keep alive those traditions. They built mansions along classical Greek and Roman lines; they filled library shelves with the works of ancient writers; they named cities Athens, Rome, and Sparta; and they held slaves.

T. R. R. Cobb applied these general historical lessons to understanding the colonial history of Georgia. "Her climate and her soil demanded negro laborers," he reasoned, "and her resources began to be developed when this demand was supplied." Like other planters, Cobb saw a providential hand in these developments: "The negro and the cotton plant seem to be natural allies, and there was something ominous in their almost simultaneous introduction into the New World." Planters prospered because their actions comported with divine and natural law.[89]

Planters also pressed science into the defense of slavery. Biology offered an analogy in the contribution made by the different parts of a living organism to the proper functioning of the whole. Masters supplied the brains, slaves the brawn. The ideologues of white supremacy on both sides of the Atlantic also developed pseudoscientific explanations for the assumed inferiority of the "colored races."[90] Georgia planters seized upon such findings to prove the "natural" suitability of Africans for enslavement.[91]

Wary of criticism, planters argued that they upheld the institution of slavery "not for gain solely, but because it had become, as it were, a part of the social system, a social necessity."[92] Suggestions that slavery be abolished conjured up images of chaos and bloodshed associated with the Haitian revolution. Only eternal vigilance could ward off the specter of anarchy. After William Lloyd Garrison began publishing the *Liberator* in 1831, the Georgia legislature passed a resolution offering a reward of $1,000 for apprehending him. The sponsor of the resolution was Eugenius A. Nisbet, a planter and attorney from Macon who would champion the cause of Georgia slaveholders through the Civil War.[93] White Georgians were determined to show that they stood second to none in opposing abolition. When they uncovered abolitionists in their midst—a regular occurrence during periods of slave unrest—they put the subversives to flight, often in a coat of tar and feathers.[94] The abolitionists' abstract professions "in the cause of *human rights*," argued Nisbet, made them "the most destructive of all the enemies of the slaves." "[T]he history of abolitionism in the United States," Cobb added, "has been the history of fanaticism everywhere."[95] For the good of the slaves and the good of society, such men insisted, this fanaticism had to be eradicated.

In a broader offensive, proponents of slavery attacked capitalist society itself. The hardships of free laborers provided an easy target, but the criticism did not stop there.[96] "All are strangers here," wrote Robert Bryan from a northern medical school to his family in Houston County. "You look in vain for that generosity of feeling, that sociability and identity of interest here that you find in beloved Georgia." Yankee traits repulsed him. "Acquisitiveness, the grasping of the dollars and cents," he observed, "is the ruling propensity—fashion and anti-slavery the only God."[97] Crude manners (and other base habits) among north-erners reflected the pervasive change endemic in that section. The opposite tendencies among southerners reflected the social stability resulting from slavery and the frank acknowledgment of racial hierarchy. Relishing their "isolat[ion] from the rest of the civilized world," planters repudiated all "desire for organic change."[98]

The most sophisticated (and brazenly self-confident) apologists for slavery even broached the delicate class question. To the consternation of northerners who insisted upon the unique egalitarianism of their section, proslavery ideo-logues described the North as a class system which, like slavery, exploited labor for purposes deemed socially useful by the exploiters. These defenders of slavery shattered the myth of social equality in the North; some even saw beyond the racial veil of southern exploitation. South Carolina's James Henry Ham-mond, for instance, argued that southern civilization rested upon "the principle & *fact* of the inequality of mankind—for policy we say *races*, in reality, as all history shows it, the truth is *classes*."[99]

Proslavery apologists also argued that slavery had in fact solved the problem of conflict between capital and labor that by the Yankees' own admission plagued their section. Cultivation of the staple crops of the South, argued T. R. R. Cobb, required "associated labor, not subject to the contingencies of 'strikes' or ca-prices." "[P]ure slaveholding communities" avoided the "excitements" and "riots" that disrupted societies like the North.[100] Robert Toombs elaborated: "Interest and humanity cooperate in harmony for the well-being of our laborers" to a degree unlike any other relation between capital and labor. In the North, where labor and capital were functionally distinct, "[e]ach individual laborer . . . is the victim not only of his folly and extravagance but of his ignorance, misfor-tune, and necessities." In the slave states, however, "labor united with capital, directed by skill, forecast and intelligence, while it is capable of its highest production, is freed from these evils, [and] leaves a margin both for increased comforts to the laborer and additional profits to capital."[101]

Slave societies succeeded where others had failed. "[T]here is perhaps no solution of the great problem of reconciling the interests of labor and capital," Cobb insisted, "so as to protect each from the encroachment and oppressions of the other, so simple and effective as negro slavery. By making the laborer himself capital, the conflict ceases, and the interests become identical."[102] All the world benefited from this prosperity. As Alexander Stephens observed, "The amount of capital invested in slaves is but a drop in the bucket compared with the much vaster amount put in motion and sustained by the products of their labor." Consequently, slaveholders held "the lever that wields the destiny of modern civilization in its widest scope and comprehension."[103] In "not a single spot" throughout the world, boasted Robert Toombs, were "all classes of society . . . so well content with their social system" as in the slave states, where "[s]tability, progress, order, peace, content and prosperity reign."[104] Against the arguments that slavery was out of step with the advanced spirit of the age, these men proclaimed its universality as guarantor of social stability and collective prosperity.

Proslavery ideologues used similar logic against northern charges that slavery subverted republican political institutions. To the contrary, T. R. R. Cobb argued, slavery had historically demonstrated itself as the premier foundation for republics. "The mass of laborers not being recognized among citizens," he observed, "every citizen feels that he belongs to an elevated class. It matters not that he is no slaveholder; he is not of the inferior race; he is a freeborn citizen; he engages in no menial occupation. The poorest meets the richest as an equal; sits at his table with him; salutes him as a neighbor; meets him in every public assembly, and stands on the same social platform." By virtue of this relationship, "there is no war of classes. There is truthfully republican equality of the ruling class."[105] Slavery was "*conservative*" precisely because it gave all southern whites a shared interest "in preserving existing institutions."[106] Eliminating class conflict within the sphere of production dissolved the potential for class conflict in all social relationships. In a word, organic society prevented the social ills—so glaringly displayed in the North—that otherwise resulted from trucking with the capitalist world market.

LIKE THEIR contemporaries in the other plantation areas of the Deep South, central Georgia planters largely succeeded in stamping society in their image. Demographically, they made great strides: the average-size slaveholding increased remarkably over the antebellum era, even as the number of planters grew. Politically and ideologically, they rallied both smallholders and nonslaveholders behind the essential principles of plantation slavery, even if they did not abolish all conflict among the different classes of white citizens.

The struggle for hegemony of central Georgia's planters paralleled similar struggles by rural elites elsewhere in the Americas. In the United States, the only group that compared with the southern planters was that presiding over the manors of upstate New York, where Dutch colonial influence lingered into the nineteenth century. Elsewhere, particularly in western grain-growing regions, rural elites tended to distinguish themselves not by the size of their holdings or the number of their hired hands, but by their commercial connections. Merchants and bankers in market towns rose to prominence promoting—not stifling—the spread of commercial agriculture and liberal-capitalist values. Freehold farmers did not differ appreciably from each other in wealth or social influence.[107]

Elsewhere in the Americas, Brazil provides the best comparative context for evaluating the success of planters' efforts to exercise hegemony over people of European ancestry. In the Brazilian northeast, the *senhores de engenho* on the sugar estates presided over a quasi-feudal hierarchy of free persons, the most distinguishing feature of which was the *senhores'* virtual monopoly of the land. *Moradores* were granted permission to squat on estate lands, in return for which they became clients of the patriarch, performing labor on demand, supporting him politically, and, when necessary, taking up arms on his behalf. Other free men, who migrated seasonally from the interior to work on coastal estates, entered similar relationships of clientage in return for employment. In southern Brazil, coffee *fazendeiros* above São Paulo, who clung fiercely to slavery during the 1870s, began employing large numbers of free laborers—mostly Italian immigrants—in the 1880s. There, too, clientage played a major part in the relations between landowners and workers.[108]

If central Georgia's planters only approximated this kind of domination, it was not for want of effort. Rather, the democratic traditions of landownership and politics in the United States provided smallholders with means of defense that the Brazilian *moradores* lacked. At the same time, no northern elite exercised the kind of economic, social, and political power that slavery made possible. Planters in central Georgia, like their counterparts in other states and such other plantation regions as Brazil, largely succeeded in constructing a patriarchal world. Few cared to admit the degree to which their world reflected the influence of the slaves whose labor made it all possible.

3

· · · · · · · ·

The World
of the Slaves,
1820s–1850s

WITHIN THE WORLD shaped by the masters, slaves created a world of their own. In countless ways the two worlds overlapped, for masters depended upon their slaves every bit as much as slaves depended upon their masters. This dependence took particular forms, such as the well-known appeals of slaves to masters against objectionable overseers. The master-slave relation rested upon the same foundation that supported other systems of bound labor: the exchange of labor services for subsistence. Yet slavery encompassed more than labor relations narrowly defined. In short, it was a way of life.

From their initial introduction into British North America, slaves relaxed and played as well as worked and ate. As slavery took on institutional trappings, slaves forced masters to concede time that the slaves could call their own. Boundaries between the masters' time and the slaves' varied by place, by season, and by task. During the colonial period certain conventions evolved, with broad differences between lowcountry Carolina and Georgia and tidewater Virginia. As noted earlier with regard to the planters, precedents from both areas profoundly influenced developments in central Georgia.

The world of the slaves itself underwent major structural transformations during the first half of the nineteenth century, as tens of thousands of new slaves trekked to the upcountry and as plantations replaced smallholdings. Slaves mastered the art of adjusting to circumstances over which they had little direct control. They stretched old customs to fit their new needs, and when that strategy failed they devised novel approaches to their problems. There can be little doubt that the masters enjoyed overwhelming advantage. They reorganized the productive process, placing a premium upon large-scale operations, strict discipline, and long hours of work. They dogged the slaves during every waking moment and even haunted their dreams. But the very process of concentration strengthened the slave community centered in plantation quarters.

THROUGH THE SOCIAL upheaval of settlement, plantation slaves enjoyed a degree of continuity with the persons, events, and institutions of the past unmatched by slaves on smallholdings. Plantation quarters served as the bedrock of slave communities, but at first plantations were neither plentiful nor scattered randomly about the countryside. Instead, they tended to be concentrated in reflection of their owners' preference for rich soil and each other's company.[1] Slaves of smallholders living on the peripheries of such concentrations no doubt frequented them, with or without authorization. But where small farms predominated, slaves might yearn for the companionship that residents of plantations took for granted.

Slaves sold to the cotton frontier from the Upper South often had difficulty adjusting to the rigors of their new surroundings. They had to draw upon reserve energy simply to keep up with the physical demands without incurring punishment. Charles Ball, a Maryland slave sold south around 1805, graphically described what Chesapeake slaves endured.[2] In comparison with tidewater tobacco fields, Ball found the labor in cotton fields more "excessive" and "incessant throughout the year." Ball experienced "much trouble" in his early dealings with mule teams, "having never been accustomed to ploughing with these animals." He found cotton picking an especially elusive art for unpracticed hands. Slaves worked under "captains" who set the pace for others to follow. Laggards were whipped, often mercilessly, in a ritual devised to impress minds more than bodies. And the slaves' basic diet did not equal the demands of their labor. Accordingly, Ball felt that cotton plantations brought to bear "the utmost rigour of the [slave] system" upon their victims.[3]

Slaves resisted the introduction of new routines for reasons of physical and mental health. After all, endurance did have limits, and it is likely that slaves suffered deteriorating health from sheer exhaustion. When planters put their slaves to work clearing and cultivating creek bottoms, for instance, microorganisms had a field day. Inclement weather brought additional disease and suffering. During one late-summer sickly season, the overseer of John B. Lamar's plantation in southwest Georgia described the prevalence of "chils & Fevers" brought on by heavy rains. Unwittingly indicating his own disregard for the health of his charges, the man noted, "As Soon as one Gets out It Rains on him or he Is In a large due or in a mud hole & Back he comes again." "[W]e are all on the land of the living," commented the overseer during another trying time, "But don't no that we will be in the morning."[4] What masters and overseers described as feigning sickness and historians have denominated "day to day resistance" suggests a process of negotiating the physical limits of exploitation.[5]

Such rigors notwithstanding, plantation slaves managed to find time for gathering plants, nuts, and berries and for fishing and hunting. In many cases, such activity was more a matter of necessity than choice, given the stinginess of masters on the make. Slaves with prior experience provisioning themselves from the wild shared their knowledge with fellow servants. Masters often capitalized on these skills—fishing, in particular—to stock the plantation larder.[6]

For many slave men, hunting served as an important arena for developing skills, socializing with relatives and friends, and supplementing the standard plantation diet. Hunters generally worked at night. Those skilled at trapping small game made their solitary rounds, and parties with dogs pursued raccoons and opossums after the day's work was done. Some slaves also worked in daylight, and a few had permission to keep a firearm. Accomplished hunters could enjoy meals of fresh game several times a week.[7] Slaves on upcountry cotton plantations also gained access to land for gardens, where they raised "corn, potatoes, pumpkins, melons, &c. for themselves."[8]

The hardships of the frontier reinforced mutual dependence among slaves. The quest for adequate sustenance magnified the importance of slave households, which, as Ball's own experience indicates, generally had a family at the nucleus, but which often included members unrelated by blood.[9] The exchange of food within the quarters linked slave households with one another. Such ties supplemented those of kinship and helped reinforce the foundation upon which the other institutions of the slave community could rest. Insofar as such subsistence networks extended beyond individual plantations, they incorporated slaves on nearby plantations and smallholdings. This web helped promote stability within the lives of mobile slaves.

The intense attention to the crop on upcountry plantations at times even encroached upon the Lord's Day. Planters required slave men to mind and feed stock (at times on a rotating basis) and to police the quarters on the Sabbath. Women had to do laundry and mend clothing. Although slaves generally turned such chores into occasions to socialize, obligations of this kind restricted the slaves' opportunities for rest, relaxation, and supplementary subsistence activity.

Where masters granted the Sabbath without restriction, slaves made ample use of the time. In early settlement days, slaves so inclined worked for wages on that day, finding no shortage of potential employers. They labored for non-slaveholders and for planters, in cotton crops and at assorted jobs, and often earned from $.50 to $1.50 per day. Ball recalled that during cotton-picking season, the intensity of competition prompted masters to "offer their own slaves one half as much as the cotton is worth, for each pound they will pick on Sunday" to prevent "them from going to some other field, to work." Ball pondered over "the moral turpitude of violating the Sabbath, in this shameful manner," but the circumstances warranted suppressing such scruples.[10]

Slaves gained more than pocket change working in this way. Ball described himself as "a kind of freeman on Sunday," whose sole object "is to get employment . . . where he can make the best wages." "[B]y the exercise of his liberty on this day," Ball observed, he was able "to provide himself and his family, with many of the necessaries of life that his master refuses to supply him with." Although this "liberty" remained severely circumscribed, the ground rules governing Sunday labor recognized the principle that slaves were entitled to compensation for labor performed on their own time. Ball noted the absence of whipping and "abusive language." None of his numerous employers "insulted or maltreated" him. Nor did they closely superintend his labor. Yet, he narrated, "I worked faithfully, because I knew that if I did not, I could not expect payment; and those who hired me, knew that if I did not work well, they need not employ me." In exchange for lost rest, slaves who worked on Sunday regained the control over their labor they had lost during the other six days. They also forced the masters to acknowledge, however grudgingly and provisionally, what the renowned traveler Frederick Law Olmsted later described as "the agrarian notion" that formed "a fixed point of the negro system of ethics: that the result of labour belongs of right to the labourer."[11]

Despite its toll upon their bodies, Sunday labor enabled slaves to purchase such necessities as salt, sugar, coffee, tobacco, handkerchiefs, and blankets. Slaves sometimes traded a portion of their rations for other goods.[12] They also bartered or sold produce and animals as well as assorted handicrafts, including moccasins, baskets, brooms, bowls, mats, mattresses, and horse collars.[13] However humble these exchanges, they held the potential to undermine as well as bolster the plantation order. Most critically, they represented a realm of production and exchange controlled by the slaves themselves. In a number of analogous circumstances, such activity gave rise to what historians and anthropologists have described as "proto-industrial" or "proto-peasant" tendencies.[14] Despite the deficiency of such terms, each accurately conveys a sense of new productive relations taking shape within the confines of an existing structure. As the

Weaving white-oak baskets, Jones County
(Courtesy of Georgia Department of Archives and History)

antebellum era advanced, the effort of central Georgia's slaves to expand their independent production fits such a description.

Not all slaves enjoyed equal access to markets for disposing of their surplus products and fulfilling their subsistence needs. As a rule, those living on yeoman homesteads had fewer advantages than those on plantations or in towns. Slaves proximate to highways and waterways could trade with itinerant peddlers and ships' crews, laws to the contrary notwithstanding. Slave wagoners and boatmen played an especially important role in promoting such exchange, but they did not monopolize it.[15] Despite their misgivings about the evils inherent in such developments, planters did not suppress this independent economic activity; after all, they benefited directly from its products, and besides, it provided a safety-valve for slave discontent. Slaves depended upon it even more as a source of goods and an outlet for creative energy.

Amidst rising cotton prices over the antebellum period, plantations grew like mushrooms, and increasing proportions of slaves lived in quarters. In 1830, for instance, one in three Houston County slaves lived on plantation-sized units of twenty or more slaves, the largest of which contained fifty slaves. Twenty years later, the proportion of slaves on plantations had doubled to two in three; five plantations contained over 100 slaves each. And in 1860, three of every four slaves in the county lived on plantations; the largest holding consisted of 343 slaves. This process of concentration framed the entire experience of antebellum slaves.[16]

Plantation slaves' efforts to control their lives centered in the quarters, where they spent their nonworking hours. Their first priority was to establish families on a sounder footing than had been possible during the yeoman-settler stage. Yet even as they welcomed the favorable environment for the development of family life presented by the quarters, slaves did not wish to abandon hard-won prerogatives. They particularly clung to the rights of taking a spouse from beyond the owner's slaveholding and of moving about for the purposes of courtship, conjugal visits, and general socializing. In short, they sought to preserve old privileges while at the same time taking advantage of openings created by the new circumstances.

They registered mixed success, as the matter of marrying off the plantation makes clear. On the one hand, slaves faced planters who saw such habits as the root of slave insubordination and placed high priority upon excising all such subversive arrangements. Fugitive slave John Brown, for instance, recalled the brutal punishment of a slave who had defied his master's wishes and taken a wife living on another plantation.[17] On the other hand, slaves encountered planters who for reasons of self-interest and paternalism allowed the old marriage practices to survive.

From the standpoint of both slaves and masters there were advantages and disadvantages in either alternative. Masters who honored the wishes of slaves to take spouses beyond the plantation necessarily encouraged mobility, which not all their neighbors appreciated. But the threat of withdrawing visitation rights provided a powerful lever of control. The separation of slave families resulting from a planter's expanding operations added another dimension to this dynamic of regulated mobility, as the slaves of Howell Cobb and John B. Lamar understood. Both overseers and slaves might bargain with each other over the privilege of visiting the old home place in return for good behavior.[18]

Such practices illustrate the frequent divergence between slave families and slave households. On smallholdings, masters and slaves may have lived together under one roof. On small plantations, a single separate dwelling may have housed all the slaves, related and unrelated alike. On larger plantations, an unrelated man or woman might have dwelt with a married couple and their children. The last-named arrangements almost always pressed against limited space and material resources, though the single person might also help ease the burden of such domestic chores as cooking and gardening. When the single slave brought skill at hunting or fishing or making handicrafts, the whole household stood to benefit. Yet more significant than the presence of such unrelated persons was the absence of a parent or a child.[19]

Coresident husbands and wives experienced the joys and strains of married life, aggravated by the routine interference of master or overseer in their domestic affairs. The masters' meddling with slave family life prompted many men to take spouses abroad. But given that masters required good deportment as a precondition for visiting privileges, these men often traded one objectionable situation for another.[20] Moreover, the ensuing strain within the family might produce argument and violence rather than harmony. But both masters and slaves had a vested interest in promoting familial peace. In any event, the progress of plantation agriculture itself had the greatest influence on strengthening slave families. Where slaves were concentrated on large productive units, they dwelt in quarters; where there were quarters, families could develop.[21]

Just as slaves faced challenges establishing families on firm ground, they struggled to keep extant families intact, often against forces beyond their control. Separation by sale figured most prominently. By the late antebellum period, planters as a rule professed aversion to separating slave families, though hard-bitten types insisted that "negroes bring less when sold in families" and accordingly subordinated paternal sensibility to cold calculation.[22] William Craft reported that his former master sold his parents and several other "aged slaves" because "they were getting old, and would soon become valueless in the market."[23] And masters routinely disposed of slaves to liquidate debts. In short, slaves of masters who adhered to the minimal standards of humanity might rest easily, but they could never lower their guard entirely.

When a planter died, the division of slaves among heirs almost invariably separated family members.[24] Slaves from large estates were parceled among surviving heirs. Administrators often divided the slaves into lots of roughly equivalent value and then matched the lots to the appropriate heir by drawing names from a hat.[25] Although officials tried to keep families intact, separation was unavoidable. Furthermore, when the deceased master left minor heirs, slaves were often hired out for the purposes of generating income, often for school expenses. Then, even before the final division of the slaves, individual slaves were separated from their families for a year at a time in a ritual that might continue for years on end.[26]

Slave families suffered additional fracture when planters made gifts of individual slaves to their children. Marriage provided a premier occasion for such presents. Planters considered this practice essential to the maintenance of wealth and power, both within families and in the class as a whole. But it wreaked havoc among slaves. Sara Crocker, a former slave from Twiggs County, recalled the uncertainty associated with such gift-giving.[27] The frequency of contact among members of fragmented black families then depended upon the frequency of contact within the white family. At times the masters' disposition of gift slaves served the interest of spite more than generosity, as the case of Ellen Craft illustrates. Her mistress seized the first opportunity to be rid of Ellen, who had been so "frequently mistaken for a child of the family." Throughout the South, mistresses in similar circumstances did the same.[28]

Besides being centers of family development, the quarters provided sustenance to such other communal institutions as churches. As social institutions, slave churches served a number of purposes, some dictated by masters, others by slaves themselves. The widespread appearance of brush arbor churches, however, indicates the importance slaves attached to controlling such areas of their lives—to removing them from the control of masters and placing them within their own protective embrace. In that context, denominational differences and the various restrictions imposed upon (or privileges granted to) black brethren by white evangelicals were largely irrelevant. Slaves simply wanted to control their own institutions, select their own preachers and other religious leaders, and interpret the Testaments as they saw fit. Although such developments would have been significant at any time during the history of slavery in North America, they were especially important during the antebellum period, as planters strove to achieve hegemony and to isolate the slaves from contact with northern notions.[29]

IN THE SHIFT from small holdings to large, slaves generally lost in the fields the measure of control over their lives that they had gained in the quarters. Under the regime of gang labor, slaves worked longer and harder under stricter supervision and greater physical force. Although they did not forfeit their determination to influence the routines of field labor, they faced an opposite number equally as determined but better armed. When and where slaves found ways to mitigate the intensity of particular tasks, they did so. But they had greatest success negotiating over the boundary between time at their master's disposal and time of their own.

Cycles of nature largely determined the dividing line. The length of the solar day, seasonal weather patterns, and the variable demands of crops shaped the nature, intensity, and duration of labor. Moreover, cotton cultivation embraced two major "slack" seasons: midsummer's laying-by time, when the cotton and corn required no further weeding prior to harvest, and winter's dead time, between the end of harvest and the start of plowing. Both lulls provided occasions for performing routine maintenance work on the plantations, including repairing fences and ditches, removing stumps, clearing land, chopping wood, and building or repairing slave cabins and other plantation buildings. But the breaks in the demand of the major crops enabled slaves to press for an extension of free time and gain the acquiescence of planters.

These departures from the norm were often accompanied by rituals of mutual interdependence, which signaled the exceptional circumstances of the dispensation while reaffirming the underlying values of the standard practice. The rituals tended to coincide with holidays, such as the week between Christmas and New Year's, when slaves customarily enjoyed a respite from work and when masters generally distributed blankets and shoes. At times slaves demanded "Christmas Gif's," or treats, begging persistently and at times noisily until rewarded. In some instances, slave children searched the grounds surrounding the big house or the quarters for hidden treats. Although masters often distributed rations of liquor at Christmas, most slaves had neither the inclination nor the means to turn the occasion into a bacchanal.[30]

New Year's Day and the Fourth of July offered similar occasions for symbolic affirmations of mutual dependence. On some Georgia plantations, slaves went to the field on New Year's morning and worked feverishly until noon, when the master made a formal promise to provide for them and look after their interests on condition they continued to work as diligently for the rest of the year. Then the entire household, black and white, spent the rest of the day celebrating.[31] In related fashion, masters commemorated the nation's birthday with elaborate barbecues for their slaves. White and black boys went fishing together; ball games, wrestling matches, music, and song accompanied the day's events; and often, just before the meal, the slaves paraded around the barbecue table, carrying hoes and leading mules hitched to plows.[32] Like the Christmas rituals, such exercises reinforced the reciprocal bonds between masters and slaves.

After dispensing with such formalities, slaves made their own use of the slack seasons. Christmas became a time of relaxing, visiting, and socializing among families and friends. Trusted slaves obtained permission to travel for the purpose of visiting relatives, as William and Ellen Craft did upon the occasion of their escape. Laying-by time brought camp meetings. Although the 1835 insurrection plot had haunted the memory of most masters, only the most suspicious or the most godless forbade their slaves to attend these gatherings thereafter. As earlier, the spirit of the campground appealed to masters as well as slaves. The meetings continued to provide a break from field labor during the hottest season of the year as well as physical and spiritual refreshment prior to the ordeal of harvest. Individual slaves still used camp meetings to decamp from their masters.[33] And both individuals and groups found cover for a host of illicit activities. In 1858, for instance, several slaves at a camp meeting in Bibb County killed a member of the slave patrol searching for liquor.[34] Most slaves, however, took other pleasures away from the meeting ground. Many a courtship and friendship originated there. And the spirit of radical egalitarianism—characterized by slaves' preaching and mourning benches that recognized no worldly distinctions—provided a soothing antidote to the planters' racist ideology.[35]

Slaves had to salt away these pleasures to carry them through the pains of plowing, hoeing, and harvesting. But even at seasons of peak labor demand, there were occasional rewards and breaks in the tedium. Slaves often collected cash payments for the special physical exertion and extended hours of labor during harvest. Corn shucking involved an elaborate ritual, which, though common enough in cooperative work settings in rural societies throughout the world, also testified to the special character of plantation slavery. When the corn was ripe, planters took turns hosting husking parties involving the slaves from all surrounding plantations. A festive atmosphere prevailed despite the seriousness of the work. The corn was usually divided in half and the slaves formed into two competing groups, each under the lead of a general or captain (either appointed by the host planter or chosen by themselves). The team that shucked its corn first won a prize, often a ration of whiskey. Teams paced their work with songs, traded insults with the opposing team, and even ridiculed the masters. For their efforts, slaves enjoyed a chance to socialize. In turn, planters got their corn shucked expeditiously. Such rituals released tension among the slaves; they also re-affirmed the authority of the planters, who, after all, owned the corn, dispensed the treats, and bent the customary rules. But perhaps most important, the shucking ritual acknowledged the principle that slaves did not labor beyond the norm gratuitously.[36]

Such after-hours labor under the eyes of masters intensified the slaves' desire for unrestricted discretion over their own time for subsistence and other purposes. For most of the nineteenth century, all southerners—black and white, slave and free—considered the subsistence resources of nature as God's gift to all humankind. From the dawn of English settlement, native North Americans

A cornshucking (Library of Congress)

and immigrant Europeans and Africans shared both knowledge and techniques of how best to take advantage of the gift. They fished with hook and line as well as net and trap; they caught turtles and assorted shellfish; they pursued small game such as squirrels, rabbits, opossums, and raccoons and large game such as deer and bears. Slaves from both the tidewater and the lowcountry carried such skills with them to the upcountry.[37] Although masters might have preferred that their slaves rest during nonworking hours, in the end they relented. After all, nocturnal subsistence activity ultimately served the masters' interests as well as the slaves'. And fishing soothed raw nerves at least as much as it strained tired bodies.

The growing body of antebellum legislation aimed at distinguishing the rights of private property holders from those claimed by society at large did not abridge the slaves' right to the bounty of nature, which stood above questions of freedom or citizenship. Fishing laws, for instance, aimed to protect the public at large from rapacious commercial fishermen. A representative law that applied to central Georgia's chief waterway, the Ocmulgee River, required "any person [or] persons, their agent or agents, slave or slaves" fishing with seines to wait at least one hour between hauls. It also banned the laying of "any seine, gil net, or other obstruction across the main channel, so as to prevent the free passage of fish."[38]

Fishermen who jeopardized life, health, or property—for instance, by poisoning the water—merited special legislation.[39] Free whites who violated such laws faced fines ranging from $50 to $200; slave or free black violators operating "without the coercion of his, her, or their owner, or overseer" suffered thirty-nine lashes on the bare back.[40] But neither slaves nor free persons fishing with hook and line or small nets violated the letter or spirit of these laws.[41]

Slaves enjoyed similar access to terrestrial game. It was not until the 1850s that opponents of unrestricted hunting began voicing their chief concern, namely, profaning the Sabbath.[42] The few laws that limited hunting aimed primarily to conserve large game such as deer in areas where it was scarce; typical legislation applied to one or two counties and banned hunting during the spring and summer, when the animals reproduced. Some laws banned camp-hunting (the ancient practice of using fire to flush animals from cover), a source of "[g]reat injury . . . arising from firing the woods," which stampeded free-foraging stock as well as game, "often destroying whole herds."[43] These laws notwithstanding, no restrictions applied to the capture of the small game that had been the preferred quarry of slave hunters from colonial times.

Individual masters often took a more restrictive view of slaves' hunting. Perambulatory slaves seemed attracted to trouble. And nighttime hunting inhibited daytime diligence in cotton fields. The hunters' canines also raised masters' hackles. "[K]ept nominally to catch raccoons," one skeptic complained, the dogs were "actually employed to catch hogs." Others cited the "half-starved" curs' penchant for sheep.[44] During the late antebellum period, lawmakers at both the state and local levels sought to restrict depredations by dogs but could devise no effective means of distinguishing dogs belonging to slaves from those belonging to planters or slaveless yeomen. Hence slaves' dogs enjoyed a degree of equality with their kind that was systematically denied to their masters.[45]

Down to the Civil War, slaves in large sections of the upcountry managed to keep alive such prerogatives of the lowcountry task system as gardening and keeping chickens and pigs for sale on their own accounts. Under this "Carolina rule," as one planter termed it, slaves could "make from ten to fifty dollars a year each, for themselves, according to their industry."[46] Most slaves worked their gardens at night and on Sundays. But some also bargained for Saturday afternoons. Others convinced their masters that tasks such as plowing were best accomplished by appropriating time from the crop and by using plantation work-stock and implements.[47] Slaves also negotiated with individual masters over various scraps of time, such as that lost to inclement weather. Although not necessarily suitable for gardening, these intervals might be employed fashioning railroad ties, shingles, barrels, bricks, horse collars, and shoes for sale or exchange.[48]

Predictably, slaves wrangled with masters over the crops to be grown in the gardens. Although slaves desired to raise whatever they pleased, masters did not generally approve of cotton or corn. Yet some slaves won such permission, often provided they sold their produce to the master. In 1851, a group of Houston County slaves collected $98.25 from their master for their corn.[49] Growing cotton was even more ticklish. With their masters' permission, some slaves planted brown-staple nankeen cotton; others raised cotton on their own account and then turned it over to their masters for marketing with the plantation crop.

The slaves of Howell Cobb and John B. Lamar fit that description. In 1856, Mary Ann Cobb (Cobb's wife and Lamar's sister) reported that "after all expenses and commissions were taken off," the slaves' cotton money "amounted to $1,965." On Lamar's plantation, extant records for 1858 indicate that thirty-nine slaves (including four women) raised cotton on their own account. Three of the four women accounted for less than 700 pounds of seed cotton each, a low figure matched by only three of the men. But the fourth woman accounted for 1,400 pounds, an amount equaled or exceeded by fewer than half the men. It appears that the thirty-nine were heads of families, and the output reflected the labor of each one's family. Just as the decision to grow such cotton in the first place involved a matter of choice, so did the mobilization of family labor power to that end. The ability to exercise such discretion and the practice of doing so, though arguably exceptional, provided slaves with important precedents for the general exercise of such rights after the end of slavery.[50]

Privileges to keep animals followed a related pattern. Chickens and other domesticated fowl did not generally pose problems, in that they pecked for much of their food and stayed close to home. But pigs were a different matter. Except just before butchering when they might be penned for fattening, the rest of the year they fed on mast foraged from the woods. Commonly held rights to the open range did not exclude the animals of slaves. By some accounts, slave-owned pigs had a particular knack for finding breaks in fences surrounding cultivated fields and feasting on the forbidden fruit. But antebellum law obligated landowners to protect their crops and exempted animal owners from liability for damages when fences did not meet strict requirements.[51] While aggrieved farmers could do little but fulminate, masters could, and did, take more decisive action. Probably most forbade slaves to keep pigs—more through fear of theft from smokehouses than of damage to crops. Masters who authorized the keeping of pigs generally insisted upon purchasing the fattened animals for plantation purposes. John B.

Lamar purchased "all of the hogs owned by the negroes" to achieve self-sufficiency in meat.[52]

Not all masters welcomed the legal complexities consequent upon slaves' ownership of property, but when they recognized that slave-grown produce could reduce subsistence costs, provision grounds and permission to keep animals made sense. So too did the realization that slaves intended to control their own food consumption, even when that meant helping themselves to plantation gardens, chicken coops, and smokehouses—what John B. Lamar referred to as "stealage."[53] Doubtless the depression of the 1840s helped make the case. It is also likely that slaves won gardening or other similar privileges from masters who abolished such practices as marrying off the plantation.[54]

It is not entirely clear how slaves divided self-subsistence activities among themselves, but they clearly mobilized their available time and energy within the framework of households. To the extent that plantations facilitated household formation, the process of plantation consolidation strengthened the slaves' ability to produce for their own ends. Husbands, wives, children, and unrelated coresidents each did a part. Some duties followed sexual lines. Nocturnal hunting and fishing was strictly the province of men, just as spinning and weaving and washing and mending clothing were women's work. Performance of other tasks depended upon the circumstances of individual households. Men, women, and children tended gardens as need dictated. Watching over pigs—like similar tasks involving animals in the woods, whether domesticated or wild—seems to have been the responsibility of men and boys.[55]

Distinctions in men's and women's work reached fullest development in the realm of skilled labor, although it is unlikely that the sexual division of labor on the plantations of central Georgia replicated the pattern that characterized Jamaica's estates. There, according to recent studies, men's access to skilled and low-level supervisory positions meant that women made up the majority of field laborers.[56] On the cotton plantations of central Georgia, there were comparatively few slave artisans on even the largest estates, where the need for skilled work was presumably the greatest.[57] During periodic building booms in Macon and the other towns, planters hired out their artisans for a year or more. But by the 1850s, as the number of white artisans and laborers available for hire increased, masters often employed skilled slaves in the field.

One group of semiskilled slave men—wagoners—managed to carve out a distinctive niche within the plantation order. At harvest time, four- and six-mule wagons clogged the public thoroughfares, moving cotton bales from gins to steamboat landings or railway stations. Moreover, as the commercial economy expanded, so did the numbers of wagons and slave teamsters. Whether they worked seasonally or year-round, slave wagoners gained an incomparable degree of sophistication.

By virtue of their various travels and dealings, they came into contact with a wider range of persons, black and white, than did slaves of virtually any other description. While on the road, they had full control of the reins, often for days or weeks on end across tens or even hundreds of miles.[58] In addition to managing their own time, they often managed their masters' money. Slave wagoners engaged in petty trade on their own account and no doubt on behalf of other slaves as well. Such dealings may not all have been above board. In 1850, the Bibb County grand jury criticized unscrupulous whites for purchasing from slave wagoners the corn and fodder furnished by owners for the teams![59]

The wagoner's "privilege" rested squarely upon his master's trust, without which he was remanded to the field. Not a few slave wagoners parlayed that trust into permission to hire their own time. Robert Anderson, whose home was in coastal Georgia, paid his master $20 a month for permission to work for himself in Macon. Surplus earnings might pave a road to freedom. After scrimping for a decade, Anderson purchased himself for $1,000. He later saved an additional $500 to free his wife. Such could be the reward of keeping the trust.[60]

Wagoners determined to be free faced little restraint. They knew the roads as potential escape routes as well as commercial arteries. They knew traffic patterns and the habits of patrollers. In 1833, the master of runaway wagoner Isaac suspected that he might have taken refuge in Macon (where he had many friends) or with the Creeks or Cherokees (among whom he had hidden two years earlier).[61] A wagoner named Bill made his bid for freedom after a four-month sojourn on the road had placed "several hundred" dollars in his hands. Other wagoners did likewise.[62] A slave named Jim who hailed from Milledgeville, though not specifically identified as a teamster, neatly expressed the world in which they moved. Before taking his leave early in 1837, Jim declared "that he preferred freedom to slavery and that from the facilities he could have from some of his white acquaintances in the neighborhood of Macon, he could spend a lifetime without detection." He did not boast idly—six months after escaping he was still at large.[63]

For this measure of control over their lives, slave wagoners paid a price. The work was often dangerous. Aside from the risk of injury caused by shifting loads, failing equipment, and bucking mules, teamsters battled assorted human adversaries. Any white person was subject to ask probing questions, and patrollers practiced harassment as an art form. Highwaymen and other sharpers accosted the wagoners with more than words. Slave wagoners carried knives for self-defense.[64] In the antebellum South, physical distance from their masters, the teamsters' stock in trade, denied them the protection of their masters—one of the fundamental rationales for slavery. The men's absence also left their families vulnerable on various fronts, an ample source of worry to fill the hours spent away. Wagoners ultimately wrestled with the trust itself: was the privilege worth the price? Not every man answered in the affirmative.

JUST AS SLAVE wagoners embodied the commercialization that accompanied the rise of King Cotton, the most obvious symbol of that process was the growth of Macon from a Creek meeting ground to the chief commercial center of central Georgia. Commercial development also spawned businesses at the respective county seats and at assorted crossroads, river landings, and railway junctions. Though clearly influenced by plantation culture, these urban areas also developed some characteristic features of their own, which profoundly affected the lives of their free and slave inhabitants. By 1860, approximately 2,800 slaves lived in the several square miles within the corporate limits of Macon.[65] Single plantations occupied more land, but only the largest contained as many as one-tenth that number of slaves. On a smaller scale, slaves in all the towns of the region experienced similar concentration.

By virtue of Macon's service function within the plantation economy, the structure of black life in the city (like that of the white urban population) differed from that in the surrounding rural areas. Although evidence regarding slave occupations in Macon is elusive at best, it is possible to make certain inferences from gross population figures and the structure of the urban economy at various points in time. In 1830, when the town was just being settled, the slave population stood at 1,183, of whom nearly 60 percent were men. Although some of those slaves no doubt worked exclusively as house servants, the small size of the white population (1,452 persons) and the modesty of dwellings would have limited such employment. In fact, given the semirural nature of the town at the time, "domestic" slaves likely worked outdoors as much as indoors. Other slaves moved the cotton about town and manned the pole boats that plied the Ocmulgee River. Still others were carpenters, masons, and construction laborers. From the early years, contractors hired slaves for such purposes, beginning the trend of attracting skilled slaves to the city that persisted through the Civil War. Finally, the city as a corporate entity owned a handful of slaves employed mostly in street maintenance.[66]

Completion of the Central Railroad to Savannah in 1843 further transformed Macon's mercantile economy. The railroad made for greater general trade, and, though the connection to Savannah markets made those in Macon largely superfluous, better access to the coast increased the volume of cotton shipped, and warehouses flourished as never before. Moreover, because the rail lines serving the city did not meet at a common terminal (a fashion typical of the antebellum South), freight had to be transferred manually from one train to another. Even beyond the handling taxes the city derived from these transfers, the railroad stimulated Macon's economy, even during the depression of the 1840s.

The white population grew from 2,296 to 3,329 over that decade, and the slave population from 1,606 to 2,353. Population growth spurred new construction, drawing additional skilled slaves to the city, and affluent cotton planters required more servants to maintain their increasingly lavish life-styles. Between 1850 and 1860, the cotton boom supported a 60 percent increase in the white population (to 5,396), but only a 20 percent increase in the number of slaves (to 2,829). Clearly, the rural demand for field hands slowed the growth in the urban slave population. At the same time, under normal circumstances, unskilled slaves were the likeliest candidates for relocation from city to cotton field. Hence the proportion of skilled slaves may well have increased in the city over the last antebellum decade.[67]

Available data do not fully clarify the picture, but 1860 federal census returns hint at the structure of slave occupations.[68] Of the 2,770 slaves belonging to household heads, 1,532 (55 percent) belonged to owners with professional and proprietary occupations. An average of six slaves, for instance, belonged to each of the slave-owning merchants. In addition to house service, these slaves doubtless also labored in their masters' places of business. Next, 1,064 of the slaves (40 percent) belonged to planters and farmers. In 1859, for instance, nineteen of John B. Lamar's eighty-four slaves maintained his residence in Macon; four of the nineteen were men. No doubt most of these slaves of planters were house and livery servants, with a smattering of skilled slaves. They generally occupied outbuildings on their master's property, often apartments above the kitchen.[69]

Only 166 (6 percent) of the slaves of household heads belonged to artisans, 27 alone to the five master carpenters and one master mason who owned slaves. The women were doubtless house servants, but it is safe to assume that at least some of the adult men worked in the trade of their masters. An additional 157 slaves (6 percent) belonged to women heading households for whom no occupation was listed. Besides serving in the homes of their mistresses, these slaves

Slave apartment over outdoor kitchen, rear of Slade House, Macon, built ca. 1827
(Historic American Buildings Survey, Library of Congress)

were presumably hired out. An indeterminate number of them were skilled. In short, perhaps several hundred of the 2,800 slaves in Macon in 1860 were skilled, but probably not more than 10 percent of the total.

Larger social changes did not particularly favor the reproduction of artisan skills within the slave population. Despite the fact that skilled slaves sold at a premium right through the Civil War, rising cotton prices prompted planters to employ their slaves in the fields and to hire artisanal services from free whites. One change begot another, as white artisans in turn attacked the competition they faced from skilled slaves. In 1846, white workingmen convinced the Macon city council to prohibit slaves from practicing trades in the city.[70] The ordinance apparently had mixed results. Masters who considered it a usurpation of their property rights continued to work skilled slaves at trades. Artisans themselves apparently flouted the ordinance: in 1860, 60 percent of the master craftsmen in Macon owned slaves, and 12 percent of the journeymen did too.[71] Still, the political tension surrounding the employment of skilled slaves surely decreased their number in the city.

Despite such adverse developments, slaves managed to hold their own in the construction trades. Unskilled slaves predominated at the brickyards, where not even the most desperate free workers would tread. Most brickyards were located near swamps, and masters hesitated to expose their slaves to the threat of respiratory problems and malaria. In 1835, the proprietor of one yard seeking hired slaves advertised that a mechanical brickmaking process minimized exposure to the customary hazards.[72] Masters willing to hire slaves to brickyards charged comparatively high rentals. For instance, six slaves hired in 1837 to work "under special exposure" drew an annual fee of $200, double what the owner charged for other slaves and approximately one-quarter of the value of the slaves.[73]

Slaves also staked out strong claims in carpentry and masonry, which required considerably more skill than brickmaking. Despite the opposition of white tradesmen to competition with slave laborers, it appears that masters placed favored, often light-skinned, slaves (who in some cases might also have been their sons) in the building trades.[74] Of course, skilled slaves—whether favored or not—could not take their positions for granted. John B. Lamar's "man Ned the carpenter" was "banished . . . to rural life" after a spree of heavy drinking and "fighting and misbehaving in every way." Miscreant slaves betrayed their master's unspoken trust. "[E]ye servants" (as Lamar described Ned) required the close and constant supervision of the plantation.[75]

Opposition by certain whites and indiscretion by certain slaves notwithstanding, the demands of the local economy continued to exert pressure in favor of employing skilled slaves down to the Civil War. William Craft was apprenticed to a cabinetmaker around 1840 and continued to work in that trade until his escape in 1848.[76] Although most butchers were white men, some black men apparently learned the trade as slaves.[77] Some slave artisans even learned the mysteries of luxury trades such as coachmaking and watchmaking during the late antebellum period. Given the paucity of free black men to fill such traditional roles as barbering, slaves routinely performed those services.[78]

Most slaves of artisans no doubt worked in close proximity to, if not right alongside, their masters, much like the slaves of yeomen. Hence they followed their masters' work patterns, governed by craft traditions no less than the weather and seasonal patterns of daylight. Beyond their regular hours slave artisans frequently worked on their own account. William Craft built boxes, cabinets, and chests of drawers, some of which graced his wife's apartment and others of which he sold.[79] Both while under their masters' tutelage and while working on their own, slave artisans clearly developed pride in their workmanship and a corresponding (even if incipient) political consciousness.[80]

In some respects, the lives of urban slaves combined features of yeoman farms and plantations. Despite their concentration within a comparatively small area, most of the slaves in Macon resided on smallholdings, in various corners of their masters' dwellings or in outbuildings on their masters' premises. Only slaves of the wealthiest planters, such as Joseph Bond or John B. Lamar, would have resided amidst twenty or more fellow servants. Such demographic and residential patterns proved disruptive to slave family life, though the high concentration of slaves proved conducive to the development of other social institutions, such as churches.

The religious life of Macon slaves underscores the kinds of opportunities that presented themselves in an urban environment, where slaves enjoyed both a modicum of control over their nonworking hours and the privilege to earn money on their own account. By the late antebellum period, slaves in Macon possessed four churches: two Baptist, one Methodist, and one Presbyterian. The Methodist church, most of whose members apparently were artisans and servants, dated from 1838. When white Methodists found the slaves' religious meetings objectionably noisy, they decided to build a new church, offering the old one to the slaves. Black communicants purchased the building and grounds, with the trustees of the parent congregation holding title to both. Black Presbyterians and Baptists eventually occupied church buildings under a similar arrangement.[81] Unlike rural slaves, those in Macon could use their savings to purchase church buildings.

Urban black churches stood somewhere between the dependence of the rural planters' churches and the autonomy of the brush arbor. The urban churches could sponsor certain religious and social events forbidden to plantation slaves. They could entertain itinerant black preachers. The churches could also exercise quasi-judicial powers, at times assuming some of the disciplinary responsibilities normally exercised by white churchmen. Black Methodists, for instance, operated a court with jurisdiction over various offenses. Although white trustees reserved the right to review its decisions, the court provided a certain structure for enforcing group norms and promoting leadership. Robert Anderson described his appearance before the court sometime during the 1840s. Anderson stood accused of defrauding a fellow drayman out of his share of $20 they had found and agreed to split. Exonerated in the end, Anderson attributed the proceedings against him to petty jealousy within the slave community. "Some thought that I was proud," Anderson later recalled, "and some thought that I ought not to wear side whiskers, and some thought that because I could read a little I thought myself better than anybody else."[82]

Although the record is not completely clear, incipient social divisions seem to have characterized black churches in antebellum southern cities. In the county seats and smaller towns of the cotton region, slaves did not form separate congregations with buildings of their own. Denominational differences among slaves largely mirrored those among their masters, with whom they worshipped. But in Macon and other cities, the more privileged slaves seem to have affiliated with the Methodist Episcopal church and the less privileged with the Baptists, though the lines were not absolute. Even as denominationalism deepened certain divisions among slaves, a similar, if less pronounced, process occurred within congregations as well. Apart from what store masters placed in church courts such as the one before which Robert Anderson appeared, these bodies served an important internal function of mediating differences among urban slaves of varying levels of privilege.[83]

ALTHOUGH CENTRAL Georgia slaves wished to be free, few achieved freedom before the Civil War.[84] Women headed most of the handful of free black households in Macon; the women made a living washing and ironing, the men working in the building trades or personal service. Occasionally, a free black person in the city would rise to a position of preeminence. Solomon Humphries, for instance, who purchased his own freedom and that of his family during the 1820s, established a mercantile business that made him wealthy. Although himself illiterate, Humphries reportedly employed white clerks and borrowed as much as $10,000 in goods at a time to replenish his stock. Travelers to Macon never ceased to marvel at Humphries's ability and his good fortune.[85]

Few other free black persons fared as well.[86] In accordance with Georgia law, they had to secure guardians to post bond for their good behavior. Free blacks at times had difficulty finding a guardian, as did Nathan, a twenty-one-year-old man with no property who in 1854 petitioned the courts to appoint one. Those who failed to register took considerable risk. The Bibb County inferior court routinely punished such infractions with fines of $100 plus costs. Inability to pay the fine necessitated hiring at public auction. In one case, the lowest bid was forty-two months' service. Even with a guardian, free blacks enjoyed a precarious freedom at best. An 1857 advertisement for a captured runaway slave described him as a former free black in Bibb County who was sold for not having paid his taxes.[87]

Another free black family originated from the long-term relationship between a planter and one of his slaves. Michael M. Healy was an Irish immigrant who became a wealthy planter. A shrewd investor in land, he once held some 1,500 acres in half a dozen Georgia counties, eventually consolidating his holdings into a 1,600-acre plantation in Jones County. Healy took as his "trusty woman" a mulatto slave, Mary Eliza, with whom he had ten children. Growing skeptical of their prospects for a fulfilling life in Georgia, in 1845 Healy penned a will that would have secured the freedom of Mary Eliza and the children and guaranteed them lifetime security through the sale of his estate. Although local lore holds that Mary Eliza moved north after Healy's death, she in fact died several months before he did in 1850. Several of the children were already at school in the North at that time. They arranged passage for their younger siblings and eventually took possession of their inheritance. The Healys subsequently achieved considerable distinction: one son served as president of Georgetown University, another as a bishop in the Roman Catholic church, and a third as an officer in the United States Navy. They apparently also arranged for the purchase of Mary Eliza's sister Nancy from the prominent Jones County ginmaker, Samuel Griswold. At the time Nancy left for New York, her husband, George, the head mechanic at Griswold's works, disappeared, presumably to join her.[88]

The saga of Peter Davis, a slave carpenter belonging to Houston County planter William M. Davis, illustrates how a convoluted path to freedom might skirt the restrictions of the law. William Davis and his family settled in Houston County during the mid-1840s. After a few years, when the time came to construct a mansion befitting the owner of more than 100 slaves, he reportedly sent Peter to Boston to study architecture, on the promise of freedom when the house was completed. Peter went north unaccompanied, learned the requisite skills, and returned. Under his direction, crews of slaves worked for four years constructing the home, which featured two parlors, a ballroom, a kitchen, a pantry, and a dining room on the first floor, five bedrooms on the second floor, and an observation post on the third floor, from which William could monitor field operations. As agreed, Peter was emancipated.[89]

Not every loyal slave fared as well as Peter Davis. In 1842, a slave stonemason named Jacob Hutchings from Jones County was, like Davis, called upon to build a monument to planter power. But Hutchings's creation was a jail house instead of a big house. Although he apparently learned to read and write—no minor accomplishment—Hutchings remained a slave until the general emancipation following the Civil War.[90]

The Healy family, Solomon Humphries, and Peter Davis were exceptional not just because they were intellectuals, entrepreneurs, or artisans in a plantation society, but because they achieved freedom. Before 1850, though few in number, free blacks were not as rare as they would become. As late as 1840, it was

Jones County Jail, built by Jacob Hutchings in 1842
(Courtesy of Georgia Department of Archives and History)

possible for a young slave woman to pass herself off as free in Macon, trading
upon her skill as a seamstress.[91] But as cotton prices soared in the 1850s, the
prospects of free blacks plummeted.[92] In all of the six counties surrounding
Macon, there were barely 200 free black persons in 1860.[93] Although some
slaves gained freedom by running away and others by performing good works,
most slaves in central Georgia—indeed, throughout the cotton South—understood that their hope of achieving absolute freedom was minuscule at best. So
they had to find what space they could to control their labor, their institutions,
and their lives within the confines of plantation slavery.

AGAINST THE BACKDROP of the capitalist world market, masters and slaves in
central Georgia interacted within a system of precapitalist labor relations. Professions of democracy and republican government notwithstanding, slaves could
neither vote nor exercise other prerogatives of citizens. Planters aspired to a
landed ideal—perhaps most closely approximated by their counterparts in Brazil—but they also favored commercial developments that in significant ways

undermined the plantation order. Like slaves and masters throughout the Americas, slaves and masters in central Georgia subscribed to a standard of reciprocal rights and responsibilities subject to past practice and the relative strength of the contending parties on any given slaveholding. The struggle over rights proceeded endlessly, though with varying degrees of intensity. In fact, it represented the mainspring of the master-slave relationship. Masters surely enjoyed the edge in this contest, but their dependence upon their slaves, coupled with the very face-to-face nature of slavery, also made them vulnerable.

Slaves wanted to be free, and with that option closed, they wanted to exercise as much control over their lives as possible in the circumstances. This effort took various forms encompassing individuals and groups. Slaves on smallholdings sought various perquisites aiming to distance themselves somewhat from the close scrutiny of their masters and facilitating their access to the larger slave community. Slaves on plantations aimed not only to achieve independent access to subsistence goods, but also to develop social institutions capable of providing solid mooring in turbulent times. Slaves in cities and towns pursued different openings still: some of these were related to the demographic peculiarities of urban life; others depended upon the growing commercial economy in which slaves found new opportunities to labor, travel, produce goods, and trade beyond the direct supervision of their masters.

This struggle for control over the slaves' time and the products of their toil assumed special significance during the 1850s, when planters aimed to promote commercial development without free labor. As the decade unfolded, slavery proved increasingly incapable of muting class conflict, and, in some respects, it even appeared to exacerbate social tension. Consequently, with northern abolitionists in their faces, planters kept looking over their shoulders at the slaves and the assortment of white citizens for whom the plantation ideal rang hollow.

4

· · · · · · · · · ·

Impending Crisis:
The 1850s

THE YEAR 1848 marked a crucial turning point in the history of the South. Regionally and nationally, 1848 represented the start of a period of economic growth that transformed the American economy. But also during that year, the treaty of peace with Mexico incorporated into the national domain a vast new territory with ominous portent for the future of slavery. Internationally, the wave of revolutions sweeping Europe polarized the forces of aristocratic privilege and popular government throughout the North Atlantic world. Among other things, it resulted in the emancipation of serfs in the Austro-Hungarian Empire and of slaves in the French and Danish West Indies.

The reverberations from these events challenged the traditional values of plantation society. Although southern partisans had long criticized the frenetic pace of change in the North, before 1848 they could do so at arm's length. In those idyllic days, southern staple producers were in the world market but not of it, realizing returns on their crops through international trade but curbing the spread of bourgeois values into the South. But after 1848, the dawn of what Eric Hobsbawm has aptly termed the "Age of Capital," the South felt the pressures of capitalist development as never before.[1]

These changes inevitably took political expression as southerners wrestled to master "circumstances that can neither be foreseen [n]or avoided."[2] From the dawn of the second party system a generation earlier, national political developments and personalities had cast a shadow across Georgia politics. Yet the primary reference point of most voters remained local. Their immediate concerns embraced neighbors and relatives, and county government provided the framework for addressing most matters of public policy. The state government seemed removed, and the government in Washington was even more distant.[3]

Following the Mexican War, however, national affairs took on new importance in the lives of Georgians. Congress became the fulcrum on which the future of slavery shifted back and forth. Congressional control over the District of Columbia made the capital "the battle field of Abolition."[4] And David Wilmot's proviso threatened to prohibit slavery from the territory seized from Mexico. The Whig and Democratic parties began splintering into sectionally based factions, with the Whigs soon disintegrating entirely. Politics at home fell apart in similar fashion. As Whiggish interests subdivided, Democrats benefited. The political awakening of upcountry yeomen also infused new life into the Democratic party, even to the point that they elevated a favorite son, Joseph E. Brown, to the governorship as the 1850s drew to a close. In central Georgia and throughout the plantation belt, slaves showed similar signs of disquiet with the paternalist social order.

THE MEXICAN WAR taught central Georgia's planters that achieving hegemony and maintaining it were not necessarily synonymous. High cotton prices during the 1850s proved both a blessing and a curse. In pursuing the lure of gold, cotton growers in central Georgia and throughout the South helped undermine what they had built over the previous generation. Large cotton crops begot rapid social change, which begot tensions that ultimately took political form.

No area of central Georgia escaped these tendencies. Developments in Houston County may be taken as prototypical. In both 1850 and 1860 the plantations and farms of Houston produced more bales of ginned cotton than any other county in the state. It boasted some of the largest plantations and wealthiest planters in the state—such pillars of the Macon elite as Eugenius A. Nisbet and P. B. D. H. Culler had plantations there, as did roughly two score other planters, each with more than 1,000 cultivated acres. Houston County's standing as premier cotton producer did not come effortlessly. Competition was intense from cotton growers on the fresh lands of southwest Georgia, where output per acre rivaled that of Alabama, Mississippi, and Louisiana. Planters on marginal and depleted lands in the eastern cotton belt of Georgia began applying fertilizers to telling effect, also increasing the competitive pressure upon central Georgia's producers. Finally, cotton culture was spreading into the upper Piedmont and wire-grass regions of the state, incorporating land that needed to be fertilized but adding thousands of cotton growers. All this meant that established planters could not rest on their laurels.

Houston County planters could still count upon reasonably good soil, not as rich as that of the Mississippi Valley, but then again, not as poor as the overworked red clay east of Macon. They could also go along with the trend to apply fertilizer to increase productivity. But they opted for yet another method, namely, sheer exploitation of their labor force. It was not that they imported large numbers of slaves from the Upper South. Between 1850 and 1860, the slave population in the county grew modestly from 9,924 to 10,755. Improved acreage increased from 145,386 to 184,132 acres. Yet cotton crops leaped from 19,362 to 28,852 bales. In other words, over the decade, 8 percent more slaves working on 27 percent more land produced 49 percent more cotton.[5]

To increase production so drastically, planters employed overseers as never before. Between 1850 and 1860, the absolute number of overseers heading households in Houston County doubled from 50 to 100. But whereas in 1850, 26 percent of overseers owned land, ten years later only 8 percent did. Without too much exaggeration, it can be said that planters displaced yeomen and then hired them to drive their slaves. Young men on the make who lacked a start in life also began their climb as overseers. They proved especially shrewd practitioners of the procreative process of accumulating slaves—seven of the ten overseers owning one slave in 1860 had a woman of childbearing age.[6] By thus investing their earnings and by courting the patronage of large planters, Houston County overseers established a reputation for rising rapidly into the ranks of polite society. Yet mere statistics on increasing numbers of overseers do little justice to the qualitative change that their presence wrought in the lives of the slaves. In a word, they must have worked the slaves ruthlessly to achieve the outputs they recorded.

The proportion of landless households increased dramatically from 30 percent to 40 percent between 1850 and 1860, but not all the dispossessed became overseers or moved west to make a fresh start (as their counterparts had done in earlier times). Instead of migrating, for example, they increasingly stayed in the area working for wages in the employ of planters with cash to spare. To the extent that masters put semiskilled slaves to work in cotton fields, vacancies in certain services appeared that dispossessed smallholders were able to fill. The three sons of William Burgamy illustrate the point. In 1850 all were farmers; ten years later one was a mechanic, another a carpenter, and the third drove a hack.[7] The planters' aggrandizement of land severed many residents of central Georgia from the soil, but the commercialization of everyday life guaranteed alternative employment to at least some.

Planters benefited disproportionately from the rise of King Cotton. In 1850, planters owning twenty or more slaves constituted 20 percent of all farmers and owned over 62 percent of the land in Houston County. On the eve of the Civil War, planters numbered roughly 30 percent of the farmers, owned 77 percent of the land, and averaged thirty-five slaves apiece. Over that same decade, the richest 10 percent of landowners (the upper crust of the planter class) prospered beyond their wildest dreams: the average value of their landholdings grew from $12,000 to $27,000 and the average size of their slaveholdings from thirty-eight to fifty-eight slaves.[8]

As the cotton economy flourished, commercial development proceeded apace. The professions swelled as factors, merchants, attorneys, doctors, dentists, teachers, and even occasional artists and daguerreotypists catered to the needs of the planter-merchant elite. Artisans and shopkeepers also settled in the upcountry to ply their trades and peddle their wares. And even laborers found employment that had not hitherto been available.

Nothing so clearly advanced these trends as the growth of railroads. Promoters of railroads linking the upcountry with the coast promised to overcome the deficiencies of river transportation. As a bonus, the railroads also made possible a growth in trade between the seacoast and the interior, which affected the upcountry in a number of ways. First, railroads expanded the quantity and variety of goods available, such that successful cotton producers could also become more conspicuous consumers. European- and northern-made trade goods, ranging from fine clothing, furniture, and housewares for planters to cloth and brogans for slaves, proliferated.[9]

Second, railroads enabled upcountry merchants to flourish as never before. This development did not, however, mark the genesis of a new class antagonistic to the planters. Merchants often had direct ties to planter families, either by birth or through marriage. Planters were the merchants' most important clients. Still, the concomitant growth of towns and trade gave rise to a commercial interest that did not always coincide exactly with the plantation interest. Moreover, merchants diversified their clienteles—or more properly, a variety of merchants appeared who filled the needs of different clienteles. Such a development augured especially well for yeomen farmers, who did not enjoy credit lines with coastal factors. Town merchants could make advances on credit for a growing variety of staple foods, hardware, and dry goods, though major expenditures, especially for slaves, still required major financing. In the end, railroads produced diversification among the merchants, who, despite the brotherhood of trade, also identified with the particular interests of their respective customers.

Third, the appearance of the railroads also contributed to a diversification of the free white population as a whole. The rail lines brought travelers and settlers to the upcountry. During the 1850s, increasing numbers of the latter were foreign born. Prominent in this group were the Irishmen who frequently sailed from Liverpool as ballast for cotton ships returning to Savannah and Charleston. These men settled in Macon and the other stops along the railroads, finding whatever employment they could.[10] The newcomers as a rule did not own land. They joined the growing numbers of native-born Georgians who, their fortunes on the land having flagged, began settling in cities and towns. The increase in commerce and manufacturing generated by the railroad made such an alternative possible.

Not surprisingly, such advantages came at a cost. Little did either railroad promoters, merchants, yeomen, or urban laborers realize the impact of the iron horse. Least of all did the planters, who wished to shape the course of social development along traditional hierarchical lines. They initially supported railroad construction to facilitate the shipment of cotton to the coast, with no clear conception of the persons, goods, and ideas that would make the return trip. Although the introduction of railroads to the upcountry fostered the development of markets in various goods and even led to the growth of a free working class, it did not signal the dawn of capitalist enterprise in the commercial centers, much less on the plantations. In fact, to the extent that railroads facilitated the process of accumulation, they deepened the society's commitment to slavery. But the impact of the railroad cut in various directions. Even slaves found ways of manipulating its effects—especially the ease of transportation and the availability of goods—to their advantage. Thus, rather than a mere sign of changing times, the railroads themselves became a battleground of change.

AS COMMERCE DREW the North and South closer together, the Mexican War and the ensuing political crisis drove the sections farther apart. Politicians everywhere acknowledged the polarizing effects of the war. As one Georgian observed, "The whole North is becoming ultra anti-slavery and the whole South ultra pro-slavery." Southern hard-liners welcomed such developments and began fanning the embers of secession. Anxious to dissolve the Union in favor of "a consolidated Republic formed of the Southern States," they desired to place slavery "under the control of those most interested in it."[11] Although most southern whites repudiated secession as potentially revolutionary, the disunionists kept up a shrill agitation.

Besides breathing new life into the ghost of disunionism, the victory against Mexico also threatened to destroy the party system developed during the age of Jackson. In response to the perceived threats against slaveholders' rights, southern politicians began to reassess the national party structure. With the Whigs largely discredited by the Wilmot Proviso, southern Democrats enjoyed unparalleled influence. But not even they could escape internal divisions. For instance, South Carolina's John C. Calhoun, whose considerable influence was waning, saw the dissolution of the old Whig and Democratic parties as the opportunity to form a new southern sectional party. Howell Cobb, on the other hand, whose influence was on the rise, favored preserving the party of Jackson by reuniting its northern and southern factions.[12] Cobb did not deny that the interests of slaveholders appeared to be suffering in the national legislative process. But he asserted that, all things considered, the Union provided the best hope for the future of slavery. Three alternatives—disunion; a new, exclusively southern party; and a rejuvenated national Democratic party—were the poles around which Georgia's politicians and voters gravitated.[13]

The particular legislative package aimed at reconciling sectional interests following the Mexican War—the famous Compromise of 1850—bought time but did not restore the status quo ante. Slaveholders winced at the admission of California as a free state and the abolition of the slave trade in the District of Columbia but took heart in the stiffer fugitive slave act. Most Georgia Whigs (like their counterparts throughout the South) favored the deal, viewing it as crucial to harmony between the sections. Democrats were more divided, however. In the assessment of compromise proponents such as Howell Cobb and John B. Lamar, the "respectable citizens," particularly "the planting interest," favored it.[14] Throughout the plantation districts of central Georgia, public meetings of old-line Whigs and unionist Democrats passed strong resolutions in favor of the Union. And in Macon, the commercial interests and the planter nabobs of both Whig and Democratic persuasions strongly endorsed the package. Although they may not have reached the mind of every voter in this way, these established pillars of wealth and respectability helped steer public opinion in favor of the compromise.[15]

Yet some Democrats resisted; for the most part, they represented three political factions. The first consisted of "old Nullifiers," who had cut their political teeth during South Carolina's nullification controversy a generation earlier. Still nursing old wounds, these men opposed what they perceived as growing federal power antithetical to southern interests, especially slavery. Upward-striving small planters from the black belt provided the second (and apparently most numerous) source of opposition to the compromise. Imbued with Jacksonian notions of frontier democracy, they viewed the compromise as a Whiggish plot to deprive them of slaves and thereby undercut their chances for economic and social advancement. The third source of opposition came from established planters in declining plantation areas, whose world seemed in jeopardy. Without strong guarantees for the future of slavery, they saw only disaster.

This coalition formed the short-lived but influential Resistance party.[16] The Resisters succeeded in defining a position of conditional unionism which, though stopping short of secession, strictly avoided unconditional loyalty to the Union. A clear statement of the new philosophy emerged from a meeting in Jones County: "[W]e love the Union, as formed by our Fathers, and will shed the last drop of blood in our veins to cherish and defend it; but we hold our liberty, equality and independence as infinitely more dear, than a Union which is alike regardless of the Constitution, our feelings, peace, rights and honor."[17]

That sentiment reached its most influential form in the "Georgia platform," which became a test of dedication to southern rights not just in Georgia but throughout the South. While professing loyalty to the Union, the platform made clear that principles—not blind faith—animated the sentiment. And while acknowledging the need for compromise, it averred that southern cooperation required protection of slavery in the territories and strict enforcement of the fugitive slave law. Any congressional action hostile to slavery would merit resistance, "even (as a last resort) to the disruption of every tie which binds [Georgia] to the Union."[18] By defining the extreme position of secession, the Resisters made conditional unionism appear moderate. At the same time, they forced the moderates to cover their flanks with professions of the ultimate right of secession.

Although unionism carried the day in 1850, the old party structure collapsed. Totally discredited, southern Whigs searched for an identity. Meanwhile, secessionist Democrats bolted the old party, while loyalists like Cobb wished to maintain their national credentials. Most Democrats no doubt took a pragmatic approach, affirming unionism in principle but reserving the right to withhold their support from particular Democratic candidates and measures. Such a program attracted old-line Whigs as well. In December 1850, former Whigs Robert Toombs and Alexander Stephens, planter-politicians of national stature, joined moderate Democrats (including Cobb) in forming the Constitutional

Union party. Such influential advocates of compromise subdued "the spirit of disunion and revolution," at least temporarily.[19]

The Constitutional Unionists charted an independent course. One such group in Houston County welcomed the break-up of the national parties, urging that "all entangling alliances with the Whig and Democratic parties be forever discarded—so that fanatics of the North, and the disorganizers of the South, may each have their own distinct organization."[20] Disenchanted with national affairs, they nonetheless believed implicitly in the Union as the source of both national strength and constitutional protection of slave property. Established planters rather than insecure upstarts, these men sought to build new organizations that would carry on the best traditions of the old ones.

That work proceeded under a new political discourse defined by the extremists. In short, politicians had to express a willingness to resist further encroachment upon slavery. Even staunch unionists such as Howell Cobb had to bow to the pressure and affirm the South's right to resist "*degradation* and *inequality*." "Nor am I particular by what name this resistance may be characterized," he declared in accepting the Constitutional Union party's nomination for governor in 1851, "whether secession, revolution, or anything else; for no one can for a moment doubt that should this fearful collision ever come, the issue will be decided only by the arbitrament of the sword. Where constitutions end revolutions begin."[21]

As the dust from the compromise settled, unionist planters perceived the danger of persistent agitation over slavery and sought to reassert their hegemony by placing slavery off-limits to political debate. An 1851 convention of Houston County unionists, for example, resolved to renounce any candidate "who favors the agitation of slavery, or who is not true to the Constitution and Compromise."[22] The following spring a similar group expressed the desire to put "forever at rest . . . all agitation and excitement upon the subject of slavery," a theme echoed in political meetings throughout central Georgia at the time.[23] Four years later, planter spokesmen were still voicing the same sentiment. "The great question now before the country," declared the editors of the *Journal & Messenger*, "is—'How can a final end be put to the slavery agitation?' "[24] From 1848 onward, slaveholders sought without success to close Pandora's box.

Tempers cooled during the early 1850s only to rise once again in mid-decade in connection with the struggle over Kansas, which white southerners viewed as a litmus test of their rights within the Union. "Kansas must come in as a slave state," concluded one Georgian, "or the cause of southern rights is dead."[25] The most determined partisans on the southern side viewed the proceedings not simply in terms of slavery in the territories, but in terms of the more fundamental issue of the sanctity of property itself. Public meetings were held to air the political implications of various actions and to raise money for proslavery settlers.[26] Unlike the Compromise of 1850, which had produced factions, the Kansas troubles drew white southerners together against the perceived enemy, northern abolitionism. A new martial spirit arose.[27]

Firebrands accused the Democrats of having "cheated the South out of Kansas" and interjected resistance into everyday political language.[28] Although the tactics of resistance still remained open to debate, no one refusing to defend southern rights in every particular escaped the brand of traitor. Increasingly, each tidbit of political news from the North or from Washington appeared to demonstrate yet another violation of southern rights. The accumulated wrongs had to be redressed. Even moderates insisted that Congress issue positive assurances protecting the rights of slaveholders in the territories.

The panic of 1857 did little to still the turbulence. On the contrary, it prompted planters to see a common source for their economic and political woes in the North's determination to direct national affairs unilaterally. Resistance would require a comprehensive economic and political initiative. To that end, early in 1858 planters from Houston County proposed a statewide convention, which met in Macon in February and formed the Georgia Cotton Planters Association. Besides advocating such short-term remedies as withholding cotton from the market until prices rose, the association endorsed direct trade with Europe.[29] For years a hobby of certain planters, direct trade was touted as a cure for all the South's ills. Selling direct to European markets would eliminate middlemen's charges and price fixing, thereby guaranteeing higher cotton prices and higher profits. And buying direct from European producers would eliminate markups and high freight rates on goods shipped through northern ports, while at the same time spurning northern manufactured goods. Although the plan threatened to increase the South's vassalage to Europe, it had the premier political advantage of frustrating Yankee business interests, an objective that appealed to the planter elite, planters on the make, and yeomen alike.

The unity of sentiment aroused by the issue of direct trade stopped there, however. For the temporary, "unnatural . . . revulsion" in cotton prices caused by the panic masked deeper concerns about the future of slavery, which different classes of white southerners perceived differently. The confluence of economic and political instability convinced established planters, particularly old-line Whigs, to control change while accommodating to what was beyond their control. Planters on the make, however, particularly the young heirs of Jacksonian democracy, wanted to secure their future prosperity by guaranteeing an abundance of cheap slaves and affordable land. They desired continued westward expansion of slavery, and they sought to revive the African slave trade.

The planter elite, whose slave forces grew by natural increase and whose investment in slave property would be devalued, vehemently opposed the African trade. John B. Lamar characterized the prospect as "an alarming idea" which would "render our negroes valueless to us."[30] The matter grew complicated with respect to the effect of cheap slaves upon nonslaveholders, for whom the prospect of ownership sank as slave prices rose. In short, as sectional tensions escalated, slaveholders questioned whether or not the loyalty of nonslaveholders would be best guaranteed by a direct material stake in the South's fundamental social institution.

Pursuing an ideological defense of slave society, Dr. Daniel Lee, an editor of the *Southern Cultivator* and professor of agriculture at Franklin College (later the University of Georgia), argued that nonslaveholders had "a moral right to own slaves" based upon the common understanding, built by "association and education," that "slaveholding is right." Anticipating that the North and the South would soon come to blows over the question, he argued that reopening the slave trade would make nonslaveholders "ready to fight for their rights . . . just as earnestly as any slaveholder will fight to defend his rights in negroes already here." "If the practice and the principle of slaveholding are worth anything," he concluded, "they must be as good for all as for a favored few."[31] In August 1859, the editors of the Macon *Georgia Citizen* argued that without renewed importations, there was "no chance for poor men to get African laborers."[32] Although Macon hosted regional meetings of slave-trade proponents, support for the notion ran shallow in central Georgia, where old-line planters carried the day against an influx of African slaves.[33]

As the future of slavery became an increasingly important consideration in national politics, struggles over a host of local issues preoccupied the residents of central Georgia during the 1850s. Although not all of these preoccupations grew directly out of slavery, they reflected the cumulative strains of a slave society undergoing rapid demographic and economic change. Not surprisingly, planters exerted inordinate influence over these proceedings. They faced some old adversaries in the persons of slaves and yeomen, but also some new ones who had entered the scene since the coming of the railroad. As the political arena grew more crowded, all participants—planters and slaves, smallholders and yeomen, lawyers and merchants, artisans and laborers—jockeyed for position. As the stakes grew, the contest became more animated.

The history of Know-Nothingism provides the clearest link between national issues and local political struggles. As elsewhere, the American party in central Georgia emerged from the disintegration of the Whig party following the Compromise of 1850. But more than simply mirroring intersectional political upheaval, Know-Nothingism reflected the social strain and class division accompanying the economic boom of the 1850s.[34] It was ironic that the Whigs' promotion of commercial development in the South created the infrastructure (particularly in the form of the railroads) that facilitated immigration. During the 1850s, a growing proportion of the electorate in central Georgia and elsewhere in the cotton South lacked the most visible sign of republican virtue—productive property in the form of land. Dispossessed native-born voters and propertyless European immigrants were changing the foundation of the political system.

To the Whigs' chagrin, these elements identified primarily with the Democratic party. Nativism held forth a promise of political resuscitation, and like fellow Know-Nothings elsewhere in the nation, central Georgia's nativists pounced upon the Irish, the most numerous, politically active, and staunchly Democratic of the new citizens. Many of the Irish were young men employed in low-paying, often disagreeable or dangerous jobs. And often they found themselves in violation of the law. Like men in similar circumstance North or South, they drank immoderately and disturbed the peace. They also traded liquor and other goods with slaves and committed more serious offenses.[35] To be sure, the Irish enjoyed no monopoly on crime, but the connection between the rising number of Irishmen and the rising incidence of crime proved too hard for many natives to resist.

The religious preference of the Irish also distinguished them from their new neighbors.[36] At a time when southerners were suspicious of all outsiders, particularly those adhering to "foreign" ideologies such as Roman Catholicism, the Irish proved ready scapegoats. And the nativists had no difficulty identifying papism with the most dreaded foreign ideology of them all, namely, abolitionism. "That the foreigners who come to this country are chiefly and for the most part Abolitionists, is an admitted fact," observed the editors of the Macon *Journal & Messenger*, who tailored their former Whiggery into new nativist garb. While asserting that "[t]hey settle in the Free States and swell the Abolition vote," the newspapermen knew better, for their eyes and ears reported that not all of the aliens had remained north.[37] Even if those in the South were not abolitionists, they were certainly Democrats contributing to the growing strength of that party in the cities. There was no mistaking the fear embedded in the late 1851 account of elections in upcountry South Carolina, wherein an "overwhelming 'Yankee and Foreign vote'" routed the small "native vote," nor in reports of the St. Patrick's Day toasts to Daniel O'Connell—Irish patriot, to be sure, but also an outspoken abolitionist.[38] To nativists, the rising number of immigrants portended subjugation to foreign powers.

While nativists viewed the Irish as pariahs, Democratic politicians began seeing them as windfall voters. To be sure, homegrown Democrats did not stoop to consider the newcomers social equals, but party kingpins perceived the benefits of courting them. Irish ballots might play a decisive part in gaining control over municipal governments in Macon and other commercial centers that had been traditional bastions of Whiggery. Moreover, the salutary care of native-born Democrats might speed the transition from Hibernian to southerner.

To forestall development of Irish working-class political bosses—whom southern elites considered the bane of political life in the North—Democratic strategists groomed comparatively privileged leaders with whom they established personal as well as professional ties. They took a particular shine to O. A. Lochrane, a physician's son from northern Ireland who had settled in upcountry Georgia to study law and whose speeches on constitutional rights meshed nicely with their views. Henry Lamar, brother-in-law of Howell Cobb, judge of the state superior court, and stalwart of the Democratic party in Macon, took Lochrane under his wing. Lochrane formed a law partnership with Lamar and one of his sons, married one of his daughters, and became a major power in the Democratic party. Remaining active in Hibernian organizations after achieving notoriety, he spoke frequently at St. Patrick's Day and other such celebrations as well as at more partisan Democratic functions. Lochrane, in effect, bridged the gap between the planter elite and his countrymen in the laboring ranks.[39]

The Democrats' dream of capturing political control of Macon materialized in 1856.[40] Although that victory may not have been entirely attributable to the growth in the Irish population over the prior decade, the relationship was more than coincidental. With victory came spoils, but the Irishmen had to settle for the relatively modest pickings of sexton, bridge keeper, and clerk of the market. As nativist sentiment waned during the late 1850s, the "opposition" party of erstwhile Whigs fielded a few Irish candidates of its own, at least one of whom won public office.[41] Although nativists despised the prospect of a free but propertyless working class, they learned from the Democrats that the lower orders could come to identify with the elite. And the lessons traveled in both directions. In establishing an urban political base, Democrats gained a new perspective on commercial development, the traditionally Whiggish preoccupation that would undergird coalition politics among the propertied classes for the rest of the century.

As THE KNOW-NOTHING agitation spent itself, the growing political awareness of sectional divisions within the state—separating "the low lands and the high lands"—began tearing at the Democratic party.[42] The political ascendancy of a slaveholding lawyer from north Georgia, Joseph E. Brown, personified the determination of the upcountry yeomen "to have their interests represented by someone they know . . . someone who is adverse to making the state government a mere machine for transfering the earnings of one class or section into the pockets of another."[43] Of course, Brown was no flaming radical. He recognized slavery as the foundation of southern society and the subjugation of black slaves as the basis for the comparative elevation of free white men. Still, his gubernatorial candidacy and victory in 1857 were perceived as rooted in sectional differences between the upcountry yeoman region and the plantation black belt. "He was nominated," explained the editors of the *Journal & Messenger* with more than a touch of resentment, to "conciliate Cherokee Georgia, and guarantee to it the spoils of office, including the State Road, once considered the common property of the State, but now held as the special almoner of Cherokee democracy." Planter-merchant interests feared calamity now that politicians with a strong constituency of yeomen controlled the distribution of government largess. For the sake of "the harmony and prosperity of our noble commonwealth," the partisans of justice for the black belt advocated stern measures against "the political traders, who, to appease a sectional and cormorant clamor for office, have ignored the rights and interests of a large portion of the State."[44]

The voters' concern over government taxation and spending encompassed a host of issues ranging from public education and poor relief to gas light systems and new courthouses. It affected rural as well as urban jurisdictions. Political differences in some cases followed, but in other cases cut across, class lines. The stakes were high; tempers often flared, and occasionally public officials resigned in protest against objectionable policies. Traditionally, planters preferred to keep public expenditures down, believing in the propriety of both low taxes and minimal government services. Active government threatened the liberty of citizens and, by extension, the well-being of society. It also smacked of a tendency planters sneeringly associated with Massachusetts and its Yankee neighbors.[45]

But as smallholding farmers and urban workers grappled with the forces of change set loose by the cotton boom, they turned to government for assistance.

Traditional political allegiance determined the stance most voters took on these issues: those of Whiggish political antecedents welcomed additional government action in certain arenas, but Democrats tended to oppose an expansion of government power. Yet matters of partisan affiliation, or even of ideology more generally, tended to fade before the major question of who would pay for the proposed activism. Whiggish businessmen and professionals in Macon, for instance, looked skeptically upon increased government expenditures. Already subjected to exorbitant taxes, they feared that additional government spending would mean even heavier levies. Ideally, the bounteous resources of the state and federal governments would provide the financial solution, as they had virtually without interruption since the War of 1812.[46] But in the absence of a steady flow of money from federal to state coffers and from state to local ones, the prospect of tax-free public improvements looked dim. Local officials had to move gingerly.

In Macon, certain improvements, such as gas lighting and an improved system of fighting fires, won voter approval without much difficulty. As was true elsewhere in the nation at mid-century, large property owners initiated such projects to safeguard their interests; if voters perceived benefits to the public at large, they granted approval.[47] Late in 1851, representatives of a New Jersey firm began promoting a plan to illuminate Macon with gas. After a year of general discussion, a popular referendum endorsed the principle without addressing the matter of funding. The economy-minded city council balked at the outcome and demanded another vote, but the results were the same. The city must not be left behind in "the race of improvement," crowed Whiggish boosters. Early in 1853, the council authorized formation of the gas company and construction of the works, and Macon entered the gas age.[48]

The same session of the city council that authorized the gas works also approved the organization of a hook and ladder company. The new unit would supplement the "utterly inefficient" system of private companies that had left the citizens "perfectly impotent" against fires. The council also provided for a system of public cisterns.[49] The following year, with the cisterns still on the drawing board, the council created the position of chief engineer with authority over all units. What the private companies lost in autonomy, the public supposedly gained in fire-fighting efficiency.[50] By the eve of the Civil War, the council went so far as to proscribe wooden structures in certain areas of the city in the interest of fire safety.[51]

Predictably, not all citizens wished to pay the price for what some of their neighbors considered improvements. In the summer of 1857, following a special mayoral election necessitated by the resignation of the incumbent, the *Journal & Messenger* noted that "[t]he questions on which our citizens divided were of a local character connected with the prospective expenses of our city"—in other words, how to solve the matter of bankruptcy that resulted from using public funds for spurious railroad schemes. Eighteen months later, when the council voted to subscribe $200,000 for the proposed Macon and Brunswick Railroad, two aldermen resigned in protest. It was one thing to pledge the city's reputation and credit for projects that would benefit the public, but another matter entirely to step willingly into "a financial labyrinth of a quarter of a century."[52]

All these issues of economy, in fact, exposed the widening class divisions within southern society—not just in the towns, but in the surrounding plantation districts as well. Two, namely, poor relief and public education, did so dramatically. Planters faced a dilemma in dealing with the growing social problem of poverty. From an ideological perspective, poverty had no place in slave society, where the enslavement of black persons provided the mudsill upon which white persons could prosper. But when reality contradicted the ideal, planters had to face the choice of pretending poverty did not exist, assuming the old system of minimal public relief supplemented by individual charity would suffice, or increasing public assistance. Once again, resolution of these issues depended upon fiscal considerations: more public support would require more taxes.

Whiggish paternalists advocated the public route despite the costs. They acknowledged that plantation society was rearing an indigenous crop of perennial paupers, for whose well-being the community bore a measure of responsibility, in its own interest as well as theirs. To avoid encouraging habits of laziness, shiftlessness, and vice that might follow from public aid with no strings attached, public charity would be tied to a system of public works. Establishing poorhouses offered the hope of providing for those in need while inculcating habits of industry.

During the 1850s, the planter elites in the respective counties of central Georgia began addressing such concerns. The articulation of these issues invites comparison with similar developments in the North earlier in the nineteenth century. If the appearance of such groups in the North can be attributed to a breakdown of traditional social structures in the face of capitalist development, the same cannot be said of the South, where the plantation household continued to function as the foundation of society. Although the planters never had it so good as they did during the 1850s, the socially marginal population grew at an alarming rate. Planters resorted to the law as an instrument of amelioration, for if left unchecked, this tendency threatened the entire social order.

In Houston County during the spring of 1853, both the inferior court and one panel of superior court grand jurors addressed the issue of poverty. Noting the "increase of paupers in our midst," the grand jurors proposed an additional 5 percent tax to support the poor fund and recommended construction of a poorhouse. The suggestions provoked a vigorous dissent from the second panel of jurors, who believed that such a proposal would "cause an additional tax upon our already high rates." "Taking economy for our guide," the dissidents argued, "we think the Poor can be as well provided for under the present system as they could be in a Poor House and at less expense to the County."[53]

The discussion of aid to the poor exposed various fault lines in plantation society. In addition to the rift between rich and poor, it portrays divisions among slaveholders themselves over how best to solve social problems. Significantly, the composition of the two jury panels differed. The first (which favored the additional tax on behalf of the poor) averaged sixteen slaves per juror, with less than half owning fewer than ten slaves. The second panel (which took "economy" for its guide) averaged eleven slaves per juror, with fully three-quarters owning fewer than ten. And if its three most opulent members (who together owned 124 slaves) are omitted from the calculation, the other jurors averaged a mere four slaves apiece.[54] In short, larger planters endorsed public spending on behalf of strengthening the paternal social order; smallholders did not.

The grand jury that sat in April 1858 settled the case. Overwhelmingly comprised of planters (the average slaveholding was thirty-six, and only one held fewer than fourteen slaves), they declared that a "well organized, and properly managed" poorhouse would both accommodate the poor and reduce county expenses. "At the same time," however, they thought it "important to have a farm connected with it, or some profitable employment, as idleness is not always conducive to health, or morality." If such provisions were not made, they feared that the poorhouse "will to some extent be made an Asylum for the lazy and improvident."[55]

Community leaders in Macon as well as the other rural counties in central Georgia wrestled with the matter of poor relief in similar fashion during the 1850s. As elsewhere, such action represented a consensus among leading citizens that private generosity was no longer equal to the task, though voluntary action on the part of citizens' groups (generally composed of prominent women) or persons with special expertise (such as the faculty of the Medical College who agreed to provide medical care to the poor) continued.[56] The factional alignments differed from town to country, although the main contours were the same. In rural areas, yeomen combined with planters on the rise and the decline to oppose higher taxes for increased government spending; in the towns, Democratic artisans and laborers took the same position. The planter-merchant elite—both Democratic and Whig—saw poor relief as crucial to social stability.

The debate over public schools, like the related one over poor relief, provides additional insight into the challenges faced by the citizens of central Georgia during a time of rapid social change. According to traditional southern practices, education was a private affair. Among the plain folk, parents taught children what literacy skills they commanded, supplemented by occasional public lessons in so-called old-field schools. Among the gentry, private tutors and academies performed the service. For children of the indigent, each county administered a "Poor School Fund," sustained by state allocations, special taxes, or sales of designated lands. Local officials had responsibility for maintaining current lists of eligible children and appropriating funds for instruction.

Despite noble intentions, the poor-school system did not work. Civil officers routinely neglected their charge, but, more important, parents of eligible children shunned the assistance for the stigma attached to it. By the 1850s, the time was ripe for change. Despite their generally defensive posture, planters had become sensitive to northern criticism of the lack of public education in the South: opponents of slavery, proponents of commercial development, and champions of democratic political institutions all decried the ignorance of the unschooled southern population. Moreover, the guardians of the social order in central Georgia discovered internal reasons (in the form of idleness and crime among youth and illiteracy and ignorance among the electorate) for a change in educational policy. On these and other grounds, the planter-merchant elite addressed the issue of general education.

The concern surfaced seriously during the early 1850s, sparked by influential reports on the need for public funding.[57] As the decade progressed, grand juries in one central Georgia county after another advocated common schools, touting the salutary effects of education upon republican political institutions.[58] A state system of common schools, Bibb County jurors declared, "lies at the foundation of, and must enter into the elements of every enlightened and popular form of government." In a formulation with the ring of a Fourth of July toast, Monroe County jurors observed that "Education, Christianity, and Freedom are mutually dependent upon each other."[59]

Proponents also claimed public education would reduce the growing crime rate. Bibb County grand jurors expressed "astonishment at the enormous expense" of administering justice. Their counterparts in Houston County apologized for shirking civil matters but claimed that "the Superior interest of Society demand[ed] that crime Should be punished & the violators of the law brought to justice." They looked forward to the time when the citizenry would "again have the character of being a law abiding and justice loving people." But given "the deplorable state of public morals," the day did not seem near.[60]

Explanations for the increase in crime were not lacking. Intoxicating liquors, grand jurors throughout central Georgia believed, were a "most fruitful source of crime & suffering." The "present retail system of ardent spirits" made liquor readily available to slaves as well as freemen. Jurors faulted unscrupulous retailers, "a class of our citizens who exercise no salutary moral influence in the community, but on the contrary, corrupt and ruin our slave property, and undermine the superstructure of all moral law."[61] In the view of other observers, crime also thrived by virtue of lax law enforcement and flaws in the system of selecting juries. According to law, petit jurors were to be chosen from lists of qualified voters. But during the 1850s, selected jurors frequently declined to appear on court day. As a result, judges had to select jurors from among the "idlers and worthless characters" making up the courthouse crowd. Representing the very persons credited with the increase in crime in the first place, such jurors were inclined not to convict.[62]

Guardians of public morality hoped that education would cure these social ills. "Without a general diffusion of knowledge among its inhabitants," ran one argument, "no State can expect to be exempt from the vices and crimes incident to ignorance."[63] Other observers pointed out that "school houses are much cheaper than Jails, Court houses, and penitentiaries."[64] An editorial sought means "to avert the scourge of an ignorant, indolent, and vicious populous," represented by the "[h]undreds of children . . . growing up to vagrancy . . . because uneducated, and unemployed." "Unless looked after," the author predicted, "they will infest and scourge the community as paupers and criminals—a reproach to the city and county, and moral contagion and death to all with whom they associate."[65] The connection between ignorance and crime appeared irrefutable. Lurking beneath the surface of the discussion, however, were points that no partisan on either side of the debate dared articulate: that growing numbers of persons simply did not fit within organic society, and that the misfits threatened the entire social organism.

Given a perceived lack of "sufficient enlightened and unselfish patriotism" in the state legislature to support common schools, counties planned for their own funding.[66] Recommendations typically called for a tax of 15 to 20 percent of the state tax.[67] In Macon, the problem was solved in mid-1858 when the trustees of the Bibb County Academy offered their annual fund of $500 if the mayor and council would match that amount. With the council's approval, preparations were made, and the school opened in mid-September.[68]

An unexpected by-product of the public school agitation of the 1850s was the growing awareness of social class divisions. To be sure, southerners had been aware of such distinctions since colonial times. But the operating assumption— one not monopolized by mid-nineteenth-century Georgians, but also one not as strongly professed in the slave states as in the free states—was that a free white man's place in society depended ultimately upon individual merit and effort rather than inherited social status. In pronouncing upon "the wants of the masses," for instance, the editors of the *Journal & Messenger* insisted that there were "no privileged classes in this free land, thank God, unless indeed, it be those, who in virtue of their industry and enterprise and providence, have rendered themselves so."[69] Education for the popular mind, the editors concluded, would be "sound political economy, to say nothing of political ethics."[70]

Yet discussion of public school education unavoidably exposed the class issue and made many southern whites squeamish. A well-ordered organic society should not have produced unemployed youth who would be tempted by crime in the absence of public schools. The very thought invoked comparison with the North. Moreover, because the issue hinged upon funding, any plan that involved raising taxes invariably touched tender sensibilities among yeomen, small-holders, and members of the planter-commercial elite. These sensibilities cut in all directions.

The planter aristocracy had moved from viewing formal education as an elite privilege to seeing it as a means of social control. But aristocrats also feared that public education might undermine privilege and level social distinctions. In 1858, Bibb County grand jurors protested an earlier panel's endorsement of such schools as places "where the children of all classes could receive a sound English Education," predicting that schools "common alike to the rich and the poor" would give rise to "jealousy between classes."[71] It was precisely to allay such fears among the Georgia elite that an influential report on public education disclaimed any intention "to excite the envy or the prejudice of the poor against the rich."[72] But not all elitists felt reassured, nor did all proponents of proper subordination place full faith in such social experiments.

Small planters, both on the rise and the fall, could not see past the increased tax burdens public education would entail and hence opposed such schemes. Yeomen also opposed taxation, but if such a system could be financed by other means, they might welcome precisely the leveling effect the aristocrats feared. Governor Joseph E. Brown, champion of the north Georgia yeomanry, devised a plan for supporting public schools with revenue from the state-owned Western and Atlantic Railroad. He touted the democratizing effect of public education: "Let the children of the richest and the poorest parents in the State, meet in the school-room on terms of perfect equality of right. Let there be no aristocracy there but an aristocracy of color and of conduct." With the support of the yeomen, he engineered passage of the 1858 general education act, which established the state's first system of public education. But the business downturn and the growing sectional crisis prevented its implementation.[73]

In sum, the unprecedented prosperity of the 1850s brought with it unimagined troubles. Slaveholders faced searing criticism from abolitionists, who, over the course of the decade, had moved from castigating slavery as morally wrong, to forming hostile third parties, to assaulting slavery with armed force. Yet planters could not let their northern troubles blind them to events in their own backyard. Demographically, central Georgia had become literally a black belt. Moreover, the social composition of the free white population also changed dramatically, as foreign-born workers settled there and native-born whites abandoned farming for assorted positions in support of plantation agriculture. The traditional consensus among free white voters began fraying, under pressure of change in the very nature of the body politic.

DURING THE 1850S, slaves in central Georgia added their voices to debates over public policy, but as denizens, rather than citizens, of the republic. As earlier, they sought to supplement their diets and earn cash, but they now contended with the planters' redoubled determination to maximize cotton production and minimize the laborers' discretionary use of time. Unlike earlier times, however, slaves devised ways of capitalizing upon the commercial development that accompanied the cotton boom. The law took an equivocal stand on the matter. The Georgia code permitted slaves to "traffic on their own account" in "articles of their own manufacture, or agricultural products of their own raising, or poultry raised by their master's permission, or articles of the like character usually permitted to slaves," provided they had "written permission of the master specifying the particular articles to be sold."[74] But larger political issues intervened.

The proliferation of commercial activity provided slaves greater facility to dispose of their products. With such new outlets for trade, masters anticipated an increase in pilferage from plantation fields, henhouses, and smokehouses and a comparable increase in their slaves' consumption of liquor and other pro-scribed items. Although this trade was not new, masters feared its unprece-dented scope and the variety and boldness of its practitioners. Besides respect-able whites, slaves' trading partners included poor whites, foreign-born peddlers and grocers, and assorted criminals, none of whom inspired confidence as defenders of the plantation order. Masters, ministers, and grand jurors railed continuously against the trade, but words had little effect.[75]

Slaves who traded on their own contradicted the paternalist image of utter dependence. Some masters opposed the "spirit of trafficking" among the slaves. "To carry this on," one argued, "both means and time are necessary," neither of which slaves "of right possessed." Another maintained that "negroes are not capable of managing [their own affairs], and that if left to themselves they would not obtain a support." Other masters of similar persuasion insisted that they be the sole purchasing agents for their slaves' surplus goods, rather than grant the slaves unimpeded access to the realm of market exchange. And many a master solved the ticklish problems of trade by simply forbidding his slaves to produce any marketable items. Slaves did not generally welcome such interposition. Whether to obtain goods of their own choosing, to turn a small profit, or to assert greater control over their lives and the products of their labor, they made market transactions on their own authority, often despite express orders to the con-trary.[76]

This struggle between masters and slaves in the U.S. South over access to local markets had no parallel in other slave societies of the Americas. Whether in the Caribbean or in South America, slaves both produced and exchanged goods on their own account, often through the institutionalized mechanism of provi-sion grounds and Sunday markets. So crucial were these products to local economies—and, by the 1820s, to the fragile peace between masters and slaves—that slaves steadily extended the scope of their marketing privileges.[77] Slaves in South American cities also enjoyed relatively fluid access to markets to dispose of the products of their labor. But in central Georgia (and the slave South generally), slaves' producing and marketing goods without the mediation of the master posed a potential threat. More than simply rights to a peculium, these practices appeared more and more as the entering wedge of free labor. In neither the Caribbean nor South America did the institutions of markets among slaves conjure up the threat of a rival political economy. Whereas masters in those areas could readily make their peace with a proto-peasantry, their North

American counterparts saw a fifth column of proto-entrepreneurs and proto–free laborers, the advance agents of Yankee capitalism and abolitionism.

As if to confirm their worst fears, planters began to view the railroads as a mixed blessing, one that facilitated marketing their cotton crops but at the same time exposed slaves to an infinite variety of temptations. Railroads opened the interior to drummers (as nineteenth-century traveling salesmen were called) and other harbingers of commercial society. Not all the notions of these newcomers comported with the planters' prized organic social order. And slaves found ways of sampling the excitement of the rails with or without authorization.

These risks notwithstanding, planters welcomed the flexibility that hiring slaves to railroads afforded. Both construction and maintenance of the railroads often provided needed employment for slaves, particularly at times when cotton prices stagnated or when a particular master's circumstances required. Construction contractors routinely hired the slaves of planters through whose property the right of way passed. Former slave Hanna Fambro from Monroe County recalled having "worked on de gradin' 'long with de other people of de plantation."[78] But many left their home plantations for a bigger world. The contract term for slave railroad workers generally spanned the year (from New Year's to Christmas). In addition to the Christmas holiday, workers were allowed to visit home periodically—a privilege that railroad overseers routinely used as an incentive to faithful labor.[79] Although some women were hired as cooks and shovel hands, men predominated. The work was heavy and often dangerous.

Some railroad workers enjoyed uncustomary privileges. Even apart from the physical mobility that was essential to the work required, hired slaves and their families at times gained permission to live on their own. In East Macon, for instance, a small community grew up around the Central Railroad's yard. In time, the settlement evolved into a haven where neighboring slaves congregated and where runaways found refuge, as the frustrated master of an escaped slave named Daniel clearly intimated.[80] Daniel demonstrated that flight was a social undertaking rather than simply an individual act of rebellion. This knowledge gave little comfort to masters, as growing numbers of slaves headed for "Ohio or some other free state," places that the railroads had brought within reach.[81] For their part, slaves thanked the commercial development attending the rise of King Cotton for their acquaintance with the highways, rivers, and railroads. When these worldly wise slaves chose to escape, they could also thank their numerous contacts, who fed and sheltered them and covered their trail.[82]

Slaveholders grew increasingly restive over the ability of slaves to parlay these contacts into long-distance escapes. William and Ellen Craft troubled the minds of slaveholders. During the spring of 1854, the escape of a slave named Ned Davis from Macon attracted national attention nearly equal to that generated by the Crafts. After reaching Savannah, Davis stowed away on a ship headed for Philadelphia. Less than thirty miles from the destination, Davis was discovered and placed in the custody of authorities in New Castle, Delaware, who thwarted the attempt of abolitionists to have Davis released. Davis's owner extradited him and put him to work on a plantation in the southwest part of the state, far beyond public gaze. But when rumors of Davis's death began to circulate, his master brought him to Macon for two days of public display. The slave's appearance, alive and bearing no signs of physical abuse, defused the excitement, and interest in the case rapidly subsided. Nonetheless, Davis's owner reportedly spent more money to recover than to purchase him but considered the expense worthwhile "to vindicate the rights of Slaveholders under the laws of the land."[83]

Even as the laws of the land bolstered slavery, the commercialization of the 1850s undermined it in some respects. Commercial development worked to the particular advantage of slaves living in and near the cities whose masters permitted them to hire their own time. In addition to finding their own employment, such slaves sheltered, fed, and clothed themselves, paying a proportion of their earnings or a fixed payment per month to their owners. Frederick Douglass was perhaps the most famous self-employed slave, but he was far from the only one.

Special circumstances on the part of the owner—widowhood, or physical infirmity, for instance—often accounted for slaves' hiring their own time. But some slaves won the right in exchange for loyal service. Slave carpenter Elbert Head from Monroe County won such permission in 1851 after having faithfully superintended his master's farm for the previous nine years. Reflecting upon the arrangement many years later, Head recalled that he and his master "got along pleasantly, without any difficulties," because "we both could trust each other." The trust held firm through the Civil War.[84] Such trust was essential to all hiring arrangements.

Occasional exceptions notwithstanding, most planters abhorred the practice of slaves' hiring their own time. They found a disproportionately high frequency of the practice in Macon and other towns and equated it with the underside of commercial development. Given the prevailing assumptions about the proper place of slaves in a hierarchical social structure, these concerns were not misplaced. If some slaves conducted their own affairs without the benefit of a master, what was to prevent all slaves from attempting the same? Grand jurors and legislators alike denounced a wide assortment of vices attributed to slaves' hiring their own time.[85] Injunctions notwithstanding, slaves continued to negotiate self-hiring arrangements with their masters. Some thumbed their noses at both masters and civil authorities, slipped away from home, and hired their time without authorization.

Quasi-independent slaves at times developed entrepreneurial skills. Slave women sold fruit and baked goods in the vicinity of railway depots. In Macon, slaves from both the city and surrounding farms supplied fresh vegetables and eggs (and perhaps poultry as well) to the public market.[86] Until the city council banned such a practice in 1853, slaves made and sold cotton mattresses.[87] Scarcely an upcountry town failed to have at least one slave-operated "grocery" purveying merchandise of every licit and illicit description. In Perry, Houston County, a slave named Landers, who belonged to an estate in probate, vexed grand jurors by keeping a "house of public entertainment." By definition these humble establishments operated beyond the bounds of the law. Civil authorities routinely denounced them as dens of iniquity, wherein slaves and disreputable whites traded liquor and other contraband articles.[88]

Judging by their frequency, these denunciations fell largely upon deaf ears, though at times actions spoke louder than words. In the fall of 1854, for instance, within the space of five weeks officials in Bibb County broke up two rings of thieves. In one case, they arrested a notorious Irishman named Powers and a slave accomplice named Armstrong; under suspicious circumstances, Armstrong "drowned" during the arrest. The other case involved two brothers named Garvis who traded liquor to slaves for stolen corn.[89] The presence of such trade networks, operating on both sides of the law, gave slaves options for procuring and disposing of goods beyond the control of their masters. In their struggle to loosen the planters' stranglehold on their lives, slaves found these niches in the widening panorama created by commercial development.

Even without passing themselves as free or hiring their own time, during the 1850s central Georgia slaves could partake of the increasing array of goods for purchase that the cotton boom had made available. If the masters' tastes veered toward the exotic, the slaves' were modest and practical. Some purchased raw materials or tools for the goods they manufactured and marketed. Prior to their 1848 escape, William and Ellen Craft purchased assorted items to effect Ellen's disguise, including a pair of eyeglasses.[90] While members of the planter elite adorned their residences with grand pianos, a group of Macon slaves invested in horns and formed a "colored brass band" that played at funerals and other suitable occasions.[91] Despite denunciations as "a public nuisance," slaves often hired buggies and horses for Sunday rides.[92] And a slave named John, hired to work in Macon, took a chance on a lottery ticket that won first prize. The sponsors of the drawing "refused to pay him & was trying to cheat him" of the jackpot (an estimated $20,000 to $30,000) "on the plea that he was a negro."[93] Although John's case was exceptional, it illustrated the logical extreme to which slaves' unrestricted participation in a commercialized economy might lead.

IN AN ERA of rapid change, planters were hard pressed to decide whether white free men or black slaves vexed them more. Advocates of racial solidarity bent to the realities of a democratic polity, but hard-core aristocrats continued to insist that hierarchy was the foundation of all social order. A bizarre incident early in 1859 illustrated these tensions. It involved Lucius Brown, an overseer, and Joseph Bond, his former employer. Bond was one of the wealthiest planters in the state; he owned six plantations in southwest Georgia, which in 1858 had produced 2,200 bales of cotton that sold for over $100,000—the largest crop recorded by a Georgia planter to that time. Colonel Bond resided in Macon, where he was a pillar of society. Among his various credits was a founding membership in the Bibb Cavalry, an elite state militia unit. Against Bond, Brown had virtually no social standing.

The trouble between the two men started shortly after the crop had been marketed when Bond accosted Brown over the whipping of a slave. With Bond insisting that the slave had been injured, and Brown insisting upon his right to strike any insubordinate slave, the argument grew increasingly heated. Bond attempted to whip Brown, whereupon the latter drew a pistol and shot his adversary dead. Following an official investigation, Brown was released from custody on grounds of self-defense and was never prosecuted.[94]

Bond's death symbolically marked the stalemate in the planters' effort to stamp society in their image. Although the plantation as a system of production was in its heyday, plantation ideals of hierarchy and deference were under assault from numerous quarters. Slaves rebelled in a host of ways, stealing, purchasing alcohol, and passing "through the country at their own liberty."[95] Although they fell short of reducing slavery to ruin, slaves expanded the boundaries of permissible behavior. If masters viewed this process as confirmation of the elasticity of slavery, slaves learned other lessons. Finding weak spots encouraged them to press harder for the breakthrough.

Among free whites, the plantation ideal failed to explain the pronounced class stratification that, to a great extent, grew organically from the success of cotton plantation agriculture. Native-born smallholders watched helplessly as the planters engrossed their land and undermined their livelihoods. The number of white wage workers, both native and immigrant, grew dramatically, and many performed labor not so clearly distinguishable from that of slaves.

Ideologues of the planter class sensed the danger. Robert Toombs, for instance, foresaw the ultimate demise of slavery in the "unvarying laws of population" operating without "regard to liberty or humanity." "The moment wages descend to a point barely sufficient to support the laborer and his family," he reasoned, "capital cannot afford to own labor, and slavery instantly ceases."[96] Although he did not predict when that fate would befall the South, the very thought shivered the spines of slaveholders. *We who are connected with the institution,*" insisted Howell Cobb of Houston County, "*regard it as permanent— perpetual.*" It was terrifying for him to think otherwise, for the end of slavery necessarily would require that "society, in all its ramifications . . . undergo a complete revolution." Cobb took some consolation in the belief that if such change did occur, it would be "brought about by Providence in gradual movements, which, causing no detriment to any, will receive the hearty approval and cooperation of all."[97] But with the specter of Haiti ever present in their minds, planters reasoned that securing the future of slavery offered the surest way to avert calamity.

Planters on the make were especially concerned that their dream not disappear just as it came within reach. Often from humble backgrounds themselves, they did not necessarily adhere to the standards of proper etiquette as defined by established planters. For them, maintaining social hierarchy among free whites was infinitely less important than maintaining the permanent debasement of black slaves. Following the Mexican War, these men took an increasingly implacable stance regarding southern rights, specifically, the right of whites to prosper by exploiting slave labor. They were willing to sacrifice everything, including the Union itself, for the future of slavery. And they managed to convince southern paternalists that, between themselves and the abolitionists, they were the lesser of two evils. Although the planter elite, aspiring planters, smallholders, and dispossessed yeomen shared a common perception of social chaos, they drew different conclusions about how best to restore order. In a remarkably rapid sequence of events, the range of solutions reduced itself to the least common denominator of secession.

5

. . . .

The Civil War and
the Demise of Slavery,
1861–1865

THERE WAS NOTHING inevitable in the destruction of slavery, even after the Civil War began. Nearly three-quarters of the white families in central Georgia owned slaves. The rest owed their livelihoods and various social privileges to slavery. Cries of individual and states' rights, resistance to tyranny, and the Spirit of '76 rallied citizens to defend this social reality. Alexander H. Stephens, who became vice-president of the Confederacy after having straddled the fence during secession, succinctly stated the case that slavery was the cornerstone of the rebellion.[1]

Georgia slaveholders perceived the multiple layers of meaning in Stephens's metaphor. As the fundamental social institution in the South, slavery was what southerners were fighting for. Moreover, because slaves performed much of the essential labor in the South, to them would fall the task of raising food and fiber to sustain both civilians at home and soldiers in the field. Nonslaveholders and slaveholders alike believed firmly that such a class of drudges in their midst would offset the North's superiority in men and machines.

Such arithmetic, of course, took for granted the slaves' cooperation. It did not anticipate the effect of what President Abraham Lincoln in a related context described as the "friction and abrasion" of the war.[2] Even in central Georgia, the heartland of the Confederate heartland, slavery was profoundly transformed even before the arrival of Sherman's legions in 1864. The roar of distant cannon made masters edgy, prompting many to take unprecedented steps to safeguard their lives and property. At the same time, Confederate war planners took advantage of central Georgia's comparative security to create an industrial base to match the agricultural one. As a result, absentee strategists in Richmond and

Washington, joined by masters and military and civil officers closer to home, began chipping away at the cornerstone.

In mobilizing for war, Confederate policymakers concentrated power in the central state apparatus in ways that not only flouted cherished southern notions of personal liberty and local government but also exceeded comparable measures by Lincoln and Congress.[3] The central government assumed wide-ranging authority over citizens and property, impressing white men for military service, drastically curtailing (and in some instances completely suspending) citizens' rights, accumulating supplies of food and war matériel through taxes in kind and outright confiscation, and ultimately overriding slave owners' cherished prerogatives in pursuit of larger interests. Governor Joseph E. Brown skirmished incessantly with President Jefferson Davis over these matters but at times adopted quasi-dictatorial powers himself. Over the course of the war, the authority of slave masters gave way to that of civilian and military officials, creating both power vacuums and competing jurisdictional claims that slaves exploited for their own purposes.

These developments left the antebellum social fabric of central Georgia in tatters. When the master-slave relationship unraveled, larger holes appeared, and the strains of war completed the destruction. Small planters, yeoman farmers, overseers, and day laborers who had rallied around the Stars and Bars during the winter of 1861 were cursing the flag long before the shooting stopped. In addition to the suffering that such men endured in the field, their families at home found it increasingly difficult to subsist. The old paternal ties, whereby planters assisted their humbler neighbors in time of need, stretched thin under the pressure of shortages. In cities like Macon, which became centers of military production, wage workers soon confronted a powerful central government, which had the power not only to impress them into armed service, but also to determine their wages and to manipulate the availability of necessary supplies. Little could Georgians, black or white, have predicted how the fight to preserve slavery would first transform and then destroy the antebellum social order.

By the same token, few could fully appreciate the broad historical panorama against which they acted, even though much of the background was clear by the time of secession. Between 1791 and 1888, slavery in the Americas expired. Death struck in two major waves, whose timing reflected key turning points in the development of capitalism in the Atlantic world. The first accompanied the age of revolution during the late eighteenth and early nineteenth centuries, which gave birth to Haiti and the United States as well as numerous South American republics. A second wave accompanied the maturation of industrial capitalism. It included the emancipation of slaves throughout the West Indies and in the southern United States and Brazil and of peasants and serfs in the Austrian monarchy and Russia. Whereas the earlier emancipations freed fewer than 1 million slaves, the later ones affected more than 6 million slaves and perhaps as many as 50 million peasants and serfs.[4]

Each of these emancipations reflected layers of local and metropolitan struggles played out within the developing opportunities and constraints of the capitalist world economy. It is not simply that slave masters recognized the errors of their ways, either morally or economically, and chose voluntarily to organize labor in conformity with an advanced spirit of the age. On the contrary, they generally resisted emancipation to the end; and in the United States and Cuba, the end meant fratricidal war.[5] As revolutionary-era slaveholders had come to understand, war jeopardized the security of slave property. Their great-grandchildren learned the lesson afresh after secession.

THE VOTERS OF central Georgia departed the Union along the path described by Michael P. Johnson's study of secession in the state.[6] Of the six counties surrounding Macon, only Monroe remained true to the Whiggish legacy of cooperation, with two of its three delegates to the state secession convention voting against the resolution to secede. Although all the delegates from the other five counties supported the resolution, this unanimity did not properly reflect the strength of cooperationism in central Georgia.[7] Differences over how best to preserve slavery and the property rights of individual slaveholders persisted.

The evidence suggests that most of the well-established planters of both Whiggish and Democratic antecedents opposed secession at first, although the political memories of 1850 made it impossible for them to deny the right of secession in principle. Whiggish planters appear to have clung to that opposition until after the state seceded; but Democratic planters, especially those close to Howell Cobb, and commercial interests of both persuasions broke ranks early and advocated disunion.[8] The plot quickly thickened. Even though Governor Joseph E. Brown favored secession, planters distrusted him. Moreover, his main constituents, the upcountry yeomen, were staunchly pro-Union. So Cobb and the alliance of planters and merchants that favored secession faced the challenge of converting—or at the least neutralizing—the cooperationism of old-line Whigs and Democratic yeomen.

As Johnson's analysis so masterfully shows, Whiggish and Democratic planters found common cause in the quest for a greater measure of home rule. Each gave some ground. In conceding defeat regarding secession, the Whigs wished to limit popular government and strengthen the black belt's control over the state apparatus. In claiming victory regarding secession, the Democrats had to acquiesce in a certain muzzling of "the people." With Governor Brown brokering the deal between planters and yeomen, Georgia left the Union.[9] Competing social classes and political factions covered their differences beneath a cloak of unity inscribed with two cardinal principles: slavery and individual rights.

The spirit of secession proved intoxicating. White citizens adopted a common language of republican virtue, claiming political descent from the Founding Fathers in a renewed quest for independence. A *rage militaire* like the one that had gripped the thirteen colonies in 1776 (and was gripping northern states in 1861) cut across social classes, creating a heady sense of solidarity.[10] Irish immigrants joined ranks with native-born laborers and smallholders and prepared for war.[11]

As war clouds gathered in the spring of 1861, the black-belt planters who had consolidated their hold over the mobilization believed that slavery was equal to every challenge. Predictably, they considered themselves especially qualified to manage the crisis. Much like managing a plantation, the secret lay in the proper combination of material and human resources. And in the eventuality of war with the North—a prospect whose likelihood increased with each passing day—they could demonstrate to the world the superiority of an organic society in which the separate and distinct parts each contributed to the welfare of the whole.

Young aristocrats would lead, bringing their martial bearing and habits of command into military service. Yeoman farmers and laborers would make up the rank and file. Planters beyond military age would hold down the home front, supervising plantations and conducting public affairs. They would be assisted by their young sons and the overseers who chose not to enlist. Townsmen marched to a similar tune, with merchants and other members of the elite serving as officers, and clerks and unskilled laborers filling the ranks.

Women on plantations and farms likewise prepared to do their part. They assumed additional chores and directed various kinds of home manufacture— spinning, weaving, knitting, and sewing—toward the goal of self-sufficiency. They managed their households frugally both to avoid waste and to reproduce the disciplined austerity that their husbands and sons were experiencing in the field. Outside the home, they formed various patriotic societies to pursue the same objectives and to provide relief for soldiers and their needy families.[12]

Whereas white men and women reordered their lives voluntarily, free black people and slaves had little, if any, choice in the matter. By virtue of the fact that

so few free black Georgians lived in the cotton belt, they did not figure prominently in the mobilization at first. But from the start, slaves were in the thick of it.
Their major contribution, of course, would be field labor and domestic service.
Slaves would aid the mobilization in other traditional capacities, particularly as
body servants of officers and soldiers and as laborers for railroads and related
enterprises.[13]

Other uses of slave laborers raised questions, if not hackles. Excepting railroad work, most masters objected to employing slaves "in any other way than in
the house or on the plantation." Their public use was "a perversion of the
institution," intoned one planter: "We do not approve of even negro mechanics
beyond plantation mechanics." The difficulty arose from bringing slaves "into
habitual contact with white men, beyond those to whom they owe obedience. It is
at the hazard of themselves and of society when this occurs."[14] Planters of
this persuasion understood clearly that the war was about slavery and that any
use of slaves outside their customary occupations—however pressing the emergency—jeopardized the ultimate objective for which the Confederacy fought.

Other planters believed that the end justified the means. The most extreme
partisans of this view went so far as to advocate placing arms in the hands of
slaves. "There is no doubt," reasoned one, "but that numbers of [the slaves]
believe that Lincoln's intention is to set them all free." By placing "ten or
twenty . . . promiscuously in each company" of Confederate soldiers, they
"might be made quite efficient in battle." But to most white Georgians, such a
proposition appeared fanciful, if not patently absurd. Slaves who wished to
experience "the frollick" could do so by accompanying their masters to the front
as body servants without upsetting customary social relationships.[15]

Short of arming the slaves was the possibility of employing them wholesale in
manufacturing, but this too raised difficulties, especially among urban artisans
and laborers, whose opposition to the practice remained intense. Despite their
larger concern to mute class antagonism among white citizens, slaveholders held
their right to employ slaves as they chose above the artisan's right to a livelihood.
"We are in troublous times," observed one master, if public opinion were to
dictate "to the owner of the negro how he shall work that negro." "As well
prescribe hours for work," he added, "as to prescribe at what work he shall be
put."[16] Even apart from the question of abstract rights, many planters considered
it no more than practical common sense that "capital and men" needed to be
redirected from cotton planting to "our various manufacturing and mechanical
necessities." "Our white boys must learn to direct all machinery [and] be the
bosses," he argued, "and our negroes do the work."[17]

Public pronouncements to the contrary, neither individual masters nor officials entirely trusted the slaves. "[T]he fidelity of our colored population depends upon our success in effectually defending our soil," explained a Macon slaveholder to Howell Cobb. "Let us falter or fail and our present security will be at an end. Northern abolition emissaries and spies are all over the South in advance of their invading army and throughout the South the Blacks are already informed of the object of that invasion." "Is anybody so blind," he concluded, "as to feel sure that a vast majority of the slaves would not with avidity escape from bondage if they felt there was a power near to secure them that Boon?"[18]

Masters took extra precautions to prevent the rise of that power.[19] In February 1861, the city council of Macon prohibited slaves from living beyond their masters' premises without the consent of both mayor and council, hiring their own time, practicing any trade (except barbering and hairdressing) except under the master's immediate control, employing or hiring out any other person, and gambling. Three months later, slaves and free people of color were restricted from entering drinking establishments on Sunday without authorization. Grand juries throughout the upcountry echoed the alarm. And state legislators did their part, holding slaves liable with their lives for obstructing or damaging railroad bridges or rolling stock and for enticing slaves from their masters. Notwithstanding the larger objective of squelching potential sedition, these measures contained tortured wording to protect the masters' discretionary use of their slave property.[20]

Even as local, state, and Confederate officials carefully planned the mobilization for war, the war itself unleashed forces that largely negated those efforts.[21] In every facet and at every phase of this process, slaves played a decisive part. The unraveling began in the least likely of quarters, namely, agriculture. The fire of secession flared hot in the cool of winter, when inclement weather interrupted chores in any event. But the approach of spring and the start of another growing season required that the concerns of practical farming supersede those of secessionist politics. In the circumstances, planters concentrated heavily upon grains.[22]

For both patriotic and pecuniary motives, they planted cotton as well. In the first place, they well understood that armies consumed vast quantities of cotton cloth (in tents, wagon covers, clothing, and the like) that would have to be resupplied. Second, cotton was the money crop, the chief source of profit to the planters and revenue for the Confederacy. And third, planters recoiled at the prospect of voluntarily conceding their virtual monopoly over world cotton markets. Politicians took sides on the issue—Robert Toombs favoring cotton and Howell Cobb advocating corn—while pundits ranging from newspaper editors through crossroads merchants to every tiller of the soil ventured an opinion.[23] In June, Macon hosted a state convention of cotton planters to address these issues; again in October a similar group drawn from across the South made a strong case for cotton as the foundation of Confederate finance and diplomacy.[24]

By the fall of 1861, as the reality of a protracted war slowly sank in, Georgians began feeling the effects of not having switched more energetically from cotton to corn. Summer gardens withered, and the demand for grain sent prices skyward. Public opposition against unscrupulous "extortioners" identified a sore spot that would only fester under the burden of war.[25] Yet the Confederate mobilization made such social tension virtually inevitable. The army consumed subsistence goods without producing any in return. Confederate currency depreciated and prices rose due to government financial policies, the machinations of private suppliers, and the Union blockade. In circumstances reminiscent of the Revolution, persons who could not grow their own food became increasingly dependent on a skewed market mechanism. Citizens and soldiers went hungry while speculators engrossed meat and meal.[26]

In a nutshell, from 1862 onward the strains of war mounted. Even from a distance, the Union army exerted a pronounced gravitational pull upon the actions of Georgians, black and white. Closer to home, the Confederate war effort also changed customary habits. In both respects, an external authority (backed ultimately by the power of arms) upset the traditional balance in the master-slave relationship. At first, both masters and slaves sought stability. When that goal proved elusive, masters hoped to retain the prerogatives of mastership even as they tried to shed certain of its responsibilities. For their part, slaves acquiesced so long as subsistence was assured.

This alternately flaming and smoldering battle between masters and slaves consumed nonslaveholding yeomen, artisans, and laborers as well. The two most obvious ways concerned the production of subsistence goods and the impact of Confederate policies regarding the conscription of men and the seizure of animals, wagons, and foodstuffs. Whereas plantations with, say, a dozen working slaves might absorb the enlistment of the master with relatively little loss of productivity in foodstuffs, yeoman households (even those with a slave or two) suffered proportionally greater loss when the man entered military service. And to the extent that yeomen and planters mutually accommodated certain subsistence needs of each other, the removal of men severed many of these customary networks, requiring a degree of self-subsistence not seen since settlement days.

When Confederate impressment officers entered the scene, smallholders assumed additional, disproportionately heavy burdens that brought many of them to the brink of starvation and despair.[27]

This process of social disintegration accelerated as the war continued. Its mainspring was the transformation in the master-slave relationship, the result of maneuvering for advantage by planters and slaves within the new circumstances created by war. The debate over cotton acreage reopened the contest between masters and slaves for control over field operations. For most Confederate strategists and many planters, the proposed reduction in cotton output boded well, not ill. Advocates of "scientific agriculture" applauded the opportunity to diversify crops and make assorted improvements to plantation fields, fences, and buildings.[28] Proponents of diversification did not underestimate the magnitude of the challenge before them, despite the obvious incentive of war. The task, argued one partisan who echoed a prevalent concern during the crisis of the 1840s, required that planters undergo "a revolution in opinion" to achieve a thorough "change in the system of the plantation."[29]

Agricultural innovators found fault with customary practices of animal husbandry. Permitting hogs to fend for themselves in the woods seemed an especially inefficient way to raise meat. Although the improving farmers did not attempt to abolish that practice until later in the century, during the war they advocated the more systematic use of corn as hog feed. They also favored the widespread conversion of bottom lands into pastures, which might produce hay during the summer and provide grazing during the winter.[30] In the same vein, more scientific sheepraising could serve patriotic and practical ends at the same time. Repeating antebellum refrains, planters blasted the unprecedented numbers of hungry dogs—especially "negro dogs"—preying upon sheep and sought passage of a dog law. But, as earlier, smallholders viewed such legislation as an assault upon their rights and blocked every bill aimed in that direction.[31]

Such advantages notwithstanding, most planters had grave reservations about abandoning cotton entirely. Most troublesome of all was the prospect of slaves with insufficient work to keep them constantly employed. "[W]hat will you have your negroes doing [with] so little cotton?" was the question of the hour.[32] The Augusta *Chronicle and Sentinel* summarized the case so succinctly as to merit quotation at length:

No grain crop in this climate needs cultivation more than four months of the year, the remainder of the working season is unemployed. Can the farmer afford to keep his negroes, horses and other capital idle and "eating their heads off" for the balance of the season? The Cotton crop employs this capital in preparing the land before the corn crop is planted, and in working it after the crop is laid by. If we plant nothing but corn, how is this capital and this time to be employed, except in the suicidal business of clearing more land, or the *up-hill* business of attempting to recuperate lands already worn out? We conclude from this reason alone, the necessity of the constant employment of a planter's capital—*that a moderate Cotton crop could be made, and at the same time a full provision crop, without interference with each other.*[33]

Given the peculiar nature of slave capital, it was more than returns on investment that prompted these concerns. Idle slaves posed a major security risk.

From the perspective of planters as well as slaves, the shift from cotton to corn offered an opportunity to renegotiate labor requirements, rights, and responsibilities. In the process, key struggles of the previous generation were replayed in reverse. Among other things, planters apparently reverted back to labor-intensive tillage techniques. Mules still did the plowing (provided that Confederate impressment officers had not seized them), but once the land was broken, hoes took over, and the assortment of cultivators that had been the darlings of agricultural reformers in the 1830s and 1840s began gathering dust and rust. But not even that strategy proved satisfactory: a greater proportion of corn to cotton meant more work during planting, cultivating, fodder pulling, and harvesting, but it did not fill in the gaps between those tasks. And nothing could take the place of cotton picking, which occupied the entire plantation force from late August into December. By late 1863, according to one observer, repeated calls for troops had "made it necessary for many plantations to be overlooked by negroes alone." "[O]ur negro population have not the disposition, had they the judgment, to conduct our farming interest," he added.[34] Slaves saw no need to maintain either the pace or the intensity of labor characteristic of the antebellum era.[35]

Given the fact that the supervision of slaves involved matters of internal security as well as agricultural production, it is not surprising that planters prevailed upon legislators to take action. In October 1862, the so-called twenty-Negro law required the presence on every plantation of at least one white man for every twenty slaves, and it modified the conscription act of the previous April by allowing exemptions for masters or overseers to achieve that goal.[36] In November 1862, Rebecca Bryan, a seventy-four-year-old widow in Twiggs County, petitioned for the discharge from service of her overseer, who had enlisted at the outbreak of the war. Like hundreds of other petitioners, she required someone "to oversee or control" her field hands (who numbered twenty-four); she felt that the overseer was "better acquainted with her business than any person that she knows of." For various reasons, including bureaucratic red tape and the reluctance of eligible men to claim exemption, the law affected only a fraction of the plantations to which it applied. As a result, women such as Bryan attempted to supervise the slaves, assisted by elderly men, disabled soldiers, and boys. They had mixed success at best.[37]

Slaves sought greater discretion over the time made available by the reduction of cotton acreage. As earlier, they produced handicrafts, both for sale and for home use, but, given the exigencies of war, provision grounds assumed unprecedented importance. The strategy of raising corn instead of cotton did not necessarily mean that there was more food available on the plantations. Confederate tax officials kept close tabs on growing crops and monitored harvests carefully to be sure they got their share. Slaves' provision grounds were by common consent exempt from such levies; therefore, it made sense from the masters' standpoint as well as the slaves' to increase food production there. But not all the changes in gardening arrangements redounded to the benefit of the slaves. In February 1863, the state legislature succumbed to pressure from Governor Brown and restricted cotton production to three acres per hand, slaves' patches included. Planters who had earlier permitted raising cotton revoked the privilege.[38]

As pork became scarcer, masters sought substitutes for bacon. Some touted the virtues of syrup; others favored vegetables. "[I]f large plantation gardens are formed," one planter theorized early in 1864, "and the negroes abundantly furnished with all the vegetables they can consume, they will pass through the year on a small supply of bacon with much less inconvenience and suffering than the peasantry of the balance of the civilized world."[39] Slaves' gardens served the same purpose.

Slaves continued to fish and hunt as they had done before the war, but the competition for subsistence from the wild became increasingly intense as the war progressed.[40] Both planters and public officials routinely charged slaves with killing pigs foraging in the woods. Given the less stringent enforcement of patrol laws, it is likely that slave hunters also ranged farther in pursuit of game. But it is just as likely that their paths crossed those of other far-ranging hunters, slave and free alike.

To reduce the glut of underemployed plantation laborers, planters with urban residences expanded their household staffs. Not all white Georgians approved of such conspicuous consumption amidst war's privations. One critic of the "[t]housands of negro men and boys and able-bodied women . . . kept ministering to the ease and gentility of private families" proposed that the "town gentry . . . work their own gardens and chop their own fire-wood" so their slaves might labor for surrounding farmers.[41] But large slaveholders had no intention of performing household chores, regardless of the circumstances.

At the same time, however, masters became increasingly fond of saving costs of support by authorizing slaves to hire their own time and provide for themselves. Although civil authorities and private citizens alike had repeatedly railed against the practice of self-hiring, they had never succeeded in banning it. "Stop negroes from trafficking about the streets, hiring their own time," intoned one master in a typical expression of the theme, "because it gives the negro facility to idle, trade and all concomitants—*interfering with the white man's rights.*"[42] Planters urged legislative action against the "evils" that resulted from the "collection of negroes in cities, sometimes nearly one hundred living in one yard and hiring out their time—their assemblage in workshops, [and] their unguarded association with irresponsible and vicious white men."[43] The community of slaves hired to the Central Railroad and their families in East Macon fit that description quintessentially.

Critics of such unlawful assemblages simply advocated the scrupulous enforcement of existing legislation. "The common practice of allowing slaves to hire their own time, rent houses, and set up establishments of their own, remote from their masters," argued the editors of the *Columbus Sun*, "is perhaps doing more to demoralize our slave population than anything else." Another journal urged steps to "prevent all practices that tend to demoralize the negro, and render him worthless, troublesome or insubordinate"; especially noteworthy was the near epidemic of nocturnal hog-stealing that "threatens to leave us almost without meat for the next year." Other kinds of "pilfering" produced similar concerns.[44]

As early as January 1863, Macon's city council aimed to reduce the number of hired slaves in the city by requiring nonresident owners to pay almost double the permit fees paid by residents.[45] Both masters and slaves routinely flouted the law, and by the summer of 1864 the council advised owners wishing to protect their slaves from arrest to provide certificates showing their name and address. Nonetheless, the Augusta *Chronicle and Sentinel* reported that large numbers of slaves roamed about Macon without such certificates, hiring their time as if they were free.[46] Employers willing to ignore the technicality of the owner's permission were in ample supply.

City fathers had little doubt that such slaves represented an abolitionist fifth column sowing chaos and sapping morale. Fire was the ultimate weapon of subversion. Early in 1863 the *Daily Telegraph* termed incendiarism "rife." "Our city seems to be doomed to conflagration," echoed the *Journal & Messenger.* "There is an enemy among us who should be sought out and made to pull hemp or cotton." But neither increased vigilance nor new restrictions proved effective; five major fires of suspicious origin flared, as did several times that number of smaller ones.[47] In the eyes of the masters, freedom-minded slaves had abandoned all civility and restraint.

Whether real or imagined, the fear of imminent doom sprang largely from one source: the federal government's new policy of emancipation announced on 1 January 1863. Georgia slaveholders could ill afford to dismiss the document as nothing more than a tinkling cymbal, for they understood its larger impact. It declared unequivocally that the war was about the future of slavery: if the Yankees prevailed, the slaves would be freed. Moreover, the proclamation served notice that federal armies operating in Confederate territory would make it their business to free slaves.[48] Most important of all, masters knew that the proclamation would exert a powerful force among the slaves, if not necessarily prompting them to risk flight or rebellion, at least bolstering their allegiance to the Union.

Slave owners did not misunderstand the nature of this threat. In time-honored fashion, they advocated closer monitoring of the slaves. A mass meeting held in Macon during June 1863, for example, resolved to organize a mounted home guard for defense against the Yankees. The meeting also recommended a night watch to prevent "improper meetings" among slaves and free black persons and to interdict communication with "mischievous or corrupt persons" and abolitionists pursuing "diabolical purposes."[49] Following the Confederate defeats at Vicksburg and Gettysburg early in July, the specter of triumphant emancipation grew larger. For the rest of the war, both individual masters and Confederate authorities at every level struggled to isolate the slaves from subversive influences.

No matter how diligently they tried to keep slaves in their accustomed place, masters and civil authorities found it increasingly impossible to do so. As the war continued, growing numbers of slaves moved about as they pleased. Temporary flight or "lying out" served as a form of protest against objectionable conditions and as a means of initiating negotiations toward amelioration, much as it had before the war. Yet the circumstances of war cast such negotiations in a new light, and not every master was willing to concede the legitimacy of this tactic. As the conflict intensified, owners who took the narrow view of flight equated a slave's absence with a treasonous bid for freedom. Such sentiment tended to rise and fall barometrically with the relative distance of the Yankees from any given plantation. But the war complicated traditional patterns of flight in several ways. Masters themselves often fled, contradicting their oft-repeated professions about the sanctity of the home place and the mutual exchange of subsistence and protection for faithful service. And before the war was over, some masters even encouraged their slaves to take shelter in the woods, to escape Confederate impressment officers no less than Yankee soldiers.[50]

As earlier, most fugitives intended to rejoin family members from whom they had been separated.[51] Railroad hands and wagoners continued to take advantage of their mobility to escape, but other slaves encountered new opportunities to run away when masters carried them off to war as servants or hired them to the Confederate government.[52] All slaves found the prospects of successful flight greater after the white men who normally provided the most salient check against insubordination had left for battle. The presence of Union troops on the coast and, by spring 1864, in north Georgia greatly reduced the distance fugitives had to travel to reach asylum. All of these elements helped to loosen the bonds of slavery, even as masters tried more frantically than ever to control their human chattels.

HIRING SLAVES directly to the Confederate government promised special security. From early in the war, strategists had been eying Macon as a potential site for military production. Aside from its excellent rail connections, the city possessed other attractive qualities. Although positioned on a waterway that flowed into the Atlantic Ocean, the city enjoyed comparative security from Union attack. The sand bars at Darien obstructed seagoing vessels, and the shallows where the Ocmulgee joined the Altamaha posed another formidable barrier. And the river provided water power as well as security.

The city's antebellum industrial establishment, anchored by the machine shops of J. H. C. D. Findlay and J. Schofield, further recommended Macon. There was a respectable core of skilled metal tradesmen and the possibility of recruiting even more from nearby towns should the need arise. Accordingly, during 1862 Confederate strategists located three major ordnance installations in Macon: an armory for manufacturing and repairing small arms, an arsenal for casting cannon and other heavy weapons, and a laboratory for making ammunition. The success of these establishments prompted the construction of a quartermaster's depot, a medical purveyor's office, and a steam bakery. All these

Anderson & Ballard Brickyard, Macon
(Courtesy of Georgia Department of Archives and History)

facilities employed slaves, by war's end nearly 1,000 of them, recruited for the most part from the plantation belt of upcountry Georgia.[53]

Most of these slaves were intended to perform menial work: making bricks, hauling building materials, performing the heavy, dirty, and disagreeable work in the shops, sweeping floors, and removing garbage. But the Confederacy also sought to employ substantial numbers of skilled slaves, especially metalworkers, carpenters, and masons.[54] In April 1862, Capt. Richard M. Cuyler, superintendent of the arsenal, began gathering his work force. Under normal circumstances, such an undertaking would have had mixed results at best. As a rule, slave rental agreements ran from New Year's Day to Christmas Day. By late spring, hired slaves had long since joined their employers and all other slaves were busy plowing and planting. But these were not normal circumstances.

Apparently in response to an inquiry from Cuyler, Findlay Iron Works reported seven white mechanics and three black ones—a machine blacksmith, a molder, and an engineer—ready for immediate service.[55] A slave owner in Houston County also offered a slave with foundry experience.[56] Another slaveholder volunteered five or six slaves provided they did not have to work "near the yankees."[57] With such offers before him, Cuyler could choose to discriminate, and he declined to hire a sixteen-year-old described by his master as "rather unmanageable" though a "smart intelligent fellow."[58] Capt. J. W. Mallet, a well-known chemist to whom Confederate chief of ordnance Josiah Gorgas had entrusted the work of producing ammunition at Macon, began recruiting laborers for his laboratory at the same time. But whereas Cuyler sought skilled slaves, Mallet sought common laborers to make bricks and assist in constructing buildings.[59]

The vagaries of war also added to the pool of slaves from which the ordnance superintendents might choose. By the spring of 1862, the success of federal forces along the coasts of South Carolina and Georgia and along the Tennessee and Mississippi rivers prompted the phenomenon described by contemporaries as "refugeeing," that is, the flight of Confederate sympathizers to the interior. Slaveholders were especially fond of the tactic as a means of securing their property. But, depending upon the haste with which they arranged the move, the distance to the intended destination, and the availability of wagons and supplies, masters did not always remove all their slaves. In many cases, they took only the most valuable ones—men and women of prime working age—leaving all others behind, sometimes under the control of an overseer, but often to fend for themselves. So in addition to a forced separation from home, refugeed slaves often endured a forced separation from loved ones as well.[60]

The black belt of Georgia offered an especially attractive destination to planters from Tennessee and Mississippi. Fugitive masters sought out relatives; when that was inexpedient, they simply looked for vacant plantations on whatever terms could be arranged. They found themselves facing the same challenges regarding crop mixes and strategies for employing slaves with which Georgia planters were contending, plus the strains of the migration and the adjustment to a new environment to boot. But in scarcely no time refugee planters and Confederate ordnance officers recognized their mutual interests.

Captain Mallet's dealings with one of Tennessee's Confederate senators, Gustavus A. Henry, illustrate the complex dynamics that governed the hiring of slaves to the Confederacy. Like numerous other planters from the west, Henry found it difficult to keep all his slaves productively occupied. Unlike his new neighbors, who feared exposing their slaves to an urban environment "at any price," Henry was willing to hire slaves to private employers in Macon. Moreover, he mixed patriotism and pecuniary interest to strike a deal with Captain Mallet.

Politics and business made strange bedfellows. Henry asked Mallet to keep his slaves confined after dark to avoid aggravating the respiratory difficulties they suffered since moving to Georgia. For his own part, Henry seemed to take a less than paternal interest in their well-being, failing to furnish them with shoes as required in the government's agreement of hire. The death of one of the slaves early in 1863 raised the issue of liability that plagued both masters and Confederate military authorities for the rest of the war.[61]

Slaves hired to the Confederate government quickly perceived potentially contradictory interests between their owners and their employers. Government officials generally tended toward bureaucratic solutions to the challenges posed by the war and often showed little concern for the cares of individual slaveholders, a stance to which the latter had a difficult time adjusting. And when it came down to the fine points of rental agreements, few officers had patience for the technicalities over which planters seemed to dote. Yet willy-nilly, the Ordnance Department superintendents, at Macon and at other facilities, found their strategic responsibilities constantly interrupted by dealings with slave owners who seemed more concerned over which party was to furnish clothing, shoes, and medical attention than over the output of arms and ammunition. Masters sought higher rates of hire, as the price of necessities rose and the value of Confederate currency fell. As late as November 1863, Captain Mallet informed a prospective lessor that the ordnance works would pay $30 per month plus rations, but financial constraints apparently forced him to revise that figure downward after the new year. Tight money also prompted Capt. James H. Burton at the armory to consider hiring slaves by the year instead of by the day. But owners increasingly spurned the rates he and his associates offered.

Hired slaves took advantage of wartime circumstances to extend the perquisites they had established in antebellum times, playing masters against hirers to achieve their objectives. Both civil authorities and white citizens generally objected to the widening sphere of slaves' "social privileges," especially that of traveling by rail to "distant localities" for purposes of visiting. As one planter explained, the practice had originated before the war through a combination of decreasing fares and "a constantly increasing confidence between master and slave." But given the wartime emergency, he argued, such practices were better overturned.[62]

Slaves who had been hired away from their families desired little more than to bolster these social privileges, and they increasingly succeeded in persuading their employers to do so, often upon the recommendation of their masters. After learning that railroad workers customarily enjoyed time off to visit their families, Captain Mallet adopted the practice "in order to use it as a stimulant to industry and good conduct."[63] One slave owner offered his two masons to Mallet, provided they could have one Saturday per month off to visit their wives. The master even agreed to pay for the lost time.[64] To the same end, Mallet inaugurated a piece-work system whereby slave workers could accumulate time off.[65] A slave couple won permission to have their children live with them at the laboratory, with the superintendent agreeing to forgo a lodging fee provided they shared their rations with the children or their master provided food.[66] By manipulating such privileges, Mallet hoped to keep the slaves—upon whose work he increasingly depended—reliable and contented. By manipulating the sometimes contrary interests of masters and employers, hired slaves aimed to keep their families together and, when possible, to gain greater control over their lives.

As the war continued, masters and employers faced growing difficulty balancing their respective interests against those being voiced by the slaves. When Dr. A. C. Rogers, a Monroe County planter and physician, contemplated sending slaves to the ordnance laboratory, he inquired closely into the terms of hire. As a rule, Captain Mallet explained, the laboratory offered "liberal" wages, rations, medical attendance, and payment of city and other taxes; masters were required to furnish clothing, shoes, and blankets. Mallet also claimed the right to discharge slaves at his discretion, but Rogers balked, fearing that too strict a policy toward temporary absences would only prod his slaves to break for the Yankees. By his own admission, they often absented themselves for a few days at a time— never more than a week, and nothing that would warrant discharge. Although the two men could not resolve their differences over the disposition of runaways, Rogers agreed to hire an unspecified number of slaves, including a carpenter and his helper.[67]

Hired slaves had to adjust to new surroundings, new conditions, and new people, often paying a heavy toll in the process. For those unaccustomed to an urban environment, there was exposure to new—often deadly—diseases, a phenomenon characteristic of nineteenth-century urban life generally, but one considerably aggravated by the war. In these circumstances, neither masters nor employers paid much heed to the potentially disruptive effect that such an apparently simple matter as a new diet might have upon the slaves.[68]

Mallet and Rogers quickly discovered the effect of that oversight. Rogers's slaves protested that the ration of fresh beef instead of pork was killing them, and this was but one of their health concerns. Making bricks in a nearby swamp wreaked havoc on their respiratory systems, and they lacked adequate medical attention. "If they can be moved and get half rations of bacon," Rogers confidently predicted, "with other necessaries I think I can satisfy them to remain." But in the absence of such guarantees, "from their extreme discontent when I saw them I believe they will be troublesome and will be *constantly* running away." Mallet offered explanations for the poor health of the slaves, but he emphatically declined indemnification for a slave who had died. When the superintendent proposed reassigning the slaves to railroad work, Rogers reluctantly agreed. The risk of injury or death there apparently did not exceed that of exposure in the swamp. And neither surpassed the challenge of keeping the slaves productively employed at home.[69]

In their effort to play masters against employers for greater privileges, slaves sometimes got caught in the ensuing crossfire. For example, when Mallet asked Rogers to furnish wool clothing for two sick slaves, the doctor questioned the need for such a dole. The slaves on his plantation had remained "perfectly healthy," he claimed, even though they had "worn cotton clothing and gone barefooted during the winter." Acting in kind, Mallet refused to advance $5 so that Rogers's slaves could purchase buttons for their trousers.[70] However skillfully slaves may have bargained for advantages, success depended upon the actions of men who had made a science of acting capriciously.

Flight remained the slaves' trump card. During the summer of 1863, all of Rogers's slaves grew discontented over their poor clothing and lack of shoes, but two slaves appeared perpetually uneasy. Clinton, whom Rogers described as "a good negro for work but his nature is such that he cannot bear much liberty," caused the most trouble, disappearing repeatedly. Bill, whom Rogers described as "an extra fine boy under *proper* management, but . . . very intolerant of abuse," also insisted upon running away. Try as they might, neither Rogers nor Mallet could either cajole or threaten the slaves into submission.[71]

While trying to retain slaves they had already hired, the ordnance superintendents also tried to increase the slave work force. Under pressure to produce more weapons and ammunition, they aimed to expand their physical facilities. Yet the shortage of workers of every description compounded their difficulties. They advertised widely and repeatedly for slave brickmakers; after having solved that problem, they still lacked bricklayers and carpenters, and once the additions to the buildings were completed, they lacked metalworkers and wood-turners. Slaves would readily fill the bill as building tradesmen, but obtaining the requisite machinists and turners required persistence and ingenuity. Although Confederate conscription legislation had provided exemptions for certain categories of skilled workers, including machinists, demand far outweighed supply, and ordnance superintendents had to resort to mobilizing skilled slaves.[72] The move had profound results, few, if any, of which were apparent at the time.

Given the number of slaves in central Georgia with prior employment in industrial settings, there was little need for panic, dire predictions to the contrary notwithstanding. To be sure, slaves in factories did experience a world much different from that of the plantations. They often worked by the task, with privileges to earn cash through overwork. And it was not uncommon for them to feed and shelter themselves out of their earnings. The Confederacy's need for self-sufficiency in armaments required unprecedented reliance upon such slaves. Confident strategists predicted no threat to the social order.[73]

Captain Burton pioneered in the use of skilled slaves, though not with great enthusiasm. From the start, slaves helped build the armory and then manufacture and repair pistols and rifles. In January 1863, when construction was not yet completed, he had fifty-seven white employees (forty-five mechanics and twelve apprentices and laborers) and seventy-nine hired slaves (twenty-three mechanics and carpenters and the rest laborers). Neither the laboratory nor the arsenal—or, for that matter, any of the other government facilities in Macon— hired so many or such a proportion of skilled slaves. At the beginning of 1863, wages of white employees ranged from $3.25 per day for mechanics to $1.50 for laborers. Unlike his counterparts who contracted for black laborers strictly on a yearly basis, Burton also hired slaves by the day, paying rates ranging from $1.85 for skilled slaves to $1.25 for unskilled slaves, with the masters responsible for all expenses, including food, clothing, and shelter.[74] Slave mechanics thus commanded a rate of hire greater than that of white laborers, and the rate for slave laborers was only slightly less than that for their white counterparts.

White mechanics rebelled at the pay scale, in some measure out of resentment against the high earnings of slaves, but more pointedly in protest against the rising cost of living.[75] Burton reported that the scarcity of labor enabled them fairly to "dictate the wages they receive." To counteract their loss in real wages, the mechanics sought pay raises nearly every month. In March 1863, they demanded parity with the Richmond, Virginia, ordnance works. Burton argued, to no avail, that Richmond's higher cost of living warranted the differential and that the rates he paid equaled those prevailing at all similar establishments in Macon. The mechanics refused to follow his logic and continued to press for higher wages. The two other ordnance superintendents faced similar demands. In mid-summer 1863, Cuyler complained that white workers at both the arsenal and the armory had resorted "to every conceivable means of getting away in consequence of the low wages." The superintendents published advertisements offering cash for the apprehension of such deserters. With the exception of a word or two, these read just like advertisements for runaway slaves.[76]

Desertion surely frustrated officials but apparently accomplished little else. Inducing a shortage of laborers in that way did not force wage rates upward, nor did it relieve the general disparity between wage rates and the cost of necessities. In fact, not just artisans and laborers felt this pinch. All urban residents did, and rural farmers and planters sympathized with their predicament. As early as the fall of 1861, grumblings of complaint against "sharpers and Shylocks" had arisen. Grand jurors in Houston County yearned to resort to "the old common law" system of punishing monopolists, and a poor farmer lambasted "the Monied power" for the high price of salt, which was essential for curing bacon.[77] By 1863, a groundswell of popular resentment attempted to unite the interests of producing farmers and consuming laborers against "overreaching speculators and extortioners" who "draw the very life blood of the country by their money schemes." Public sentiment waxed most sympathetic toward soldiers' families. To supplement the numerous agencies of private relief, early in 1864 Macon's city council authorized a "City Store" with authority to buy provisions wholesale and sell them cheaply to soldiers' families. These popular campaigns on behalf of a moral economy, wherein speculators were treated as pariahs and public officials influenced the distribution of foodstuffs, clearly were the last gasps of an older social order. Under the pressure of war, inflation, and the growth of market exchange, cash replaced custom as the main desideratum.[78]

Through 1864 rising inflation aggravated the wage dispute, causing widespread disaffection among white employees of the ordnance facilities. "The men generally are so much dissatisfied with the wages allowed them," reported Captain Burton in March, "that it is impossible to get them to apply themselves to their work in anything like a satisfactory manner." Detailed soldiers, especially, tried to get away to rejoin their regiments, where they reportedly received higher pay. Burton recommended wages of $7 per day for skilled operatives and $6 for carpenters and bricklayers, more than twice the rate of the previous year. Later he still had occasion to criticize the shoddy quality of work in the pistol repair shop, attributing it to demoralization wrought by low pay. The women operatives at work in the laboratory also took up this spirit of protest. Mobilized to relieve the shortage of men, they too found it difficult to support their families in the context of rising prices and depreciating currency. Accordingly, in the fall of 1864 they struck for a raise in wages from $5 to $7 per day and won the endorsement of the *Macon Telegraph*, even if not that of the laboratory superintendent.[79]

This unrest among wage workers in government employ reflected the much greater level of dissatisfaction with the declining fortunes of war after mid-1863. It was not simply that the loss of life and limb had taken such a dreadful toll, but also that the quest for subsistence had become a daily struggle. Households that suffered the death of the soldier-father battled almost insuperable odds, but all soldiers' families fared badly. Although they hoped that the soldiers' wages would contribute to their subsistence, they faced the problems of irregular pay and depreciating Confederate scrip. Finally, the notion that purchased food could fill shortfalls in home production took into account neither the uneven development of markets in foodstuffs before the war nor wartime speculation. Privation bred disaffection with the Confederacy, which manifested itself in desertion, evasion of conscription and tax officials, and theft.

IF THESE TRIALS were not enough, early in 1864 Georgians heard the news—greeted with joy by some and with horror by others—that federal armies under Gen. William T. Sherman had departed Chattanooga in the direction of Atlanta. For the rest of the year (if not the rest of the century), Georgians could speak of little else than Sherman and his hordes of grizzled troops. Aside from the Yankees' propensity to destroy what they could not devour, they added new instability to the master-slave relationship. Yet that result derived more from the actions of Georgia slaves than from those of Union soldiers. To be sure, the Yankees brought hope of freedom wherever they advanced. But throughout their sojourn in the state, they subordinated freeing slaves to demoralizing Confederate sympathizers. Sherman's troops did not necessarily greet escaped slaves with open arms, and in one notorious case, they abandoned several hundred in their train to the mercy of pursuing Confederates.[80]

Simultaneous with the movement of federal armies out of Tennessee, Georgia's agriculturists also abandoned their winter quarters for the field. Although Governor Brown had failed to convince the legislature to further restrict cotton acreage to one-quarter acre per hand, by the spring of 1864 few farmers failed to understand the importance of growing food. Regardless of the army's needs, uncontrollable inflation suggested the wisdom of raising, rather than purchasing, foodstuffs. Accordingly, planters apportioned their arable land among various kinds of edibles for man and beast. Die-hard cotton growers also planted up to the maximum of three acres to the hand.[81]

As Sherman's campaign advanced, central Georgia planters became increasingly edgy. They threatened slaves contemplating escape with brutal punishment. Interdicting the flow of information from the front, they painted the invaders as barbarians or, worse yet, heartless speculators who sold captured slaves to Cuba. By spinning such a cocoon around their slaves, planters in effect tried to seal them off from contact with the outside world. They had little hope of success. The fall of Atlanta shook central Georgia, prompting masters to move their slaves and other possessions to southwest Georgia, deeper into the hinterland. Former slave Bob Mobley of Crawford County remembered being refugeed to Dooly County (south of Houston). According to another former slave, Sara Crocker of Twiggs County, white families east of Macon also felt unsafe and fled to other parts of the state.[82] Masters who were unwilling to leave central Georgia took shelter in the woods, as did the owners of George Womble of Jones County, through which part of Sherman's army eventually passed.[83] The movement of slaves against their will further tarnished the masters' image of omnipotent protector. And their image of provider disintegrated completely when they removed slaves from familiar fields and gardens and hunting and fishing spots at a time of such extreme uncertainty.

Predictably, slaves ran away. Young men set out for the Yankees.[84] But few found a straight path to freedom. George Carter, for instance, fled from Confederate impressment in hopes of reaching Union lines. Captured by Rebel authorities, he made it known that he had had antebellum experience as a fireman on the Central Railroad, and he was put back to that work for the rest of the war.[85] Other slaves aimed to rejoin family members from whom they had been separated, reversing the movement of slaves to fresh land before the war and to military installations and places of safety since the fighting began.[86] Still others joined the federal army. Fifteen-year-old John Sparrow fled from Jones County in June 1864 and succeeded in reaching the Yankees above Atlanta. He returned home after the war, wearing the Union uniform and bearing federal discharge papers.[87] But not even the federals could offer foolproof protection. Ell Robinson, a former slave serving as a federal scout in Virginia, was captured and sold into slavery in central Georgia. Only three full years after the surrender did he manage to return home.[88]

Whether consciously or not, Sherman helped crystallize a process that had been underway from the start of the war. Simply put, he forced both civil and

military officials to define certain matters in the public interest, irrespective of
the wishes (or even cherished property rights) of individual citizens. The official
actions of Governor Joseph Brown, the perennial thorn in the side of Richmond
authorities intent upon centralizing power, illustrate this dynamic, as he played
his own version of Jefferson Davis to Georgia slaveholders. In March 1864, he
unsuccessfully sought legislation to compel removal of slaves from areas threatened by federal invasion upon penalty of seizure by the state. "No man has a
right," he declared, "to use his own property as to weaken our strength, diminish
our provision supply, and add recruits to the army of the enemy."[89] Such
pronouncements played well in the yeoman region of north Georgia but, if
anything, made planters question the governor's commitment to their fundamental rights.

The reaction of Confederate military officials to Yankee invasion similarly
undermined the master-slave relationship. From the start of the campaign for
Atlanta, the Confederates depended heavily upon the output of factories and
fields in and around Macon. The ordnance works played an especially important
part, and the superintendents did not misunderstand their responsibility. Both
Burton at the armory and Mallet at the laboratory rushed to produce more arms
and ammunition.

Construction of new buildings required both skilled and unskilled slaves, an
increasingly scarce commodity at the rates authorized by the Ordnance Department regulations. At the beginning of 1864, the superintendents of the works
had attempted to fill their quotas, but with mixed results at best. No shortage of
patriotism afflicted slaveholders, but growing dissatisfaction with the terms of
employment did. The unsuccessful effort of Burton and Mallet to hire 275 slaves
to make bricks illustrates the mounting frustration on the part of hirers and
owners. The officers' first offer of $18 a month produced eighty slaves; increas-
ing the rate to $24 per month added only nineteen more. With the hired slaves
falling sick in "an unusual number," masters grew even more aloof, a sentiment
that slaves seem to have shared. To overcome the resulting inertia, in June 1864
the Confederate War Department authorized the impressment of 120 slaves to
make bricks. Public need superseded private rights.[90]

As Sherman's pressure on Atlanta intensified, Confederates appealed to yet a
higher order of necessity. Scarcely had Burton and Mallet gained authorization
to impress slaves when they in turn were ordered to relinquish one-third of their
force to work on the besieged city's fortifications.[91] Burton protested that such a
use of hired slaves would invalidate the government's contract with their masters.
But with little patience for such technicalities, the post commander at Macon

ordered the impressment of twenty-three "laborers and mechanics" for a week's service. Burton successfully appealed to Ordnance Department officials for an exemption, but his victory was short-lived.[92]

Sherman's army exposed Georgia's (and the Confederacy's) underlying manpower deficiency. Ordnance superintendents manipulated their supplies of white workers, even as they combated persistent "discontent" regarding pay and indifference regarding the quality of work.[93] And the need for laborers at Atlanta exacerbated shortages of hired slaves in Macon. When the draft of slaves came again early in August, contractual formalities provided masters little protection. The following month Burton offered to pay $4 per day for fifty slaves, lamenting that their "labor is very much needed in consequence of nearly all my force being sent to the front."[94] Resentful of the Confederacy's high-handed disregard for their fundamental property rights, masters refused to hire at any price.

Predictably, slaves sent to Atlanta often made straight for the Yankees, to the consternation of Burton and their masters.[95] The families of several such escapees had earlier prevailed upon Burton for permission to live at the armory, and he continued to let them do so. Paternalism took on a new face as strangers provided for slaves whose masters had abdicated the responsibility. In settled times, slaves might well have transferred their loyalty from the old to the new provider. But in the circumstances of war, paternalism itself lost legitimacy. Slaves filled the gap with a growing sense of their own ability to survive without a master and of the propriety of doing so.

Free black conscripts encouraged this self-assurance among their slave counterparts even as they struggled to protect their own tenuous rights. Precisely because the free black population of upcountry Georgia was small, it was vulnerable. Lacking masters or other advocates, free black persons stood little chance of escaping the search for warm bodies to work on fortifications. Simultaneous with the federal advance toward Atlanta, military authorities in Georgia took steps to harness free black men. Enrolling officers in the respective counties identified the able-bodied and, as need required, sent them to a rendezvous point—in Macon, denominated the Camp of Instruction—for dispatch to the front. Traveling unescorted, only a fraction reached that destination. When those who did report were directed toward Atlanta—or even across town to the ordnance establishments—few completed the journey.[96]

Free black men stood with little to gain and much to lose from service at the front. After all, Yankees could not offer them freedom, but dangers to their families and meager property abounded. The risk of jail or physical punishment did not deter flight. And those who could not escape the dragnet harbored intense resentment, a feeling they readily shared with their fellow laborers who were slaves. However necessary to Confederate defensive strategy, conscription made free black persons active partisans against the slaveholders' rebellion.

As the battle for Atlanta reached the critical stage, federal commanders contemplated a bold stroke behind Confederate lines to free federal prisoners held at Macon and Andersonville. Union Gen. George Stoneman underestimated the adversary. After being stopped by Confederate forces at Macon, Stoneman began to backtrack. On the last day of July, Confederate cavalry serving under a native of central Georgia, Gen. Alfred Holt Iverson, laid a trap which, when sprung, resulted in the defeat and capture of Stoneman and approximately 500 federal cavalrymen. Among the captives was a former slave from Jones County named Minor, who had escaped to the Yankees and was serving as a guide. Swiftly and unceremoniously, the Rebels hanged Minor.[97]

Georgians sensed instinctively that Sherman would march to Savannah via Macon. Accordingly, Howell Cobb, then commander of the state defense forces headquartered in Macon, ordered the conscription of 500 slaves to work on fortifications, and masters began systematically hiding supplies, animals, and valuables.[98] Despite the lure of transportation and manufacturing facilities there—not to mention the imprisoned federals who had been Stoneman's undoing—the main body of Sherman's army passed northeast of the city, crossing Jones County en route to Milledgeville, the state capital. Approximately ten miles from Macon at Griswoldville, site of the large antebellum gin works of Samuel Griswold, which had been converted to a pistol factory early in the war, Confederate state militiamen chose to join battle. The motley assortment of inexperienced, overaged and underaged Georgians were soundly trounced, suffering heavy casualties at the hands of Sherman's seasoned veterans.[99]

The federals burned the pistol factory to the ground, destroyed much of Clinton and the other towns along their line of march, and generally "loaded up and carried off everything that was eatable for men or beast and then burned what was left."[100] "Everything has been swept as with a storm of fire," observed a Macon newspaper. "The whole country around is one wide waste of destruction." After castigating the Yankees for destroying food supplies, taking the clothing from the backs of "contrabands," and defiling "female servants," a resident of Jones County concluded, "Many of us are utterly ruined."[101]

Sherman reportedly took "especial pleasure" informing escaped slaves that they were free, but only a modest number—3,000 by one reliable estimate—arrived at Savannah with his army.[102] This figure scarcely conveys how thoroughly the March to the Sea transformed the lives of Georgia slaves. The immediate presence of Yankees stripped away the veneer of paternalism in ways that distant events could not possibly do. Howell Cobb, for example, reportedly removed the able-bodied slaves and stock from his plantation near Milledgeville, leaving "some fifty old men—cripples—and women and children, with nothing scarcely covering their nakedness, with little or no food, and without means of procuring it." They, like other slaves in Sherman's path, were told the Yankees would kill them. "A more forlorn, neglected set of human beings," remarked a federal officer, "I never saw."[103]

Although Union soldiers did not encourage slaves to follow in their wake, neither did they refrain from proclaiming freedom. But the lilt of the word did not linger long in the air; it was part of the general din that accompanied the movement of the army. One elderly slave captured the ambiguity of this kind of freedom when he observed to Sherman, "[Y]ou'se 'll go way to-morrow, and anudder white man 'll come."[104] But for all its limitations, this brush with a new world left indelible impressions. Slaves saw their masters and themselves in a new light; the old ties were stretching thinner and the possibility of a new structure of social relationships growing stronger. Yet masters were not willing to concede either the wisdom or the expediency of this insight.

The change registered immediately in the slaves' behavior, even in Macon. By casual observation, the work at the Confederate ordnance facilities appeared to continue as before. On the last day of 1864, Burton reported that the slaves hired to the armory were busy "grading land, making and hauling brick, waiting upon bricklayers & carpenters, cutting wood, burning coal," and whatever odd jobs needed doing.[105] This impression of order disguised his growing fear that the slaves would run away, to assuage which he ordered them housed within the armory enclosure instead of outside as before.[106] But not even these precautions removed the fear.[107] And, as earlier, running away hinted at other grievances. One slave expressed dissatisfaction with working at the armory because he had no opportunity to earn money for himself there. When neither the superintendent nor his master took remedial action, the slave decamped with a group of fellow servants of the same owner.[108] During the closing months of the war, other slaves also ran away to escape odious labor, visit families, or simply experience life on their own. Slave relations of production were falling rapidly apart.

BOTH INDIVIDUALLY and collectively, these actions of slaves demonstrate the internal dynamic of emancipation. Probably nowhere—least of all central Georgia—did President Lincoln's celebrated new birth of freedom begin on 1 January 1863. Instead, it developed slowly over the course of the war, with certain large turning points, to be sure, but with countless small struggles that in the end decisively shaped the outcome of events. The unwitting role of Confederate strategists and even masters in these proceedings must not be underestimated. In attempting to fight a war to preserve slavery while relying so heavily upon the labor of slaves, they sowed the seeds of their own destruction. When they abandoned cotton for corn, they undercut the carefully constructed regimen of disciplining slaves through constant work. And to the extent that the mobilization of white men for military service created shortages of skilled civilians, Confederates relied increasingly upon slaves for industrial as well as agricultural labor.

Matters grew more complicated as slaves exploited these contradictions. From early in the contest, slaves made it clear that their loyalty could not be taken for granted. They pressured both masters and Confederate strategists to expand gardening privileges on the plantations and visiting privileges, time off, and overwork payments in the workshops and factories. This process assumed a dynamic of its own due to the strains of the federal blockade, the depreciation of Confederate money, and, ultimately, the march of Union soldiers. Having legitimated the process of exacting concessions, slaves returned repeatedly to the bargaining table.

Slaves assumed major burdens under the guise of extended privileges. As the war progressed they increasingly had to feed, clothe, and shelter themselves. They occupied vacant land, constructing makeshift dwellings and cultivating garden patches. Those living in cities also sought remunerative employment in an uphill struggle to obtain the necessities of life. Enduring the worst of both worlds, such slaves were freed from the protection and largess of their masters and were obligated to subsist themselves in an imperfectly functioning market mechanism straining under the unprecedented demands of war. In the circumstances, it is not difficult to understand why most central Georgia slaves stayed close to home.

In stripping away the aura of the masters' invincibility, the Civil War also exposed the nature of freedom. Slaves in central Georgia understood that freedom was not an absolute state so much as a contest that might sway backward as well as forward. The abstract rights of property remained to be settled by federal bayonets and federal courts, but the most pressing practical matter concerned the struggle for subsistence. As masters increasingly abdicated this responsibility, slaves had little choice but to take it up. The closing months of the war drove home the lesson that had been building all along: subsistence depended upon access to land.

To be sure, masters cringed at the implications of Appomattox, just as slaves vicariously shared the victory of John Sparrow and his federal comrades-in-arms. But the defeat of the rebellion did not signal either the paradise some expected or the apocalypse others feared. It did, however, decisively affect the dynamics of struggle at the grass-roots level. Former masters would not again enjoy the privileged access to the persons and the products of labor of their work force. Former slaves would not again be bought and sold. These changes mattered for everything, setting in motion a thorough reconstruction of southern society.

6

. . . .

The Origins of
Compensated Labor,
1865–1868

IN THE SPRING OF 1865, cotton bound the future of central Georgia, much as it had bound the past. Despite significant industrial development in Macon during the war, military production ended with the Confederate surrender. But the transformation in the master-slave relationship, which military mobilization had helped to initiate, proceeded at a faster pace and toward a more radical conclusion. Clearly, the North's victory necessitated the substitution of free labor relations for those of slavery. But the larger story entailed devising a labor system that would both subsist the population and produce a marketable surplus. In central Georgia, as in most of the black belt, cotton was crucial.

Planters and agricultural workers occupied central places in the unfolding drama. As their struggle played out, a dynamic process of class formation, reformation, and conflict radiated throughout society. Antebellum tensions between yeoman farmers and planters resurfaced in intriguing new ways after the war, as the former gained unprecedented access to the labor of persons of African descent. Moreover, the continuing evolution of the commercial economy made for the development of a class of merchants of diverse roots, whose interests were more properly bourgeois than agrarian.[1] And even among the freedpeople, emancipation set loose a process of class differentiation, whose outlines had been discernible before the Civil War but whose development slavery had stunted. In short, changes in the master-slave relationship necessitated by emancipation transformed both the social structure and the habits of interaction wherein citizens of every description ordered their dealings with each other.

There were a few precursors of these changes but no real precedents. The most obvious example, northern agriculture, was characterized by widespread proprietorship and reliance upon the labor of family members, assisted by machines of an astonishingly wide array. Tenancy and wage labor figured more or less prominently in different sections at different times, largely as the lower rungs of an "agricultural ladder" whose uppermost rung was proprietorship.[2] In time, cotton growers would come to rely upon both tenants and seasonal laborers, though not upwardly mobile ones.

If northern agriculture offered few concrete precedents for the South's transition from slavery to free labor, the experience of other societies that had previously undergone the process of emancipation offered even fewer. The Haitian precedent was no precedent at all, for the government in Washington would never have countenanced the annihilation of the white planter class, seizure of the estates, and reversion to subsistence agriculture. The experience of the British West Indies, while less terrifying, was no less sobering. Apprenticeship was a failure, agricultural production had fallen drastically as the emancipated slaves evolved into a subsistence-oriented peasantry, and indentured labor not only depended upon access to subject populations (ideally, "coolies" from various parts of Asia) but also led to complicated new racial politics among persons of European, African, and Asian ancestry. Jamaica's Morant Bay Rebellion of 1865 extinguished most surviving notions among northern or southern whites that they might have anything to learn from the British West Indian experience.[3]

As a result, the reunited nation made its own way through the revolutionary social process of emancipation, confident that slavery was dead but less certain of the exact contours of the new social order. The ambiguity derived from the fact that free labor was neither an absolute nor a uniform condition. Rather, it represented a social relationship between persons with productive property (especially land) and persons who possessed little or nothing more than an ability to work. This relationship presupposed that the laborers were free of all claims by a master and that their labor was their only means of support. The evolution of this relationship would be monitored by emissaries of the victorious North, who would impose their visions of a properly functioning free-labor system upon the vanquished. But these guardians were far from unanimous regarding what the process entailed; moreover, the stewardship did not last long, nor did it extend to every nook and cranny of central Georgia, much less the South.[4]

By virtue of the war's outcome, former masters and former slaves had to learn to resolve their different interests through market mechanisms—the residual of battered antebellum and wartime practices laced with new ones imported from the North. Under the scrutiny of federal officials, planters would negotiate terms of employment with laborers. Other social classes might also enter the action, with yeomen, for instance, gaining access to potential laborers on a scale unthinkable under slavery. Accordingly, every resident of central Georgia had a sizable stake in the new labor system. Although planters and freedpeople occupied center stage of the contest, no one qualified as a mere spectator.

In these circumstances, capitalist social relations—the defining feature of which was the separation of the labor force from the means of production—developed to a remarkable degree over the first postwar generation. The process was far from complete even in 1880; moreover, it moved in fits and starts, sideways and even backward, rather than in steady linear progression. Yet its essential features are unmistakable: after the war, the planters evolved by several routes into an agrarian bourgeoisie and the freedpeople into a rural proletariat. Antebellum yeomen who lost their land as a result of the war often became tenants, in many respects no different from their black neighbors. Some, however, became improving tenants who rented large parcels of land, hired black laborers, and clawed their way up the social ladder.

In the cities, similar developments occurred, with white men tending toward the more privileged positions in business and finance, and black men toward less skilled, lower paying, and dirty or disagreeable occupations. Although selected freedmen made steady inroads into the artisanal trades and women as well as men opened small businesses, the continuing commercialization of the upcountry undercut many of these gains. In all of these developments, the key transformations occurred during the immediate postwar period.[5]

HOWEVER MUCH they curtailed the public expression of their feelings, freedpeople in central Georgia, like their fellows throughout the South, viewed emancipation as the dawn of a new era and formulated their expectations accordingly.[6] These centered around the establishment of certain rights embracing individuals, family members, and, ultimately, all who had been delivered from slavery. Underlying all these aspirations was the premise of equality among former slaves and former masters. Whatever its limitations, this egalitarianism directly contradicted the ideological foundation of antebellum society. It had profound implications for the new labor system.

True to the ideals of the republic, individual rights embraced life, liberty, property; in practical terms, these translated into the freedom of personal mobility, the integrity of the individual and the family, and compensation for services rendered. Apparently simple actions often affirmed fundamental rights.

Take the reuniting of families, for instance. Piecing together broken families entailed countless labors of love, but the consequences extended far beyond mere emotion. Reconstituted nuclear (or extended) families provided a new model for living arrangements, social relations, and the organization of production. Ideally at least, men would labor in the fields, women would tend to domestic duties, and children would perform light chores and attend school.

Both the conceptualization and the actualization of this familial ideal grew out of the larger struggle over the meaning of emancipation and the shape of the new labor system. When black parents claimed the rights of parenthood, for instance, they did so both to limit the prerogatives of the former masters and to affirm their own rights to raise their children and to dispose of the children's labor as they chose. One freedwoman politely but firmly informed her former master that "he warn't gwine brush none of her chilluns no more."[7]

Much of the freedpeople's concern over the etiquette of freedom—the new ground rules that would govern the behavior of equals—grew out of their insistence upon security of persons against arbitrary physical violence. This issue assumed such overriding importance because of the place of whipping in the old labor system.[8] As northern traveler Sidney Andrews remarked of the Georgia upcountry shortly after the war, "[T]he whole struggle between the whites on the one hand and the blacks on the other hand is a struggle for and against compulsion."[9]

With so much at stake, it is little wonder that the contest continued for years. In Houston County, freedmen made the point emphatically. Thomas W. Brock, town marshal of Fort Valley, complained that "several negroes" armed with Enfield rifles had "ben making threats that they don't intend that any negroe shall be Tyed up by the thumbs."[10] In Monroe County, freedman Aaron English refused to let his former master tie him up, insisting "before I cross my hands I want to know what it is for. I will die first right here before I will allow myself to be tied unless I know what it is for." English paid his life to establish the principle that such treatment was "a relic of slavery" that no self-respecting freedperson would tolerate.[11] Freedman Silas Woodfolk suffered a blow to the head with a rail for having declared that "whipping has gone up."[12]

Such heroic stances convinced employers that physical force would not serve as the primary form of motivation. But nonetheless, the violent passions unleashed during the war continued to roam at large after the surrender. Frustration among Confederate partisans accounted for much of it, as did a pervasive unwillingness among white citizens to recognize the freedom of the former slaves. Although much of the violence was random, most incidents originated in the uneasy adjustment to the new system of labor. Historians have properly cited the birth of the Ku Klux Klan as a turning point in this regard. Yet disguised night riders accounted for only a fraction of incidents that freedpeople reported to federal authorities. Their testimony suggests that murder and mayhem were the background noise accompanying the evolution of compensated labor.[13]

Many planters commenced the era of freedom clinging desperately to the cherished notions and habits of the past, trying to preserve paternalist ideology in a world without slaves. Believing themselves inherently superior to persons of African descent, they acquiesced to slave emancipation reluctantly at best. "In my judgment," wrote Howell Cobb shortly after the return of peace, "[t]he institution of slavery . . . provided the best system of labor that could be devised for the negro race."[14] "Under our beneficent despotism," observed Absalom H. Chappell, a prominent planter-attorney in Macon of antebellum Whiggish pedigree, the Negro "was reclaimed from the grossest barbarism and superstition and trained up to a degree of civilization and religious culture from which it is yet uncertain whether the gift of freedom will carry him up higher or drag him down lower."[15]

While the jury remained out, such paternalists hoped to retain their influence, notwithstanding the defeat of the Confederacy. "We understand the character of that class of people, their capacities, their instincts, and the motives which control their conduct," declared Herschel V. Johnson, the Democratic planter-politician who had been Stephen A. Douglas's running mate in 1860. Accordingly, he hoped that federal officials would "simply let us alone."[16]

While paternalists lamented their loss of personal influence over the labor force, a small but increasingly influential group of agricultural and commercial interests began devising ways to make the most of the end of slavery. The *Macon Telegraph* served as an important mouthpiece of this group, whose members numbered former Whigs as well as Democrats. Its concession late in May "that remuneration for labor will hereafter be necessary" marked a new direction, dedicated to neither nostalgia for the dead past nor quixotic assaults against the authority of the conquerors. The partisans of this approach tailored antebellum paternalism to fit the new circumstances. "The law which freed the negro, at the same time freed the master," reasoned the editor of the *Southern Cultivator*. "At the same moment, and for both parties, all obligations springing out of the relation of master and slave, except those of kindness, ceased mutually to exist."[17]

Planters of every stripe shared with northern officials a strong desire to keep former slaves engaged in commercial agriculture. The well-being of the South, declared the *Telegraph*'s editors, required the former slaves to perform "self supporting labor." "The great question now before our people is how to appropriate all the African labor of the country" in a way consistent with "the best possible good." Short of that, the South stood to "lapse into primeval forest, like Hayti, Jamaica or any other of the West Indies."[18] Believing implicitly that "the negro will not labor except on compulsion," former slave owners had only to determine what form the compulsion would take.[19] Federal officials considered contract labor—with employers promising compensation, food, and shelter, and employees pledging faithful labor through the harvest—as the method of choice. New South planters were willing to give it a try. Unreconstructed planters were more skeptical. A freedman from Twiggs County, for instance, reported that planters had vowed to "whip the dam negro when ever we meet him unless he has a ticket from his Master."[20]

Like the former masters and northern newcomers, freedpeople conceived of the new labor system largely in relationship to the old. Despite their general indictment of slavery, they saw no logical contradiction in preserving what suited their postwar needs, such as the planters' provision of shelter and medical attention. After all, their primary concern was access to the means of subsistence. To some extent this reflected a priority common in agrarian societies throughout the world, especially those undergoing rapid social change.[21] It also testified to the recurring subsistence crises slaves had endured at various times, especially in the closing phase of the war.

In addition to such guarantees regarding necessities of life, former slaves expected drastic departures from the objectionable ways of the old order, particularly those affecting work. They resented close supervision and sought greater control over their own labor. Testimony from J. D. Collins, one of Howell Cobb's overseers, vividly illustrates the tension between traditional patterns and new expectations. "[Y]our propersition to hier them has no effect on them at tall," he informed Cobb's son. "Some of them go out to work verry well   others stay at thier houses untell & hour by sun   others go to their houses an stay two & three days   Say enny thing to them the reply is I am sick but tha air drying fruit all the time   tha take all day evry Saturday without my lief." After visiting his plantation in southwest Georgia, the elder Cobb wrote his wife in the same vein, reporting that "nothing satisfies them. Grant them one thing, and they demand something more; and there is no telling where they would stop." Cobb vowed to cease planting altogether, declaring himself "thoroughly disgusted with free negro labor. . . . There is no feeling of gratitude in their nature." In one of the more memorable characterizations to emerge from this memorable period,

Collins expressed the combination of exasperation and contempt among those accustomed to commanding black laborers: "[Y]ou had as well Sing Sams to a ded horse as to tri to instruct a fool negrow."[22]

Freedpeople had no doubts about the ultimate link between access to subsistence goods and access to productive resources, especially land. The imperfect development of markets in labor power—due partly to cash and credit shortages and partly to the legacy of the past—made it unwise to work for the mere promise of future payment.[23] Moreover, the imperfect development of markets in necessities, and irregular supplies of such goods even when markets existed, encouraged self-sufficiency. Land provided the key. The desire for land has accompanied the emancipation of bound rural laborers—whether slaves or serfs—throughout the modern era. In much of western Europe and the United States, that hunger was supplemented by the belief that civic virtue rested upon economic independence, ideally demonstrated by property ownership. The freedpeople's desire for land never blinded them to the specific attributes of individual parcels. Nonetheless, access to land—preferably with titled ownership—offered subsistence, family security, control over both labor and its fruits, and economic and political independence.[24]

The debate over land came late to central Georgia and similar areas of the Confederate heartland. Yet developments along the Georgia coast, where Gen. William T. Sherman had staked out an area for the exclusive use of former slaves, influenced events in the upcountry. The promise of forty acres and a mule contained in the Freedmen's Bureau bill deepened the expectation of redistribution.[25] A Macon freedman reportedly offered to buy land from an employer who had told him to work or leave. Another freedman proposed to sell back to a white man his anticipated share of the latter's estate. But this longing did not reflect a sense of absolute property rights whereby an individual might exploit the land and dispose of it at will. Instead, it reflected a communal tradition that viewed the land as the birthright of those who worked it and as a medium for reinforcing social ties within families and communities.[26]

With a clear view of the stakes involved, planters throughout the plantation belt beseeched federal authorities to suppress the "clamoring for land." In the summer of 1865, a group from Houston County requested assistance to disabuse freedpeople of a "delusion," namely, the belief that they held "title to the real estate and stock of their former masters." Echoing fears voiced throughout the South, planters raised the specter of "indiscriminate slaughter" among an "unarmed population." Striking another major chord, they protested the removal of federal troops who might positively influence the freedpeople, even as they excluded from this category black soldiers who would only "influence the spirit of discord already of alarming proportions."[27]

In the fall of 1865, President Andrew Johnson's decision to restore confiscated and abandoned land to its original owners virtually destroyed the prospect of a general allocation among freedmen. It also signaled the growing federal commitment to economic reconstruction based upon compensated labor instead of proprietorship. Yet the dream of landownership did not die so easily. During Radical Reconstruction, freedpeople pressed for land whenever political circumstances offered hope.[28] Possessing land continued to provide a powerful standard of independent subsistence and associated civic virtue.

CLOSING OFF the prospect of land distribution hastened the development of a system of compensated labor to govern the production of cotton and underlay the new social order. Federal military officials—first those under Gen. James H. Wilson, who had occupied Macon late in April 1865, then those associated with the Freedmen's Bureau—assumed the responsibility of oversight. Wilson's troopers enforced the public peace and, prior to President Johnson's appointment of a new government in June, also administered civil affairs. But even after Provisional Governor James Johnson took office, military courts could both initiate proceedings and overrule the judgments of civilian courts.

General Wilson favorably impressed Macon's aristocrats, but the feeling was not always mutual. He suspected the planters' intentions, describing some as anxious to reestablish slavery in modified form "similar to peonage." Criticizing the "dehumanizing and vicious tendencies of the present comunal system of labor," Wilson advocated a system of tenancy wherein each freedman would be granted "a life lease upon as much land as he and his family could cultivate . . . paying a fair rate of rent either in money or in kind to the proprietor." "[T]he protection of the law and the privilege of free schools" would guarantee "the development of independence, respectability, and healthy morals."[29]

At the practical, as opposed to the theoretical, level, Wilson's policies were much more modest. He insisted that freedpeople work, preferably for their former masters, and that employers pay them "either in money or the products of the soil." General orders he promulgated in July designated former masters as "guardians" of dependent former slaves and prohibited the expulsion of those unable to labor. He also forbade brutality and outlawed the dismissal of freedpeople without compensation for work they had already performed. He left it to "the employer and servant" to agree upon the wage rate, counseling the latter "to expect only moderate wages" and, in the event the employer could not pay cash, "to be contented with a fair share in the crops to be raised."[30]

Lest the freedpeople conclude that Wilson's program invited idleness, military provost marshals began combating vagrancy with compulsory labor, the time-honored means of promoting habits of industry among juridically free workers.[31] The provost marshal offered positive and negative inducements: on the one hand, he opened an "intelligence office" to serve as a clearinghouse for employers seeking laborers; on the other hand, he rounded up able-bodied vagrants and put them to work repairing railroads and cleaning up Macon. Those who resisted were arrested for petty crimes, fined beyond their means, and then bound out to employers willing to pay the fines.[32]

The provost guard especially targeted the estimated 1,000 freedpeople residing in the shantytowns that had sprung up around the city over the previous decade. These included former slaves from Tennessee and Mississippi whose masters had refugeed them to central Georgia during the war. Some were persons who had left the countryside at their former masters' admonition to "go to the Yankees and let them support you." Many were women with small children whose husbands worked on the railroads or on outlying plantations where accommodation was denied to nonworkers. Some simply desired to be "whar I can go an' cum, an nobody says not'ing," as one told a northern reporter. Relying on aid from Macon's black community, growing what food they could on land adjacent to the shacks, and working odd jobs, they had managed to survive. However precarious their existence, squatters preferred it to either the shackles of slavery or the strictures of contract labor. In this regard, they exhibited the same desire to control their lives that freedpeople throughout the Americas did in the aftermath of emancipation.[33]

Planters and civil authorities joined the provost marshal's assault against this floating population.[34] As freedpeople drifted in and out of the camps, former masters—begging, cajoling, threatening, and ranting about the absence of gratitude—followed hard on their heels, trying to lure them back to the countryside. In mid-June, the city council supplemented that action with a vagrancy act that empowered the mayor to take up "all idle, mischievous and disorderly negroes" and impose "ball and chain, bread and water, work on the streets, public works, [or] confinement in the guardhouse and stocks." Other restrictions followed.[35]

Freedmen's Bureau officials, who began arriving on the scene simultaneously with the campaign against vagrants, preferred the intelligence-office approach to finding employment for "surplus freedmen." They even persuaded an African American carriagemaker and minister named William D. Banks to open such an office in hopes of dispelling freedpeople's misgivings. But neither the bureau nor the planter-commercial elite endorsed the proposal by a group of freedmen to purchase a lot and build an asylum for destitute former slaves. Antebellum policies regarding relief would continue to apply to white citizens, but freedpeople would have to perform honest labor whatever their constitution or circumstances.[36] As a result of all these efforts, the black population declined from a high of about 5,000 in late summer to roughly 4,300 by early 1866, still nearly a 60 percent increase from 1860.[37]

However draconian, these efforts speeded the development of a market in labor power in Macon proper and in the nearby countryside, as did the purposeful movement of freedpeople in search of better wages and amenities. The structure of urban life assisted in this transformation. Both before and during the war, businessmen and landlords had made arrangements with slaves mediated by cash, but what had been peripheral to slavery became central to the system of free labor. Employers could hire and fire as need (or whim) dictated; although laborers could seek the most advantageous situations, in most circumstances they would have to provide for their own subsistence.

The negotiation of these relationships, whether entered into voluntarily or through official persuasion, reinforced the economic fabric patterned after the capitalist North. Those who wished to exchange commodities through the medium of cash developed awareness of their interests and acted accordingly. In fact, freedpeople with entrepreneurial talent or ambition could exercise that option. Persons who had acquired skills of one kind or another before the war, such as carriagemaker William D. Banks, watchmaker Moses Pollock, and tailor Jefferson F. Long, opened establishments of their own. Men with the requisite skill and capital might open blacksmith shops, groceries, or butcher stalls or hire their services independently as carpenters, bricklayers, and draymen. Women might operate boardinghouses and laundry services or hawk "chicken pies and goober peas" on street corners or at the public market. Although none grew rich, many prospered. As a result, Macon's black community diversified, with distinctions that had originated in slavery growing larger.[38]

But whereas such "open market" qualities developed relatively quickly in the city, they evolved more slowly in "Country Districts." There, according to a bureau officer in Macon, planters were able to take "advantage of the ignorance of Men, who have not yet learned the value of their own labor."[39] Matters could scarcely have been otherwise during the first six months after the war, when the circumstances of Confederate defeat most aggravated the general unfamiliarity with Yankee ways. Vanquished on the battlefield, planters sought to reassert

Ells & Laney Grocery, Macon
(Courtesy of Georgia Department of Archives and History)

control over the land and the labor force, in some cases by rushing a crop of cotton into the ground as the war came to a close. Former slaves, allies of the victors, sought subsistence and more to accompany freedom. While awaiting federal action on their behalf, they continued to provision themselves as they had during the war, either on their own or by agreement with a landowner. The terms took as many idiosyncratic forms as minds grappling with unprecedented social chaos could devise, but their basic feature carried over directly from slavery: the exchange of shelter and food—with access to supplemental means of subsistence—for labor. In fact, when bureau agents arrived in central Georgia, these arrangements were already several months old. For the most part, they remained in force for the rest of the year.[40]

THE MAKESHIFT arrangements of freedom's first summer pleased no one, least of all federal officials. Freedmen's Bureau inspectors reported at the end of 1865 that most freedpeople in the region had worked for minuscule wages or mere rations. Those who worked for shares averaged only a one-tenth share of a meager harvest. In addition, much violence attended the settlement, as planters defrauded laborers of earnings in full knowledge that the civil courts would take their side.[41] Even when judgments were rendered against them, however, planters procrastinated settlement. Even with the most strenuous exertions on the part of bureau officials, many freedpeople got nothing for their labor.[42]

To prevent repetition of these problems in the future, the new assistant commissioner of the Freedmen's Bureau for Georgia issued strict guidelines governing plantation employment. Gen. Davis Tillson, a Maine-born artillery officer with prior experience among the freedpeople of Tennessee, aimed to guarantee compensation to former slaves and a reliable and industrious labor supply to planters. Speaking before the state constitutional convention late in 1865, Tillson described his role as "not the champion of the negro but the disinterested umpire between him and the white race," whose role was "to reconcile conflicting interests, and to adjust properly the great question of free and coloured labor." He implicitly assumed that "labor like any other commodity" would "sell itself, in the open market to the highest bidder." In a long letter to a black-belt planter, Tillson reiterated his determination to construct a labor system upon the principles of capitalist social relations. "Labor, like all other articles for sale, has a market value. Cheap laborers will certainly be found unprofitable laborers. Let me urge you not to make your own failure certain in the attempt to manage free laborers, by giving inadequate wages." "The material salvation of the white people of this State as well as the black," Tillson concluded, "depends upon the success of the free labor system."[43]

Notwithstanding such laissez-faire economic assumptions, Tillson soon recognized the need for prescribed wages to compensate for the faulty operation of the nascent market mechanism. Hence, for 1866 he required compensation of $12 to $13 per month for first-class men in upper and middle Georgia ($8 to $10 for women), and $15 for men ($10 for women) in southwest and coastal Georgia. Planters bristled at these rates but purred when Tillson appointed civilian agents and demanded that freedpeople "make contracts and work industriously for the old planters." Employers expressed "great confidence" in the bureau as the "means whereby the industry of the country was to be promoted."[44] And well they should have, given the number of ex-Whig planters among the appointees. Taking their cue from Tillson, bureau agents did little to dispel that confidence.[45]

The agents soon discovered that general orders alone could not call the new labor system to life. Capt. Louis Lambert, the subassistant commissioner sta-

tioned at Macon, criticized the planters' "strong disposition . . . to Contract with
the Freedmen for unsufficient remuneration." Claiming that "the land cannot
stand" Tillson's proposed $12 minimum, they offered $8 to $10 per month
instead. A few planters had even "endeavored to make Contracts for Food and
Clothing only." Lambert showed like impatience with freedpeople who, in the
words of one planter, held "high notions of freedom" and demonstrated "a
stubborn unwillingness" to contract: he considered such persons "entruders,"
who "must at once obtain employment or be considered Vagrants and treated
accordingly." "[T]he Negro," he insisted, "must have a visable and proper
means of livelyhood."[46]

As a result, freedmen on plantations as well as in the cities and towns learned
how to bargain over terms of employment and to play prospective employers off
against each other. "Impossible to get hands here for part of the crop," a
frustrated Howell Cobb, Jr., informed his father early in 1866. "All *demand*
'*wages*' and generally are high in their self-esteem. None listen to less than
($150.00) one hundred and fifty dollars a year, in money, and their '*board &
clothes*,' that is food & clothes, and $12.00 twelve dollars per month." Freedmen
on plantations lying close to the city enforced a similar scale, but those farther
away enjoyed much less success. A freedman from Macon reportedly caused
great consternation in Monroe County by advising freedpeople that refusing to
contract would drive up wages.[47]

As such sophistication spread, clearer outlines of a system of compensated
labor began to emerge in the plantation districts. Freedpeople who prized their
independence had grave misgivings about a labor system resting solely upon cash
wages. They specifically resented the equation of the wage laborer with a
hireling—a virtual automaton, devoid of volition and unquestioningly obedient
to the employer. They sought variations from strict cash wages to embody their
aspirations. One alternative was share wages, wherein workers contracted collectively for a predetermined share of what they produced and then divided the
proceeds among themselves.[48] During 1866, most plantation hands in Monroe
County apparently worked in this way for one-third of the crop. Yet elsewhere,
either planters or freedpeople or both preferred wages.[49] And on individual
plantations, some workers might work for wages, while others worked for shares,
and still others worked for a combination of the two.[50]

From the landowners' standpoint, the share system had a number of virtues.
For one, it resolved the knotty problem of care for dependent freedpeople by
making them the collective responsibility of all who worked.[51] More important, it
enticed the freedpeople to invest more than their labor power in the production

Hoeing cotton, Jones County
(Courtesy of Georgia Department of Archives and History)

process—generally by feeding themselves or assuming part of the cost of feeding work animals—in exchange for a larger share.[52] Lacking credit, share-renters generally petitioned Freedmen's Bureau authorities for advances. Not every official (much less every landowner) appreciated the sturdy independence they demonstrated. A bureau agent recommended that one such group seek employment with "responsible parties," thereby assuring their support and avoiding prosecution as vagrants for persisting "in their unreasonable and foolish intentions."[53]

As recent studies have established, the shortage of credit—more so than of cash—best explains the origins of crop-sharing arrangements.[54] Even employers who contracted for wages rarely paid more than half in cash each month. As merchants spread throughout the countryside and planters began opening plantation stores, a system of credit governed the compensation of even those laborers nominally working for wages.[55] Under both share and cash systems, the settlement of accounts at the end of the year was intended to induce laborers to stay through the harvest, the period of peak labor demand.

The freedpeople who rejected the emphasis upon cash wages in favor of shares presumed continuing access to the subsistence resources of nature. Plantation laborers thus supplemented their diets of cornmeal and fatback pork with various plants, fruits, nuts, and game from the wild, much as they had done as slaves. But the mere survival of such subsistence activity from the era of slavery to that of freedom does not suggest that little change resulted from the Civil War. On the contrary. Aside from the handful of freedpeople who found it possible to feed themselves entirely in this way and thus escape plantation employment altogether, self-subsistence provided leverage to freedpeople that slaves never enjoyed. Specifically, it enabled them to take days off (either when they wished to hunt or fish or when their larders appeared sufficiently full) and, in time, to opt for seasonal employment on the plantations. No slave, no matter how accomplished a hunter or a gardener, could exercise such options.[56]

The Whiggish planters who most rapidly adjusted to emancipation well understood the importance of state power in achieving social ends and maneuvered along those lines to guarantee their interests. Under the protective umbrella of the provisional government created by President Johnson, they attempted to legislate freedpeople into a peculiar state of dependency, which preserved some of the personal features of domination that had been the hallmark of slavery even while extending limited citizenship rights. The black code of 1866 embodied the essence of this Whiggish-planter strategy.[57]

Supplementary legislation focused pointedly upon freedpeople as laborers. In a measure that promised to facilitate collection of revenue while attaching workers to their employers, lawmakers obliged the latter to pay their employees' poll taxes and to charge the deduction against wages due. The new legislation prescribed stiff punishments for laborers who broke their contracts and made enticement of employed hands a misdemeanor. Although the latter provision aimed primarily to prevent railroad contractors and Mississippi Valley planters from siphoning off Georgia's work force, it also suggests competition for laborers among planters and between large and small landowners—a phenomenon unknown under slavery.[58]

Freedpeople made the best of this competition. It was never an easy task, however, for employers sensed the potential danger of divisions within their ranks. Still, labor requirements differed, often substantially, from one employer to another. Whereas planters with large landholdings required numerous employees, small farmers might need only one or two or, at most, a family of black workers. The interests of planters and farmers in the labor of the freedpeople did not diverge absolutely, of course. But landowners who during the 1850s had been priced out of the slave market often proved willing to negotiate terms of employment that antebellum planters considered objectionable. Farmers did not necessarily care, for instance, where their employees resided or what they did during nonworking hours, provided they worked industriously.

To limit workers' options, the Whiggish planter-legislators began chipping away at traditional rights to subsistence from the public domain. They broadened the definition of criminal trespass to include cutting wood without permission and squatting, whether the land be unenclosed or enclosed, public or private. The act in question provided a ten-day grace period and exempted wayfarers but nonetheless portended ominous changes in deeply held common rights to unenclosed land. Lawmakers also curtailed customary land and water rights crucial to African Americans' subsistence both before and after the war, beginning with restrictions on seining fish in particular waterways during stipulated seasons. A hunting act banning Sunday hunting in sixty-two counties—all but one in the black belt and including Houston, Jones, and Twiggs in central Georgia—neatly complemented the mandatory six-day work week required of farm laborers. Subsequent legislatures passed laws that restricted hunting seasons in precisely the same way the early fishing laws did.[59]

Each of the new acts marked dramatic changes from antebellum practices, underscoring the Whiggish planters' significant role in fostering more narrowly defined—more properly bourgeois—notions of private property and the public's access thereto, though the lawmakers no doubt saw themselves merely as attempting to deny propertyless vagrants the means to avoid honest labor. The legislative program represented a compromise strategy that appealed to both old- and new-style planters. The former, still imbued with a lingering sense of paternalism, wished to keep the freedpeople dependent upon them for all of life's necessities. The latter, devoid of maudlin sentimentality, wished simply to make the labor force as vulnerable to control and exploitation as possible. Freedpeople would have to understand that, in the idiom of the times, they would have to "work or starve."[60] As the planters either drifted or steamed toward such Yankee notions of political economy, they scarcely anticipated the ultimate consequences. Among other things, they could not have predicted the political explosion that followed white smallholders' being drawn into the vortex of change.[61]

Although Georgians (like other southerners) continued to hunt and gather wood on unimproved private property, the presence on the books of laws enjoining such behavior enabled both employers and civil authorities to clamp down on independent-minded citizens whether white or black.[62] The strategy of keeping dependent members of society in their place, of course, had antebellum precedents, but federal authorities abolished whips and patrols along with slavery. To be sure, planters did not always resort to the nicety of law to curb behavior they deemed objectionable, but their willingness—indeed, their perceived need—to do so suggests how drastically emancipation transformed the planters' world and, in fact, their essential nature as a class.

THE FREEDPEOPLE'S insistence upon hunting and fishing rights suggests that they also adapted other antebellum practices to the needs of the new order. In addition to receiving a one-fourth share of the cotton crop, for instance, the forty freedpeople employed by one Bibb County planter raised and sold to him fodder for his stock, an arrangement that hints strongly of origins during slavery.[63] Other former slaves similarly pressured employers for such perquisites, not always successfully. Like their prewar equivalents, such arrangements could both reinforce the personal nature of the relationship between employers and employees and make possible the laborers' independent involvement in impersonal markets.

But in fundamental contrast with the old ways, when an employer refused to come to terms over such perquisites, the employees had the right to seek one who did. "Let any man offer them some little thing of no real benefit to them, but which looks like a little more freedom," Howell Cobb fumed to his wife, "and they catch at it with avidity."[64] Some of the little things that so exercised Cobb were far from trifling. A freedwoman named Biney, for example, convinced a Crawford County landowner to grant her access to a one-acre cotton patch. And freedman Aaron Bowman contracted for a five-acre corn patch and a garden plot for his wife in Twiggs County. An up-and-coming planter from Houston County allowed his twenty employees garden patches and the privilege of electing their own foremen.[65]

The terms of employment to which freedpeople agreed sometimes involved subjective judgments about the character of particular employers independent of wage rates. Northwest of Macon, a bureau agent reluctantly approved contracts for 1866 that did not offer "fair compensation" because the freedpeople preferred "to live with those with whom they had contracted at the wages offered than to receive higher wages at other places."[66] Once having won concessions, freedpeople considered them standards to which they would hold other planters. Antebellum agricultural societies worked in the opposite direction, building solidarity among planters. Those who snubbed their neighbors and accommodated the freedpeople faced indictment for violating the enticement act.[67]

Besides the mode and amount of compensation and access to subsistence goods, planters and laborers disputed who would be obligated to work. Landowners insisted that every man, woman, and child who had labored as a slave continue to do so as a freedperson. Former slaves wanted to keep all but able-bodied men out of the field. Battle lines were drawn.

Former masters felt that their vested right to shape black family life had not ceased with the mere formality of emancipation, as the history of apprenticeship illustrates. Planters acted like well-heeled bourgeois in their disdain for supporting persons incapable of labor, but they professed deep paternal concern for healthy "orphans" of working age. In most circumstances, former slaves cared for orphan children within networks of extended families or the old slave quarters, as they had done for generations of children separated from parents by sale or death.[68] But former owners now saw a chance to prolong the dependence of young workers. For the right to appropriate the labor of youths without compensation, they gladly agreed to supply food, clothing, and shelter. In line with Tillson's orders and as proof of their good will, the new masters even tossed the rudiments of an education into the bargain.[69]

An 1866 apprenticeship law granted masters the compulsory labor services of indentured orphans until they reached their majority (for boys, age twenty-one; for girls, eighteen) that they might learn the "business of husbandry, house service, or some other useful trade or occupation." It also authorized parents to bind their children; in the event that the parents were absent from the county or "[f]rom age, infirmity or poverty . . . unable to support them," the law empowered county officials to place the children. The law provided certain safeguards for the child but also gave great authority to the master. Most important, it invalidated all other claims to the apprentice's labor during the term of indenture.[70]

Apprenticeship invited corruption. At times, planters paraded all the "orphans" and "abandoned children" on their plantations before county officials for indenture. They routinely falsified ages to increase the years of service. And, even if the truth were told, young men and women in their teens were often capable of supporting themselves. According to Edwin Belcher, a bureau agent in Monroe County, planters there took to driving off the father, then swearing that he was "out of the County and the Mother unable to support the Child," and producing "witnesses to Corroborate their statement." Others persuaded one parent or the other to consent to the proceedings. One man even used apprenticeship to gain control of his illegitimate mulatto children. With all these tricks at their disposal, during the early postwar years former masters apprenticed large numbers—in Monroe County, reportedly one-third of the black children in the county.[71]

Most freedpeople viewed the practice as a "new slavery." Belcher commented that the only distinction between the old and the new was that "formerly it was perpetual servitude now it is for a term of years." Deeming it "as cruel in all its aspects as the Institution destroyed by the Mighty arm of the Loyal people of the United States," he recommended that the bureau ban apprenticeship. Freedman Jack Gill wrote in a similar vein: "I think very hard of the former oners for Trying to keep My blood when I Kno that Slavery is Dead." Seeking custody of his granddaughter, Gill indicted the system that so favored the interests of "the Rebels" who "Did evry thing they could to Demolish this Govenment and to make the negro a Purpetual slave."[72]

Civil officials administered the apprenticeship law, but Freedmen's Bureau officers scrutinized apprentice cases with authority to nullify those that violated the freedpeople's rights. Tillson's decision to appoint civilian agents compromised the bureau's impartiality. On occasion, these men even apprenticed children to themselves. Jesse D. Havis, an agent from Houston County who had been a prominent Whig planter before the war, bound a freed girl to himself in April 1866. Although he had followed proper procedures, freedpeople placed little confidence in his judgment in apprenticeship cases. Instead, they hiked the twenty miles or so to Macon, carrying their grievances before subassistant commissioner N. Sellers Hill, a Union army captain.[73]

The racially neutral wording of the apprenticeship law enabled some freedpeople to protect vulnerable young relatives.[74] Henry Johnson successfully petitioned for custody of his two grandchildren so that he might "care for [them] as his natural offsprings." Another freedman sought custody of his wife's twelve-year-old brother "to get him out of bad company and to train him up honest."[75] The federal Civil Rights Act of 1866, which opened southern courts to the testimony of black persons, effectively denied bureau officers the power to intervene unilaterally, though they could still enter civil suits as "next best friends" of freedpeople seeking custody. Practically speaking, the new law meant that the same civil authorities who had winked at or conspired in the original indenture now adjudicated the claims of parents and other kin.

With the law so pliable, virtually every master ignored the mandate to teach apprentices to read. Some masters also flouted the law's prohibition against excessive physical punishment. Ransel Daniel of Houston County insisted upon beating a black girl whom he had apprenticed, eventually prompting her to run home. Daniel followed her, became embroiled in an argument with her father, and then shot the man dead. Perceiving masters and courts arraigned against them, freedmen resorted to such expedients as seizing their children and running away. Thereupon they were charged with violating the enticement act![76]

Despite its popularity during the early postwar years, apprenticeship proved unequal to the planters' needs under the new system of free labor. For one thing, orphans constituted a negligible proportion of the work force. Even had they succeeded in binding every child within a county, planters would have failed to secure sufficient working hands. And if they had first to drive away the fathers, then the short-range objective would subvert the long-range one. In short, apprenticeship served limited utility as a means whereby individual smallholders and elderly planters might gain the services of a young worker or two. But for planters, it fell far short of framing a labor system to take the place of slavery.[77]

The freedpeople's objection to apprenticeship fit into their larger desire to control the allocation of labor within their households. Children's labor illustrates the case. Planters tried first to command the labor of children. Parents refused, insisting instead that the children attend school or perform chores around the home. Planters then cut off rations to children who did not work, a tactic that bureau officials did not favor even though they did permit employers to charge parents $1 per month for each child under twelve.[78]

In a much more significant bid for control over who would work, black women undertook a virtual exodus from field labor beginning in 1866. Many refused to enter contracts at the beginning of the year, and those who did soon regretted having done so. Bureau agent Jesse Havis in Houston County described them as "dead heads" who had not worked enough to support themselves. They were "lazy . . . exceedingly sensitive and ungovernable," and their insubordination, he claimed, accounted for nine-tenths of the cases brought before him. Employers tried in vain to make the women work diligently; they "universally concur in the resolution," Havis reported, "not to imploy the women next year at all, but only men." Freedwomen throughout the South similarly emancipated themselves from the field at this time.[79]

On a superficial level, the women's protest suggests a determination to imitate white women, who customarily did not labor in the fields. But even if they remained entirely out of the cotton crop, freedwomen still performed the time-consuming and tedious chores of farm households: raising children, cooking, doing laundry, and tending gardens and assorted barnyard animals. Rather than signaling women's withdrawal from labor altogether, the protest reflected the desire that the women's labor serve the needs of the household instead of those of the plantation. This principle was an important precondition to family-based tenancy, even though a by-product in many cases was a new domestic patriarch, insisting upon controlling the labor of his wife and children.[80]

In combination with urban and westward migration—much of the latter being bureau-sponsored—the withdrawal of women and children from the fields dramatically reduced the number of laborers, thereby increasing the bargaining power of those who made contracts. Between 1867 and 1872, the number of field workers fell from 4,201 to 2,846 in Houston County and from 3,458 to 1,240 in Monroe, to cite but the most precipitous declines.[81] In time, poverty forced many women back into the fields, but the success of the original withdrawal opened new options. For one, women could choose to work temporarily, during the harvest, for instance. Better yet, they could gain access to plots of land as lessees rather than as hired laborers.[82] As such independent producers, freedwomen worked under their own supervision and within the framework of the household economy, not at the bidding of an employer.

Such arrangements provided black women a measure of security. Single women and widows who had to work for wages remained prey to sexual advances and other forms of intimidation; married women working within a household economy did not. Freedwoman Mary Flower, for example, reported that her former owner, Jess Flower, took her as his slave concubine and fathered her five children after his wife had died. Since emancipation, he ordered her not to marry yet refused to support her or the children and threatened to kill her if she complained to the Freedmen's Bureau.[83] Another black woman complained that her employer had twice offered her money to live with him and had also propositioned her daughter. When the mother ran away following the second offer, he had her arrested, but bureau authorities successfully intervened. In a world that took little cognizance of white men's sexual abuse of black women, bureau agents provided unprecedented protection. But the surer protection lay in avoiding labor contracts.[84]

Related to the question of who would work were those of who would supervise the labor process and what kind of labor would be performed. Contract terms for 1867 suggest the evolving contours of that struggle, with both freedpeople and planters desiring formal understandings with regard to contested issues. Specifics about supervision continued to loom large. Planters demanded absolute obedience, imposed heavy fines for unauthorized absences, required laborers to tend stock and perform other such chores on Sundays and to maintain fences, ditches, and plantation buildings, and either withheld the pay of laborers who violated regulations or simply dismissed them. As they had done in days of old, planters extended their control over the nonworking lives of their employees,

most of whom continued to live in antebellum quarters (often the same structures they had occupied as slaves) within view of the overseer's dwelling. Employers often restricted visiting rights, forbidding the entertainment of relatives
or "freed Friends" without permission.[85]

As earlier, freedpeople saw access to land as the key to both independent
subsistence and discretion over their own labor. Early in 1867 a planter observed
that they "will almost starve and go naked before they will work for a white man if
they can get a patch of ground to live on and get from under his control."[86] When
the ideal proved elusive and former slaves had to contract for wages or a share of
the crops, they objected to practices that planters either took for granted or
considered their prerogative to dictate unilaterally. Freedpeople strongly opposed working under overseers and, when forced to do so, defied their authority
at every turn. But even when supervised by landowners, former slaves strained
for greater control over their actions in the fields. To counter, employers imposed
tight contractual restrictions backed by monetary fines of $.50 to $1.00 for such
infractions as tardiness, breaking tools, and insubordination. A $10 monthly
wage could not long sustain such deductions.[87]

A contract dispute in Jones County illuminates other aspects of this struggle
between employers and employees. Farmer Jeremiah Miller granted freedman
Harry Barrington the use of "seventy five acres of land or so much thereof as he
and his family can cultivate." Directly addressing matters of ongoing disagreement, Miller specified that Barrington would "be controlled by him in all matters
relating to the labor of himself & his children—to work when he directs where
he directs & upon what he directs." The contract also obligated Barrington "to
do all the plantation work on the entire farm of the said Miller such as black
smiths work making plow stocks gates &c."[88]

Barrington chafed under the restrictions from the start and registered his
objection by leaving the field early on Saturdays. Matters came to a head after he
first refused to plow a certain field as directed and then quit work without
permission to attend Fourth of July festivities in Macon. For good measure, he
instructed his children to take the day off too. Miller complained to the local
Freedmen's Bureau agent, who submitted the case to arbitration (each side
choosing a representative and the agent selecting a third party), a common
method of resolving such disputes. The arbitrators ruled against Barrington,
ordering him to relinquish rights in his crops of corn and cotton and to vacate
Miller's premises.[89]

Barrington's dispute with Miller reveals the contours of the contested terrain.
Freedmen wanted to control their own labor. They wanted a shorter work week

than obtained during slavery; they wanted the discretion to take an occasional day off to observe national holidays, to attend religious and political meetings, or to conduct personal business (with the Freedmen's Bureau, for instance). "[T]hey seem to be under the impression," observed a bureau agent in Houston County, "that there time is there own and they can work when and how they please."[90] And they increasingly resented having to perform such chores as cutting wood for the household use of the landowner and constructing or repairing ditches, fences, and buildings without additional compensation. Ultimately, they sought control over all phases of the cotton economy, from preparing the soil to ginning and marketing the harvested crop.[91]

THE HISTORY of free labor in the South took a dramatic turn in 1867, due not so much to any improvements in the cotton economy as to the beginning of Radical Reconstruction. In March, when the Reconstruction Acts established military rule and granted southern black men the right to vote, the struggle for control over labor intensified.[92] In the eyes of planters, politics would distract freedmen from their work and resurrect the hope of land redistribution, both of which fears proved true.[93] Most important, black suffrage would turn the state apparatus into a battleground: whoever controlled the government would have power to shape the developing free-labor system.[94]

Disgruntled employers attempted to use contractual leverage to neutralize the voting strength of black workers. In contracts dating from the start of spring planting—coincidental with passage of the acts—a new series of provisions prohibited freedmen from having guns. Although such a strategy never assumed the level of state policy as it had in Mississippi during 1865, the new departure clearly aimed to check the threat of armed, paramilitary political clubs that freedmen in the plantation districts were rapidly forming.[95] Employers also increased the fines against unauthorized absences (some to as high as $5 per infraction) and enforced them with special diligence against freedmen absenting themselves to attend political meetings, to register, or to vote.[96]

For their part, freedpeople viewed the Reconstruction Acts second in importance only to the Emancipation Proclamation. They were determined to exercise the right to vote, even at the peril of life and limb. They cherished the suffrage in its own right, but the intensity of the former masters' opposition enhanced its value. The vote benefited freedmen in other, more practical ways as well. Although it proved unequal to the task of effectuating a distribution of land, it gave freedpeople—the southern working class—powerful leverage in the form of an electoral majority in plantation areas such as central Georgia. The full implications of that development remained to be seen. But even before the first freedman cast the first ballot, the weight of congressional favor tipped the scales, however slightly and precariously, in the direction of the former slaves.

By the end of 1867, the freedpeople's desire to manage their own labor and subsistence forced a radical restructuring of plantation agriculture.[97] The reconstructed black family stood at the heart of this transformation. Freedpeople insisted that individual families, rather than aggregated gangs, constitute the fundamental social unit of labor. Family farms would approximate landownership as closely as circumstances would allow. Moreover, they would make apprenticeship, and the mandatory labor of women and children, essentially obsolete.

Although few freedpeople had the animals and tools to rent land independently, the large numbers who reached accord with the landowners on the principle of shares thoroughly transformed the underlying assumptions as well as the physical structure of plantation agriculture. Freedpeople rationalized this system as "co-partnership." The term itself was not new; even before the Civil War, business advertising routinely referred to "co-partnerships."[98] Not so much a form of tenure in its own right as the foundation underlying all tenures, co-partnership implied that the partner performing the labor had just as much a say in farm management as the partner supplying the land. This partnership also implied co-ownership of the growing crops. Gaining even contested recognition of the principle marked a pivotal achievement.

Some planters stoutly criticized co-partnership for such "new-fangled ideas [as] scattering negro houses all over plantations, and working them in small squads." Others found the deeper implications more unsettling. "Negroes left to their judgment, and their own volition must fail," one believed, "for with a very few exceptions they have neither; and where you work 'on shares,' they are beyond cavil co-partners, and they have a right, and in the fullness of their conceit, exercise that right, to have a say so in everything." Conceding defeat on the matter of labor unrelated to the present year's crop, this planter regretted "having no one to cut and haul your family fuel, or go on errands, or haul anything for your family, or repair a gate, or hang a fallen door, or put up a fence blown down that does not enclose their crop, or do anything, except to cultivate the crop."[99] "The all absorbing subject, agitating the Southern mind," insisted a correspondent of the *Southern Cultivator*, was "the highly important question of the management of the labor system in our country."[100] And freedpeople seemed to be getting the upper hand. "The prevalent idea," a planter explained, was "that it was better to take the chances of obtaining a small remuneration, than to allow the land to be idle, with the certainty of no return."[101]

In time cotton planters throughout the state bowed to the inevitability of family-sized farms. Making the best of a situation not entirely to their liking, some found the new arrangements useful in pitting families against each other to increase productivity and to separate the industrious from the lazy.[102] Structural pressures in the larger cotton economy (including declining prices and poor harvests during the early postwar years), coupled with higher fixed costs to compensate for deteriorating soils, induced others to acquiesce. All in all, most planters would have preferred other options had circumstances and the persistent demands of freedpeople for autonomy not necessitated co-partnership.[103]

THE EXPIRATION of the Freedmen's Bureau act at the end of 1868 threatened to reverse many of the freedpeople's advances in the area of plantation labor. Freedmen and bureau officers alike feared for the future. The agent in Houston County, for instance, predicted "that the freed people are going to have pretty hard times." Many planters vowed revenge for injustices they felt they had endured; even those who professed no such spirit gloated in the prospect of acting free from federal oversight. Confident that "the Bureau is played out," they invited Yankee bureau agents to "go to hell." Petitions from former slaves seeking an extension of the "Bureau of our peace" fell upon deaf ears.[104]

Withdrawal of the Freedmen's Bureau marked the end of a crucial period in the development of free labor in the South. Freedpeople became more vulnerable to local landowners and civil officials. Against that background, co-partnership stands out as a structural safeguard for the security of black families and the household economy, which, despite its numerous drawbacks, helped slow the full transformation of former slaves into proletarians. For a time at least, it provided a foundation for the laborers to claim control over their labor and its products. It also reflected and helped advance the parallel struggle to revolutionize the concept of citizenship. In all those respects, the experience of freedpeople in the American South differed markedly from that of their counterparts anywhere else in the hemisphere.

7

· · · · · · · ·

Creating a
New Body Politic,
1865–1867

EMANCIPATION IN THE American South was unique in two important respects. First, the defeat of the Confederacy relegated southern planters to a position of subordination to the dictates of an army and government whose stated objective was freeing the slaves. In addition to an armed occupation force, the national government dispatched agents of the newly created Freedmen's Bureau to oversee the transition from slavery to freedom. And the president appointed provisional governments, whose actions were subject to close scrutiny and ultimate veto by officials of the federal government.

Among the other slave societies of the Americas that experienced emancipation during the nineteenth century, only Cuba did so in a context of civil war. But even there, emancipation did not follow immediately upon conclusion of the Ten Years' War for independence in 1878. Furthermore, slaveholders aligned themselves on both sides of the struggle in more complicated ways than characterized the American Civil War. And the future of slavery never hinged directly upon the outcome of the fighting.[1] American slave emancipation was also unique in that it occurred within a society committed to the principle (if not always the practice) of popular government. A broad electorate of adult white men would be entitled to their say. Moreover, by virtue of the traditional guarantees of individual rights (as best expressed in the Bill of Rights to the U.S. Constitution), even nonvoters could shape public policy.

Hence the future role of the emancipated slaves in the reconstructed body politic would be determined by three major constituencies: 1) federal authorities—both military and civilian—who were beholden ultimately to the northern electorate; 2) the southern electorate; and 3) two groups of disfranchised citizens, the freedpeople and the antebellum elite (men with taxable property worth $20,000 or more in 1860, who were deprived of the vote by President Andrew Johnson's Reconstruction Proclamation of May 1865). During the first three postwar years this struggle to reconstruct civil society loomed as large as the struggle to devise a new labor system.

DURING PRESIDENTIAL Reconstruction, Georgia's old-line Whigs reversed the defeat they had suffered during the secession crisis. They succeeded in presenting themselves to President Johnson as conservative moderates and, as such, the persons best suited to cooperate with federal Reconstruction. Predictably, their ranks included numerous mainstays of the antebellum planter aristocracy, such as Alexander H. Stephens, Herschel V. Johnson, E. G. Cabaniss, and Absalom H. Chappell, all of whom had begun their political careers as Whigs. But, in a process of reverse political identification, former Democrats also rallied around the banner of rule by the "best and wisest men."[2] Urban Democrats in particular, including O. A. Lochrane and the editors of the *Macon Telegraph*, with impeccable ties to the plantation establishment but with rising commercial aspirations as well, styled themselves Conservatives and found common ground with the Whigs. The final group of antebellum Democrats to join the Whig bandwagon was small but disproportionately influential. Led by former governor Joseph E. Brown, these men championed a strategy of cooperation between northern and southern capital in the interest of a stable business climate.[3]

With the old-line Whigs at the helm, planters had no reason to fear that their interests would not be represented. And, despite his earlier bombast, President Johnson proved sympathetic to their continued hegemony. He appointed as provisional governor James Johnson, a lawyer from Columbus with an impeccable record of cooperation during the secession crisis. When the Reconstruction constitutional convention met in November 1865, the Whiggish planters obligingly acquiesced in emancipation, repealed the secession ordinance, and repudiated the Confederate debt. On that basis, they won authorization to form a government.[4]

The new governor, Charles J. Jenkins, had also opposed secession until the state left the Union. The legislature that met in December was likewise inclined toward cooperation with the president, as were all but one of the seven men selected to represent the state in the federal House of Representatives. It was doubtless in this spirit that the legislators chose as U.S. senators two giants of antebellum Georgia politics, Alexander H. Stephens and Herschel V. Johnson.

Although both had opposed disunion prior to passage of the secession ordinance—Stephens with considerably less animation than Johnson—after secession each held prominent office in the Confederacy, the former as vice-president and the latter as a senator. Whatever the intention of the Georgia legislature, Congress and the northern public viewed these appointments as deliberate acts of defiance.

Under the guiding hand of the old-line Whigs, the lawmakers went directly to the task of defining the civic condition of the former slaves. The resulting black code gave freedpeople the right to marry but kept in place the antebellum restriction against interracial marriage. It authorized former slaves to make and enforce contracts, to sue and be sued, to testify (in civil cases wherein a person of color was a party, and in criminal cases wherein a person of color was the defendant), and to possess and convey real and personal property. Notable by their absence were provisions entitling persons of color to serve on juries or to vote.[5]

Scarcely had the ink dried on these laws when the federal Civil Rights Act of 1866 overrode their discriminatory provisions. In addition to enjoining both states and private individuals from discriminating, the act empowered federal officers to arrest transgressors and to adjudicate cases wherever state courts refused to recognize the rights of freedpeople. In Georgia, as elsewhere, this responsibility fell largely upon the shoulders of the Freedmen's Bureau.[6]

With regard to establishing the civil rights of the freedmen, planters clearly were guided by prewar precedents. The 1866 black code, for instance, was largely a modified version of antebellum legislation regarding free black persons. But the "termination of the long existing patriarchal relation"[7] both necessitated and made possible changes in old-style paternalism, one clear sign of which was the rapid disintegration of the procedural safeguards that had earlier surrounded slaves brought before the bar of justice. It is not simply that emancipation undermined the property rights upon which the master-slave relationship had rested; after the war former masters took deliberate steps to isolate former slaves so that they stood as unattached—and, in the nature of the case, unprotected— individuals without an intercessor before the state. If Yankees wished to assume the mediator's role, dispossessed masters reasoned, let them also take up its burdens.[8]

This view of society reflected the planters' continuing belief in the inherent inferiority of the freedpeople. In this respect, of course, they drew heavily upon antebellum proslavery ideology. But emancipation required changes. Persons of African descent clearly could no longer be described as divinely appointed for slavery—at least not by anyone wishing to avoid trouble.[9] But they could be—and were—described as a class whose racial character and social condition rendered them preeminently suited to manual labor. Ex-masters throughout the Americas formulated similar descriptions of ex-slaves. Eastern European lords also detected similar qualities in peasants, as did northern industrial employers in assorted groups of wage workers. What is remarkable in these descriptions of such widely divergent groups is their common resort to racial or ethnic phenotyping and stereotyping, especially of workers recently removed from rural backgrounds.[10] The legacy of antebellum racism lived on, not to prop up a system of property in human beings, but rather to support a system of economic, social, and political inequality among free men and women.[11]

The planters' resort to racial ideology, apparently without missing a step from antebellum days, suggests how rapidly they perceived their potential loss of social influence once slavery was destroyed. Their fears were not misplaced, for, even apart from the effects of the northern presence in the South, planters experienced divisions in their own ranks from the very beginning of the postwar period. These divisions reflected the persistence of antebellum differences, though often in new alignments. Such organizations as planters' clubs and the Democratic-Conservative party served in part as mechanisms for mediating conflicting viewpoints.

These divisions among planters barely hinted at those between planters, on the one hand, and smallholders, urban artisans, and laborers on the other. Certain issues drew particular attention to the differences. The first was legislation to provide relief to debtors. Upcountry yeomen especially favored such measures, but planters were divided. Most old-line Whigs believed such action either just in the abstract, given the extraordinary circumstances, or necessary in practical terms to avert unrest. But a number of Democrats turned against their yeomen constituents on this issue.

Howell Cobb best expressed the rationale of such Democratic planters when he explained that legislative relief would undermine the sanctity of contracts.[12] Such action would further weaken a society that was already reeling from the blow of uncompensated slave emancipation. Responding in kind, the upcountry yeomen who clamored for relief from their own obligations felt little compunction for the losses experienced by the planters. But for yeomen in the black belt, who remained reciprocally tied to planters through notes of credit, the matter of debt was not so cut and dried. Accordingly, black-belt yeomen were much less vociferous in demanding repudiation of private debts than were their counterparts in the upper Piedmont.

Black-belt planters had less luck discouraging destitute smallholders from seeking relief from the government in Washington. To the planters' embarrassment, when the Freedmen's Bureau arrived in the upcountry in mid-summer 1865, its agents began to provide relief of last resort to suffering smallholders. Not to be outdone, the Georgia legislature appropriated some $300,000 to provide corn, in particular for the families of Confederate soldiers, but more generally for white destitutes. Still, Yankee cereals threatened to drive a wedge between the planters and the smallholders.[13]

When it came to bolstering the loyalty of the urban artisans and laborers to the rule of the planter-commercial elite, the old-line Whigs benefited from the antebellum experience of aristocratic Democrats. On the positive side, they could count upon the workingmen's strong—indeed, virtually unflappable— allegiance to the Democratic party. Moreover, artisans could no longer blame the planters for manipulating the supply of skilled slaves to their disadvantage. Instead, they could focus their animosity directly upon the skilled freedmen. Although the workingmen might well have resented the paternal style of the most aristocratic planters, they welcomed the attention to commercial development exhibited by former Democrats and former Whigs alike.[14]

The planters' anxiety over the potential for class division among white citizens prompted them to dust off the political settlements reached on the eve of the Civil War regarding such matters of public concern as education. Despite the chaotic condition of the state's finances, in 1866, with hardly any discussion, much less dissent, the legislature pledged to inaugurate a system of publicly financed education for every white child in the state commencing in 1868. Although Radical Reconstruction interfered with the implementation of that plan, it aimed to bolster the allegiance of workingmen and smallholding farmers to the Whiggish planter elite—rather than the Freedmen's Bureau or northern benevolent associations—as the proper dispenser of public services.

NEITHER FEDERAL officials nor Georgia Conservatives understood how committed the freedpeople were to being fully incorporated into the new body politic. The men who made policy at both national and state levels simply assumed that they would make the critical decisions affecting the freedpeople's lives, but they miscalculated. Whatever internal divisions prevailed among African Americans, the legacy of slavery produced remarkably unified expectations of freedom.[15]

The freedpeople's conception of citizenship rested squarely upon their understanding of the rights enjoyed by free citizens of the republic. It embraced expectations that the government would guarantee full enjoyment of these rights: security in their persons and property; freedom of speech, association, assembly, and worship; access to the judicial process as jurors as well as witnesses; access to government services such as schools and asylums; access to the ballot box. Many freedpeople also associated the enjoyment of these rights with possession of land—a kind of freedom dues warranted by their years of unrequited toil and their loyalty to the Union during the Civil War. But even short of a distribution of land, freedpeople viewed emancipation as a commitment to personal rights over property rights. In pressing this point, former slaves and their Radical Republican allies revolutionized the prevailing concepts of citizenship and of the proper relationship between individual citizens and the state.

During the immediate postwar period, when the shape of the new body politic was least decided and most susceptible to influence, the freedpeople struggled at two interrelated levels to achieve these objectives. The first was that of the community, where the challenge was to fashion organizations and leadership structures equal to the demands of the new order. For many purposes, existing institutions served, but new circumstances often required novel measures. The second level was that of society in general, where freedpeople had to choose allies and articulate demands upon policymakers. The interconnection between these levels is best illustrated by examining two crucial institutions among the freedpeople of central Georgia—the church and the public school—and by tracing the effects of institution building upon the more general pursuit of full citizenship rights.

The freedpeople's struggle to control the key institutions in their lives began precisely where antebellum struggles had left off, as the history of the church clearly demonstrates. Before the war no less than after, churches formed the institutional backbone of plantation and urban communities alike. Yet the divergent nature of antebellum religious experiences of urban and rural slaves influenced postwar patterns. Consider the matter of church buildings. Fully two years after the end of the war, freedpeople in the rural areas of central Georgia had only a handful of church buildings: two each in Houston County and Bibb County (excluding Macon), but not a single one in Crawford, Jones, or Monroe counties (though land had been purchased for church purposes in the last named). Amidst grinding poverty, they found it difficult to acquire land, despite the most determined efforts.[16] In Macon, however, black Christians fared better, as did their counterparts in metropolitan areas elsewhere in the state and the region. At the dawn of freedom, four congregations possessed their own church buildings: two Baptist, one Presbyterian, and one Methodist. Although the latter two congregations answered to higher church authorities, the Baptists functioned autonomously for the most part, except for loose associational ties with white Baptist congregations. In either case, possessing a building created options envied by rural church members.

Whether housed or not, churches served a variety of critical needs. Foremost was their role in strengthening the family. Ministers sang the blessings of marriage.[17] Churches commemorated such key events in the collective lives of their members as weddings, births, and deaths. Insofar as the church thus strengthened the freed black family, it indirectly entered the contest between former masters and former slaves over the shape of new labor relations. As that struggle unfolded, churches played an especially important role in preserving the sense of community that was lost when old plantation quarters gave way to cabins scattered about the plantations.[18]

The road to religious freedom was lined with friend and foe alike. Planter paternalists, who from slavery days had attempted to manipulate Christianity in their struggle to control the minds and hearts of the labor force, predictably stood out. White ministers to the freedpeople repeated antebellum exhortations regarding industry, sobriety, chastity, and marital fidelity. Other traditional themes included the God-ordained inferiority of African-derived persons, the civilizing effect of slavery, and the continuing benevolence of former masters. Although planters believed that slaves had internalized these messages, no harm and potentially much good would result from a refresher course.[19]

Church courts also continued to exert their traditional disciplinary roles, especially in the Baptist congregations of the plantation districts. Monroe County's Smyrna Baptist Church, which had not expelled any "black brethren" since the unsuccessful slave revolt of 1835, dismissed three soon after the war "for leaving their master and going to the Yankes." In the summer of 1865, Houston Factory Baptist Church revived the practice, suspended since 1858, of holding separate disciplinary meetings for black members. In a revealing slip of the pen dated August 1865, the church minutes referred to a disciplined black brother named Wash as "the property of Sister Moore." In congregations such as this, old habits died hard.[20]

Understandably, former slaves quickly grew resentful of such oversight and began withdrawing from antebellum congregations both individually and in groups. This process of separation suggests a strong desire among the freedpeople to control the critical institutions in their lives. They wanted to choose their own minister, to determine their own polity, to worship as they pleased, and to interpret for themselves the relevance of the Christian gospel to their lives. At the very least, they sought greater congregational autonomy within a loosely federated church structure. When white churchmen balked, they insisted upon a clean break.[21]

A brief survey of several Protestant denominations indicates the strength of this impulse to separate. Within rural Baptist congregations, the departure of the black brethren occurred gradually, congregation by congregation, over the first several postwar years.[22] Black Presbyterians sought a more general solution in keeping with the church's more centralized organizational structure. Having grown "restive" early in 1866, black communicants of Georgia's Hopewell Presbytery petitioned for independence. In April, church officials granted the request, provided that the separatists remained subject to Hopewell's authority until a black presbytery could be formed. That same month, the church ordained its first three African American ministers, one of whom was Macon resident Robert Carter, formerly a slave of Howell Cobb.[23]

The experience of the former-slave members of Macon's Methodist Episcopal (ME) Church, South, comported with that of their coreligionists throughout the states of the former Confederacy.[24] Emancipation broadened the traditional antebellum constituency of servants and artisans to include the emerging strata of black professionals and shopkeepers. Desiring independence, soon after the war they decided to affiliate with the northern-based African Methodist Episcopal (AME) church, whose radical political and social views irked white church elders. Facing a rash of such actions, leaders of the ME Church, South, devised guidelines for dissolving old ties. The Georgia General Conference, for instance, authorized freedpeople to organize "entirely independent of us and self-governing in every respect."[25] But these pronouncements stopped short of offering title to the church property that black Methodists had purchased before the war. Accordingly, tensions rose.[26]

In Macon, the simmering dispute boiled over in November 1865, when the freedpeople requested the title and announced that they had chosen one of their own, William Campbell, to serve as pastor. Officials agreed on condition that the congregation sever all ties with African Methodism. Infuriated at such a blatant "infringement of their religious liberty," members appealed to the Freedmen's Bureau for assistance. Capt. Louis Lambert, subassistant commissioner at Macon, decried this new "species of 'religious intolerance'" and advised the freedpeople to retain possession of the property until civil courts decided the case. Assistant Commissioner Davis Tillson ruled that the trustees had "no right, legal or moral, to eject the colored congregation or prevent their using the property." Astonished at such "uncharitable" behavior, Tillson ordered the arrest of anyone interfering with the black Methodists.[27]

Two years later an internal dispute within the congregation brought the property issue back to the forefront. During the late spring of 1868, Campbell—who had relinquished the pastorate to New Jersey–born Theophilus G. Steward while remaining an elder—led a splinter movement out of the church. Newspaper reports at the time attributed the fissure to political differences.[28] Seeing an opportunity to regain control over the property, white Methodists declared Campbell's faction the original congregation and sued for possession of the building. In mid-February 1869, the sheriff produced a warrant ordering Steward to vacate the premises. That night the church burned to the ground. Authorities suspected arson, and the white public suspected Steward's congregation. Undaunted by such adversity, Steward and his followers raised nearly $3,000 within the next few months and constructed a church on a new lot. Just the same, they refused to abandon their claim to the disputed property, and late in 1870 the Bibb County Superior Court resolved the case by selling the land and dividing the proceeds equally between the two contending parties.[29]

Nearly overshadowed by the property dispute, the black Methodists' insistence upon organizational autonomy demonstrated the strong determination of the freedpeople to control their institutions and their lives. Controlling church organizations had several implications. Superficially, it simply involved style: church members associated on the basis of doctrine, liturgy, and—perhaps most important—preaching style. At a deeper level, congregations sought to develop structures for grooming leaders equal to the challenges of the postslavery era. To be sure, black ministers served as spiritual leaders, but they also provided guidance through the complex ways of the new world.

The church produced a diverse corps of leaders to address the challenges of revolutionary times. Certain denominational differences are apparent. The large number of Baptist and the handful of Presbyterian ministers tended to be former slaves who had lived for years, if not their whole lives, in Georgia. Few had had any formal schooling, though most had learned to read and write. Rural Baptist preachers tended to farm six days a week, just as their Baptist and Presbyterian brethren in the towns and cities supported themselves as artisans or shopkeepers. In Macon, for instance, William Banks operated a carriage shop, Isaac L. Primus was a carpenter, and Lewis Smith was a grocer.[30]

AME ministers differed substantially from these men. Henry M. Turner and Theophilus G. Steward were freeborn and educated and had lived in the North before the war.[31] The native Georgians of the group had all been slaves. Although some were "untutored" and "very poorly equipped for [their] task," as Steward characterized Thomas Crayton, most resembled the wagoner Robert Anderson in having lived and worked in urban artisan communities before the war.[32] Three circumstances contributed to the uniqueness of the AME ministers. The first was the comparative degree of skill and property ownership among their communicants. In short, Methodists had certain aspirations of self-improvement for themselves and their children and possessed a modicum of property around which they might organize their efforts. If nothing else, the church building provided a meeting place. The AME church in Macon hosted local political gatherings and statewide conventions of political and educational organizations from the earliest postwar days. No doubt it served the same purposes for the assorted men's and women's clubs and associations that characterized freedpeople's communities throughout the South.[33]

Second, the Methodist practice of itinerancy favored the development of an activist ministry with a larger than parochial vision. Turner, for instance, traveled throughout the black belt and upper Piedmont of Georgia, eventually becoming presiding elder of the North Georgia Conference of the church. Although he centered his ministry in Macon, he frequently spent weeks at a time on the road preaching, baptizing, ordaining ministers, and establishing congregations and schools, with a measure of support from the Freedmen's Bureau for his educational work. He enjoyed singular success among urban freedpeople—particularly the class of independent professionals, proprietors, and artisans.[34] At the start of Radical Reconstruction, he organized freedmen into the Republican party with the same zeal, simply adding a partisan political dimension to his religious and educational work.[35] Like Turner, Steward organized schools and political clubs as well as churches in the leading towns of upcountry Georgia. Other denominations sponsored missionaries of their own, but none touched the incipient political consciousness of urban freedmen as did those of the AME church.[36]

Last, but by no means least, the AME ministers' ability to support themselves from their ministry gave them an unparalleled degree of freedom from intimidation and control by unfriendly whites. That AME ministers were beholden only to the church for their financial support goes a long way toward explaining their political independence. But that autonomy had drawbacks as well as advantages. Leaders immune to threats to their livelihoods faced threats to their lives instead.[37]

THE SECOND institutional tool with which the freedpeople sought to remake the body politic was the school. By all accounts, former slaves throughout the South had an insatiable desire for education. Although partly rooted in antebellum prohibitions against reading and writing, this passion also stemmed from the common understanding of how important schooling would be in the new world of freedom. Education was "the safe-guard of human freedom, and the only source of individual and national happiness and prosperity," declared the resolutions of a freedpeople's educational convention that met in Macon.[38] Former slaves used every opportunity to master literacy skills. Those who had stolen such knowledge as slaves passed it along, often merely a step or two ahead of their pupils. Persons of every age eagerly attended classes. "We work all day," said adult students observed by a northern traveler, "but we'll come . . . in the evening for learning."[39]

Education also had practical benefits. Although much of the rural culture of the nineteenth-century South was oral, reading was more than simply a luxury. Vital information was communicated in printed or written form. Military authorities posted various notices, as did government officials and a host of private organizations and individual citizens. Whatever their biases, the *Telegraph* and the *Journal & Messenger* printed items of general importance. In addition to advertising and public notices, such information included transcriptions of state and national laws and legislative debates. And upon the appearance of newspapers overtly sympathetic to the cause of the freedpeople—first the *Colored American* and the *Loyal Georgian*, both of which were published in Augusta, and later Republican party organs from all the major cities of the state—the rewards of literacy were never higher.

But whereas churches could survive on faith alone, schools required teachers, buildings, books, and other materials, all of which necessitated money. Long before the last Confederate had trudged back from Appomattox, the freedpeople began cobbling together stray bits and pieces of what they hoped would become a school system. Given their poverty, the rural freedpeople's sacrifices on behalf of education border upon the incredible. Teachers' salaries (though proverbially modest) strained financial resources. Communities dug even deeper to purchase land and buildings, for renting accommodations left education "entirely in the hands of the white citizens," as James B. Deveaux of Jones County explained; if public sentiment changed, the pupils would be "turned out of doors."[40] On occasion a prosperous freedman or a sympathetic white landowner would donate land for school purposes. After money had been raised for building materials, the members of the community would erect the structure themselves.[41]

Not surprisingly, ministers took the lead in educational matters. They made church buildings available for schools, often paying expenses out of their own pockets and serving as teachers. They functioned as intermediaries between the freedpeople and northern benefactors. During the first summer of freedom, all four of the black churches in Macon hosted schools taught by black teachers. Lewis Smith, pastor of one of the Baptist churches and a grocer, paid all building expenses.[42]

The paucity of rural church buildings obstructed educational progress. In time, freedmen in the county seats and rural commercial centers overcame the "impoverished condition" of the people and purchased lots and buildings for church and school purposes.[43] Compared to the surrounding countryside, rural towns offered an enviable degree of security and accessibility. But even at that, the teacher in one such school remarked that her "Pupils have from (9) to (10) miles a day to walk."[44]

Throughout central Georgia, freedpeople formed educational committees both to raise money and to monitor the schools. Black businessmen and artisans generally assisted the ministers in this work. They conducted subscription campaigns, often contributing substantial sums of their own money.[45] Behind the scenes, individuals and clubs, women and men, parents and other interested community members contributed time and money. One typical group of sub-scribers pledged sums of $.20 to $1.00 per month to "open a Public School & take all the cullard children that may come to Said School."[46] The school committees also functioned as overseers of the schools, monitoring both the progress of the students and the good conduct of the teachers and taking remedial action when necessary.[47]

In cities such as Macon, teachers brought diverse backgrounds and experiences to their classrooms. In addition to the ministers already referred to, an unnamed pressroom hand at the *Macon Telegraph* apparently got up an informal school right after the war. Among the teachers at the schools sponsored by the churches were two carpenters, Isaac L. Primus and John Bentley, who taught "only . . . for the good they thought [they] were doing," inasmuch as they could each earn three dollars per day at their trade.[48] R. M. Mitchell, who had never been to school himself, felt "called upon to do . . . this Glorious & all important work which has been committed to my charge," namely, "doing the very best I can to edgucate the People of my color."[49] In rural areas, however, the number of persons capable of teaching was limited.[50] Still, by the end of 1866 Georgia freedpeople reportedly supported fifty-six schools and a like number of teachers entirely on their own.[51]

Given the magnitude of the task before them and the modesty of the resources at their disposal, freedpeople necessarily turned to outside financial assistance.

From the summer of 1865, the Freedmen's Bureau and the American Missionary Association (AMA)—an organization committed to proselytizing on behalf
of Congregational religion and Christian education—distinguished themselves
in this regard. The Western Freedmen's Aid Association and the Peabody Fund
also offered some aid.[52] Without this support the educational aspirations of the
freedpeople of central Georgia (if not the whole South) would have faced
insuperable financial obstacles in the crucial first years after the war.

Northerners pursued a number of objectives in fostering education. Obviously, they wished to banish the ignorance, degradation, and backwardness
enforced by the slave regime, so that the former slaves could take their place as
free workers and citizens of the national republic. Education would elevate them
on the scale of civilization: "They may be taught to respect the marriage-vow,"
predicted John E. Bryant, former captain in a regiment of black soldiers and the
bureau's first agent in upcountry Georgia, and "[t]he barbarous habit of eating
hominy from the pot in which it is cooked may be broken up." At their best,
northern sponsors of freedmen's education envisioned a total "reformation . . .
that will extend throughout the South." One measure of success would be the
degree to which the freedpeople behaved as dark-skinned Yankees.[53] More than
that, however, education also formed a cornerstone of the Radicals' political
program. As George L. Eberhart, the first state superintendent of education for
the Freedmen's Bureau, insisted, without education the rights and immunities of
citizenship "may prove rather a curse than a blessing."[54] The southern states
needed to follow the northern lead and establish general systems of free common
schools.

The Freedmen's Bureau and the AMA addressed many complementary
needs of the freedpeople, but the two agencies were far from duplicate copies of
each other. By virtue of its close ties to the Congregational church, the AMA
retained a strong missionary flavor that, while not altogether absent in the
bureau's work, was comparatively more subdued. Moreover, the AMA recruited
its own teachers among northern Congregationalists, and these included large
numbers of women. Though at first suspicious of entrusting classroom responsibilities to freedpeople, the association's reluctance subsided over time, particularly following the establishment of Atlanta University in 1867. From the
start, the AMA focused its efforts in the urban areas, which sat well with rural
planters. But the teachers' habit of fraternizing with freedpeople infuriated
native white Georgians to the virtual ostracism of the northerners.[55]

By the late summer of 1865, the AMA had established itself in Macon,
operating its own school staffed by its own teachers, who by the end of the year

numbered approximately a dozen. The school was graded, with the most advanced students receiving additional instruction so that they might assist the teachers and prepare to conduct classes on their own. With the proliferation of schools, parents organized a board of school visitors, consisting of twelve men— three from each of the four churches—and a financial committee to raise funds.[56] The AMA schools took a summer recess, prompted in large measure by the Yankee teachers' desire to escape the heat. When schools reopened in the fall, they had to compete for students against a number of tuition schools that freedpeople had begun during the interim.[57]

The bureau fared somewhat better than the AMA did sponsoring schools outside the major cities. Under the energetic direction of the successive superintendents of education (George L. Eberhart, Erastus A. Ware, and Col. John R. Lewis), bureau agents disseminated much advice and some money, though this effort remained largely confined to the county seats and market towns where the agents kept their offices. The bureau's two African American school organizers, ministers Henry M. Turner from Macon and William Jefferson White from Augusta, enjoyed considerable success organizing schools in churches, which, again, favored the towns over the plantation districts. Still, urban areas proved most conducive to the success of schools. Whereas from 1866 through 1868 approximately 1,000 black children in Macon regularly attended classes, all the schools in all the counties surrounding Macon combined could not claim 1,000 students.[58]

The white residents of central Georgia witnessed this exploding educational movement with mixed emotions but prior to the summer of 1866 did little but exhort the freedpeople to entrust the future to their true best friends. According to a group of leading citizens from Macon, good intentions regarding freedmen's education had been there from the end of the war but "the exhausted condition of the State" frustrated all plans to adopt "a system of public instruction for the negro." Such appeals were disingenuous given the absence of such authorization from any official body and the general antipathy among whites against common schools for black children.[59]

The spokesmen for the urban planter-merchant elite grounded their opposition upon traditional values. Although most believed that education would spoil plantation laborers, they also recognized the inevitability of schools for freedpeople. Some impetuous former masters in Jones County reasoned "that as the Yankees set the negroes free, they should educate them,"[60] but new-style paternalists rejected such shortsightedness. If the freedpeople were to be educated, then the work must be in trustworthy hands. Northern missionaries and philanthropists did not fit that description.[61]

During the summer of 1866, prominent residents of Macon decided to take the matter in hand. After a series of public meetings, these leaders issued an address on the subject of educating freedpeople, whom they characterized as a "numerous race—ignorant, capricious, indolent, without property, without habits of self-control, and without any just sense of obligation to civil authority." The address credited former masters with having elevated Africans from a state of pagan savagery to one of Christian civilization. "Had their slave *status* continued," these leaders opined, "the race would in a few generations, have attained to a point of moral elevation, equal to that of the uneducated laboring classes of any of the States of Europe."[62]

On the strength of that antebellum experience, they believed that "[t]he native population have advantages for the instruction of the colored people far superior to all others." "We understand their character, their wants, their habits, and therefore know better how to minister to their and our own necessities than anybody else." The freedpeople themselves were even beginning "to rely upon their former owners as their friends" in educational matters. Even without public financing, "the Christians, and benevolent, patriotic citizens" had the ability to "devise and put into operation a local system of instruction, equal to the accomplishment of great good"—provided that it were "disconnected from all others, and under our exclusive control."[63] In the same vein, a handful of rural paternalists were even willing to grant freedpeople property and control of the schools on condition that they not employ Yankee teachers.[64] But promises flowed more freely than money.

As much as Georgia freedmen depended upon the Freedmen's Bureau and the AMA, they relied even more upon the Georgia Equal Rights Association (GERA), an outgrowth of the January 1866 convention of freedmen in Augusta. In October 1866, due largely to the intensity of political opposition against the association's political program, strategists decided to change the emphasis and the name of the association to the Georgia Education Association (GEA). John E. Bryant, its president, raised money in the North and worked tirelessly to organize educational associations throughout the state, using the pages of the *Loyal Georgian*, which he edited, in the effort. As Bryant explained in the association's printed prospectus, he and "a few white friends" began assisting Georgia freedpeople after they "became satisfied that the ruling class of that State would not provide for the education of their people; that the Northern Societies could not educate all, and that, unless they entered upon the work themselves, a large majority must remain in ignorance." This required monumental energy, sacrifice, and courage. Subordinate associations in the various counties organized committees to "establish the schools, provide the school-houses, [and] employ and pay the teachers; the scholars and their parents pay the expenses." In Bryant's estimation, support for such schools amounted to $2,000 per month.[65]

During 1867, the association sponsored two conventions to advance its work, both held at the AME church in Macon. The proceedings featured county-by-county reports. Whereas cities like Macon, Augusta, and Savannah boasted nine to eighteen schools, 1,100 to 1,600 pupils, and substantial northern support, plantation counties fared poorly. In all of Monroe, for example, there were only four schools with 112 pupils, and in Jones only one school with 35 pupils. With nothing to report, some plantation counties sent no delegates. In mid-1867, after visiting Crawford County, William J. White described the freedpeople as "exceedingly poor, but very anxious to have schools and . . . willing to do what they can." Such enthusiasm notwithstanding, no school operated in the county until 1868. In Twiggs County, the educational effort likewise struggled—and declined precipitously when its prime mover, S. Ashley, led a group of emigrants to Liberia.[66]

Resolutions of both conventions declared strongly in favor of a state system of free schools.[67] The appearance of such provisions in the new Republican constitution adopted in 1868 (and in similar documents from the other reconstructed states) culminated the antebellum political struggle. The diverse objectives of education for social control and education for self-improvement were reconciled in the general understanding that public education benefited both society and the individual students; this proposition in turn won acceptance only after Yankees and liberated slaves had thrown their weight into the debate.

Victory came at the expense of several important compromises, which, though justified on the grounds of political expediency, established precedents whose future results would subvert the objective of common schools for all. The first was a constitutional provision that the new system be financed from poll taxes, which soon made the schools hostage to political battles for votes. Just as damaging over the long run was the tacit understanding that when the system went into operation—which it did during the early 1870s—it would provide separate schools and unequal resources for white and black children.[68]

THE THIRD KEY component of the struggle to define the new body politic entailed citizenship rights, including the suffrage. A close look at this struggle during Presidential Reconstruction reveals the challenges faced by former slaves everywhere at the moment of their liberation: Who were their best friends? With whom might they build alliances? Who in their own ranks were best qualified to lead the struggle? What kinds of organizational form should the struggle take?

Understanding the freedpeople's quest for equal civil and political rights requires distinguishing between ideals and practice. From the eighteenth-century age of revolution, the nineteenth century inherited the concepts of the natural rights of citizens, which, along with protection of their property, included government by consent of the governed. Yet the practical meaning of representative government remained contested.

In the antebellum North, as the hierarchical domestic economy dissolved in the face of developing capitalism, adult men whose life prospects did not appear to include achieving the status of freeholder pressed for a new conception of social responsibility and worth. Disputing property qualifications for voting, this conception viewed adulthood and residency as sufficient conditions to exercise the franchise. By the 1830s, this revolutionary notion of citizenship rights had swept the North and most of the South as well.

Even that achievement left several important issues unsettled, particularly with regard to the eligibility of certain segments of the population, specifically, illiterates, foreign-born persons, and persons of African descent. Moreover, old-line Federalists and others of similarly aristocratic backgrounds never accepted the proposition that hirelings could exercise the suffrage independently or responsibly. (Few seriously considered the notion that women might vote.) The struggle over the meaning of citizenship turned around how the principle of representative government was to work in everyday life.

Exactly the same kind of process began in central Georgia and throughout the South in the wake of slave emancipation. Numerous interests representing assorted social classes of local and national provenance vied to influence the outcome. Through that thicket the politically disfranchised and inexperienced freedpeople had to chart a course and choose allies. Their actions often demonstrated uncertainty over the best path to take.

Having witnessed as slaves the operation of a society founded upon the rule of law, freedpeople looked eagerly to establish their rights before the bar. Two tribunals—civil and military—adjudicated cases, though the two did not always function in harmony. Given the biases of most civil officers, former slaves looked to the army and to the Freedmen's Bureau for legal protection. In a typical appeal, a Twiggs County freedman who declared that he and his fellows had "no chance to get justice at the courts" implored a Freedmen's Bureau official to "see us all righted."[69]

During the first two years of freedom, the freedpeople's struggle for equal citizenship encompassed political as well as civil rights. Former slaves from both plantation and urban areas joined forces. This coalition was a natural by-product of the freedpeople's lives. Persons seeking work moved back and forth between city and countryside. And just as they had done during slavery, plantation laborers visited Macon (as well as the rural towns) on weekends to conduct business, to socialize, or to attend church services.[70] By the same token, urban freedpeople visited rural relatives and worked as day laborers on plantations. Institutions reflected this interaction.

Because all roads led to Macon, the city became a special locus of the freedpeople's struggle for civil and political rights. Artisans, entrepreneurs, and professionals there, like similarly situated groups throughout the Atlantic world during the nineteenth century, provided the cadre.[71] The city's large contingent of Yankees, which included soldiers, Freedmen's Bureau officials, missionaries, and teachers, offered support. And the former slaves enjoyed strength in numbers. Mass political gatherings proved electrifying.[72]

To further the cause, former slaves affiliated with northern groups such as the Union League (or Loyal League), a network of secret political societies organized during the Civil War. Emissaries of the league began working in Georgia following Gen. William T. Sherman's capture of Savannah in December 1864. After the surrender, black league organizers fanned throughout the upcountry, organizing freedmen on behalf of equal rights. Black representatives of the Georgia Equal Rights Association did likewise after the organization's founding convention in January 1866.[73]

The influence of such men notwithstanding, freedpeople in central Georgia, like their counterparts elsewhere, looked chiefly into their own ranks for leaders. Ministers frequently applied their skills to secular affairs, testifying both to their ability to respond to the needs of their congregations and to their relative economic independence.[74] Leaders who lacked a formal tie to the ministry nonetheless enjoyed a modicum of economic independence as craftsmen, proprietors, professionals, or landowners.[75]

Freedpeople in central Georgia made their first collective political expression on Independence Day, 1865, when a hitherto secret Union League club staged an elaborate parade through the city followed by a dinner at the Methodist church. The proceedings included a business meeting at which officers of the league were chosen and by-laws drawn up, with the whole audience—women as well as men—voicing opinions and voting on general questions. In mapping strategy, speakers reportedly "stoutly resisted the idea of colonization," encouraging the freedpeople instead to stay where they were because "they had acquired rights which must be respected."[76]

Even apart from the strategic planning that occurred at the meeting, it was remarkable for other reasons. It was doubtless the largest assembly of African Americans that Macon had ever witnessed. Antebellum state ordinances had limited unsupervised gatherings of slaves and free persons of color to a maximum of seven; supervised church services or social events might have turned out several hundred at most. But when over 1,000 attended this meeting, both former masters and former slaves understood that the old order was dead and gone. Among other things, it signaled the start of a contest over public space that would rage for years after the end of the war.

The gathering on the Fourth of July also affirmed the freedpeople's appropriation of the most sacred national holiday as their own. White residents of Macon had last celebrated the nation's independence in 1860 and, following Confederate defeat, felt little inclination to do so again soon. In seizing the day, the former slaves affirmed their identity with the American political tradition. They were the political descendants of the Sons of Liberty; their cause was the Spirit of '76. Over time, freedpeople would add other ceremonial occasions to their calendar of holidays—election day being the most significant.

The evident success of the radical Union League drew out more moderate leaders. In September, William D. Banks, the carriagemaker and minister, challenged the league's political program. Resisting the rush to political rights, Banks counseled honest hard work instead.[77] This difference in strategies persisted in central Georgia for years and in many respects echoed similar conflicts among African Americans throughout the nation both before and since emancipation.[78] Banks's ties to the white elite reveal one source of this tension; a local newspaper endorsed his establishment as meriting "a share of the public patronage" inasmuch much as he was "a quiet, well-behaved freedman." Former slaves with comparable business ties tended to take a comparable political stance, despite other links they maintained (through the ministry, for instance) to the freedpeople's community.[79]

Over the next few months, developments at the state level helped promote political consciousness locally, even while fostering the growth of factions. In January 1866, the first state convention of Georgia freedmen met in Augusta; from this meeting emerged the aforementioned Georgia Equal Rights Association. Banks and Lewis Smith, a black minister and grocer from Macon, represented Bibb County, and Henry M. Turner, at the time still an army chaplain, also attended. The delegates resolved, among other things, in favor of impartial, rather than universal, male suffrage and the disposition of government lands at rates that freedpeople could afford rather than gratis.[80] Not all freedpeople appreciated the delegates' apparent pandering to their "friends at the North" as reflected in their equivocal stance on these crucial issues.[81]

Whatever influence northerners may have had upon the proceedings, the delegates ultimately answered to their home constituencies. Black leaders forgot this at their peril. In February 1866, a freedman from Macon complained that Lewis Smith had yet to report publicly on the convention. Smith's constituents rejected his excuse that he was awaiting receipt of the printed proceedings.[82] Their future depended upon full acquaintance with the key issues of the day, and there was no time for delay.

The Augusta convention deepened the split among black leaders in Macon by exposing their different political strategies. Lewis Smith favored full citizenship rights and urged agitation to that end; William Banks advocated education, relief for the destitute, and respect for former masters. In March 1866, Smith engineered a minor coup in which he replaced Banks as GERA vice-president for Bibb County. Smith reportedly first lobbied on his own behalf and then called a mass meeting to repudiate Banks. Moses H. Bentley, a Union League organizer from Savannah who eventually settled in Macon and taught school, and George Washington, a soldier in the 103d U.S. Colored Infantry stationed at Macon, argued against internal dissension. Despite an eloquent claim by Banks that "my whole object and aspiration in life" was "the amelioration and bettering of the conditions of my race," the meeting voted 1,007 to 7 in favor of Smith.[83] Leaders whose ties to the white elite dictated accommodationist politics were ushered to the rear.[84]

Smith paid a heavy price for his political activity. In mid-April 1866, Jones County authorities accused him of taking part in the attempted rescue of a woman being transferred from the Macon jailhouse, where she had been imprisoned since 1863 for poisoning her master's family. When freedmen witnessed the woman being led by a rope around her neck, they feared a possible hanging and set out in pursuit. They soon abandoned the quest, but not before exchanging gunfire with the party. Officials arrested fifty-three men suspected of involvement. Smith, who had argued in favor of restraint, turned himself in voluntarily and posted a $1,000 bond. But his ordeal did not soon end. Arrested on a charge of carrying a concealed deadly weapon, Smith feared attempted assassination by some "unknow[n] party." His culpability for the events of April 1866 lingered inconclusively in the courts for a year, at which time he was acquitted and his bond returned.[85]

Events surrounding the attempted rescue demonstrate both the strengths and weaknesses of Macon's freed black community. On the positive side, the incident made clear that forces could be mobilized quickly in an emergency, especially from among the artisans and shopkeepers.[86] On the negative side, Smith's prosecution indicated the freedpeople's vulnerability. The arrests threw freed-people onto the defensive and, among other things, succeeded in taming Smith's militancy. Early in the spring, the Macon press considered him one of the key conduits of northern radicalism to the freedpeople. But by late summer, "Jones County" delighted in reporting a speech in which Smith had urged freedpeople to be industrious, honest, and respectful toward whites, their true best friends. Smith also won points for encouraging freedpeople to form charitable associations to aid the poor and, most significantly, for discouraging suffrage agitation in favor of relying upon the generosity of whites.[87] Even if Smith had intended only to appease his enemies, he also succeeded in confusing his friends.

To complicate matters even more, Smith's remarks conformed with the changing position of the GERA itself on the question of political agitation. In a climate of intense and violent opposition, delegates to the state convention in October 1866 decided to concentrate their efforts on education rather than political organization during the upcoming year. In short, the pressures bearing on Smith similarly affected black leaders and their radical white allies all over the state.[88] Their strategic objectives remained the same, but the survival of the organization and its individual members required a temporary shift in tactics.

Precisely during this crisis in the state's progressive leadership, freedpeople in central Georgia implemented an explicitly nationalist political strategy, in the form of a Liberian emigration movement. Early in July 1866, a committee of three men from Macon (Wyatt Moore, Moses Pollock, and James M. C. Logan) wrote to the American Colonization Society (ACS) requesting transportation to Liberia and back for a party to investigate prospects for settlement. Claiming to be "heartily sick of affairs here since tis in our power to better our condition," they explained that they were "tired of the unprovoked scorn & prejudice we daily and hourly suffer." They vowed not to "continue to kiss the chains that binds us from what other men are." Moore wrote again explaining that "the spirit of Emigration seems to be Rising" because "we can never be what we desire to be in this Country." The ACS soon agreed to sponsor not an advance guard, but a group of permanent settlers who would depart from Savannah or Charleston in November.[89]

Shortly after the association observed Liberian Independence Day on 26 July, a split arose between Pollock and Moore, president and secretary, respectively.

After conjecturing—incorrectly, as it turned out—that migrants would have to pay their own transportation and support, Pollock lost interest. He insisted that the persons most anxious to migrate could not pay their way to Savannah, much less Liberia. Even after learning that the ACS would pay transportation, Pollock withheld his endorsement, fearing that "as certain as we make a move the rest will be throwed out of employment." He did "not want to do something that [would] cause those who stay behind to suffer."[90]

As the summer progressed, Moore and the prospective emigrants resisted pressure from Freedmen's Bureau officials to resettle on Florida homestead lands instead of in Africa. They sought "an asylum," Moore explained, and were willing to "Loose Life in the attempt." Only Liberia would do. Overcoming difficulties at every turn, the resolute emigrants, who represented approximately 5 percent of Macon's black population, left for Charleston in October and embarked for Africa the following month. With the fire of emigration still ablaze, another group laid plans to depart for Liberia in April 1867.[91]

The ACS journal, the *African Repository*, listed the occupations of the adult men who migrated in November 1866: of those from Macon, 35 percent were tradesmen, 26 percent farm workers, 18 percent laborers, 4 percent professionals, and 2 percent servants.[92] The Macon emigrants contained a considerably smaller proportion of farmers than other groups that sailed either with them or on future society-sponsored voyages.[93] The first wave of migrants from Macon reflected the impatience for more sweeping social change among skilled urban freedmen.

Unlike the early group, the April 1867 emigrants consisted mostly of farm workers, in apparent reflection of deteriorating conditions in the countryside. Nonetheless, the second wave expressed no less determination than its predecessor to enjoy the full fruits of freedom. Wyatt Moore wrote from Liberia, extolling its virtues to Lewis Sherman, initiator of the 1867 migration. "Talk about Freedom," he boasted; "When A man Comes to This Country he is Free sure enough." "The White man has not part nor lot in this Land," Moore explained. "[I]t is the Black man Land   We have our negro President negro vice President negro Cogressmen and Every Thing belongs to negroes and that is one thing That excites my Curiosity   to behold A negro nationality." At a time when freedpeople held neither land nor full citizenship rights, such sentiments resonated powerfully through the towns and rural areas of central Georgia.[94]

The "negro nationality" Moore beheld in Liberia fit squarely within deep-rooted traditions of both black nationalism and American republicanism.[95] In the fall of 1867, for instance, James M. C. Logan, one of three signers of the original inquiry to the ACS, explained the political basis of the emigrationist spirit: "Our people declare they will not remain here in a disfranchised condition, in other words they will go out of the country unless even-handed justice is extended to them." Logan likened disfranchisement to a fate worse than slavery; it was better to "fight it out . . . till the battle's lost or gained." If the time should come when no hope remained, former slaves would move to Liberia, for they "had better be dead than to remain in the South with no rights which white men were bound to respect."[96]

The case histories of two prominent leaders in the African emigration movement add perspective to the freedpeople's political development. Moses Pollock, who chose not to move to Liberia even after having served as first president of the emigration association, was a watchmaker who apparently operated his own shop. For entrepreneurs like him, emancipation held forth hope of a bright future that migration might put into jeopardy. Yet unlike the carriagemaker Banks, the watchmaker Pollock was not so dependent upon white patronage that he could not chart an independent political course, struggling openly for equal rights and identifying himself conspicuously with northern Republicans, even if ultimately rejecting migration to Africa.

Lewis Sherman, on the other hand, reported "prime-mover" of the April 1867 emigration, was a painter whose brother had apparently migrated to Liberia before the Civil War. For men like him, the pervasive cloud of racial discrimination blocked off all hope for improvement in the United States. "I Still Beleave Liberia to Be the Home the only Home for the Black man," he wrote from Africa. "[I]t is His own Country he is Second to None Hear I find more Happiness Among them Hear than I Have Seen in the States." But within a year Sherman returned, bearing lurid tales of suffering and hairbreadth scrapes with death. Moving from nationalism to full-blown political conservatism, he affiliated with the Democrats and began roundly denouncing the Radicals.[97]

The experiences of Pollock and Sherman illustrate the subtle relationship between black republicanism and black nationalism in the postbellum South. Both tendencies had strong roots in the antebellum past, but emancipation made possible for the first time an open debate over the relevance of the respective traditions of struggle. These discussions indicated that, while republicanism and nationalism shared many of the same formal goals, they envisioned profoundly different paths to those ends. Ultimately, the key question dividing black nationalists from black republicans was whether or not the American polity could extend full equality to persons of African descent. Depending on how they answered that question, individuals and groups chose either to depart or to struggle for change in the United States.

Over the next decade and a half, migrationist sentiment waxed and waned. The promises of Radical Reconstruction drove it underground from 1868 to the mid-1870s, but with the end of Reconstruction, republicanism retreated and nationalism surged periodically for the rest of the nineteenth century. Postreconstruction emigrationism, however, showed little influence of the skilled freedmen's earlier impatience with the slow pace of progress. As the craftsmen found a social niche, emigration appealed largely to poor, unskilled, and increasingly disfranchised plantation laborers who saw scant hope of improving their lot in Georgia.[98]

It was not for frivolous reasons that southern freedmen cast their fate with northern Radicals during Presidential Reconstruction. The old-line Whigs had proven themselves something other than best friends. Professions by their leading men (such as Benjamin H. Hill and E. G. Cabaniss) on behalf of "equal and absolute civil rights and protection under the law" did not accord with reality. And "we never felt," explained Hill, "that the negro was in a condition, either for his own good or for that of the country to be clothed with equal political rights in the shape of suffrage, and the right to hold office."[99] In the circumstances, Georgia freedpeople had no difficulty discerning a more friendly alliance with the Radical Republicans, who—whatever their ultimate motive—offered to grant voting rights. A political controversy in Twiggs County on the eve of Radical Reconstruction illustrates the connection between parochial developments and larger national issues and suggests how freedpeople in the deepest depths of the rural South came to view federal authorities as the guarantors of a democratic polity.

Late in 1866, county officials decided to relocate the seat of government from Marion, in the plantation region where most freedpeople lived, to Jeffersonville, in an area dominated by white smallholders. Before the Civil War, planters throughout the South had routinely resisted such moves, but the prospect of inconveniencing the soon-to-be-enfranchised freedmen overcame all earlier objections against inconveniencing themselves. The proposal clearly reflected a concerted attempt on the part of the planters to strike an alliance with the yeomen on an issue that the yeomen and the freedmen viewed from diametrically different perspectives. In a January 1867 referendum on the question, planters joined yeomen in overwhelming approval of the move. Freedmen urged bureau agent Henry M. Loyless to challenge the vote on the grounds that they had no voice in the outcome. Loyless ordered the county seat to stay in Marion. The following summer the state legislature approved the relocation, whereupon Gen. John Pope, commander of the newly formed Third Military Reconstruction District, which embraced Georgia, sustained Loyless's ruling. This outcome strongly encouraged freedpeople's faith in the federal government as an agency of social change. And for a time it would appear that their hope was well placed.[100]

IN TAKING SUCH an important part in the creation of the new body politic, freedpeople in central Georgia left a number of legacies whose importance extended far beyond the purely local level. From their own standpoint, they staked out a program to enjoy the full fruits of citizenship and then mobilized their collective energy to achieve it. In the process, they built and maintained an infrastructure of institutions, rooted in the slave past but designed to meet the challenges of freedom. Moreover, they devised means to cultivate leaders from among their own ranks to carry the struggle forward when Congress inaugurated Radical Reconstruction.

8
· · · · · · · · ·

The Rise and Decline
of Radical Republicanism,
1867–1872

RADICAL RECONSTRUCTION inaugurated what W. E. B. Du Bois described as an experiment in democracy of world-historical proportions. The Reconstruction Acts of 1867 established military rule in the former Confederate states and required the formation of new governments (based on the principle of universal manhood suffrage) and passage of the Fourteenth Amendment as preconditions for readmission to the Union. The political history of Radical Reconstruction in the South turned around the unprecedented participation of African American men in public affairs.[1]

To be sure, there were emancipations of slaves and serfs that removed the shackles from millions of bound laborers. Perhaps the most dramatic, Czar Alexander II's Edict of Emancipation (1861), freed an estimated 22 million serfs; but while it provided for a distribution of land, it left both the structure and the practice of aristocratic rule untouched. On much less sweeping, but nonetheless impressive, a scale, Brazilian abolition affected more than 2 million slaves, who received neither land nor political rights by proclamation, though they often gained both as clients of aristocratic landowners. In no other American society (except Haiti and, in vastly different circumstances, Martinique and Guadaloupe) did emancipated slaves gain a fraction of the influence over the state apparatus achieved by freedmen in the southern United States.[2]

Still, in no southern state—Georgia perhaps least of all—did freedmen exercise political domination through the electoral process. Even in South Carolina, where the party of Lincoln remained in power until 1876, where persons of African descent formed a majority of the population, and where former slaves and former free men of color held a comparatively large number and wide range of state-level offices, at no time did they effectively control the machinery of state.[3] Thus, perhaps ironically, the relatively quick collapse of Republican rule in Georgia created conditions remarkably like those prevailing in areas undergoing emancipation outside the United States: landed elites controlled local government, with little, if any, independent input by the former slaves. This lesson is instructive for two reasons. First, it did not take the other southern states long to fall into the same situation—nowhere did the Republicans stay in power for as long as a decade. Second, during modern times (again, with the exception of Haiti), no agricultural laboring class (whether slaves, serfs, or peasants) succeeded in winning control over a state until the twentieth century. Even then, few could go it alone; they struggled as parts of coalitions with other working or bourgeois classes.

The Republican party stood as the premier ally. Freedmen took comfort in the growing influence of Radicals over Reconstruction. If at first freedpeople miscalculated the role of northern finance capitalists, who anchored the party's Moderate wing, the Moderates' commitment to creating governments friendly to industrial development orchestrated by a strong central state soon became clear.[4] The question remained, however, whether viable coalitions of former slaves, northern immigrants, southern unionists, and antebellum free black persons could be forged to create such governments.

Over most of the South, the Republicans faced a determined, sophisticated opposition, which, though not without internal divisions of its own, was united behind a program of social hierarchy whose central tenet was the unfitness of freedmen to exercise the franchise. The planters and merchants who articulated this viewpoint accused congressional Radicals of forcing unrepresentative government upon the traditional electorate. At the same time, they laid out a case explaining why freedmen were unqualified. The foundation of the argument was the innate inferiority of persons of African descent. Emancipation might well do away with slavery, but no mere edict could make freedmen fit to vote. Over time, they found an increasingly receptive audience in the North, among Moderate Republicans as well as Democrats.

If so much of Georgia's story replicated that of its neighboring states, within months of the start of Radical Reconstruction, Georgia departed from the pack. Before the Republican government had been in office three months, both houses of the legislature expelled their black members. For that action, Congress imposed another round of military occupation and supervised Reconstruction during 1870 and 1871; no sooner had that ended than Democrats gained control of the legislature and Republican governor Rufus B. Bullock fled the state rather than face certain impeachment and civil prosecution on corruption charges. Following hastily called elections, Democrat James M. Smith assumed the governor's office in January 1872, thereby ending the brief but tumultuous Republican reign.

UNDER THE protective canopy of military rule, Republican parties sprang up throughout the South. In Georgia, the men who pioneered the effort were in some ways like, but in other ways unlike, their counterparts elsewhere. Among the white men who assumed leadership of the party, there was only one bona fide carpetbagger, John Emory Bryant from Maine, the veteran of both the Union army and the Freedmen's Bureau who had headed the Georgia Equal Rights Association since early 1866. The rest of the key leaders consisted of a group of native northerners who before the Civil War had settled in the Augusta area, where they entered business or the law and dabbled in politics: Rufus B. Bullock, Foster Blodgett, Amos T. Ackerman, and Benjamin F. Conley.[5] They quickly became known as the Augusta Ring, and they enjoyed disproportionate influence over the party throughout Radical Reconstruction. Although Bryant would qualify as a Radical, the other men were Moderate Republicans of Whiggish antecedents. Committed to Congressional Reconstruction, they nonetheless steered well clear of any program of land confiscation; they also opposed any wholesale attempt to disfranchise former Confederates lest such action promote eternal enmity rather than rapid reconciliation.

The Republicans attracted only a handful of white men in central Georgia. Conspicuous at first were the Yankees associated with the Freedmen's Bureau; though they actively encouraged the political mobilization of the freedpeople, most returned North at the end of 1868.[6] In Macon, a few immigrants and aristocrats also affiliated. The most prominent convert to Republicanism in the region was Joel R. Griffin, a Civil War hero descended from an old-line Virginia family. An uncompromising Radical, Griffin opened a law office on his plantation to assist the freedpeople of Houston County; he held a number of minor local offices and even a seat in the state legislature. He endured constant ostracism and numerous threats upon his life.[7]

No native Republican, either in central Georgia or anywhere else in the state, cast a longer shadow than former governor Joseph E. Brown. Hardly a Radical— indeed, at first scarcely even a fellow traveler—Brown saw Congressional Reconstruction as the chance for Georgia and the South to make economic progress. The old guard of Whiggish planter-attorneys and merchants who predominated during Presidential Reconstruction would have to yield power to business and commercial interests with a more pronounced capitalist orientation. Brown saw his traditional constituency, the yeomen of the upper Piedmont, as a vital component of the Republican coalition and one ripe for plucking away from the Democratic-Conservatives. Like other party kingpins, he took for granted that freedmen would cast Republican ballots.

Out of this melange of interests emerged a program pitched all at once toward pleasing congressional Radicals, securing the loyalty of the freedmen, and attracting Georgia's yeomen and capitalists. Not all aspects meshed neatly. Although few freedmen or Yankees would have disputed the tenets upholding civil and political rights and expanded government services (especially in the form of state-supported education), the yeomen did not feel as strongly about those issues as they did about debt relief and a homestead exemption limiting what could be seized for debt. From the time he began flirting with the state's Republican leadership, Brown demonstrated the uncanny ability to make different—at times even conflicting—promises to the different constituencies of the party without being called to task.

When Congress passed the Reconstruction Acts, establishing military rule and enfranchising the freedmen, differences quickly surfaced among Democratic-Conservatives regarding an appropriate strategy of opposition. The minority faction, led by Governor Charles J. Jenkins, appealed to the U.S. Supreme Court to nullify the acts. Failing that, its members refused all cooperation with the military regime on the grounds that the actions of Congress were unconstitutional and that the proposed new state government was illegitimate. "We are upon the verge of a consolidated centralized despotic empire," Alexander Stephens lamented. "We are fast abandoning the Teutonic systems on which our institutions were based and are lapsing fast into the Asiatic system of empire." "[T]he two races cannot coexist in their proportions in this country on this basis," he concluded. Howell Cobb feared that the Yankees intended "to make our former slaves *our masters*."[8] Disfranchised Conservatives found it especially objectionable that former slaves would vote while they were disqualified. And they appealed to other social classes—yeoman farmers, small planters, and urban merchants, artisans, and laborers—to resist the measures imposed by Congress.[9]

The majority faction, whose preeminent spokesman was another old-line Whig, Benjamin H. Hill, shared the minority's view that Reconstruction was unconstitutional. But rather than principled noncooperation, these men preferred mobilizing opposition against every specific Reconstruction measure.[10] In time, they concluded to cooperate with the letter of the law, but not its spirit. E. G. Cabaniss, another Whiggish planter-attorney who served as state Democratic chairman, perfected this technique and urged it upon the party faithful.[11]

Residual Whiggish influence appeared prominently in another favored tactic of the cooperationists: presenting themselves as the "best friends" of the freedpeople in an effort to undermine the Republican coalition.[12] A meeting in Jones County during the summer of 1867 offers insight into the dynamic. Col. Isaac Hardeman, one of the most prominent planters in the county, addressed the gathering, thanking the freedmen for "the kind feelings" they had expressed toward the former masters. Taking a legal tack, he warned: "If the party in power at present had any right to violate one principle of the Constitution, the party in power to come would have the same right to remand them back to slavery." Taking a religious tack, he proposed that the Bible's "corner-stone love" and its "superstructure peace and good will towards all men" be their guide toward eliminating "strife and hatred and bayonets." In short, he suggested that planter-paternalists knew what was best for the freedpeople.[13]

Within this majority was a group of businessmen from Macon and other railroad towns who yearned for the return of order and did not relish the prospect of a long, drawn-out dispute with federal authorities. Instead, they wanted to get down to business, including business with the freedpeople, transformed by emancipation into a vast untapped population of direct consumers. Some of these commercial visionaries followed Joe Brown into the Republican fold.[14]

One last element completed the Democratic-Conservative roster. It consisted of both established and up-and-coming planters from before the war, especially from the party's antebellum strongholds south and east of Macon, who viewed straightforward oppression of former slaves as the key to economic revitalization. States' rights advocates to the core, they detested Reconstruction; if they could not convince Congress to abandon the scheme, they would undercut it by terrorizing the freedpeople into inactivity. These are the men who took part in Ku Klux Klan attacks specifically and who proffered the most violent opposition against federal authority generally.

The freedpeople of central Georgia approached this assortment of Democratic-Conservatives gingerly, often with conflicting signals emanating from head and heart. Indeed, one of the banners displayed at a mass meeting of freedmen gathered in Macon to celebrate the new era proclaimed, "If we must Live and Vote in the same State, let us be friends." Former slaves of this mind pledged to act "meritoriously," serve their employers faithfully, and improve themselves through education.[15] In return, they expected cooperation with Washington.

Untroubled for the time being by what the opponents of Reconstruction might attempt, General Pope set about registering the new electorate defined by Congress. He divided Georgia's 136 counties into forty-four districts, each presided over by a board of three registrars, one of whom was to be black. Pope looked to white unionists and black leaders for prospective registrars and fielded recommendations from both interested parties themselves and their sponsors. The nomination by Samuel A. Cobb, a black Republican leader from Houston County, of Drury M. Cox, a white hotel keeper who before the war had owned no land but several slaves, suggests the revolutionary dimensions of this new political order. Noting his long acquaintance with Cox, Cobb certified him "in every respect a union man" who had "opposed secession with all his might." On behalf of "many of my Coloured friends," Cobb predicted that Cox "will see we Coloured people altogether justified and righted in all our dealings with the white man." In the topsy-turvy postemancipation world, former slaves testified to the character of former masters![16]

If a successful registration of voters required trustworthy registrars, it depended upon sound organization even more. For various reasons, General Pope could not lead in that effort, however much he might assist it. White and black Republicans would have to undertake the work themselves. Thanks to the mass mobilization of freedmen during Presidential Reconstruction, there was no shortage of volunteers. Crucial in this regard was the Georgia Education Association, which, despite its shift of emphasis away from political agitation during the fall of 1866, still championed more than the single-issue program that its name implied. In May 1867, the association's third statewide gathering adjourned into a Republican convention that resolved to press for equal political rights, safeguards for labor, protection of persons and property, nondiscriminatory jury selection, and free churches and schools. It also laid plans to form local party organizations throughout the state. Over the next several months such groups developed, many out of preexisting Loyal League and GEA chapters.[17]

During the voter registration campaign of mid-1867, the clubs met frequently to strengthen collective resolve. Both leaders and members alike enforced standards of acceptable political conduct, encouraged the weak-hearted to persevere in the face of adversity, and bitterly censured—even ostracized—those who broke ranks. Planters spread fear by circulating rumors of bizarre fates, such as sale to Cuba, awaiting black registrants and by threatening freedmen with discharge or heavy fines for leaving work to register.[18]

Civil authorities routinely harassed the meetings. In Houston County, Thomas W. Brock, the constable of Fort Valley, took special pains to monitor the freedmen's political activity.[19] In November 1867, he and his henchmen broke up a meeting at which a group of black Republicans had begun "ridiculing others about not voting and threatened to hurt them." When one of the arrested leaders threatened Brock, a deputy shot the man dead and then fled. Freedpeople scraped together a reward, but civil authorities displayed no interest. Although military authorities pursued the man, white residents of the county refused to cooperate. Hence the killer never saw justice.[20]

The struggle against such arbitrary violence provided background to the drama of Reconstruction, even as other struggles occupied the foreground. Black and white Republicans offered strategic leadership, which was subject to the scrutiny of not just black voters, but the entire population of former slaves. Mass meetings, though hardly the monopoly of Republicans, proved an especially effective vehicle for mobilizing mass support. Towns such as Macon, with good rail connections and a large black population, hosted innumerable gatherings of this kind. At one such meeting in Macon late in August 1867, an estimated 6,000 to 8,000 freedpeople attended, the equivalent of every black person then living in the city.[21]

As earlier, women and children attended as well as men. The festivities began with picnics, followed by parades of bands, fraternal organizations, and political clubs, and ended with speeches. Besides building solidarity, the meetings provided occasions for rank-and-file voters and party leaders to exchange ideas. At the August meeting just referred to, for instance, the head of the state's Union League, Henry P. Farrow, spoke of matters to be addressed at the upcoming state constitutional convention. Unlike the Democratic opponents of Reconstruction, he advocated a constitution based upon equal civil and political rights for all citizens. Because "[t]he majority of the people were but day laborers," he opposed taxes on the necessities of life and poll taxes. He favored instead taxes on property, especially luxuries. Taking up the gauntlet thrown down by Benjamin Hill, Farrow accused "the aristocrats of the South" of favoring franchise restriction "among the poor whites" as well as the freedmen. The auditors also heard the more moderate views of Henry M. Turner. Addressing his remarks to former masters as well as former slaves, Turner strongly opposed confiscation of private property but offered to "take the hand of all white men who will give us our rights." Without equal rights, he argued, "our freedom amounts to nothing."[22]

At other political meetings during this time, black speakers echoed similar themes. In Jones County, for instance, Lewis H. Smith and Henry Fyall proposed that "Southern men—white men" represent the interests of the freedpeople.[23] Moderation and cooperation also rang out from a meeting of freedpeople in Upson County, situated immediately west of Crawford and Monroe counties. The featured speaker, Aleck H. Gaston, a barber in Macon, "advised the colored people to cultivate friendship with their white neighbors and live in harmony with their former masters, as their interests were mutual and the same." He recommended against running "any of their own color for office yet, as they were not at present competent," preferring that they place their trust in "some good Southern white man" who supported "equal political and civil rights."[24]

The resolutions of the meeting largely reflected this tone, advocating harmony and opposing "disfranchisement, confiscation or other punitive measures for alleged disloyalty." They affirmed the right of "all men born in the United States" to vote and "hold offices in the Government," but they opposed debtor relief, the Republican party's major initiative to the yeomen of the upper Piedmont. Declaring themselves "in favor of honest and prompt compliance with lawful contracts," they denounced "the doctrine taught by some" that "the present situation of our people" made it acceptable "to repudiate their just indebtedness." "Any doctrine which teaches us that we may, under any conceivable circumstances, with propriety refuse to pay a just debt" not only contravenes "God's word," they reasoned, but ran the risk of "demoralizing the people, destroying their material interests, and disgracing them before the world."[25]

Finally, in one of the most startling declarations of the period, this assembly of freedmen laid out a radically bourgeois vision of the suffrage, which contradicted prevailing practice among both former masters and former slaves. Declaring it "inconsistent with the character of freemen to be bound by obligations which may constrain their consciences," they pronounced themselves "opposed to all leagues and associations whose aim is directed at the securing of votes rather than the securing of liberty." Few freedmen had the luxury of such a purist view of the ballot.[26] Loyal Leagues and Republican Clubs were their only hope of voting as they wished.

Yet concerted action among former slaves alone was not enough, as the proceedings of the state constitutional convention that met from December 1867 to March 1868 clearly demonstrated. By virtue of the Democrats' boycott of the election for delegates, only 46 staunch representatives of their party numbered among the 169 men chosen. But by the same token, only 37 black men were elected (barely one-fifth of the total), even though freedmen constituted nearly half of the electorate.[27] The proportion of black delegates in the Georgia convention contrasts sharply with that of the neighboring states of South Carolina (where they made up nearly three-fifths of the delegates) and Florida (two-fifths).[28] This outcome suggests a strong feeling among the freedmen that responsible white men could represent their interests. Voters in central Georgia elected three black men to the convention: Henry M. Turner from Macon and Samuel A. Cobb and Isaac H. Anderson from Houston County.

Despite the evident influence of such men as Turner and Aaron A. Bradley, both of whom, though born in the South, had lived in the North before the Civil War, ex-slave delegates of narrower experience did not follow them blindly.[29] Turner's conciliatory tone toward antebellum aristocrats played especially poorly.[30] He opposed the debtor relief and homestead exemption measures that formed the core of Republican appeals to upcountry yeomen.[31] That stand typified his belief that the "best element" of antebellum society represented the freedpeople's most desirable allies. And he saw no need to specify the freedmen's right to hold public office, a stance he soon regretted. Most of his black fellow delegates—and most freedpeople—disagreed. They viewed the convention as an opportunity to create a new social and political order, not to resuscitate the old one.

Consistent with the wishes of Radical leaders in Washington, Republican delegates to the Georgia convention aimed to remove the vestiges of the old order that hampered the development of a liberal capitalist social order. Accordingly, they applauded the demise of slavery, abolished imprisonment for debt, and eased antebellum restrictions on incorporation. To woo yeomen to Republican ranks, they provided a generous homestead exemption, which safeguarded up to $2,000 in real estate and $1,000 in personal property against seizure for debt, and endorsed the existing stay law. They took a much more casual approach to cementing the loyalty of black voters.[32]

The shortsightedness of this approach proved immediately apparent. First, the proposed system of public schools was to be financed by a $1 poll tax, notwithstanding the warnings from innumerable observers that such taxes would weigh heavily upon poor freedpeople. Second, and more seriously, the constitution failed to guarantee the freedmen's right to elective office. Amidst debate over the issue on the convention floor, Joseph Brown—who attended the proceedings, though not as an elected delegate—lobbied Moderate Republicans to accept the Democratic approach of following the letter of congressional guidelines, which were silent on the subject. Although some prescient delegates predicted the difficulties that would follow upon such a course, most—including

Election day (Library of Congress)

all but three of the black ones—considered clauses expressly to that effect unnecessary.[33]

Most Georgia freedpeople simply refused to believe that the new constitution would allow them to vote but not to sit on juries or hold elective office. Accordingly, they were stunned as events unfolded. In Crawford County, black Republicans adjourned a meeting when told by their white allies that they could not hold office. And at a mass gathering in Macon, John T. Costin, a freeborn man originally from Washington, D.C., cited the need for black justices of the peace without for a moment considering that the prerogative of elective office would be denied.[34] Yet before long the omission of the office-holding guarantee would paralyze the government and eventually entail a third Reconstruction of the state in 1870.

Among its other accomplishments, the convention also gave new life to "land fever." Early in 1868, with the convention still in session, reports from throughout Georgia indicated that freedmen were refusing to make contracts in the hope that "as soon as the new law came, they would soon own the land themselves." Black political leaders operated under strict instructions from their constituents to learn the status of land redistribution plans. "[T]he negroes believed," according to one commentator, "that by voting they were going to get a division of the land and stock of the country." Landowning promised the independence that emancipation ideally conferred, and politics offered a means to achieve that end. Georgia freedpeople, like their counterparts throughout the South, drew sustenance in the struggle for economic and political rights from the republican tradition of small-propertied independence.[35]

Not all freedmen interpreted the struggle, or the tactics for pursuing it, the same. A small but highly visible number allied with the Democrats instead of the Republicans. Most of these men had been personal servants before the war and retained their privileged status after the war, as landowners or tenants, for instance. A few enjoyed regional exposure. Joseph Williams, for example, toured his home state of Tennessee and Georgia on behalf of the Democracy and made several appearances in the Macon area. Because "[y]ou are dependent upon the Southern whites for your bread and meat," he counseled the freedpeople in a typical refrain, "your best friends [are] your employers." He perceived a "mutual dependence" in this relationship—"they have the land and need your labor"— that could work to the advantage of the freedpeople. Bucking that reality would only lead to "a war of the races, which must result in the extermination of your race."[36]

Of the homegrown black Conservatives, disproportionate numbers hailed from Twiggs County. John Dupree described himself as a former "servant boy" of a prominent planter. Cornelius Shelton was even more obsequious: "These good Southern white people I love, and I love to serve them." "I want good white people to be my leaders," he affirmed, "and I propose to make myself a good citizen in their midst. By thus doing, I know I shall have money and every comfort necessary to make me happy."[37] Dupree lambasted Republicans for betraying their promises, especially regarding land.[38] He advised freedmen "to trust matters of State importance" to their southern "white friends."[39] Dupree formed a Colored Conservative Club, which for a time met weekly in the courthouse of Wilkinson County, which lies immediately east of Twiggs. He also appeared at Democratic meetings in Jones and Twiggs counties.[40]

Another black Conservative from Twiggs, Henry Armstead, blended appeals from both the republican and the black nationalist traditions. He advised the freedpeople that "[t]hese dark and gloomy days will pass over us if we only adhere to the principles of that great instrument formed by our fathers' protectors, which gives us liberty and preserves our rights." Central Georgia freedmen appreciated his invocation of the Constitution but deprecated his advice that "[i]n sickness or in health, in joy or in sorrow, we fly to our old masters for aid."[41] Former masters did, in fact, provide aid and comfort. When a man named Butler formed a Conservative Club in Macon, white Democrats threatened Jefferson F. Long, a prominent black tailor and kingpin of the Republican party in Macon, with retaliation for any violence directed at the members. Yet black Conservatives did not always follow their own prescriptions. Houston County's William C. Smith fled to General Pope for protection from freedmen who had threatened to shoot him "off the stand" unless he expressed acceptable views. "Knowing under your orders that I was entitled to the freedom of speech," Smith argued, this treatment was "a great outrage."[42]

Despite superficial similarities, Conservative and Republican freedmen differed fundamentally over the relationship between the black citizenry and the government. The former opted for the continued mediation of the former masters, whereas the latter wanted a direct, unmediated relationship. Voters beholden to former masters were not truly free, and governments built upon such an electorate were not truly representative. In one sense, the Conservatives represented a variation on the theme of absolute freedom of political conscience expressed by the Upson County freedmen, but one wherein bourgeois rights reinforced paternalist practices. By late 1868, as it became clear that the freedmen wanted nothing of warmed-over paternalism, the black Conservatives disappeared from the political scene.

For the freedmen of central Georgia and their counterparts throughout the South, the Republican party was a major weapon in the struggle to complete the social revolution initiated by emancipation. A black Republican from Houston County, Cupid H. Cupid, made this clear in justifying the harassment of Conservative speaker William C. Smith. Cupid portrayed Smith's actions as "the first attempt by negroes (hirelings) to warp our minds from our true interests." Denying Smith's claim of free speech, Cupid asked General Pope to arrest him for disturbing the peace. "Our Color is largely in the ascendency here," Cupid claimed, and freedmen enjoyed a precarious electoral margin. Disavowing any desire for trouble "with our white neighbors many of whom are on the very best terms with us and who we have the highest respect for," Cupid nonetheless sought federal protection: "Give us then but the rights of Citizens Sir we want no more, we dont want the rights of the whites to drag in the dust, but they to stand where they are and we pull up to them and be their equals before the law."[43] Like him, other black Republicans championed equality rather than dependency. "He was no nigger now," announced George H. Clower, the leading black Republican in Monroe County. "He was a citizen and was going to have all the rights of the white man, and would take no less."[44]

With the new constitution in hand, Republican organizers began stumping for ratification. Predictably, they faced stern opposition from the Democrats, who claimed the document would "establish the supremacy" of "ignorant negroes from the cornfields."[45] A Republican mass meeting held in Macon at the end of

March 1868 illustrates the character of similar assemblies throughout the state. The affair began with a procession that included bands and representatives of fraternal and benevolent societies carrying their respective banners. One of the wagons in the parade reportedly carried a gallows with the effigy of a black victim inscribed, "Every Man Don't Vote a Radical Ticket this the Way we Want DO Him. Hang Him by Neck."—a stark departure from the sentiment of the previous spring.

Approximately 1,000 persons, including many women and children, attended, and a festive atmosphere prevailed, with venders selling fruits and sweetcakes moving through the crowd. Speakers Jefferson Long and Aleck Gaston reportedly threatened violence to renegades. George Wallace, a minister from Milledgeville and recent delegate to the constitutional convention, asserted that if freedmen held to their Republican principles, white voters "would wheel into line with them." Theophilus G. Steward, the New Jersey–born pastor of the AME church in Macon, spoke on the significance of the constitutional provisions concerning equal rights and debtor relief. Robert Carter, a wheelwright and one of the first black Presbyterian ministers ordained in Georgia, reportedly "came out flat-footed on the Radical platform" and warned against the machinations of black Conservatives.[46]

The editors of the *Macon Telegraph* roundly criticized the proceedings. While denouncing the gallows scene, they also harped upon the complexion of the black speakers, suggesting that light-skinned political leaders—specifically Long, Gaston, and Wallace—were manipulating the darker-skinned freedmen, aiming to sell votes "to the highest bidder" for their own selfish purposes. But the editors tactlessly headlined the discussion "Look Here, You Black Scoundrels!," thus compromising their intended objective.[47] At the same time, they clearly demonstrated the strategy that seemed most appropriate to the rising business elite's immediate political circumstances.

Recognizing that the freedpeople would hold their meetings with or without authorization, the city fathers accommodated in hopes of exerting a moderating influence. It was not unheard of for Mayor George S. Obear to attend the gatherings, even to make brief remarks. The elite also sponsored mass meetings, at times hosting black speakers. At one, resolutions conceded the abolition of slavery and expressed the desire "to return to the Union of our Fathers, and obey its laws and enjoy the protection of the Federal Constitution." Pledging to guarantee "the rights of person, property, character and opinion," they proclaimed the freedmen "entitled to vote . . . according to their own best judgment, uncontrolled by bribery, threats or coercion." Robert Carter spoke, no doubt with advance understanding that he would favor "peace and harmony"; but when he objected to the use of the term "freedmen" instead of "colored citizens" in the official resolutions of the meeting, the body obligingly made the change.[48] As Henry M. Turner later testified, Macon boasted "the best moral sentiment . . . among all the citizens, anywhere in Georgia," largely because city officials were true to their pledge of fair elections. Accordingly, in April Republicans polled a majority in favor of the constitution.[49]

WHILE OLD-LINE Whig planters who predominated in Monroe County (and those lying to the east of Jones in middle Georgia) continued to believe that the freedmen would be susceptible to their paternal influence, the ultimate strategy of Democratic success emerged from Houston County, where old-line Democrats held sway. Even the most established planters there, including antebellum paternalists, despised the theory and practice of black suffrage. With a strong infusion of passion from the smaller planters as well as the firm backing of the planter-merchant elite of Perry and Fort Valley, the Democrats devised a strategy to overcome the freedmen's electoral majority.

The program began with firm unity of purpose. "[W]e had the utmost perfect unanimity, harmony and concert of action," one of its architects explained; "all past political differences of opinion were entirely forgotten." The next ingredient was time and energy, in short, "all the efforts in our power . . . to accomplish the end desired." Democrats were omnipresent at the polls, haranguing individual freedmen when they could not get a group hearing and denouncing the constitution and its Republican sponsors. They criticized the Radical relief and homestead measures as "humbug" of no benefit to the freedpeople. They upbraided the Republican candidates for local office, contrasting one—"a negro trader" who had "parted husband and wife, parents and children"—with their own "popular men, well known to the people and beloved by the colored people." The Democratic slate included two black grocers, Jefferson Swift and Solomon Jackson, running respectively for tax collector and tax receiver.[50]

Collectively, the Democrats strove "to undeceive the negroes—to show them that we are not their enemy because we deemed them unfit to manage the affairs of government." In sum, the old-line Democratic planters and their allies pledged themselves to secure "good government," that is, "constitutional government, carried on and administered by wisdom, intelligence and virtue—not by ignorance and vice. And hence we say this should be a white man's government, doing at the same time full justice to the colored men."[51]

In time, these New South Democratic planters would gain the adherence of both old-line Whig paternalists and urban commercial interests behind their program, but for the time being, the strategy simply piqued the curiosity of such groups.[52] The freedpeople, however, took a different view of the matter, and as Republican leaders within Houston County prepared for battle, reinforcements also arrived from Macon and beyond. At a political meeting at the county seat early in August, white Republicans warned of a possible return to slavery if Democrats carried the fall elections. Aleck Gaston declared that the time was near to draw blood.[53] Tensions between black Republicans and white Democrats remained high through the November election and beyond.

Houston County's Democrats prevailed in April 1868 even though the Republicans carried the state. The Houston Democrats would not have succeeded had they followed the advice of state party leaders and boycotted the election. That strategy aimed to defeat the constitution by assuring its failure to win approval by a majority of registered voters. Seeing through the ruse, Congress approved the new constitution on the basis of a majority of votes cast, and the Republican government took office in July. The new legislature included three black senators (out of forty-four) and 29 black representatives (out of 172). Only two black men from central Georgia—Henry M. Turner from Bibb County and George H. Clower, a schoolteacher and political activist from Monroe County—won legislative seats.[54]

The victorious Republicans had good reason not to rest on their laurels. For one thing, their strategy of appealing to the yeomen had mixed results, apparently succeeding best among the debt-ridden smallholders of northern (or Cherokee) Georgia but failing miserably among denizens of the central black belt and of the wire-grass region in the southern part of the state. Moreover, even in Cherokee Georgia the platforms of debtor relief and homestead exemptions did not purchase the yeomen's permanent allegiance to the party, even when coupled with strong assurances from Joseph Brown that the freedmen would not hold elected offices. Most unsettling of all, the party could not long avoid the contradiction of simultaneously preaching a white man's government to the yeomen and equal rights to the freedmen.[55]

Within weeks the contradiction became the preoccupation of the new legislature. Under the sponsorship of Democratic members in both the senate and the house, resolutions were introduced to examine the credentials of members with an eye toward categorically excluding all persons who fit the legal definition of Negro as specified by the 1866 black code. Moderate Republicans, who held majorities in the legislature as well as the party's leadership, sat on their hands lest they be suspected of trying to Africanize the government. At bottom, the native southern Moderates—from both old-line Whig and commercial Democratic backgrounds—did not disagree with the proposition that black men had no right to hold office. As Radical Republicans abandoned the party's professed ideals in favor of practical politics, the outcome appeared more and more certain. In September, the legislators voted to expel all but four of the colored senators and representatives; the four were so light complected that they appeared not to qualify as Negro before the law.[56] The shock of expulsion transformed black politics.

None reflected that transformation more clearly than Henry M. Turner. Infuriated at the betrayal by the freedmen's nominal friends, Turner admitted the bankruptcy of allying with the antebellum ruling elite but held Republican Moderates in no higher regard. He called a convention out of which emerged the Georgia Civil and Political Rights Association, pledged to achieve full and uncompromised citizenship rights. Addressing Congress in words bearing Turner's heavy hand, the association announced the political reawakening of black Georgians. Expulsion from the state legislature, they claimed, resulted from nothing other than "the deep-rooted prejudice of caste, the inveterate hatred of our race." Former masters wanted to resurrect the old order, making the freedpeople "submit to law as enacted and enforced by those who, though they might love us as their property, as they love their sheep and oxen, hate us as freemen." Rather than share the reins of power, "[t]hey must be our legislators, our judges, our jurors, and, in spite of our constitution, in spite of all that a loyal Congress has done for us, they must be our masters."[57]

The Georgia Civil and Political Rights Association marked Turner's political coming of age. Frustrated in his efforts to cooperate with white aristocrats, he moved increasingly in a nationalist direction. Following the collapse of the Bullock regime late in 1871, the pace of this development quickened. He moved to Savannah, utterly frustrated with the prospect of effecting change through normal political channels. In 1876, he accepted a vice-presidency in the American Colonization Society, and from then till his death nearly four decades later, he was the leading black proponent of African emigration in the United States. Although Turner had chosen to keep arm's length from the migration fever of 1866 and 1867, he clearly took to heart the movement's demand for immediate and full citizenship rights, if not in Georgia, then in Liberia. Turner's own nationalism emerged more slowly, but when it did, it erupted with volcanic force that continued to surge for the rest of his life. The legislative expulsion brought those fires to the surface.[58]

Expulsion shook, but did not shatter, the Georgia Republican party. The members of Turner's Civil and Political Rights Association continued to consider themselves Republicans, more by virtue of their trust in congressional Radicals than to any sense of confidence in Georgia's Moderates. But until early 1870, when Congress imposed a third Reconstruction and ordered the reseating of the original 1868 legislature, their political future stood in limbo. Meanwhile, as Democrats worked tirelessly at overturning the Bullock regime, black Republicans rallied to his and their party's defense. The presidential election of November 1868 would prove a crucial test of the strategic alliance between freedmen and yeomen.

Early signs were not promising, in that party Moderates seemed to have learned nothing from the debacle of expulsion. Presuming that freedmen would vote Republican come hell or high water, Moderates clung to the strategy of special appeals to white voters. Under cover of the expulsion, Republican strategists could present a preponderance of white candidates, thereby appealing both to white office-seekers whose livelihoods might have suffered because of their politics and to white voters who refused to vote for a black man.[59]

Given those circumstances, it is no wonder that black Republicans wanted the party to accommodate them more. Even apart from the matter of expulsion, the fact remained that not a single black man had been nominated for (much less elected to) a state executive office or the national Congress, despite the overwhelming majority of black voters in the party. This record proved especially galling to freedmen in central Georgia, Macon especially, who from the end of the war had been active partisans of Reconstruction. Yet when they challenged party policy, they met obstinacy rather than understanding. Further partisanship and factionalism along color lines resulted, as the proceedings of a regional nominating convention in September 1868 showed.

Jefferson Long supported the nomination of Henry M. Turner for Congress. James Fitzpatrick, an Irishman from Macon who was Long's chief rival in the county Republican organization, also sought the nomination. At one level, the contest underscored the potential racial rift within the party. One white delegate argued that he and his fellows "wanted a white man nominated so that he could hold in the Radical party the few white men already in it," because "if a negro was put forward he would only receive the votes of that race and would be defeated." But other considerations, ranging from the larger strategic objectives of the state and national parties to the narrower interests of control over patronage and genuinely different estimates of the popular mood, also weighed into the decision. As battle lines were drawn, defectors appeared. When George Wallace, one of the expelled state senators, crossed over to support Fitzpatrick, Turner was vanquished. A Democratic observer reported such "confusion, hard feeling and violent denunciation among members" that Fitzpatrick's candidacy was "utterly hopeless."[60]

Despite their growing differences, Republicans of all colors recognized the paramount importance of winning the November election. As they awaited favorable action by the federal government to resolve the matter of the legislative expulsion, black leaders redoubled their organizing efforts. Henry M. Turner addressed a mass meeting at Macon City Hall for four hours, exploring the political difficulties facing Georgia freedpeople. As he saw it, the matter boiled down to "whether the negroes should be free men indeed or should be perpetual hewers of wood and drawers of water to the whites—without the opportunity of social or intellectual development and improvement." Turner's speech provoked a two-column response from the editors of the *Telegraph*, in which they advocated letting "public opinion," the "final and paramount law," settle all questions regarding the future of the freedmen.[61]

Both Democrats and Republicans waged a no-holds-barred contest that was especially vicious in the countryside. Statewide, strategists from both parties recognized the importance of plantation freedmen's votes. Having failed with the carrot, Democrats turned to the stick. Employers threatened to impose heavy fines or to discharge any laborer who voted Republican.[62] Most freedmen defied these threats, but the boldest planters responded as promised, at times evicting families whose menfolk were absent at elections or political meetings. Planters routinely declared "they had no use for radicals." The Crawford County Agricultural Society aimed to turn back the hands of time, pledging to hire only laborers who subscribed to the standards of "organic society," which categorically ruled out radicals. The Democratic Club of Wilkinson County resolved "that Democrats sustain & hire democratic Labour, and no other."[63]

Civil authorities supplemented the work of private employers, as did the Ku Klux Klan. Planters aiming to subordinate their laborers frequently masterminded such violence, but the revolutionary social implications of emancipation also help explain the involvement of whites of considerably lesser means. After the war, white wageworkers and tenants viewed freedmen eyeball to eyeball instead of down their noses as before. And, despite their open and often heated competition for laborers, small-scale employers shared with planters a common interest in exploiting the labor power of former slaves. As Henry M. Turner had learned in 1866, the "lower and more imbittered class of whites" took to discharging freedpeople during laying-by time, when it had become clear "that the crops were cut short by the drought, and fears entertained of being unable to pay the freedmen."[64] Small and large farmers alike resorted to the same tactic in subsequent summers to save the expense of wages during the time that crops no longer needed weeding. More politically focused Klan violence, especially that beginning in 1868, aimed to annihilate the rural leadership cadre and destroy the dense network of Republican political organizations popularly known as Grant Clubs. The overall objective was to guarantee a tractable source of cheap labor that had absolutely no interest in government affairs.[65]

In most rural counties, as in Macon itself, artisans, professionals, and other comparatively independent freedmen served disproportionately as both political leaders and targets of Klan attacks.[66] In Houston County, Isaac H. Anderson, who made his living as a carpenter and a Baptist minister in Fort Valley, assumed prominence among black Republicans, serving successively as voter registrar, delegate to the state constitutional convention, and state senator. Isaac L. Primus, another carpenter-minister, also taught at the freedmen's school, along-side George Ormond, who apparently supported himself solely as a teacher. Both men assisted Anderson and Samuel A. Cobb in organizing Grant Clubs. All these men operated in daily fear for their lives, and the clubs offered them a measure of protection. Aside from the security of arms, the clubs provided additional shelter. One served as something of a benevolent association, report-edly assessing monthly dues of twenty-five cents to defray inevitable legal ex-penses.[67] The clubs also reinforced family and community ties among the men who had been slaves on the same plantations or who worked for the same employer.

In the months leading up to the fall election, Houston County became a battleground. White residents of the county persuaded military authorities to take action against the Grant Clubs that had been parading about in military formation.[68] On several occasions, white persons interfered with authorized meetings, but matters came to a head in mid-July, when a Grant Club member inadvertently walked between two white women and the man escorting them on a sidewalk. Despite the freedman's apology, a scuffle ensued that resulted in his arrest. Club members secured his release after threatening to pull the jailhouse down. Frustrated at their inability to intimidate the club, the Democrats threat-ened the lives of Ormond, Cobb, Anderson, and Primus. In a tone of dignified rage, Ormond and Primus reported the incident to Freedmen's Bureau authori-ties. Claiming that club members had behaved peaceably at every meeting, they declared "we want nothing but Justice . . . we dont intend to trouble the white people if they let us alone."[69] But as the local bureau agent observed, the planters "think if they do not get him [Ormond] out of the way, their chances of electing their democratic ticket are small."[70]

In Jones and Monroe counties, black Republican leadership and organizational patterns followed those of Houston. Jones County freedmen organized a club under Jacob P. Hutchings, the stonemason responsible for building the county jailhouse in 1842. Similarly, black voters in Monroe County organized Grant Clubs under William Travis, one of the voter registrars in 1867, George H. Clower, one of the expelled members of the state legislature, and Jerry W. May, an artisan.[71]

In counties like Twiggs that lacked such a class of independent artisans and professionals, plantation freedmen seem to have raised political leaders from their own ranks to preside over distinctively paramilitary political clubs.[72] Of those from Twiggs County about which information is known, each apparently consisted of approximately fifty men.[73] The members of one reportedly "formed a Secret Band or company" and pledged themselves to kill any white person who struck a black person. In April 1868, after a white man named Burns hit a freedman with his cane, the members went on a shooting spree. When witnesses sounded an alarm, a crowd of irregularly armed freedmen assembled to the accompaniment of fife and drum. Although they attempted to have Burns arrested, the sheriff refused, instead ordering a posse to disperse the crowd. In the confusion Burns bolted, drawing fire from club members who shouted, "[K]ill [him]   he Struck one of our color   kill him   God Damn him." Burns escaped unharmed. An army investigator criticized the sheriff for not having arrested Burns, but military authorities took no action. Irate whites throughout the county vowed to exterminate the organization perpetrating such "riotous behaviour."[74]

They got their chance later in the summer. Toward the end of August, two black men working in a cornfield began a dispute that ended in one's death. When word spread, members of a Loyal League club pursued the killer, intending to punish him. Following an altercation between the leaguers and the man's former owner, sheriff's posses swept the county apprehending league members, most of whom surrendered peaceably. Two, however, attempted resistance; both were shot and killed. One, Berry Hill, reportedly led a sixty-man military company.[75]

Fearing for their lives, a delegation of freedmen visited Freedmen's Bureau subassistant commissioner N. Sellers Hill in Macon seeking protection. When he insisted that they had nothing to fear, they considered sending a representative to Atlanta to lay their case before the governor. The Macon *Journal &*

Messenger condemned these "secret, oath-bound political organizations," which "quickly learn to assume the functions of the State and its regular officers" such that "when any one of their members commits an excess, a collision . . . immediately follows." Although silent when Klansmen assumed such state functions, the newspaper recommended suppressing all such associations of freedmen. It also implicated black Republicans in Macon as the spirit behind the unrest in Twiggs County.

Authorities in Twiggs County wasted no time in Macon pursuing the conspiracy theory, opting instead to round up suspects at home. In October, the county superior court held its deliberations, convicting twenty-eight men and acquitting five. Two of the men found guilty were sentenced to six months in jail plus fines of $100 and costs, and the other twenty-six to lesser fines and jail terms. Democratic planters could hardly have found a more effective means of crippling black political organization. In the atmosphere of repression, Berry Hill's club disbanded, as did Alfred Flemming's.

The November election tested Republican convictions and political organizations to the limit. Freedmen voted with the least intimidation in Macon, yet even there, "the authorities allowed the negroes to be very much troubled by persons challenging their votes."[76] Everywhere else in central Georgia, black voters encountered intense opposition. Although most of the difficulty resulted from the determination of New South Democrats to win the election by whatever means necessary, Republicans created needless complications for themselves. The most costly one centered around the provision of the 1868 constitution requiring payment of the poll tax (a levy of $1 per annum to support public education) as a prerequisite to voting. Under an 1866 law, employers paid their employees' taxes, deducted the sum from wages due, and kept the tax receipt until accounts were settled at the end of the harvest. As a result, planters had a ready means to disfranchise their workers.

The poll tax patently demonstrated the intimate connection between economic and political independence. Only a few freedmen—artisans, proprietors, professionals, landowners, and prosperous tenants—had the wherewithal to pay their own tax. Victory in November 1868 would depend upon poor black laborers, most of whom were tax delinquents under the law. To solve the crisis (and further ingratiate the Republican party with the freedmen), Governor Bullock suspended tax collections until the legislature met again in 1869.[77]

Democrats either ignored the governor's order altogether or used the resulting confusion to defraud the Republicans of votes cast by freedmen. Events in Houston County illustrate the tactics employed. As election day dawned, prospects for a Republican victory looked excellent. The Grant Clubs, "which composed a large maj[ority] of the freedmen," according to a bureau agent, "were all well organized and the Presidents Generally marched their men up in line, handed them their tickets and made [them] stay in line until they had voted." But the Democratic election managers kept two ballot boxes, one for men who had paid their tax, the other for those who had not, and then refused to count the tickets in the latter, virtually all of which were Republican votes cast by plantation freedmen. "[I]f a fair count had been made and no delay and bother made and the freed people not deceived," the agent concluded, the results would have shown an overwhelming vote "for Grant & Colfax. But, as the ballot boxes were entirely in the hands of the opposite party every thing was at their disposal." He described the freedpeople as "hurt" by these proceedings, but the apparent indifference of Republican officials to the "outrageous frauds perpetrated upon the Colored people" hurt even more.[78]

The scene was much the same elsewhere, as election managers employed a host of schemes to deny freedmen a voice in the outcome. In Monroe County, Jerry May's Republican Club assembled at the polling place in Forsyth with Grant badges prominently displayed. Hostile Democrats demanded that they remove the badges and disperse. May tried unsuccessfully to vote and then attempted to go to Macon, but roughnecks seized and held him until after the train had left.[79] At Clinton, Jones County, Democrats employed a different tactic to prevent freedmen from voting. Election officials declined to open the polls on the grounds that they could find no one willing to serve as election judges. Two black freeholders volunteered, but they could not find a third, so the polls stayed closed. Thereupon Jacob P. Hutchings, one of the two volunteers and president of a 900-member Grant Club that had marched to town, walked with several hundred fellow partisans the twelve miles to Macon and voted there. By virtue of there being "no white republicans in the county," Hutchings observed, "I have a hard time in all the campaigns." His experience typified that of other black Republican leaders outside of Macon.[80]

When the vote was tallied, Republicans won a majority in Bibb, Jones, and Twiggs counties but lost in Crawford, Houston, and Monroe.[81] Republicans also carried the state, but the election conveyed ominous signs. Democrats showed their determination to win by means of intimidation, obstruction, fraud, or violence, as they saw fit. And, although they took special pleasure in turning the poll-tax provision of the Republican constitution against its creators, Democrats had no idea that the tactic would prove so effective in disfranchising the freedmen. As they had done in the election of April 1868, the New South agrarians of

Houston County pointed the way. Their success in silencing the freedmen's political voice won them the admiration of other groups who shared their disdain for black voting but who, for one reason or another, had shied away from such a blunt and uncompromising approach.

Just as it drew Democrats together, the November election drove Republicans apart. Taking the long view, black voters grew even more suspicious of the motives of their white allies and even less confident in Governor Bullock's ability to guarantee their right to vote, much less to hold office. In the circumstances, it is not surprising that black leaders began distancing themselves from Bullock's administration. Some pursued the lure of federal patronage. Henry M. Turner sought the postmastership at Macon, and men as widely divergent in background and interests as Edwin Belcher and Aaron A. Bradley sought positions in the internal revenue and customs branches of the federal government.[82] But for others, the hope of elective office still burned brightly, as much perhaps for its potential to shape public policy as for its modest livelihood. Rank-and-file black Republicans also kept their eyes on who ran for office as an indicator of the party's commitment to equity and social change. Meanwhile, Republican leaders pursued an increasingly narrow program aimed at little more than perpetuating themselves in power.

Confined by that strategy, black leaders struck a new alliance that frankly acknowledged the special interests freedmen possessed as workers. During 1869, the most politically active artisans, proprietors, and professionals among Georgia's black Republicans affiliated with the Colored National Labor Union (CNLU), the first national organization of black workers. At both the national and local levels the organization represented the economic and political interests of artisans and artisan-entrepreneurs more so than those of unskilled laborers. Although organizers made strong appeals to plantation workers, the most active participants hailed from the ranks of independent artisans and shopkeepers. In central Georgia, Jefferson Long stood at the forefront.

In advance of the union's first national convention scheduled for December 1869, local groups throughout the country met to select delegates. Georgians met in Macon in October; 236 delegates from fifty-six counties attended.[83] The convention laid plans to organize local associations throughout the state. Resolutions demanded higher wages, pay for labor performed, civil justice, and better educational facilities and advised black women to abandon field work. Meanwhile, the hostile *Macon Telegraph* branded the proceedings so much "mischief" and exhorted "owners of the soil and employers" to establish "a dominant influence over the negro, by showing him that we are not only his best friends, but actually and truly the only friends" capable of furnishing "regular supplies of food, clothing and money." Although the meeting—like its counterparts else-where—articulated the political aspirations of the black working classes, it failed to provide a formula whereby the freedpeople could translate their strength in numbers into meaningful political power.[84]

IN JANUARY 1870, when Congress inaugurated Georgia's third Reconstruction and ordered the original 1868 legislature to reassemble, it looked as though the Republicans were once again on the rise. To be sure, the return of the black legislators created a different tone from the one that had prevailed during their absence. And there was much mischief to be undone. Early in 1869, for instance, over the strenuous objections of some white Radicals, including Governor Bullock, the New South planters had enacted a law banning the sale and purchase of agricultural products at night in two plantation counties southwest of Macon. When the black members rejoined the legislature in 1870, they suc-ceeded in repealing this law, which was aimed so clearly at preventing freedmen from trading in plantation crops.[85] They had less success, however, attempting to outlaw discrimination in public carriers, to require employers to pay wages due, to abolish the convict-lease system, to revamp the district court system, to deny county ordinaries the power to indenture children, and to eliminate the word "white" from the state code.[86] Given their small numbers, they had com-paratively little influence upon the legislative process. The best they could hope for was a rearguard action that might check the most outrageous overtures by their political enemies.

The Republicans' return to power under federal bayonets only briefly dis-tracted from the party's internal weakness. Factionalism spread, with color providing an important line of demarcation, but not the only one. As earlier, Republicans of all hues allied with each other on specific policy matters. During 1870, the Butler Bill, which would have postponed state elections slated for December and thereby perpetuated Governor Bullock's rule, deepened the split. Most Republicans, black and white, favored keeping Bullock in power, not because he was an ideal governor, but rather because he was seen as the only viable check upon a rising Democracy. In some regards he merited wide acclaim among Republicans—for instance, in his use of the pardoning power. As Henry M. Turner testified, although Bullock "had his faults," he showed great gener-osity toward persons unjustly convicted of crime. "There are scores at liberty to-day," Turner calculated, "who would have been in the penitentiary but for him."[87] But the honorable exercise of executive clemency by itself could not support a regime. White Moderates and independent-minded black Radicals favored holding the elections to test the party's mettle. The latter also saw an opportunity to run black candidates.

In the Macon area, Jefferson Long and T. G. Steward pressed hardest for black officeholders, taking special interest in one of the congressional seats to be filled in the December elections.[88] Late in the summer, J. Clarke Swayze, a former Freedmen's Bureau agent and then editor of the Republican *Macon American Union*, responded to this pressure in an editorial declaring "although I do not object to a man because of his color, I do object when he is unfit, the same as I would if an unfit white should present himself, and especially when his color will jeopardize the success of the party." Swayze rejected the notion that freedmen be entitled to leading state offices simply because "the majority of the Republicans in the State are colored," even as he affirmed the party's persistent "war against the assumed rights of whites over blacks." Seeing the issue not as one of proportional representation, but as one of race, he predicted that if black Republicans pursued the matter, he and "every white Republican" would rush "to the defense of our own race." The party's commitment to "equal rights" for every man, he explained, implied "an equal chance in the race of life" and nothing more.[89]

The issue that had festered among central Georgia's Republicans now exploded into the open. All over the state, Democratic newspapers seized the heaven-sent moment, reprinting Swayze's statement with extensive comment.[90] His remarks deepened the disenchantment of freedmen—precisely what the platitudes about qualifications for office and equal chances in the race of life aimed to avert. Black Republicans in Macon rejected Swayze's logic but, in the end, had to accommodate to its force in the form of a compromise. The district nominating convention agreed to put forward the name of Jefferson F. Long for the short term of the Forty-first Congress—which would last barely six weeks, from mid-January to early March 1871—on condition that a white man be nominated for the full two-year term of the Forty-second Congress. The *Telegraph & Messenger* charged Republicans with offering "half a negro for two months' service in Congress" as "bait" to keep freedmen loyal to the party.[91] Regarding who was best fit to govern, the Republicans seemed to be converging rapidly with the Democrats.

Long won the seat, but, like the opposition press, Henry M. Turner took a skeptical view of the accomplishment. He attributed Long's success to two factors. First, leaders in neither party placed any value in the short congressional term. Second, political opponents of the freedpeople delighted in the prospect of sending a prominent black leader to Washington, where he would have no real power to effect change yet would be far removed from local affairs. "They do not care so much about Congress admitting negroes into their halls," he explained, "but they do not want the negroes over them at home."[92]

As Democrats laid plans to topple the Bullock regime, they took their cues from the most successful practitioners of neutralizing Republican majorities. In central Georgia, these were the New South planters of Houston County. When Macon's Democrats adopted such tactics during the national and state elections of November and December 1870, violence was a forgone conclusion. Both elections resulted in "riots."

In the former, the fracas began, according to a prominent Democratic judge from the city, when a black Republican was arrested for having voted twice, at which point "a most terrific effort was made by the black people to rescue him." Stephen Mangum, a minister, then reportedly encouraged the assembled freed-people to "[s]hoot every damned rebel you see" before he was arrested. Women also took up the cause, verbally harassing black Democrats—in the case of one, threatening to "burn his damned arse off." Despite the confusion, Republicans still polled a majority.[93]

The trouble in December began on the second day of the three-day campaign. After a black man had cast a Democratic ticket and was leaving the polling place escorted by several prominent white Democrats, Republicans "hollered, and jeered, and laughed at him." The escorts responded in kind, but soon the shouting escalated to cursing and then beyond. The Democrats brandished a pistol and commenced shooting into the crowd, whereupon the Republicans seized a wagon load of wood and began throwing it about.

A troop of federal soldiers soon appeared and restored order, but, as Henry M. Turner observed, "from that time, a kind of bitterness began to develop itself." Democrats gathered in numbers to intimidate black voters, and for the entire third day they commandeered black men to vote the Democratic ticket, among other things marshaling the entire crew of a circus that had come to town, seizing the driver of every wagon that entered the city, and "changing the dress of the few democratic negroes they had there" so the men could vote repeatedly. White Democrats also cast multiple ballots, openly boasting of their deeds. At the conclusion of the voting, Democrats took custody of the ballot boxes, tampered with them freely, and, with but three exceptions, pronounced their candidates victorious. Republicans challenged the results before the legislature, but the investigating committee refused to take action.[94]

Elsewhere in central Georgia, Republicans did not fare as poorly as they did in Macon. In Monroe County, when longtime political organizer George Clower declared his intention to vote for Democrats rather than lily-white Republicans, he hoped more to awaken the latter than to mollify the former. The tactic worked, at least to the extent that in the fall of 1870, Republicans chose him and another freedman, a blacksmith named Paul Austin, to run for the state legislature. Clower reportedly toured the county making inflammatory speeches, vowing that freedmen would burn the county seat to the ground if denied full enjoyment of their civil and political rights. Both Clower and Austin lost.[95] In other counties of central Georgia, black Republicans also competed, at times successfully, for local and state offices. In Jones County, Jacob Hutchings lost his bid for the legislature, but several candidates won positions in the county government. And James H. Deveaux, teacher of the freedmen's school in Clinton, won a seat in the state senate. Isaac H. Anderson of Houston County did the same.[96]

Black Republicans in Crawford County also ran for a variety of county offices and the state legislature. All lost.[97] The significance of the Crawford election lay not in the defeat of the black candidates, but in their very candidacy. From the dawn of freedom, Crawford County freedpeople had been comparatively inactive. Rarely did they send delegates to political meetings, even those that met in Macon. And black organizers from elsewhere in the state repeatedly called attention to the extreme poverty and backwardness in the county.[98] That freedmen should have progressed so far within five years of freedom as to run candidates for office suggests the potential that Radical Reconstruction embodied—and which, once suppressed, took nearly a century to resurrect.

The Bullock regime collapsed when the governor fled the state in October 1871, but escape was not so easy for central Georgia's freedpeople. Jefferson F. Long continued to provide the focal point of black Republican politics in Macon, but internal and external obstacles mounted. Though Long at first was a critic of Bullock, his election to Congress in December 1870 injected him with a newfound loyalty to the Republican machine. When he returned from Washington in March 1871 after his brief congressional term, many of his constituents found him politically unrecognizable. Despite his earlier stance in favor of black nominees for national offices, he now supported the party's preference for white candidates. Not all freedmen stayed in step with his about-face. They continued to demand black candidates at least in proportion to their voting strength, which remained a central preoccupation of active black Republicans—whose numbers steadily declined—throughout the 1870s.[99] But their efforts paid few dividends.

GEORGIA'S REPUBLICANS left a mixed legacy from their short tenure in office.[100] The 1868 constitution established the structure for the development of a liberal political economy, but its numerous loopholes created endless problems. Perhaps most seriously, Republican leaders failed to fulfill their promises to the majority of the party's constituents, that is, plantation freedpeople. Education languished, and the political waffling that resulted in the expulsion of black members from the legislature left the party ill-equipped to block the planters' legislative program. Internally, the political shortsightedness of party leaders also contributed mightily to their own demise. Although the strategy of attracting white yeomen showed great initial promise, its architects took black voters for granted. In the end, it failed miserably.[101]

Despite these shortcomings of Radical rule, Reconstruction profoundly influenced the postbellum social order in countless ways that speeded the development of capitalist social relations. The effect upon the freedpeople was especially significant. In one sense, Reconstruction represented an effort to apply republican ideals of an independent, responsible citizenry wholesale to a vast population of former slaves. Many Republicans believed, naively perhaps, that dependent laborers could exercise an independent political voice. But even if the experiment failed, it had to be tried: republican ideals themselves required it.

Once begun, the experiment quickly descended from the realm of the ideal to that of the real. And it was precisely at that juncture that freedmen in central Georgia and throughout the South made their major contribution to the political reconstruction of the former slave states. They demanded a democratic political system responsive to the needs of the electorate, many if not most of whom were propertyless workers. They required services from government and considered it not only legitimate, but also consistent with the noblest traditions of the nation's past, to expect their taxes to satisfy those needs. But most of all, they demonstrated that in a system of compensated labor, workers required the franchise, if not to revolutionize the distribution of property, then to counter their employers' influence over the legislative apparatus.

The experience of black political leaders during Reconstruction underscores other aspects of the development of capitalist social relations. From 1865 onward, the class of relatively independent artisans, proprietors, and professionals enjoyed unique ability to rise to positions of political leadership. For many, their political careers became inseparable from how they made their living, in part due to patronage, but to a greater extent because their political constituents and their business clienteles were one and the same. Accordingly, Radical Reconstruction enabled these men to establish a sound foundation in their respective communities. Progressive segregation during the 1870s, both formal and informal, also worked to their advantage in a business sense, and, even after Republican politics became largely a matter of window dressing, their positions of leadership in church and civic organizations solidified their influence within the community of freedpeople, and at times in the larger community as well.

Yet the birth of this "black bourgeoisie," while not without enormous significance, also marked the stillbirth of a truly democratic polity in Georgia and throughout the South. Although the principle of "one man, one vote" was implicit in the new political order, most freedmen viewed voting not as an individual act of conscience, but as a way to reinforce family and community ties and to work collectively for a better future. It was precisely for that reason that white Democrats—led by the New South agrarians of such plantation areas as Houston County—overcame various social and political differences to unite in a phalanx pledged to stifle the collective aspirations of the freedmen. The politics of race emerged supreme, and capitalist agriculture evolved with the owners of the means of production enjoying a virtual monopoly over the state apparatus.

9

. . . .

Capitalist Transformation,

1872–1880

WHEN DEMOCRATS regained control over Georgia's government at the beginning of 1872, they presumed that their resurgent political power would translate into greater economic power. But they failed to take into account the larger forces that affected their lives and actions. From the standpoint of the national political economy, Republicans in Congress fashioned monetary and tariff policies designed to promote the development of northeastern and midwestern industrial interests at the expense of southern and western agricultural interests. With little or no political leverage at the national level, vanquished secessionists were powerless to resist.[1] On a larger scale, they had even less control over falling cotton prices that followed the panic of 1873.

Just as the depression of the 1840s had enabled central Georgia's planters to consolidate their position as a powerful slaveholding oligarchy, the depression of the 1870s advanced their transformation into a class of agrarian capitalists. To be sure, New South planters assumed that economic prosperity and social order required reducing the freedpeople to dependency. Urban commercial and manufacturing interests had similar hopes of a golden future based upon expanding commerce and responsible government. These propertied classes assumed that white artisans, unskilled laborers, and yeomen farmers would share the same ideals.

Related presumptions that the freedpeople would acquiesce quickly proved erroneous. Democrats found it difficult to dissuade black men from voting, even with threat of dismissal from employment. Because independent artisans and landowners were not as vulnerable to such threats, they voted routinely. Perhaps even more important, freedpeople on the plantations clung to the principle of co-partnership. This insistence produced divisions within the ranks of the planters that followed traditional lines. The Whiggish paternalists—most of whom by 1870 were middle-aged or older—tended to rent out their estates, conceding management prerogatives to the lessees and effectively transforming themselves into rentiers. Although there were exceptions to the rule, few of these men and women (largely widows) considered freedmen capable of managing their own economic or political affairs. But they saw no practical alternative. Good laborers could often only be had upon co-partnership agreements. And in any event, they had little taste or energy for the day-to-day management of farming affairs. Hence tenancy thrived in the old Whiggish strongholds north and east of Macon as well as in the areas surrounding the cities and towns of the region.

The old-line Democratic planters took a different approach. Like their Whiggish counterparts, they doubted freedpeople's competency, but rather than acquiesce in tenant partnerships, they redoubled their efforts to maintain control over plantation management. They preferred to operate their plantations under modified versions of the antebellum gang system supervised by resident managers. They had few reservations about exerting physical force, if not in broad daylight as a routine accompaniment of field labor, then after dark in disguise as a means of terror. They resented competition from neighbors and more distant employers for the services of the freedpeople. As earlier, these men turned to the law for assistance. By means of a friendly ruling from the state supreme court, they were able to treat sharecroppers as the statutory equivalent of wage laborers rather than tenants, with no proprietary rights in growing crops. New South planters also undertook a systematic assault upon the traditional rights of subsistence as represented by the open range and by unrestricted hunting and fishing. In short, the Democratic planters found themselves favoring exactly the kinds of changes in property law that business-men and industrialists North and South found congenial. This desire to control a recalcitrant labor force by nonmarket means was not essentially different from similar measures by landlords in England or New England from the seventeenth through the nineteenth centuries.

In these latter overtures, the Democratic planters ran afoul of the black-belt yeomen, who had consistently refused to ally with the Republicans, but who found themselves voting with the freedmen against the planters after Reconstruction. "Redemption" surely made strange bedfellows. The yeomen looked to past practices to resist the planters' social design for the future. The former slaves also resisted, both by looking forward toward landownership and independent tenures and by looking backward toward independent subsistence.

DESPITE THE overall boundaries of development imposed by the world economy and by Republican policymakers in Washington, capitalism evolved unevenly in postbellum central Georgia, with the plantation areas somewhat behind Macon, and with pockets of subsistence-oriented agriculture surviving in certain rural areas even after capitalist labor relations came to predominate on the plantations. Nonetheless, just as the political history of the city during the postwar period cannot be understood apart from the interaction between town and country, neither can its economic history. Developments in one area profoundly affected those in the other.

Republican rule did not appreciably alter Macon's economy; the city remained a clearinghouse for upcountry cotton, a regional entrepôt for trade goods, and an industrial center specializing in grain milling, cotton manufacturing, and machine making and repairing. In 1870, the machine shops accounted for approximately 30 percent of the value of goods produced in the city.[2] But prosperity was not strictly a matter of shrewd investments or hard work. The depression that began in 1873 wreaked havoc in the city no less than the countryside, with especially devastating effects upon construction and machine building. Despite the economic downturn, however, the Bibb Manufacturing Company opened a massive cotton mill that managed not only to survive, but also to prosper during the hard times. By 1880, it displaced the machine shops as the most important component of the urban economy, accounting for one-third of the value of goods produced in the city.[3]

The similarity of Macon's antebellum and postbellum economic structures must not disguise the radical changes that emancipation set loose, as the experience of black workers makes clear. Although the black population increased only modestly between 1870 and 1880—from 6,200 to 6,600—the latter figure represented a numerical majority of the city's population for the first time. Changes in occupational structure accompanied this demographic breakthrough. Large numbers of former slaves were firmly ensconced as proprietors and professionals, and nearly one-third of the male household heads were artisans, with a preponderance of shoemakers, blacksmiths, and building tradesmen. Some black women also were entrepreneurs—hucksters and boarding-house keepers, for instance—although most employed black women were servants. The depression took a heavy toll, reducing the black artisanry to less than one-quarter of the male household heads by 1880.[4]

Among white citizens, the occupational portrait changed just as drastically. Over the decade of the 1870s, white men tended to vacate the skilled trades in favor of clerical, professional, and proprietary positions in the economy. Although most white women avoided compensated labor, some operated boarding-houses or groceries. Perhaps the most significant change in the pattern of employment among white workers was the growing number of unskilled operatives—men, women, and children—employed at the Bibb Manufacturing Company's cotton mill. Compared with other fall-line cities, Macon's occupational structure did not stand out.[5] Yet compared with its own past, these were significant changes clearly marking the process of capitalist development.

Within this framework, social classes reshaped themselves. The elite, for example, promoted commercial advancement even while maintaining firm ties with the plantation economy, wherein the region's prosperity—as well as its families' roots—lay. As the depression continued, Macon's businessmen found themselves competing for commercial supremacy against their counterparts in Atlanta, an upstart city, whose superior rail connections they envied and whose association with the former Republican government they loathed. Yet this competition did not represent antagonistic visions of capitalist development; rather, it was simply a matter of commercial rivalry between different regions.[6]

In terms of local, as opposed to statewide, politics, Macon's business elite faced little opposition. To some extent, the changing occupational demography strengthened its political power. The declining numbers of white artisans eroded whatever threat might have lingered from the antebellum agitation against competition with skilled slaves. Moreover, the near cessation of foreign immigration to central Georgia after 1861 meant that the separate ethnic consciousness of persons born in Europe would fade over time. Finally, despite the ominous growth in the number of cotton mill operatives, through the 1870s these workers expressed no independent political voice.

Not content to let demographic changes alone diffuse the likelihood of political challenge from white working people, the Democratic elite took deliberate action. Lest any hint of political elitism be suggested in choosing candidates for the 1872 local elections, the *Telegraph & Messenger* advocated an open nominating meeting rather than a private caucus. "To act otherwise," the editors observed, would run the risk of destroying "all union and concert of action among the whites."[7]

The freedmen of Macon worked with equal determination to build solidarity among themselves, as their political activity following the return of Democratic rule makes clear. One tactic involved petitioning the new governor, James M. Smith, for authorization to form militia companies. Smith, a native of Culloden, a community in Monroe County created during the 1830s by Whig planters, retained paternalist tendencies despite his partisan conversion. In the spring of 1872, a small but articulate group of professionals and artisans pressed for greater advantage from the state's new Democratic administration. Led by N. D. Sneed, a cotton sampler and cashier of the Freedman's Bank branch, and Frank Disroon, a grocer and city alderman, several dozen black men from Macon formed a company, naming it the Lincoln Guards.[8] Complaining of "old and mostly unserviceable" arms, they requested state aid from Governor Smith. Advising the governor that the revised federal militia act forbade states to make "distinctions . . . on account of color" in arming and equipping militias, Sneed also reminded Smith of his earlier promise to furnish arms to companies of freedmen. Bursting with anger, Sneed pronounced the governor's conduct "unworthy of the Executive of a great state" and vowed to take the matter to federal authorities for redress. "*We will purchase arms*," Sneed predicted, "and your conduct will have the effect of inducing colored men to organize all over the state into military companies independent of and not subject to your jurisdiction," which was questionable in any event, in that it had been obtained "by the grossest frauds ever perpetrated upon a free people." Disroon, who served as second in command, tried a more circumspect approach, apologizing for Sneed's insolence and asking for state recognition and arms. Governor Smith consented.[9]

Inspired by the success, other Macon freedmen attempted to form a militia company, but their selection of the name Central City Blues ignited a powder keg. A company of the same name had fought for the Confederacy, and its veterans resented the "humiliation that a company, bearing such a part in the war for Southern rights, and having so proud a record, should have their name taken from them and assumed by a company so antagonistic in sentiment & feeling." Not surprisingly, Smith refused recognition to the black Central City Blues.[10]

The Lincoln Guards soon learned that the governor's blessing alone did not convey legitimacy among white citizens. In the spring of 1876, in anticipation of their fourth anniversary celebration, the Guards obtained permission to use the city park. The appointed day began with a parade and target shooting; then a large crowd of relatives and supporters proceeded to the park, where they encountered a white Sunday school picnic. A line of pickets styling itself a "death line" stood guard, threatening to kill any black person who dared cross it. William S. Scarborough, a Macon native who had graduated from Atlanta

University and returned to teach school in the city, considered the confrontation premeditated and concluded "that democratic ascendency means none other than death to the colored man."[11]

Whether or not it portended wholesale death, Democratic ascendancy did prompt an increase in violence. Early in the autumn of 1872, as partisan passions rose, black Democrats and black Republicans clashed at a camp meeting.[12] At the federal election several weeks later, politically motivated scuffling prompted Jefferson F. Long to urge freedmen to seize the polls, whereupon the police opened fire, resulting in the deaths of one white Democrat and three black Republicans.[13] Following the debacle, the *Telegraph & Messenger* opined that "there can be nothing more unsatisfactory than scrambling and wrangling with negroes for the very fundamental conditions of public order and safety."[14]

After first issuing warrants for Long's arrest, federal court officials decided instead to indict about half a dozen whites for violating the Congressional Enforcement (or Ku Klux Klan) Act prohibiting interference with the civil and political rights of freedmen. The indicted men appeared before the U.S. Circuit Court at Savannah in April 1873, but amidst intense opposition from the Georgia press and a reported attempt on the life of Henry P. Farrow, the U.S. district attorney prosecuting the case, the charges were dropped.[15] Flushed with the success of violent tactics, Democrats resorted to them freely again in 1874, resulting in what the *Telegraph & Messenger* trumpeted as "a glorious popular uprising in behalf of liberty and the white race."[16]

As Democrats consolidated their position, Republicans bickered among themselves. At their 1876 gubernatorial nominating convention held in Macon, two black men, William H. Harrison of Hancock County and William A. Pledger of Clarke County, played pivotal roles. Harrison, who during the Civil War had been implicated in a slave conspiracy, demanded that the party declare its unequivocal support for civil rights to "the colored as well as the white man, and all other laboring men." Accordingly, he wanted a Republican candidate willing to challenge Democratic interference with elections. Pledger, editor of the *Athens Blade* and protégé of John E. Bryant, shared Harrison's larger objective but favored nominating a Democrat on the grounds that a Republican "could not enforce the law if elected."[17]

After Bryant spoke in favor of nominating a Republican, Jonathan Norcross, an antebellum Whig originally from Maine, was selected. Delegates constructed a platform calling for free schools in each militia district, denouncing lawlessness, and demanding that the state government protect the citizens' rights to life, liberty, and property. Seeking greater control over the party, they soon engineered Bryant's appointment as chairman of the state executive committee. But the combination of internal factionalism and deep disagreement over the strategy of supporting Democratic candidates left them profoundly divided and unable to present a solid platform before the electorate.

Choosing Norcross failed not only to attract white voters, but also to halt Democratic violence. In August, Macon police disrupted a Republican meeting called by James B. Deveaux.[18] At the October state election, Democrats let Republicans vote unmolested until after noon when they realized that Republicans might carry the contest. Preliminary challenges—including one in which a ninety-year-old man was disqualified as being underage—had not deterred black voters. When Democrats closed the polls, black voters adjourned to City Hall, where they elected a board of election managers to receive their votes. City officials later refused to count those ballots. A *New York Times* correspondent reported that in the face of such intimidation, freedmen vowed to vote for Rutherford B. Hayes the following month "or die in the attempt."[19]

The *Telegraph & Messenger* made one last appeal to the freedmen to align with their "best friends and employers in their efforts to secure an honest government and good laws."[20] Election managers even agreed to set aside the polls at City Hall for the exclusive use of black voters. But intimidation and violence were the order of the day. After white Democrats in the rural districts prevented freedmen from voting, they converged upon City Hall. Even with those ballots adding to the Republican total, Democrats won handily.[21] Increasingly viewing black Republicans as a "public evil," Democratic strategists sought a remedy that would remove black voters from the electoral process altogether.[22]

As the commercial elite adopted these tactics, planters in Houston County and other Democratic strongholds were busy devising new ones to match their own evolving struggle with the former slaves. These innovations in part represented responses to perceived divisions among rural employers themselves. To some extent, these divisions followed traditional political tendencies, but the combination of opportunities and constraints imposed by slave emancipation and the economic depression also produced new patterns. The clearest fault line separated planter-rentiers from planter-managers. The former, largely old-line Whig paternalists, acquiesced in the freedmen's insistence upon co-partnership, rented land to former slaves, and either lived off their rental income or supplemented that with what they earned practicing law or medicine or operating a dry goods or grocery business. These men and women tended to be of middle age or older; they cultivated paternalistic ties with their black tenants and customers; and they felt a certain degree of civic responsibility for their social inferiors within what they believed to be a modified version of the old organic society.

The men committed to close management, in contrast, tended to be old-line Democratic planters, both established and up-and-coming, who viewed the new social order in distinctly less sentimental terms than former Whigs did. They perceived the competitive nature of producing cotton with free laborers, scoffed at the freedmen's insistence upon the prerogatives of co-partnership, and strove to reduce the labor force to a condition of utter subordination to the landowners.

Some planters advocated a frontal assault against "the pernicious habit of farming in co-partnership with hands." When "properly utilized," one planter argued, the labor of freedmen had no peer, for it was "simple slave labor . . . born, bred, and educated to respect, obey and carry out the dictum of the white man." But to realize its full potential, the landowner had to possess full control.[23] In a similar reaction against partnerships, an "Old Style" planter recommended a system of cash wages, paid monthly. The editors of the *Telegraph & Messenger* concurred, suggesting that tenures be reserved for white farm families. The "great body of negro tenants," claimed the editors, were "practical nuisances" and poor farmers to boot. Yet the journalists also conceded the "unavoidability" of extending tenures to "every applicant." The intensity of competition among landowners enabled freedpeople to play off one against another for better terms. The *Telegraph & Messenger* proposed a more effective enticement act as a practicable way of undercutting the freedpeople's bargaining position.[24] But that remedy had been tried before without effect.

When Democrats regained control over the legislature, these New South planters and their allied commercial interests saw an opportunity to act. They pursued three parallel paths: modifying the criminal law to make plantation workers inordinately susceptible to arrest, conviction, and a prison sentence; stripping sharecroppers of rights to growing crops, thereby reducing them to the legal equivalent of laborers; and curtailing customary rights to the bounty of nature, thus denying propertyless citizens access to traditional means of subsistence.

Perhaps unwittingly, the Democratic planters advanced their own transformation into an agrarian bourgeoisie as they attempted to reduce the freedpeople to an agricultural proletariat. Even less consciously did they intend to alienate the black-belt yeomanry from the strategy of reducing freedpeople to mudsill status. Yet that is exactly what happened, and sooner rather than later. The alienation began with an 1872 measure to permit voters in the respective counties to decide by local option whether or not to amend the antebellum fence law and require

Picking cotton, Jones County
(Courtesy of Georgia Department of Archives and History)

stock owners to pen their animals instead of obliging planters to enclose their crops.[25]

During the depression of the 1840s, improving planters had experimented with new fencing materials and innovative designs, but they did not tamper with the rationale of the law. The Civil War revolutionized their thinking. Fences took a terrible beating, from neglect and more purposeful destruction. By 1865, if not earlier, both slaves and free citizens were using fences for firewood, and Sherman's army elevated fence-burning to a high art. Dwindling timber supplies hindered repairs, even when no other obstacles stood in the way. Conceding those difficulties, the 1866 legislature declared it a misdemeanor to tamper with the enclosures that the residents of one particularly hard-hit county had had to build "for the confinement of their stock, in order to plant the crops necessary to subsist the people."[26] However inauspiciously, this measure pointed the way of the future.

The local-option law passed in 1872 authorized an election to take place when fifty freeholders petitioned county authorities to that effect. If another fifty freeholders signed a counterpetition, the proceedings ceased unless an additional twenty-five proponents petitioned. What followed could scarcely have been predicted, as developments in Houston County demonstrated. The process began auspiciously enough in February 1873, when sixty-four men requested the referendum. They represented the old-line Democratic planter elite from the central and southern parts of the county and its planter-merchant allies in Perry and Fort Valley. Only six of the forty-five petitioners identifiable on 1870 federal census returns owned neither land nor personal property; ten owned over $10,000 worth of real estate (the equivalent of approximately 1,000 acres). The twenty-six identifiable on 1860 federal census returns collectively owned 885 slaves, twelve possessing thirty or more and only two holding none.[27]

Two weeks later, county officials received a counterpetition bearing the names of sixty-one freeholders, overwhelmingly representing the traditional yeoman areas in the northern part of the county. Only a handful had owned slaves before the war, and the three who owned twenty or more all lived amidst the yeomen. Even more revealingly, more than half of those identifiable on census records were young men in their twenties and thirties. Not one owned more than $6,000 worth of real estate (or 600 acres) in 1870; six owned neither real nor personal property, and another twelve owned only personal property (livestock, in all likelihood). One signer may have been a freedman.[28] This petition clearly voiced the black-belt yeomen's interest in preserving the open range.[29] Yeomen found themselves once again in a strange alliance with freedmen, but this time under independent instead of Republican auspices.

By submitting a petition with an additional fifty-five names, proponents of the referendum forced the issue, and county officials scheduled the election for the first Monday of July. When the vote was tallied, the count stood 1,628 to 98 in favor of the traditional practice. The freedmen and yeomen had turned back the Democratic planters' assault upon customary rights, for the time being at least.[30]

TEMPORARILY DEFEATED on the issue of the new fence law, New South planters moved in other directions. In one approach, which they had already sampled during the absence of black legislators, they reintroduced the ban upon trading agricultural products at night. But whereas the earlier measure had applied to only two counties southwest of Macon, the new one applied to forty-two plantation counties, including Crawford, Houston, Jones, and Monroe in central Georgia. For the rest of the century, planters from other black-belt counties jumped on the bandwagon.[31]

These restrictions hint at the planters' desire to control the development of market mechanisms in the postbellum period. Several dimensions of this issue raised concerns. One was related to the legal maneuvering between landowners and merchants for the rights of first lien, which black-belt planters ultimately resolved in their favor.[32] Another dimension, the one most frequently cited by the planters, concerned the likelihood of theft associated with the nocturnal trading of agricultural products and their subsequent exchange for liquor. By the late 1870s, the New South planters took more concerted action against the illicit liquor trade that had vexed them since at least the 1840s; by local option they began passing prohibitions on the sale of ardent spirits.[33]

Democratic legislators supplemented this effort at subordinating the labor force by modifying the criminal code. Aimed at "Negro crimes," these measures followed the path charted by the 1866 black code. In 1871, as the Republican regime neared collapse, legislators extended the sweep of the 1866 law declaring insurrection a capital offense to include incitement to insurrection. The same legislative session also broadened the definition of arson to include burning fences, fodder, and crops, but this did not prevent what one source described as a "holocaust" of gin-house burnings during the 1870s.[34] The notorious pig law passed in 1875 made stealing a hog the equivalent of stealing a horse or mule and thus punishable by two to four years imprisonment.[35] Later in the decade, a series of laws banning cruelty to animals barely disguised the attempt to hold farm employees criminally responsible for injuries to work stock.[36] Another law made it a misdemeanor to ride a horse or mule without permission of its owner.[37] The legislatures in neighboring states also busied themselves enacting similar measures during the 1870s.

These laws placed enormous power in the hands of local authorities, particularly rural sheriffs, but not exclusively so. Officials in Jones County, for instance, appointed three men in each militia district to report "vagrants" to the superior court for prosecution.[38] The new criminal code worked hand in glove with the convict-lease system, which, though originally intended by its Republican sponsors as an economical way of promoting internal improvements, quickly evolved into a weapon for terrorizing the black labor force.[39]

In 1872, the state supreme court made an important contribution to this legal assault on the rights of agricultural workers by undercutting the foundation upon which freedpeople had rested the principle of co-partnership. Deciding that sharecropping constituted merely another mode of wage labor, rather than a form of tenure, the court at once denied croppers decision-making prerogatives and legal rights to their growing crops.[40] Thereafter, only tenants proper (that is, those who rented for cash, a fixed amount of cotton, or a share of what they produced) had valid claim of ownership to unharvested crops. Lacking such ownership, croppers got their share only after landlords and furnishing merchants had taken theirs. In disputed cases, croppers could scarcely afford the cost of legal proceedings and, accordingly, got nothing.

The ruling legitimated a sizable reappropriation of wealth from those who worked the soil to those who owned it. But even more important, it struck down the principle whereby croppers had considered themselves joint managers of the enterprise. The decision pointed a direction for courts and legislatures in other southern states, where New South planters were also devising means to undercut the principle of co-partnership and to reduce sharecroppers to a condition of subservience.[41]

The final legislative piece of this effort entailed restricting traditional access to land for the purposes of gathering wood, hunting, and fishing.[42] If the Democratic planters could win these changes, the freedpeople's ability to subsist themselves independently would be seriously curtailed, thus practically requiring that they resort to remunerative labor. In effect, these laws broadened the rights of individual property owners at the expense of the community at large.

Not accidentally, the burden of these changes fell heaviest upon former slaves, but yeomen were not immune. The crucial component of this legislation was redefining public rights to privately owned but unenclosed land. A preview of this tactic had appeared in the 1865 act that redefined criminal trespass and banned the cutting or gathering of wood without the landowner's permission.[43] By the early 1870s, hunters were required to obtain a landowner's permission before hunting on his land.[44]

In a broader attempt to restrict the lower classes' access to subsistence on the commons, legislators also sharply curtailed public hunting and fishing rights. New legislation extended the 1866 ban on Sunday hunting to new counties and restricted the capture of stipulated prey to certain seasons of the year. One measure designed to promote conservation by protecting wildlife during propagating seasons also cited "eminent medical experts" to the effect "that the flesh of deer, partridges, wild turkeys, etc., when obtained by trapping, or when killed during the breeding season, is, for sanitary reasons, improper as an article of food." Curiously, the legislature chose thus to safeguard public health only in three black-belt counties. Such a thin disguise hardly conceals the underlying purpose of denying plantation laborers access to independent subsistence.[45] But the new laws also demonstrated the development of bourgeois notions of private property rights in the crucible of struggle between planters and freedpeople. In time, the yeoman farmers in the white-majority areas of the upper Piedmont found themselves under a similar attack, which reached its legislative culmination in the 1890 game law that applied to the entire state.[46]

ANOTHER FACET of the New South Democrats' strategy for reducing the labor force to subservience involved gaining control over the freedpeople's schools.[47] When the Freedmen's Bureau ceased its educational operations in 1870 and the American Missionary Association strained to pick up the slack, northern sponsors of freedmen's education throughout the South welcomed the assistance of state authorities. By the terms of Georgia's Radical state constitution of 1868, that aid should already have been forthcoming. But Republican political maneuvering resulted in a suspension of tax collections and, consequently, of plans for organizing common schools. When Democrats regained power, they presented themselves as the true friends of freedpeople's education. Events in Bibb County illustrate the significance of this campaign in the larger effort to mold a tractable labor force.

The first Democratic legislature began the initiative, passing laws that empowered county grand juries to establish school boards consisting of five freeholders and that fixed the school term at three months.[48] At first, it appeared that freedmen's schools would prosper, perhaps as never before. County school commissioner W. D. Williams, principal of the Georgia Academy for the Blind in Macon, proposed making the American Missionary Association's John R. Lewis High School (built in 1868 and named for the state's first commissioner of education) the keystone of freedmen's education.[49] But with no funds immediately available, continued success would depend upon substantial support from the AMA.[50]

The tables turned later in 1872 when the legislature granted school boards taxing power. The Bibb County board reopened negotiations with the AMA, offering to support Lewis High School while permitting the association to furnish teachers of its own choosing. Lewis High School was no small prize: its eight white teachers and 500 black pupils substantially outnumbered the one white and five black teachers and 300 pupils in the three schools funded by the board.[51] But no sooner had the AMA accepted the offer than the board began exacting concessions. The self-proclaimed "best friends" of the freedpeople moved "to get full possession of the building and employ Southern teacher[s]," observed the school's principal.[52]

As the process of consolidation inched forward, the board took up the banner of economy. County school superintendent B. M. Zettler reported that the black enrollment did not warrant supporting three schools in addition to Lewis High School. "At no time since I entered my duties," he remarked ominously of the school in the AME church, "has there been a necessity for this school." Black parents had good reason to question his arithmetic. In 1874, there were 728 pupils (approximately 40 percent of the school-age population), but available facilities could accommodate only 450. White parents arguably had similar cause for concern inasmuch as 826 white students (more than 50 percent of those eligible) crowded into facilities designed for 620.[53] Zettler's desire to close schools seemed to make little sense. Nonetheless, the AMA offered use of Lewis High School to the county board. During the summer of 1874, black parents petitioned against the plan, forcing a compromise wherein the school board assumed financial responsibility while the AMA maintained control over instruction and administration.[54]

The county board manipulated school funds to promote subservience and undercut independence. In July 1875, the trustees of a rural district, who styled themselves "dependent upon the white people for nearly all the educational privileges we have," requested aid. Criticizing those who challenged the board's administration of the schools, the trustees expressed satisfaction "with our schools and the provision made for our welfare." Meanwhile, they claimed "no sympathy with those of our race who are disposed to push themselves into places and positions for which they are not fitted, or who are clamorous for privileges that would disturb the present social relations of the white and colored races." Not only was the memorial "just and true in itself," declared the board, but it was also "a good answer to the wicked misrepresentations of the temper and conduct of the Southern whites in respect to the colored people."[55]

At the same time, the feud in Macon escalated when the board announced plans to operate the city's schools for freedmen on a June through September term instead of an October through June calendar, as previously done. The board also planned to discontinue support for Lewis High School and for the northern teachers employed there, unless the AMA authorized the appointment of southern teachers. The proposed changes were ominous. Arguably, operating the schools during the slack agricultural season favored families whose children customarily picked cotton during the fall. But this apparent advantage was illusory inasmuch as these were the poorest families, whose children had to work at odd jobs the rest of the year as well. Thus the change did little to increase the number of black schoolchildren, though it did eliminate a potential alternative to harvest employment. Even more galling, Macon's black artisans, proprietors, and professionals—who from the summer of 1865 had provided the backbone of the city's public school system—understood that the new calendar bore no relationship to nonagricultural labor. Hence it represented an especially insulting blow to their educational aspirations.

Black parents were incensed by the proposals. At a public meeting they "pleasantly" informed Superintendent Zettler that "they had no confidence in him or his plans." They sent a deputation to the board of education requesting that Lewis High School remain open, that the board continue to support teachers approved by the parents, and that the board restore the old school calendar. They also offered to mediate between the board and the AMA over repairs to the building and the amount of monthly rent. Zettler and the association soon agreed to terms that included restoration of the old school calendar. Zettler wasted no time making clear the implications of the agreement, denying to black Congregational minister W. A. L. Campbell use of a room in the school for meetings of his YMCA. In gaining control over the building, the board intended to monitor its use closely.[56]

To thwart these plans, black residents of Macon formed a "compact" to make Lewis High School entirely self-supporting. They established a "Board of Responsible Managers" consisting of three men from each of the four largest churches; members included Moses Pollock, Jefferson F. Long, and other well-established leaders from the ranks of the artisans, shopkeepers, and professionals as well as a new generation represented best by William S. Scarborough, a teacher who had graduated from Atlanta University. Officials at the national office of the AMA snubbed the proposal, instead heeding the advice of the newly appointed Congregational pastor in Macon, S. S. Ashley, who had observed, "The Colored people cannot yet go alone—they are not yet ready to emerge from the Wilderness." Northern philanthropists showed no greater desire to grant freedpeople ultimate control over the schools they helped fund than did southern paternalists.[57]

The following year, the opposition of black voters helped defeat a legislative proposal that would have turned over control of freedmen's schools to boards of county commissioners charged with supervising all public finances. Just the same, the Bibb County board of education continued to pinch its funds. Figures for 1875–76 indicate that while there were 1,589 white and 1,564 black pupils enrolled, thirty-four teachers served the former, but only twenty-two the latter. Similarly, the board spent $20,116 on the white schools and only $5,705 on the black ones, and for the rural schools the grossest discrepancy prevailed: $2,835 for the former, but only $900 for the latter. The board also inaugurated a July-to-November school calendar for black children in the countryside. In Macon, freedmen's schools retained their eight-month term beginning in October but suffered cuts in both numbers of teachers and teachers' salaries.[58] The next year, the board agreed to continue supporting Lewis High School provided it appointed the principal. The AMA capitulated, and the board achieved its objective of total control.[59]

ALTHOUGH THE FULL impact of these developments remained to be seen, freedmen in Georgia's plantation belt had no doubts that the return of Democratic rule coupled with the onset of the depression greatly narrowed their political and economic options. As they had done repeatedly since 1865, they sought relief in the quintessential prerogative of freedom: the right of physical mobility. In Macon as well as the plantation districts of central Georgia, former slaves contemplated emigration to the West. Agents for planters in Mississippi and Arkansas told persuasive tales of high wages on the rich alluvial lands. Attachments to central Georgia did not rule out seeking better conditions elsewhere, especially in areas where Republicans still ruled or where local black communities exercised a degree of self-determination.[60]

The ebb and flow of such sentiment, especially in the extreme form of African emigration, clearly charted the freedpeople's perception of their prospects for improvement. In the spring of 1867, Radical Reconstruction suspended interest in Africa, but that sentiment returned stronger than ever during the mid-1870s, in part due to the exceptional energy and influence of Henry McNeal Turner. A desire to move westward appeared periodically under Republican rule: for instance, in 1869 among men associated with the Colored National Labor Union and its search to improve the status of southern black workers, and again in similar circles during 1871 as a tactic against landowners who "utterly refuse to sell or rent lands" to freedpeople.[61]

Emigrationist sentiment also arose locally in response to particularly unfavorable conditions or events. A pervasive sense of frustration inspired black residents of Clayton County south of Atlanta to seek "a colonization somewhere." In similar fashion, some 2,000 freedpeople reportedly left Houston County following the contested campaign of 1874, wherein the New South planters had employed open terror to prevent Republicans from polling an electoral majority. Democratic governor James M. Smith insisted that the migrants later returned more destitute than ever and less tempted to seek their fortunes elsewhere, but his words failed to comfort former slaves in the plantation districts.[62]

Deteriorating economic and political conditions fueled emigrationist sentiment. In the view of some freedmen, the effort on the part of the state Grange to lower wages from $100 to $60 per year was "nothing short of an intention to get us to steal," the punishment for which was a stint on the chain gang. Others reopened the quest for land only to have their hopes again frustrated. When a state convention of freedmen voiced this sentiment in 1874, Governor Smith insisted that there were "thousands of acres" available at reasonable prices and urged former slaves to "be quiet, honest, hard-working citizens, and let me protect you." Spurning the offer, the convention adjourned into an emigration association to assist prospective migrants.[63]

As the depression deepened during the summer of 1875, fires of hope erupted in violent form. As in days gone by, the merest murmur of unrest called forth the specter of Haiti. When white residents in several middle Georgia counties fantasized that the freedpeople intended to kill them and divide their lands, hysteria spread. It soon reached westward as far as Houston County, and the entire upcountry black belt braced for a conflagration.[64]

Authorities in Washington County acted first to root out the alleged conspiracy. Superior court judge Herschel V. Johnson, an old-line Democrat with strong paternalist sensibilities, spearheaded the effort, counseling calm, deliberate action but insisting that the conspirators face justice. "I am convinced," he wrote, "that the Combinations & Conspiracy are extensive, embracing several Counties." From "papers & Confessions" he deduced a purpose "as diabolical as if it were the Scheme of devils." Although charges were eventually dropped against the seventy-five persons who had been arrested, the prosecutor claimed a "moral . . . conviction." Henry M. Turner commended Johnson for his timely intercession. "I simply did my duty," Johnson replied, in the interest of "harmony and good feeling between the white and colored races."[65] Such sentiments notwithstanding, freedpeople from the affected areas began moving to South Carolina, where Republicans still held power.

The spirit of migration rose higher at the state convention of freedmen that met in Augusta in October 1875. Representatives from virtually every black-belt county attended. Opinions diverged. Some delegates favored "amicable relations" between laborers and employers in light of their "mutual dependence" and the "unseparableness of their destiny." But others considered migration the only solution, especially from areas where "the landed aristocracy or capitalists refused to recognize their manhood rights and appreciate their faithful labor." They breathed new life into the emigration societies organized the year before, though they disagreed over the most appropriate destination. Growing numbers proposed Africa, with Turner emerging as the chief spokesman of this group.

Arguing that the whole nation was abandoning the commitment to the freed-men's political rights, Turner looked toward Africa as the place where former slaves could possess land, form their own government, spread Christianity, and build a great civilization.[66] Other delegates repudiated African migration. James H. Deveaux, a former state senator from Jones County, argued that Georgia freedmen should stand their ground and demand their rights, and then the federal government would intercede. Although other delegates echoed Deveaux, the majority desired results, not platitudes. The meeting adjourned into an emigration society, which, like its predecessor of the previous year, appears to have quickly collapsed.[67]

The recurring interest in migration suggests both the possibilities and con-straints of free labor during the 1870s. Freedpeople were not so bound to the new plantation order, by either poverty or debt, that they could not consider fleeing from intolerable conditions, whether defined economically, politically, or otherwise. But they had few viable destinations. The lure of Africa was more symbolic than real. South Carolina and Florida offered political attractions, and Mississippi and Arkansas offered fertile land and higher wages. But the seg-mented labor markets in the nation at the time effectively confined the likely alternatives to other plantation regions of the South.[68] And other constraints—ties to extended families, in particular—discouraged freedpeople from mov-ing.[69] In short, migration was not a tool of individual upward mobility, but a collective strategy for survival of an oppressed laboring class.

NEW SOUTH PLANTERS used the financial stringency resulting from the panic of 1873 to undercut the homestead provisions of the 1868 constitution. Like the fence law, however, that protection benefited yeomen as well as freedmen. So the planters' strategy had to avoid the appearance of adversely affecting the former. The impetus for such change appeared early in 1874, when creditors began requiring waivers of homestead exemptions as a precondition for advances. When smallholders and tenants balked at such terms, a stalemate resulted.

Planters and merchants alike sought a remedy. Democratic leaders, led by Robert Toombs, the archfoe of everything Republican, proposed a constitutional convention to resolve this and other grievances lingering from Reconstruction days. Toombs assumed a radically laissez-faire, states' rights view that reflected a powerful strain of planter agrarianism: minimum government that neither bur-dened its citizens with high taxes nor lavished them with social services. It took for granted a hierarchical society presided over by the plantation elite.

That Toombs's views prevailed in the revised constitution of 1877 has been a source of endless fascination and no little confusion. In a state that from before the Civil War had prided itself in being the Empire State of the South, Toombs's version of old-style plantation agrarianism seems out of step with New South industrial and commercial boosterism. And his particular assault upon concentrated power in corporate form has led some recent commentators to see him and like-minded planters as charting a "Prussian Road" of economic development.[70] Even apart from the larger issues of national configurations of economic and political power that such a characterization does not address, it also fails to take into account the radical transformation of the planters, which Toombs's militant refusal to be reconstructed contradicted rather than represented.[71] A brief look at state and local politics helps clarify the confusion.

Toombs proved a master of orchestrating popular unrest over the financial panic. But being the shrewd politician that he was, he understood that different classes bore different burdens. His main concern was to promote the interests of commercial agriculture, and though he surely resented the political power of New South industrialists represented by the renegade Joe Brown, he also had to chart a course that would win popular support among the state's sizable yeomanry. To describe the results as a political coup scarcely does justice to his wizardry. But to describe it as a victory of agrarian over industrial interests misses the point.

Representing the interests of planters of every description, Toombs spearheaded the attack on the homestead, fully cognizant of its deep appeal among the yeomen. He played the familial chord, claiming that the Republican measure did "not secure a sound, substantial real homestead to the women and children of the State." His objection also reflected the planters' traditional concern for a stable social order—a more modest exemption would enable such dependents to escape being "thrown on society houseless and homeless and penniless, outcast and wanderers, subject to all the temptations to crime in the worst forms, and finally to become tenants of jails and poor houses."[72]

Toombs's attack on the homestead represented but one facet of his broader assault upon Republicanism. Faulting the 1868 constitution as the work of "hungry, hostile, alien enemies, domestic traitors, and ignorant, vicious, emancipated slaves," he pronounced the "present government" of the state "a usurpation," with "no moral or legal claim to the support or obedience of the people." The 1868 constitution "denies the right of the states," he claimed, subordinating them to "their agent, the federal government." To reassert state sovereignty and eliminate the residue of Radical rule, Toombs recommended substantive changes in every branch of state government. But "the great defect in the constitution," he insisted, "is that it does not protect the property of the people against invasion of the legislative power." A new constitution was necessary to "remark and plainly define the dividing line between individual rights and public authority." He especially faulted "gigantic corporations" whose influence upon government "violates justice, transfers the sweat of the poor to the coffers of the rich, appropriates the public fund to private use and profit, and opens the flood gates of fraud and public demoralization."[73]

Woven through that anti-Republican agenda was Toombs's opposition against the other major change that Reconstruction had inaugurated, namely, extending voting rights to "ignorant, vicious, emancipated slaves."[74] This characterization, he hoped, would align the yeomen behind a new constitution, even if it reduced their homestead exemption. Freedmen in central Georgia saw the handwriting on the wall. In the summer of 1876, a black delegate to a Republican convention in Macon quoted Toombs as boasting that if a constitutional convention were called "the nigger would never be heard of again."[75] And recent elections demonstrated the growing sentiment against freedmen's voting, even among former moderates such as Macon's commercial elite.

In the shrewdness of their political imaginations, racist aristocrats seized upon another provision of the 1868 constitution, the poll tax, as the key to silencing the freedmen's political voice. As eventually presented to the voters, the new constitution would require proof of payment of all poll taxes since the last election as a condition for voting.[76] Accordingly, freedmen rallied against it, in Houston County, for instance, returning a 700-vote majority opposed. Black voters throughout the state did likewise, but, nonetheless, the constitution won approval, imposing new economic and political burdens upon poor whites as well as former slaves.[77]

The new constitution reduced the homestead exemption, from $2,000 to $1,600 in real estate, with the option to waive everything except $300 in wearing apparel. This provision accomplished the intended objective of easing restraints upon credit, but at the expense of those for whom Toombs professed such solicitation. Creditors routinely insisted upon homestead-exemption waivers as a precondition for every description of loan, whether cash to purchase a mule or credit for food and fertilizer. To add insult to injury, borrowers were required to pay a $2 filing fee to record their waivers.[78]

Under cover of these affidavits, creditors could dispossess smallholders and tenants of all they possessed save the clothes on their backs. If deteriorating soils and falling prices were not challenge enough, now the entire rural work force had to fear being "cleaned out" for what generally amounted to trivial financial considerations.[79] Not surprisingly, black tenants and laborers bore a disproportionately heavy load of the discrimination, but white ones also found themselves increasingly at the mercy of merchants. To compound the burden, the cumulative poll tax decimated the black electorate. In the 1880 national election, the *Telegraph & Messenger* noted the small turnout compared with previous years and attributed it "to the large number who are disqualified by non-payment of taxes."[80]

AGAINST THIS MASSIVE effort to reduce them to a propertyless, disfranchised proletariat, freedpeople employed several strategies. In one, they scrimped and saved to purchase work animals and tools to make a go of renting. The deck was clearly stacked against black cash renters. That freedmen were able to gain cash tenures indicates the depth of their determination to labor independently. That they were able to retain cash tenures hints at a monumental level of self-exploitation to finish each year with a positive account balance and thus to avoid foreclosure. As the experience of Ned Cobb indicates, cash renters supplemented their farming with various sidelines such as making white-oak baskets, cutting cross ties and shingles, and hauling lumber during slack seasons of the cotton cycle.[81] But not even the greatest ingenuity and exertion could guard against the vagaries of nature and world market conditions, or the planters and merchants who opposed too much independence on the renters' part. Yet, if in 1870 not more than 5 percent of black household heads in central Georgia possessed a mule, the sine qua non of rental tenancy, ten years later approximately 20 percent met that qualification.[82]

The ability of black renters to maintain their tenure also depended upon the resources of individual households and extended families. Obviously, the father's farming skill counted for much, as did the number of teenage sons capable of performing field labor. The mother's domestic skill in the area of caring for young children, keeping the kitchen garden, and tending chickens and other such barnyard animals (which sometimes included a cow) provided the other pillar upon which successful tenancies rested. If the mother or one of the children had mastered reading and writing, that proved an additional advantage. At the very least, it might lessen the likelihood of being legally hoodwinked by an unscrupulous landowner, merchant, or creditor. With a measure of good luck, some of these families managed to purchase land.[83]

The social structure of Houston County, central Georgia's quintessential

A hog killing on farm of William Means's family, Houston County
(Courtesy of Georgia Department of Archives and History)

plantation county, in 1880 provides a vivid picture of the freedpeople's struggle for economic independence.[84] Black residents of rural areas occupied a variety of positions in the agricultural economy, based to some extent upon personal choices that they exercised, but to a greater degree upon the arrangements that they collectively devised with landowners in particular areas. As noted earlier, freedmen living close to a town or in districts wherein small planters had predominated before the war enjoyed the greatest likelihood of farming as cash renters. Conversely, the districts characterized by large plantations before the war continued to be so characterized after the war.

In areas containing the choicest land, the New South planters had thoroughly resisted the freedpeople's pressure for co-partnership and continued to operate with gang labor under overseers. There most adult freedpeople—women as well as men—worked for wages, and children also worked in the fields during the cotton harvest. In Houston County's two wealthiest plantation districts from before the war, for instance, 47 percent of the black household heads in one claimed the occupation of farm laborer, as did 89 percent of their counterparts in the other. Little cash changed hands, however, regardless of the agreed-upon wages. Laborers might obtain advances of a dollar or two on a regular basis during the year, but with advances of provisions and other necessities as well, few would have emerged from the postharvest settlement with much to show for their year's labor. In other plantation districts of the county, freedpeople worked on shares instead of for wages, but thanks to the 1872 state supreme court ruling, there was little practical difference between the two.[85]

Patterns of personal property ownership among freedmen in Houston County suggest several strategies for obtaining work stock and thereby escaping wage labor. As early as 1870, a pattern emerged wherein the freedmen with $50 or more in personal property (the value of a mule) tended to share the surname of one of the leading planter families. Given the idiosyncrasy with which freedpeople chose surnames, this correlation may be entirely accidental, but that is unlikely. The pattern suggests the afterglow of antebellum paternalism, wherein the animal owner had commuted his favorable relationship with a planter into a kind of freedom dues. Other animal owners appear to have been fathers and sons living in close proximity to each other, suggesting a process whereby families facilitated the accumulation of animals, tools, and other necessities. More often than not, however, the accumulation process reflected patient saving over time and, no doubt, a lot of luck.[86]

Cash renters differed from croppers in a number of important ways. In 1880, in the counties surrounding Macon, renters were, on average, four years older than croppers. Although the former tended to have smaller families than the latter (itself partly a reflection of the age difference) and thus could muster fewer workers, their wives also worked less frequently as hired farm laborers than did the wives of croppers. Nevertheless, cash renters throughout central Georgia worked larger farms on more valuable land and outdistanced croppers in both total crops produced and yield per acre in virtually every category, cotton not excepted.[87]

Although the manuscript federal census records tend to convey an impression of rigidity in the tenure structure, it was nothing if not fluid. This is not to endorse the popular notion of a tenure ladder, upon which young, unskilled farm laborers supposedly progressed steadily upward through the stages of cropper and renter until they reached the pinnacle of proprietorship. As it happened, farmers moved down the ladder as well as up. In fact, most planters posited a variant on the tenure ladder model, taking into account what they perceived as inherent disabilities of black laborers. That view presumed perpetual oscillation back and forth between renting and cropping. It also presumed benevolence on the part of the landowner: a desire to see croppers and laborers advance and to

impart farming skills and financial assistance to that end. But once the black
renter commenced functioning on his own without constant oversight, problems
began. Then, according to the planters' stereotype, laziness, shiftlessness, or
profligacy took over, leading quickly to debt, foreclosure on animals and tools,
and the renter's return to cropping or wage labor, where, under the benevolent
guidance of the landowner, the cycle would begin again.[88] Planters thus re-
fashioned familiar racial ideology in their struggle for power over the emancipated work force.[89]

One of the most striking developments in postbellum central Georgia was the
growth in the number of white tenants. The structure of white tenancy in
Houston County in 1880 closely parallels the structure of black tenancy. Share
tenures predominated in both the antebellum plantation and antebellum yeoman
districts, and cash tenures took the lead in the town districts and in those
characterized by variegated landholdings. As tenancy enabled white farmers
whose fortunes were flagging (from depressed land values, low crop prices, and
resultant debt) to remain on the land while they marshaled their resources, their
strength, and their wits for another go at proprietorship, it also enabled aspiring
planters to gain experience farming and managing free laborers. Over the last
quarter of the nineteenth century, the former tended in the direction of a
debased white peasantry, while the latter displayed characteristics of a new class
of southern kulaks.[90]

For many dispossessed whites, share tenancy represented a dead end, where,
deprived of their land, and lacking credit or sufficiently large families, they
worked hard raising cotton to satisfy landlords and furnishing merchants and
scratched what subsistence they could from the soil. Such tenants tended to be
older than cash tenants (though not as old as owners) and to have fewer family
members and numbers of workers in their households than both cash tenants
and owners. They worked farms of inferior value to those of all other farmers or
tenants, white or black, spent less on hired laborers, and raised fewer crops than
all but black share renters.[91]

The kulaks, though younger, did not trouble themselves over fielding large
families. Their strategy involved leasing large plantations, either splitting the
crop with the landlord or paying cash rent, and hiring black laborers to work the
cotton and corn. Some owned their own animals; others simply viewed animals
and tools as other factors of production to be rented or purchased as the situation
dictated. Agricultural entrepreneurs par excellence, they staked their futures to
the exploitation of free black laborers. Some rose and others fell, but unlike
many antebellum planters who viewed the confiscation of their slaves as the end

of their world, the kulaks clearly understood how emancipation created a new world for them. Landownership and its perquisites would follow upon the careful mobilization of productive forces and, most important, upon the efficient exploitation of black laborers.[92]

Other white tenants, share and cash alike, merely represented young men just breaking into farming, who aspired to nothing more than farm ownership and opted for share or cash tenures depending upon the work stock and tools at their disposal, the preference of landowners, and prevailing tenure patterns in various locales. Landowners at times found it convenient to play white tenants against black, and in some sections of the plantation belt it appears that planters deliberately recruited white tenants from the upper Piedmont for precisely such purposes.[93] Some landowners preferred white tenants for their supposed superior industry, but others loathed their comparatively greater subsistence needs, their insistence upon certain amenities, and their stubborn, intractable independence. "White man not worth a d—n in a cotton crop," a Jones County resident telegraphically observed in the mid-1870s.[94]

The development of tenancy forced a restructuring of social relations among rural whites. Among other things, it placed tenants in a position of subordination to landowners that was both much more pervasive and much more complete than anything experienced by antebellum tenants. The key change resulted from the furnishing system that had developed since the war, with tenants indebting themselves for advances of supplies and fertilizer, both the practice and the principle of which would have been unthinkable to antebellum tenants. Perhaps most ominous of all, white tenants stood in a similar relationship of dependence to that of black tenants. Such structural equality of black and white was something new. Among other things, it made possible the tactical alliance between white yeomen and tenants and black tenants and farm laborers opposed to the new fence law.

In another strategy of escaping the clutches of the New South planters, growing numbers of freedpeople opted for day labor in the interstices between the rural and urban wage economies. For the right to control their lives to some degree, these African Americans paid a heavy price: none of them prospered, and most lived in abject poverty. To escape the burdens of sharecropping— yearlong commitments, increasingly restrictive conditions, debt—they combined seasonal work on the plantations during the harvest with odd jobs and hunting, fishing, gathering, and other self-subsistence activities during the remainder of the year. Success required contributions from every member of the household. Yet considerable numbers of these casual workers managed to subvert all the planters' schemes, however intricately designed or comprehensively drawn, to reduce them to steady employment. The very nature of the capitalist labor market demanded such a floating population, so it persisted and even grew. "[M]any of them," observed a disgruntled Houston County planter, "have been able to squat about on the lands of others . . . satisfied if they can be let alone." Others were the farm laborers whom the 1880 census takers found residing in Macon and the various rural towns of the black belt.[95]

NOTWITHSTANDING the many advances registered by the capitalist-minded planters, they did not entirely get their way. To be sure, they had political power and time on their side, as evidenced, for instance, by the 1881 fence law, which amended the 1872 act to allow voting at the level of militia districts within counties. The change was largely intended to overcome the difficulties of achieving countywide approval, especially in the black belt.[96] The strategy worked. Late in 1883, following a flurry of such referenda, the *Atlanta Constitution* lamented that the stock law "suffers a great number of defeats because the negroes in every instance vote to maintain the prevailing order of things." But where large planters had the power to influence black voters—keeping them from the polls, if nothing else—the new system came into vogue. At the time of the *Constitution*'s survey of fencing legislation, in central Georgia only Jones and Bibb counties still clung to the traditional system.[97] As black voters in the plantation districts were being vanquished seriatim, the scene of struggle shifted to the upper Piedmont, where white yeomen continued to resist the change. Their continued political unrest over the issue fed directly into the Populist movement of the 1880s and 1890s.[98]

Besides curtailing a traditional source of subsistence, closing the range also restricted the ability of freedpeople to keep work animals, a precondition of true tenancy. Denied grazing rights on the commons, renters would have to build pens and provide feed for their stock, often at considerable cost in time and resources. And by making animal owners legally liable for damages caused by their roving stock, the new law increased the likelihood that animals would be seized in consideration of such damages.[99] Individual black households suffered, but the significance of the stock law lies in the effective transfer of hitherto public resources into the hands of private landholders. It also obliged propertyless citizens to acquire forage or grazing rights contractually, paying in cash, in kind, or in labor services, or to risk criminal prosecution for stealing what had previously been theirs by customary right.

In their effort thus to create an agricultural proletariat, the planters re-created themselves as an agrarian bourgeoisie. In some respects, it might be considered ironic that the largest planters, with the strongest antebellum commitment to slavery and the strongest wartime commitment to secession, would pioneer these changes. Yet within the context of struggle over the dwindling fruits of plantation agriculture under the federally imposed rubric of compensated labor, the planters' actions make perfect sense. Free labor, after all, implied legal equality among contracting parties, not economic equality between employers and employees. Once planters understood this, they devised both legal and political mechanisms to promote economic inequality. As a result of this particular history of struggle, the planters of central Georgia remained an agrarian elite, but one with little in common either with their antebellum forebears or with their contemporaries in Brazil or the Caribbean.

Although the New South planters were making great strides toward reducing the plantation work force to the status of agricultural proletarians, they had not entirely achieved that objective by the end of the period under consideration. Moreover, they continued to encounter freedpeople determined to avoid complete proletarianization, through either cash tenancy or day labor. The former slaves seeking autonomy on the land had counterparts in the cities and towns among the artisans, entrepreneurs, and professionals. Though far from independent in an absolute sense, these freedpeople kept alive the struggle on behalf of Reconstruction ideals.

CONCLUSION

. . . .

From Slavery to

Agrarian Capitalism in

Larger Perspective

ALTHOUGH THE FOREGOING events took place within a relatively small compass, they provide a keyhole through which to observe processes shaping much of the Atlantic world during the nineteenth century. The central theme of antebellum southern history was the rise of the planter class during an era when merchant capitalism was giving way to industrial capitalism.[1] The opening of the Georgia upcountry to settlement by Anglo-Americans and their slaves occurred in the context of rising demand for raw cotton that resulted from the Industrial Revolution. Certain demographic features of late colonial society created a popular clamoring for land throughout the original thirteen states, and as Georgians trekked to the backcountry of their state, their counterparts as far north as New England were doing the same, fanning throughout the coastal plain and the Appalachian foothills and even pushing the Indian frontier west of the mountains to the valleys of the Ohio and Tennessee rivers.[2]

During the pioneer phase of this settlement process, most migrants of European ancestry stood in general economic and political parity with each other, especially if they were sedentary agriculturists. Households provided the structure within which labor was performed and persons related to civic society. Through the first quarter of the nineteenth century, most household labor served the end of subsistence rather than production for either local or distant markets. Although households were hierarchically structured, reproducing inequality between men and women and between the household head and his assorted dependents (children, servants, apprentices, slaves), political equality obtained among household heads.

North of the Mason-Dixon line, traditional urban and rural economies began bending under the pressure of commercial change in the late eighteenth century. Although the process had numerous dimensions to which no brief summary could possibly do justice, commercial markets extended in both range and depth. Growing numbers of persons began producing goods for these markets and partaking in market exchange involving an increasing variety of products and services. As a result of these changes, household production in the cities and rural towns of the northeast gave way to a putting-out system under the direction of urban merchants or a factory system controlled by merchant-manufacturers.[3] Even in rural areas, the growth of commercial agriculture transformed traditional social relations based upon reciprocal exchange and complex networks of personal and familial contacts.[4]

Among its other effects, this commercialization generated social differentiation with clear overtones of diverging class experiences and interests. By the late antebellum period, a permanent class of laborers, with little if any hope of acquiring a competency in land, had taken shape in all the cities and in many farming communities as well. Laboring men gained full citizenship rights (including the suffrage), but in a public arena increasingly characterized by economic and social distance between the wealthy and the humble members of society.[5]

South of the Mason-Dixon line, these developments played out much differently because of slavery. In two superficial respects, the history of Anglo-American settlement of central Georgia and comparable southern areas looks much like that of newly settled regions in the North, namely, that most households farmed and that a crude equality obtained among household heads. But there the similarity ended. The nature of southern farming became bifurcated in ways that had no clear parallel in the North. Commercial farmers, who concentrated upon growing cotton for the world market, occupied choice lands in what came to be known as black belts. Subsistence farmers settled on less valuable lands, consciously avoiding production for world markets and deliberately perpetuating the complex of social relations based upon the exchange of goods and services among kinfolk and neighbors rather than upon the purchase and sale of commodities among strangers.[6] So, as household production grew weaker in the North, it grew stronger in the South, supporting the economies of both yeoman-farming and plantation regions.[7]

Slavery accounts for this disparity between North and South and between commercial and subsistence farming in the South. Having gained new strength as a result of the Industrial Revolution and the provisions of the U.S. Constitution, the "peculiar" institution became the defining feature of antebellum southern developments between 1789 and 1865 and increasingly preoccupied national politics as well. It took a bloody civil war to destroy the principle of property in humans.

Producing cotton for English manufacturers with the use of slave laborers enabled a comparatively small number of southern planters to garner enormous wealth and political power both locally and nationally during the antebellum period. To be sure, a substantial number of southern white households had a direct stake in slavery, but this does not negate the fact that slavery was at bottom a class relationship undergirding a class society. It defined both the narrow sphere of productive relations between slave owners and their laborers and the more general sphere of social relations between masters and slaves, between free white and free black persons, and among different classes of northern and southern whites. Despite the professions of equality in the Declaration of Independence and the U.S. Constitution, southern planters enjoyed special advantages. Even apart from believing this a fitting perquisite of mastership, they wished to guarantee their disproportionate ability to shape public discourse and policy regarding slavery. To a remarkable degree they succeeded, although in the end they failed.[8]

Popular understanding of both the success and the failure of the planters stops well short of understanding the context of day-to-day political struggles in which the plantation elite found itself incessantly embroiled. And least clearly understood of all is the important role played by slaves, who by law and custom were excluded from the body politic. Yet, like free white persons, slaves lived and worked in constant exposure to the political culture of the nation, and they legitimately wondered why the constitutional guarantees of life and liberty did not apply to them. In pursuing a more inclusive definition of who constituted "We, the People," they forced themselves into political affairs at the national as well as the local level.[9]

Even while freedom remained over the horizon, slaves in central Georgia and throughout the South struggled for control over their labor and their lives after working hours. This struggle for control bore a certain resemblance to that preoccupying antebellum northern factory operatives, who resisted the efforts of merchants and manufacturers to strip them of land and other productive property (including artisan skills). But the term "wage slavery" was more a rhetorical device than an accurate description of reality. After all, the essence of the wage relationship was the fact that the laborer's ability to work, not his person, was the commodity being exchanged for the wage.[10]

The slaves' struggle more closely resembled that of bound laborers elsewhere in the nineteenth-century world, particularly Caribbean and South American slaves and European serfs and peasants.[11] Although the slave quarters on central Georgia's plantations were large in comparison with the cabin or two dotting the yards of smallholders, they were modest in comparison with the quarters on West Indian plantations or with European serf villages. By the same token, central Georgia's slaves did not enjoy either the control over their labor and domestic life that Russian serfs did or the gardening and marketing privileges that Jamaican slaves did. But all these bound laborers shared a common struggle against masters who were capitalizing on commercial opportunity in the world market.

With no legal right to withhold their labor power from the person who owned their bodies, slaves had to find points at which their masters' property interests rendered them vulnerable. The provision of subsistence constituted precisely such a point. As masters otherwise subjected slaves to greater discipline, a harsher work regimen, and a sophisticated ideological assault upon their humanity, slaves clung to the prerogative of supplementing their diets by cultivating gardens, tapping the bounties of nature, and pasturing hogs on the open range. They also preserved the right to exchange their surplus products both on and off the plantations. And as the commercial development of the southern interior accompanied the rising fortunes of King Cotton (and the rising wealth and expanding consumer tastes of his minions), slaves succeeded in gaining entrance to these new trade networks, both with and without authorization. After all, planters could not have their cake and eat it too. If the railroad was an essential component of their prosperity, then they would have to live with its less desirable functions—as a means of transportation for propertyless European immigrants and illicit liquor and literature, as well as a means of escape for runaway slaves.

Even apart from the likelihood of successful flight, which was remote in any event, slaves in central Georgia found some distance from their masters by producing and trading on their own account. If such production tied them to the plantation order, it also helped sustain their health, their cultural life, and their ability to direct their own affairs. But it created problems for their masters—political problems rather than simply nagging annoyances. Although commerce provided the lifeblood of the slave system, planters feared that runaway commerce would destroy, not nourish, the social organism.

In abolishing slavery and the antebellum planter class that was its chief beneficiary, the Civil War removed the legal and political obstacles to capitalist development in the South. The South remained an agricultural region, to be sure, and many antebellum landholders retained their land; but the postbellum proprietors bore a fundamentally different relationship to the labor force than had their antebellum counterparts. The laborers were free to move about in search of employment and living accommodations and to bargain with employers over rates of pay, hours of labor, and a host of related issues. For a fleeting moment, the prospect of a redistribution of land also presented itself, only to disappear in a barrage of fears that the former slaves would forsake commercial agriculture for subsistence and thereby assure the collapse of the South into a state of economic decay, and perhaps political and social anarchy.

The slaves would be free—to work or starve—but Reconstruction would not even attempt to address the persistent and growing inequality between the owners of productive property and the propertyless. The victorious northerners cleared the field for the evolution of a free-labor system and even oversaw its functioning for several years through the instrument of the Freedmen's Bureau. But the tenets of laissez-faire economics, not to mention federal fiscal exigencies, all but guaranteed that this process would be short-lived. Federal policymakers would establish certain structures—markets in labor power, for instance—and even coach the novitiates in the proper habits of behavior. But sooner or later, landowners (and other employers) and laborers would have to make free labor work on their own.

During the postwar years, labor arrangements assumed a variety of forms but tended toward tenancy on the one hand and proletarianization on the other. From the perspective of the Americas, this trend was not unusual, though the rapidity with which it emerged is unique.[12] In the British West Indies, for instance, where the slaves were freed during the 1830s, former slaves opted out of sugar cultivation wherever they could gain access to land. They raised and marketed produce, evolving in the direction of peasantry. In territories where planters succeeded in denying land to former slaves, most stayed on the plantations, nominally working for wages, but in fact living close to the margin of subsistence.[13] From the perspective of Europe, this pattern very much resembled the development of capitalist agriculture in seventeenth- and eighteenth-century England, down to improving landlords, impoverished workers, and laws aimed at promoting industry and subordination in the free labor force. In that comparison, too, proletarianization occurred relatively quickly in the southern United States, central Georgia not excepted.[14]

This evolution of free labor in postbellum central Georgia and elsewhere in the South also reflected the strong influence of developments in the North during the late antebellum period. Federal policymakers made any number of analogies to northern free-labor precedents, both industrial and agricultural, to make the case that permanent wage labor was not inconsistent with republican ideals and institutions.[15] By that same logic, they extended voting rights to the freedmen. Although former slaves throughout the Americas shared many similar struggles in their effort to give meaning to freedom, nowhere did they enjoy the civil and political rights of the freedpeople in the United States.[16] But by the same token, nowhere else did they face the vicious assault against these rights mounted by the planters of the southern states. The former slaves' insistence upon first-class citizenship guaranteed that the struggle would continue into the twentieth century. Although Congress extended the suffrage to freedmen for various motives (including partisan political considerations), the principle of enfranchising approximately one million former slaves, most of whom had no property and only very few of whom were literate, represented an important precedent regarding the qualifications for exercising the franchise.

With votes in their hands, freedmen claimed a formal voice in public affairs. Even had the black electorate not consisted so overwhelmingly of laboring men, it is unlikely that postbellum southern politics during Reconstruction would have been any less preoccupied with relations between former masters and former slaves. But in association with northern Radical Republicans who had settled in the South, black voters helped lay the legal infrastructure for the development of a liberal capitalist polity in Georgia and the other former Confederate states. Among other things, they removed the standard antebellum obstacles to incorporation, provided for public schools, and aimed to promote economic development along explicitly capitalist lines.

During Reconstruction such development inched forward. As much as the planters opposed building industrial capitalism on the ruins of slavery, they soon welcomed capitalist social relations, which—as they learned in the crucible of struggle—promised a way of regaining some of the control over the labor force they had lost as a result of emancipation. Specifically, planters discovered how to use the state apparatus (especially its legislative and judicial branches) to undermine the freedpeople's traditional ability to subsist themselves independently. By curtailing public rights to the open range and by redefining the prerogatives of individual proprietors at the expense of the public at large, large landowners obliged former slaves to seek plantation labor as the key to subsistence. Numbers of freedpeople resisted this slide into proletarian status—much as northern workers did. In attempting to speed the process, southern planters transformed themselves into an agrarian bourgeoisie, comparable in that respect to the northern industrial bourgeoisie.

Toward the end of the period under review, white smallholders in the Georgia upcountry found themselves losing both their land and their independence.

Victims of the same legislation that curtailed the customary rights of the freed-people, they too sensed themselves entering into new social relationships that compromised the independence that had been the hallmark of their existence. After having observed Reconstruction from the sidelines, they began voicing their political concerns in the 1870s and by the 1890s had the whole South in an uproar.[17] As a perceptive student of Virginia politics has noted, popular movements of southern freedmen and of southern yeomen surged powerfully after the Civil War, but at different times.[18] The yeomen gained the podium only after the freedmen had been driven from the stage.

THE PLANTATION WORKERS of central Georgia left a powerful and moving legacy. Both before and after emancipation, they struggled mightily (but ultimately without success) to resolve the contradiction between the political ideals of human equality and the persistent reality of economic inequality, hoping all the while that the latter would bend to accommodate the former and not vice versa. After five generations, the contradiction persists, but the flame of hope that it can be resolved continues to burn.

APPENDIX

. . . .

White and Black Populations in Jones, Twiggs, Bibb, Crawford,
Houston, and Monroe Counties, Georgia, 1810–1880

JONES

Year	White	% Total	% Change	Black	% Total	% Change
1810	5,571	65	——	3,026	35	——
1820	9,620	58	+ 73	6,950	42	+130
1830	6,471	48	− 33	6,874	52	− 1
1840	4,417	44	− 32	5,648	56	− 18
1850	3,899	38	− 12	6,325	62	+ 12
1860	3,084	34	− 21	6,023	66	− 5
1870	2,991	32	− 3	6,445	68	+ 7
1880	3,753	32	+ 25	7,860	68	+ 22

TWIGGS

Year	White	% Total	% Change	Black	% Total	% Change
1810	2,756	81	——	649	19	——
1820	7,096	67	+157	3,544	33	+446
1830	4,495	56	− 37	3,536	44	0
1840	4,214	50	− 6	4,208	50	+ 19

TWIGGS (*Continued*)

Year	White	% Total	% Change	Black	% Total	% Change
1850	3,517	43	− 17	4,662	57	+ 11
1860	2,930	35	− 17	5,390	65	+ 16
1870	2,913	34	− 1	5,632	66	+ 4
1880	2,844	32	− 2	6,074	68	+ 8

BIBB

Year	White	% Total	% Change	Black	% Total	% Change
1830	4,139	58	——	3,015	42	——
1840	5,355	54	+ 29	4,447	46	+ 47
1850	7,009	55	+ 31	5,690	45	+ 28
1860	9,458	58	+ 35	6,831	42	+ 20
1870	8,831	44	− 7	11,424	56	+ 67
1880	11,429	42	+ 29	15,700	58	+ 37

CRAWFORD

Year	White	% Total	% Change	Black	% Total	% Change
1830	3,591	68	——	1,722	32	——
1840	4,412	55	+ 23	3,569	45	+107
1850	4,342	48	− 2	4,642	52	+ 30
1860	3,407	44	+ 22	4,286	56	− 8
1870	3,284	43	− 4	4,273	57	0
1880	3,940	46	+ 20	4,716	54	+ 10

HOUSTON

Year	White	% Total	% Change	Black	% Total	% Change
1830	5,161	70	——	2,208	30	——
1840	4,861	50	− 6	4,850	50	+120
1850	6,510	40	+ 34	9,940	60	+105
1860	4,828	31	− 26	10,783	69	+ 8
1870	5,071	25	+ 5	15,332	75	+ 42
1880	6,024	27	+ 19	16,390	73	+ 7

MONROE

Year	White	% Total	% Change	Black	% Total	% Change
1830	8,838	54	——	7,364	46	——
1840	7,804	48	− 12	8,471	52	+ 15
1850	6,810	40	− 13	10,175	60	+ 20
1860	5,753	36	− 16	10,200	64	0
1870	6,409	37	+ 11	10,804	63	+ 6
1880	6,693	36	+ 4	12,115	64	+ 12

Source: U.S. Census Bureau, *Compendium of the Ninth Census*, 34–37, and *Statistics of Population* (1883), 385–87.

NOTES

. . . .

ABBREVIATIONS USED IN NOTES

ACS	American Colonization Society Papers, Correspondence, Library of Congress, Washington, D.C.
Acts	Georgia General Assembly, *Acts*, 1820–1880
AMA	American Missionary Association Papers, Georgia Records, Amistad Research Center, Tulane University, New Orleans, La.
DU	Perkins Library, Duke University, Durham, N.C.
GDAH	Georgia Department of Archives and History, Atlanta, Ga.
Jnl. & Msgr.	Macon *Georgia Journal & Messenger*
RG 29	Record Group 29, Records of the Bureau of the Census, National Archives, Washington, D.C.
RG 60	Record Group 60, Records of the Department of Justice, National Archives, Washington, D.C.
RG 94	Record Group 94, Records of the Adjutant General's Office, National Archives, Washington, D.C.
RG 105	Record Group 105, Records of the Bureau of Refugees, Freedmen, and Abandoned Lands (Freedmen's Bureau), National Archives, Washington, D.C.
RG 107	Record Group 107, Records of the Secretary of War, National Archives, Washington, D.C.
RG 109	Record Group 109, War Department Collection of Confederate Records, Chapter 4, Ordnance Department, National Archives, Washington, D.C.
RG 393	Record Group 393, Records of U.S. Army Continental Commands, National Archives, Washington, D.C.
SHC	Southern Historical Collection, University of North Carolina, Chapel Hill, N.C.
Telegr.	*Macon Telegraph*
Telegr. & Msgr.	Macon *Telegraph & Messenger*
UGa	Special Collections Division, University of Georgia Library, Athens, Ga.

INTRODUCTION

1. Details of the escape of William and Ellen Craft come largely from William's account, *Running a Thousand Miles for Freedom*. See also Blackett, *Breaking against the Barriers*, chap. 2, esp. 87–89; Ripley et al., *Black Abolitionist Papers*, 1:243–44n, 246–49, 271–75; Quarles, *Black Abolitionists*, 203–4.

2. [Craft], *Running a Thousand Miles*, 27.

3. Following his escape, William learned that his mother had purchased her freedom and was endeavoring—with considerable difficulty—to secure the release of his sister from a Mississippi slave owner. See Ripley et al., *Black Abolitionist Papers*, 1:275n.

4. [Craft], *Running a Thousand Miles*, 17–27 (quotation on 26).

5. See the letter of John Knight, an agent of the owners, in *Jnl. & Msgr.*, 13 Nov. 1850, and that of Robert Collins to the Attorney General of the United States, 1 Nov. 1850, Letters Received from Ga. Private Citizens, Attorney General's Papers, RG 60. See also Blackett, *Beating against the Barriers*, 93–94.

6. Ripley et al., *Black Abolitionist Papers*, 1:330; Blackett, *Beating against the Barriers*, 94–123, and "Fugitive Slaves in Britain," 41–62.

7. See Blackett, *Beating against the Barriers*, 124–37; Shadgett, *Republican Party in Georgia*, app. C.

8. *Jnl. & Msgr.*, 22 May 1867.

9. For the fullest elaboration of these changes as they affected the slave-plantation regions of the Americas, see Fox-Genovese and Genovese, *Fruits of Merchant Capital*, chaps. 1–2.

10. Crosby, *Ecological Imperialism*, esp. chaps. 7–10; Wallerstein, *Modern World-System III*, esp. chap. 3; Wolf, *Europe and the People without History*, pt. 3; Hobsbawm, *Age of Revolution*, esp. chaps. 1, 8, 9; Chirot, "Growth of the Market."

11. Wallerstein, *Modern World System III*, chaps. 2–3.

12. For the best general overview of these trends, see Hobsbawm, *Age of Revolution*.

13. See E. Foner, *Tom Paine*; Wallace, *Rockdale*; Dublin, *Women at Work*; Prude, *Coming of Industrial Order*; Wilentz, *Chants Democratic*; Hahn and Prude, *Countryside*; Stansell, *City of Women*.

14. A rich literature, highly seasoned with the spice of scholarly debate, describes this process. See esp. C. Clark, *Roots of Rural Capitalism*; Lemon, *Best Poor Man's Country*; Barron, *Those Who Stayed Behind*; Hahn and Prude, *Countryside*; Henretta, "Families and Farms"; Merrill, "Cash Is Good To Eat"; C. Clark, "Household Economy"; Rothenberg, "Market and Massachusetts Farmers." Good recent overviews of the debates are Pruitt, "Self-Sufficiency," and esp. Kulikoff, "Transition to Capitalism." On developments in the West, see Faragher, *Sugar Creek*, which supersedes M. Bogue's still-valuable *Patterns in the Sod*. The importance of the Revolution to these developments is especially clear in Henretta, "War for Independence."

15. See Clemens, *From Tobacco to Grain*; Fields, *Slavery and Freedom*, chap. 1.

16. On the colonial origins of the planter class, see esp. Morgan, *American Slavery, American Freedom*; P. Wood, *Black Majority*; Isaac, *Transformation of Virginia*; Rutman and Rutman, *A Place in Time*; Gallay, *Formation of a Planter Elite*; Klein, *Unification of a Slave State*. Despite the disagreement among historians over the minimum number of slaves

necessary to qualify a slave owner as a planter, the prevailing criterion of twenty or more slaves will be the standard for this study. The intention is to define the minimum slaveholding that would allow for gang labor under the direction of the owner or an overseer and would guarantee the slaveholder a measure of status among his peers. Of course, the use of a twenty-slave designation does not eliminate all ambiguity. If a hypothetical planter's twenty slaves consisted of only three or four able-bodied adults, the rest being children or old or disabled persons, the term "gang" hardly seems appropriate. Moreover, certain regions of the South might call for different criteria. In the alluvial Natchez District of Mississippi and Louisiana, for instance, it seems appropriate to designate planters as owners of thirty or more slaves, among whom the owners of fifty or more represented the planter elite (see Wayne, "Old South Morality Play," 848). Such a standard, however, would obscure, rather than illuminate, important developments in central Georgia.

17. The best recent study of southern yeomen is Hahn, *Roots of Southern Populism*, which perceptively analyzes how the political system served as an arena wherein yeomen and planters addressed—without always resolving—their conflicting class interests. For studies that view southern politics as an arena in which yeomen and planters reaffirmed shared values, see Thornton, *Politics and Power*; Ford, *Origins of Southern Radicalism*; and Oakes, *Ruling Race* and *Slavery and Freedom*.

18. For general overviews of this process of institution building, see Blassingame, *Slave Community*, chaps. 2–3; Fogel, *Without Consent or Contract*, chap. 6. On specific institutions, see Gutman, *Black Family*; Burton, *My Father's House*, chap. 4; Raboteau, *Slave Religion*; Webber, *Deep Like the Rivers*; Sobel, *Trabelin' On*. On the broader theoretical implications of the process, see Genovese, *Roll, Jordan, Roll*, esp. 159–284. Studies of slaves elsewhere in the Americas illustrate the similarities and differences in the cultural lives of persons of African descent. See esp. Mintz and Price, *Anthropological Approach to the Afro-American Past*.

19. See esp. P. Morgan, "Work and Culture"; Innes, *Work and Labor*.

20. Virtually every study of Caribbean slave societies notes the significance of slave provision grounds. See especially the work of Mintz.

21. For a fuller elaboration of this relationship between privilege and right with respect to gardens, see Genovese, *Roll, Jordan, Roll*, 535–40.

22. Critical insights into these processes appear in Thomas, *Confederacy as a Revolutionary Experience*, and (from the perspective of the evolution of central state authority) Bensel, *Yankee Leviathan*.

23. See esp. Cox, *Lincoln and Black Freedom*, chap. 1.

24. E. Foner, *Reconstruction*, esp. xxiv–xxvi.

25. For an early exploration of relevant themes, see Woodward, "Emancipations and Reconstructions." More recent overviews include E. Foner, *Nothing But Freedom*, chap. 1; Moreno Fraginals, Moya Pons, and Engerman, *Between Slavery and Free Labor*; Richardson, *Abolition and Its Aftermath*; Mintz, "Slavery and the Rise of Peasantries"; and Engerman, "Economic Adjustments to Emancipation" and "Slavery and Emancipation."

26. For an incisive contemporary assessment of the relationship between central state authority and the citizenry, see Brig. Gen. J. W. Phelps to Capt. R. S. Davis, 16 June 1862, in Berlin et al., *Destruction of Slavery*, doc. 63. More generally, see Bensel, *Yankee Leviathan*.

27. For treatment of changes in the ideology and practice of free labor in the North during the Civil War era, see the works cited in n. 15, above. The implications of these changes upon rural communities are addressed in Barron, *Those Who Stayed Behind*; Hahn and Prude, *Countryside*; Faragher, *Sugar Creek*; C. Clark, *Roots of Rural Capitalism*; and Ferleger, *Agriculture and National Development*.

28. The most thorough exposition of these points is found in the work of E. Foner: *Reconstruction, Nothing But Freedom*, and *Politics and Ideology*, esp. chap. 6, "Reconstruction and the Crisis of Free Labor."

29. See Wilson, *Black Codes*.

30. For fuller discussions of these developments, see Woodman, "Post–Civil War Southern Agriculture"; Fields, "Nineteenth-Century American South"; Hahn, "Development of Capitalist Agriculture"; and Reidy, "Capitalist Transformation of Southern Agriculture."

CHAPTER 1

1. The choice of this area as the focus of the study rests upon a number of considerations, both analytical and methodological. For analytical purposes, the area encompassed the heartland of Georgia's antebellum plantation belt and a major upcountry commercial center. Moreover, Macon has traditionally served as a convenient meeting place, for both the surrounding countryside and the state as a whole. This was especially the case during the politically tumultuous 1850s, 1860s, and 1870s. Methodologically, the focus upon central Georgia made possible the extensive use of local sources. Foremost among these were the newspapers from Macon and the voluminous records of the Freedmen's Bureau and other agencies of the federal government during the Civil War and Reconstruction. Although few plantation records from central Georgia are accessible to scholars, county records hold treasure-troves of invaluable information that social historians of the nineteenth century have only begun to examine. But the prospecting itself is exhausting, so some kind of geographical limitation is an essential research strategy.

2. On the origins of slavery in Georgia, see B. Wood, *Slavery in Colonial Georgia*; Ver Steeg, *Origins of a Southern Mosaic*, esp. 7–32, 125–27; Flanders, *Plantation Slavery*, 3–22; Wax, "Georgia and the Negro"; Miller, "Failure of the Colony of Georgia."

3. Callaway, *Early Settlement*, chap. 6.

4. For explanations of the various land cessions and the disposition of the ceded lands, see Phillips, *Georgia and State Rights*, chap. 2; Flanders, *Plantation Slavery*, 55–64; Banks, *Economics of Land Tenure*, 15–20; Heath, *Constructive Liberalism*, 69–158; Dobbins and Andrews, "History of Houston County, Georgia," GDAH.

5. Butler, *Historical Record*, chaps. 1–4; Hickson, *Land So Dedicated*, 49–105; Central Georgia Genealogical Society, *First Hundred and Ten Years*, 2–45; Governor Treutlen Chapter, DAR, *History of Peach County*, chap. 2; C. Williams, *History of Jones County*, chaps. 3–4.

6. Although steamboats had captured much of the cotton trade by the 1830s, pole boats (which enjoyed the advantage of shallower draft to counterbalance the disadvantage of smaller capacity) survived along the Ocmulgee until the completion of the Central

Railroad in 1843. A typical company consisted of two boats and fifteen slave men. *Georgia Messenger*, 24 Oct. 1829.

7. Two classic accounts describe the settling of the backcountry: Bridenbaugh, *Myths and Realities*, chap. 3, and Owsley, *Plain Folk*, chap. 2. More recent studies include Beeman, *Evolution of the Southern Backcountry*; Klein, *Unification of a Slave State*; Ford, *Origins of Southern Radicalism*; J. Moore, *Emergence of the Cotton Kingdom*. For Georgia, see Gallay, *Formation of a Planter Elite*, and Chaplin, "Creating a Cotton South." For a comparison of the newer works with Bridenbaugh and Owsley, see Tillson, "Southern Backcountry."

8. Hall, *Travels*, 2:258–60.

9. See Central Georgia Genealogical Society, *First Hundred and Ten Years*, 7. Biehle, "Edward Oxford," chronicles Oxford's moves from Wilkes to Baldwin to Jones and, finally, to Henry County (all in the lower Piedmont) between 1800 and 1830. See also Owsley, *Plain Folk*, 52–58.

10. J. R. Coombs, "Recollections of a Twiggs County Planter," manuscript dated Apr. 1867 and 23 Jan. 1868, typed copy at DU. See also Owsley, *Plain Folk*, 50–77.

11. U.S. Census Bureau, *Compendium of the Ninth Census*, 34–37. See also Phillips, "Origin and Growth."

12. U.S. Census Bureau, *Aggregate Amount . . . 1810*, 81, and *Census for 1820*, 28–29.

13. Flanders, *Plantation Slavery*, 62, 66. Summary figures on Macon's cotton receipts from the earliest days to 1877 appear in the *Telegraph & Messenger*, 30 Oct. 1877. The *Telegraph*'s account noted that Macon's marketing role peaked in the early 1840s but began to decline in October 1843, following completion of the Central Railroad to Savannah. Thereafter, cotton merely passed through Macon en route to market in Savannah. On the Central of Georgia Railroad, see Phillips, *History of Transportation*, 252–302.

14. In 1830, at the dawn of settlement in Houston County, 26 of 315 slaveholders (8 percent) qualified as planters, and approximately 33 percent of the 2,200 slaves in the county lived on their plantations. Calculated from ms. federal population census schedules, Houston Co., Ga., 1830, RG 29. Similar patterns prevailed throughout the region.

15. See Houston Co. Court of Ordinary, Inventories and Appraisements, bk. A, GDAH. See, for example, the property holdings of Fauntleroy F. Chavis, p. 38, and of William Harril, p. 61.

16. Ibid.; in addition to the inventories of property cited in n. 15, see those of Benjamin Lewis, p. 39, and A. M. Scarborough, pp. 12–15.

17. Virtually every estate inventory listed arms, ammunition, and a coffee mill, though only a few contained supplies of coffee. Luxury items appeared among the possessions of slaveless yeomen, even if less frequently than in the case of large slaveholders. See ibid. For general discussions of consumer culture in the late eighteenth and early nineteenth centuries, see Perkins, "Consumer Frontier," and Jaffee, "Peddlers of Progress."

18. Compare the inventories of the following three men, of varying means, who died during the mid-1830s. William Harril, who was slaveless, possessed no tools other than farming implements; Fauntleroy F. Chavis, who owned two slaves, had a tool kit consisting of several axes, a hand saw, a drawknife, and a hammer; and James H. Killen, who owned twenty-eight slaves, possessed a "Sett of Blacksmiths Tools" in addition to the

following carpenters' tools: a froe, a drawknife, a foot adz, a screwdriver, a bevel, a brace and bit, a hand vice, a pair of compasses, two broad axes, and assorted augurs, chisels, gauges, squares, saws, and planes (jointer, smoothing, sash, and moulding). Houston Co. Court of Ordinary, Inventories and Appraisements, bk. A, pp. 61, 38, 71–72, GDAH.

19. Except for Hahn, *Roots of Southern Populism*, there is little on the domestic economy of southern yeoman farms to compare with the rich literature on the North, cited in n. 16 to the Introduction, above. See also Burton and McMath, *Class, Conflict, and Consensus*; Ferleger, *Agriculture and National Development*.

20. Calculated from ms. federal census returns, Jones County, Ga., 1820, RG 29. Contrast Oakes, *Slavery and Freedom*, 94, which finds a "clear preference for adult males" among owners of a single slave.

21. *Jnl. & Msgr.*, 30 Sept. 1857.

22. Kulikoff, "Uprooted Peoples," 149, table 1, estimates that 52,000 slaves were imported to upcountry Georgia between 1790 and 1810 and that of this number 48,000 were Africans. If this proportion holds true for each of the two decades and for the upcountry counties severally, then approximately 2,800 of the 3,000 slaves in Jones and Twiggs counties were African-born. The imprecision of nativity information about slaves makes confirmation of this figure impossible, but it seems remarkably high, given the absence of commentary to that effect by white settlers and travelers.

23. *Jrnl. & Msgr.*, 13 Mar. 1827, 29 Aug. 1829, 24 Jan. 1833, 27 Aug. 1835, 4 Aug. 1836. It is impossible to estimate the proportion of skilled slaves in the total slave population; it is likewise impossible to ascertain the skill level of these slaves. But such skilled slaves as resided in central Georgia were more likely to live in a town or on a plantation than on a yeoman-settler's homestead.

24. See esp. Berlin, *Slaves without Masters*, chap. 1; Clemens, *Atlantic Economy*; Fields, *Slavery and Freedom*, chaps. 1–2; Kulikoff, *Tobacco and Slaves*, chap. 4.

25. Blassingame, *Slave Testimony*, 575; Coombs, "Recollections," 5, DU. Migrants were particularly susceptible to disease for the remainder of the antebellum period. See the account of a frightful cholera epidemic among two families of migrants from Crawford County to Texas in 1854, which killed thirteen of fifteen whites and thirty-nine of sixty slaves. *Jnl. & Msgr.*, 15 Mar. 1854.

26. See Ball, *Fifty Years in Chains*, 36–37, for a description of restraining devices, and ibid., chaps. 3–5, for a graphic account of the journey south in a slave coffle. In the *Georgia Messenger*, see the notice of apprehension of two unnamed women, 20 Mar. 1827, and the runaway advertisements for Isaac, 18 Sept. 1827; Bob and Lucy, 7 Feb. 1830; Jim, 22 May 1830; Isaac, 28 Feb. 1833; and Harrison, 25 Sept. 1834.

27. Genovese, *Roll, Jordan, Roll*, 91, uses the term "reciprocal rights." Faulkner similarly refers to an "unspoken gentlemen's agreement" between master and slave. *Go Down, Moses*, 262.

28. Rawick, *American Slave*, ser. 2, vol. 12, pt. 3, pp. 166–69 (Pattillo); and Rawick, Hillegas, and Lawrence, *American Slave*, suppl. ser. 1, vol. 1, pt. 1, pp. 223–29, quotation on 226 (Crocker). See also Harris, "Organization of Work" and "Portrait of a Small Slaveholder."

29. Hall, *Travels*, 2:260.

30. Testimony of Catherine Beale in Blassingame, *Slave Testimony*, 572–80.

31. See minutes of the following churches, all on microfilm at GDAH: Richland Baptist Church (Twiggs County), Sharon Primitive Baptist Church (Monroe County), and Smyrna Baptist Church (Monroe County). The Smyrna congregation first admitted slaves in 1824 and at some unspecified time before 1835 also began licensing slave preachers.

32. Blassingame, *Slave Testimony*, 579. For a white woman's perspective on camp meetings, see Sarah Pope to her sister Deborah, 20 Aug. 1827, Pope Family Papers, GDAH. More generally, see Mathews, *Religion in the Old South*, and Boles, *Masters and Slaves*.

33. *Georgia Messenger*, 4 Aug. 1836; Joseph McGhee to John B. Lamar, 8 Oct. 1839, Cobb-Erwin-Lamar Family Papers, UGa.

34. Advertisements in the *Georgia Messenger* for Dunwoody, 12 May 1823; Pindar, 21 June 1826; Isaac, 28 Feb. 1833; Jake, 21 May 1835.

35. More generally on patterns of slave flight, see Stampp, *Peculiar Institution*, esp. 109–30; Mullin, *Flight and Rebellion*, chaps. 2–3; Gutman, *Black Family*, chap. 7; Genovese, *Roll, Jordan, Roll*, esp. 648–57; Kolchin, *Unfree Labor*, esp. 285–91.

36. Advertisements in *Georgia Messenger* for Bob and Lucy, 7 Feb. 1830; Daniel and Margaret, 4 May 1837; Austin, 1 July 1841; Jacob, 20 Sept. 1848; and Jerry, 7 Aug. 1835.

37. [John B. Lamar] to Howell [Cobb], 16 Aug. 1837, typescript copy, Cobb-Erwin-Lamar Family Papers, UGa.

38. *Georgia Messenger*, advertisements for Jim, 15 Nov. 1848; Jacob, 13 Aug. 1831; and Tony, 3 July 1850; and notice of apprehension of unnamed slave, 24 June 1841. For an insightful analysis of late-eighteenth-century advertisements for runaway slaves and servants, which focuses especially upon their clothing and personal effects, see Prude, "To Look Upon the 'Lower Sort.'"

39. *Georgia Messenger*, 10 Jan. 1829, 21 Nov. 1839.

40. Ibid., 29 Aug. 1829, 7 Aug. 1830, 25 July 1833, 25 Sept. 1834, 14 July 1836.

41. Advertisements in *Georgia Messenger* for Fountain, 27 July 1837; Sarah (described below), 27 Feb. 1840; Wiley, 8 Apr. 1841; Dick, 16 Jan. 1840; John, 28 Mar. 1849.

42. [Craft], *Running a Thousand Miles*, 26–27; advertisement for Emily and Mary, *Jnl. & Msgr.*, 16 July 1856.

43. *Georgia Messenger*, 3 July 1827; Young, Gholson, and Hargrove, *History of Macon*, 89; Butler, *Historical Record*, 103–5; Bonner, *Milledgeville*, 62.

44. The history of slave insurrections in the American South has generated as much bitter debate as any topic in U.S. history. Phillips's treatment of the topic within the rubric of "slave crime" (*American Negro Slavery*, chap. 22) established the early parameters of discussion. Deliberately revisionist works by Wish, "American Slave Insurrections," and Aptheker, *American Negro Slave Revolts*, added depth and breadth to understanding the frequency and larger significance of revolt. More recently, Genovese, *From Rebellion to Revolution*, and Craton, *Testing the Chains*, have placed the phenomenon of modern slave revolts in a global historical framework, much as Finley, *Ancient Slavery and Modern Ideology*, chap. 3, has done for revolts in the ancient world. Kolchin's comparison of slave revolts in the United States with peasant wars in Russia (*Unfree Labor*, 244–57) illuminates still other dimensions of resistance. Despite the large volume and high quality of such scholarship, confusion persists. Even apart from ongoing debates about the veracity

or extent of various rumors of revolt, vexing analytical issues, especially with regard to geographical and chronological patterns, have yet to be resolved. In this vein, see esp. Kilson, "Towards Freedom." As Genovese and others have suggested, larger economic and political developments in the Atlantic world provide the essential context for understanding these patterns. At the same time, the innumerable studies of individual revolts completed over the last three decades make abundantly clear the importance of national, regional, and local contexts. In the absence of large concentrations of Africans from the same ethnic group (an important precondition of revolt elsewhere in the Americas) or of a revolutionary crisis (such as the one that gripped Saint-Domingue), slaves in the United States plotted revolt when bondage appeared intolerable and freedom seemed within reach. In central Georgia, such a conjuncture occurred in the mid-1830s—before planters fully consolidated their power—but not again until the eve of the Civil War.

45. *Georgia Messenger*, 8 Oct. 1835.

46. The reference is to Georgia's two leading political factions: the Jacksonians under John Clark and the anti-Jacksonians under George M. Troup. See Phillips, *Georgia and State Rights*, chap. 2.

47. *Georgia Messenger*, 22 Oct. 1835; Monroe Co. Inferior Court Minute Books, Oct. 1835 Called Term, GDAH.

48. Minutes, Smyrna Baptist Church, 24 Oct. 1835, microfilm, GDAH. Church elders also deemed it "inexpedient to Licence any black bro to preach."

CHAPTER 2

1. Although cotton prices declined overall from a peak in 1817, generally rising prices characterized the early 1820s, most of the 1830s, and from the early 1840s to the Civil War. See Hammond, *Cotton Industry*, app. 1; Phillips, *American Negro Slavery*, chart facing 370.

2. The classic works of the "Owsley school" are Owsley, *Plain Folk*; B. Clark, *Tennessee Yeoman*; and Weaver, *Mississippi Farmers*. Recent interest was sparked by Oakes, *Ruling Race*, and has been kept alive by Ford, *Origins of Southern Radicalism*, and Oakes, *Slavery and Freedom*.

3. The case for seigneurialism is most comprehensively made by Genovese, *Political Economy of Slavery*, *World the Slaveholders Made*, and *Roll, Jordan, Roll*; and Fox-Genovese and Genovese, *Fruits of Merchant Capital*. But see also the important supporting arguments made by Hahn, *Roots of Southern Populism*, and Fields, *Slavery and Freedom*. The case for capitalism is made most forcefully by Fogel and Engerman, *Time on the Cross*; Fogel, *Without Consent or Contract*; Oakes, *Slavery and Freedom* and *Ruling Race*; and Shore, *Southern Capitalists*. Ford, *Origins of Southern Radicalism*, adds supporting evidence.

4. See nn. 9–11 to Introduction, above, for relevant references.

5. See esp. Genovese, *World the Slaveholders Made*, 71–95; Graham, "Economics or Culture?," 118–24.

6. See Genovese, *World the Slaveholders Made*, pt. 1, esp. 95–102; Fox-Genovese and Genovese, *Fruits of Merchant Capital*, chaps. 1–2.

7. Estate of James A. Everett, Houston Co. Court of Ordinary, Inventories and Appraisements, bk. B, GDAH; Hickson, *Land So Dedicated*, 84–86; Governor Treutlen Chapter, DAR, *History of Peach County*, 68–70.

8. On the Lamars of Georgia, see Andrew J. Lamar to John B. Lamar, 21 Dec. 1842, and list of the property holdings of John B. Lamar, 1859, in Cobb-Erwin-Lamar Family Papers, UGa; John B. Lamar to Mrs. H. Cobb, 2 Dec. 1845, in Phillips, *Plantation and Frontier Documents*, 1:173. See also Thornton, *Politics and Power*, chap. 1; Cauthen, *Family Letters of Three Wade Hamptons*. The most sophisticated analysis of antebellum planter families is Fox-Genovese, *Within the Plantation Household*.

9. Coombs, "Recollections," 3–6, DU; Andrew J. Lamar to John B. Lamar, 21 Dec. 1842, Jonas Smith to John B. Lamar, 5 May 1851, Mrs. Howell Cobb to Howell Cobb, 21 Dec. 1856, Cobb-Erwin-Lamar Family Papers, UGa; Hickson, *Land So Dedicated*, 83–84; Central Georgia Genealogical Society, *First Hundred and Ten Years*, 7–9, 45; C. Williams, *History of Jones County*, 35–37.

10. Quoted in *Jnl. & Msgr.*, 31 May 1838. Additional criticisms of the practice appeared in ibid., 29 June, 18 July 1839, but the infamous hard cider presidential campaign of 1840 silenced the critics. The classic analysis of such electoral practices is Sydnor, *Gentlemen Freeholders*, chap. 4.

11. For more general discussions, see Fox-Genovese, *Within the Plantation Household*; Clinton, *Plantation Mistress*; A. Scott, *Southern Lady*.

12. Local lore has it that some of the most prominent antebellum families in Houston County traced their lineage to overseers, but the incidence of such rags-to-riches transformations was small. Even during the prosperous 1850s, only a handful of overseers became landowners. Two notable success stories were G. W. Singleton and Patrick Carroll, both of whom began the decade landless and finished with real property worth $8,000 and $12,000, respectively. But overall the fortunes of overseers seem to have declined rather than risen. Of those who headed households in 1850, 26 percent owned land; of the same group ten years later, only 12 percent did. Figures compiled from ms. federal population census returns, Houston Co., Ga., 1850 and 1860, RG 29. On overseers more generally, see Scarborough, *Overseer*; on the social and political constraints that bound even upwardly mobile overseers, see Wayne, "Old South Morality Play."

13. Dobbins and Andrews, "History of Houston County, Georgia," GDAH; Hickson, *Land So Dedicated*, 62–105 passim; Harris, *Plain Folk and Gentry*, esp. chaps. 3–4.

14. Houston Co. Court of Ordinary, Inventories and Appraisements, GDAH; Hickson, *Land So Dedicated*, 65–105; C. Williams, *History of Jones County*, chap. 3. Isaac, *Transformation of Virginia*, chaps. 2–5, describes similar developments in eighteenth-century Virginia.

15. In Monroe County the process of concentration was not quite so dramatic, with the proportion of planters increasing from approximately 9 to 16 percent over the boom period. Ms. federal population census returns, Jones Co., 1820, and Houston and Monroe counties, 1830 and 1840, RG 29.

16. Quoted in Gray, *History of Agriculture*, 1:557.

17. *Southern Agriculturist* 7 (Aug. 1834): 404.

18. See, for instance, Blassingame, *Slave Testimony*, 132.

19. See Ball, *Fifty Years in Chains*, 149–50.

20. *Southern Agriculturist* 5 (Apr. 1832): 181–84. For a closely reasoned defense of tasking as a key component in the proper "Management of Slaves," see ibid. 6 (June 1833): 281–87, esp. 286–87. More generally, see Berlin, "Evolution of Afro-American Society," esp. 65–67; P. Morgan, "Work and Culture" and "Black Society in the Low-country"; Armstrong, "From Task Labor to Free Labor"; Joyner, *Down by the Riverside*, 43–45; J. Smith, *Slavery and Rice Culture*, 45–46, 61–63.

21. See James M. White to Editors, *Jnl. & Msgr.*, 21 Nov. 1860.

22. *Southern Agriculturist* 10 (May 1837): 240. Thanks to Leslie S. Rowland and Steven F. Miller for this reference. See also Phillips, *American Negro Slavery*, 259–60.

23. [Brown], *Slave Life*, 76, 58.

24. The best sampling of prescriptive advice on the "Management of Negroes" is Breeden, *Advice among Masters*. This compilation reprints Foby, "The Management of Servants," *Southern Cultivator* 11 (Aug. 1853): 226–28, and Robert Collins, "Essay on the Treatment and Management of Slaves," ibid. 12 (July 1854): 205–6, which bear particularly upon central Georgia. (The latter author, incidentally, is the same Robert Collins whose wife owned Ellen Craft.) See also Rose, *Documentary History*, 345–63, and Mullin, *American Negro Slavery*, 151–82, 189–90.

25. [Brown], *Slave Life*, 36–38.

26. Ibid., 38–39.

27. Geo. W. Grise to I. L. Brookes, 17 Nov. 1846, in Iveson L. Brookes Papers, SHC.

28. Hiram West Diary, 21 May 1829, typescript in Hiram Warner Collection, GDAH.

29. Fogel, *Without Consent or Contract*, esp. 26–29.

30. This preoccupation with managing nature, man, and beast permeated Georgia's influential agricultural journal, the *Southern Cultivator*, from its inception in 1843. Journals published elsewhere in the South reflected the same interest. See, for instance, the *Southern Agriculturist* (South Carolina) and the *Farmers' Register* (Virginia).

31. Wm. L. Gwyne to Col. H. Brown, 30 Dec. 1840, Hamilton Brown Papers, SHC.

32. *Georgia Messenger*, 4 Jan. 1838, 18 June 1840, 30 Dec. 1841; Heath, *Constructive Liberalism*, 266; Phillips, *History of Transportation*, 244–45, 266–69, 272–77.

33. In Monroe County, the number of owners fell from 933 to 831 while the number of slaves increased from 7,355 to 10,170. See ms. slave census schedules, 1830, 1850, RG 29. Phillips cites figures (derived from county tax digests) for Hancock County; between 1821 and 1844, the number of slaveholders decreased from 678 to 445, and although the total slave population also decreased (from 6,331 to 5,787), the average size slaveholding grew from 9.3 to 13.0. Phillips, "Origin and Growth," 809. The *Georgia Messenger* contains countless advertisements of liquidation sales; see, for example, 16, 23 Dec. 1841. On depressed prices, see ibid., 3, 17 Mar. 1842. On the general process of consolidation, see Phillips, "Origin and Growth," 811–12; Flanders, *Plantation Slavery*, 71.

34. Flanders, "Two Plantations and a County," 5 (Tooke) and 13 (Everett). See also Houston Co. Court of Ordinary, Inventories and Appraisements, GDAH. See Flanders, *Plantation Slavery*, 120, for the comparable experience of Farish Carter of Baldwin County.

35. Flanders, *Plantation Slavery*, 67–69, 85–92; Bonner, *History of Georgia Agriculture*, 62; Bonner, "Profile of a Late Ante-Bellum Community," 675; Phillips, "Origin and

Growth," 799; and Range, *Century of Georgia Agriculture*, 22–31. Compare with Wright, *Political Economy*, 15, 17, and Craven, *Soil Exhaustion*.

36. See *Southern Cultivator* 4 (Aug. 1846): 127; *Southern Agriculturist* 10 (May 1837): 239; *Southern Cultivator* 5 (Apr. 1847): 60–61. For illustrations of improved machinery, see *Southern Cultivator* 5 (Nov. 1847): 161.

37. Hilliard, *Atlas*, maps 64–75, illustrate the growth in the number of mules over the antebellum period. See also the comments of "A Planter" in *Southern Cultivator* 1 (26 Apr. 1843): 62–63. Estate inventories document the correlation between mules and improved implements. When he died in March 1843, Moses Roundtree owned twenty-four slaves and farmed with six mules drawing an assortment of scooter plows, shovel plows, turning plows, and sweeps. Estate of Moses Roundtree, Houston Co. Court of Ordinary, Inventories and Appraisements, bk. A, GDAH. Farmers who relied upon oxen for animal traction rarely had such an array of implements; a typically nondescript entry in an inventory of such an estate would read "1 Lot Plows & Gear." See, for instance, estate of William F. Jenkins, ibid.

38. Lawson is quoted in Hickson, *Land So Dedicated*, 70. See also Phillips, *American Negro Slavery*, chap. 12; Gray, *History of Agriculture*; Raper, *Tenants of the Almighty*, 44–45; Destler, "David Dickson's 'System of Farming,'" 30–39, esp. 31; Bonner, *History of Georgia Agriculture*. On fences, see *Southern Agriculturist* 1 (Feb. 1828): 306–8; *Southern Cultivator* 2 (1844): 19, 173.

39. Completion of the Western & Atlantic Railroad in 1846 effectively linked central Georgia with the grain- and stock-raising area of the Tennessee River Valley.

40. *Southern Agriculturist* 3 (Mar. 1830): 123.

41. Ibid. 11 (Oct. 1838): 512–13.

42. Ibid.

43. Faust, *James Henry Hammond*, 74–75 and chaps. 5–6. On another plantation not far from Hammond's, the prominent Georgia planter Alexander Telfair permitted tasking in work that was conducive to that kind of organization; the size of the task depended on the "state of the ground and the strength of the negro." See Phillips, *Plantation and Frontier Documents*, 1:126. For contemporary accounts of upcountry planters who tasked their slaves, see *Southern Agriculturist* 1 (Dec. 1828): 529.

44. *Southern Agriculturist* 7 (Aug. 1834): 406–7.

45. Ibid. 5 (Mar. 1832): 118.

46. Ibid. 7 (Aug. 1834): 408.

47. Foby in *Southern Cultivator* 11 (Aug. 1853): 227.

48. Ibid.

49. Testimony of Fannie Hughes in Rawick, Hillegas, and Lawrence, *American Slave*, suppl. ser. 1, 3:331–32.

50. *Southern Cultivator* 11 (Aug. 1853): 227.

51. [Brown], *Slave Life*, 29–39. The slave, John Glasgow, was a freeborn British subject enslaved in 1830 for violating Georgia's Negro Seaman Act. See also Ripley et al., *Black Abolitionist Papers*, 1:261, 266n, 267n.

52. *Southern Cultivator* 11 (Aug. 1853): 225–27. The Georgia code eventually recognized the right of slaves to hold personal property and trade it with their owner's permission. Clark, Cobb, and Irwin, *Georgia Code*, 368–69.

53. Estates of James A. Everett and Joseph Tooke, Houston Co. Court of Ordinary, Annual Returns and Vouchers, bks. C and D, GDAH; Flanders, "Two Plantations and a County," 6–7, 18.

54. Phillips, *American Negro Slavery*, 268, 277; see also Olmsted, *Cotton Kingdom*, 482. On the phenomenon of slave theft more generally, see Lichtenstein, " 'That Disposition to Theft.' "

55. *Southern Cultivator* 11 (Aug. 1853): 227.

56. In addition to Fitzhugh, *Cannibals All!*, which is the most sustained exposition of these themes, see *Southern Cultivator* 11 (Aug. 1853), 226.

57. Smyrna Baptist Church Minute Books, 1 Dec. 1827, 14 Jan. and 16 Sept. 1832, 17 Aug. 1833, 24 Oct. 1835, 14 May 1836, and 16 July 1836; Sharon Primitive Baptist Church Minute Books, 13 Dec. 1833, 9 July and 10 Sept. 1831, 2 May 1833, 12 Mar., 11 June, and 9 July 1842, all on microfilm, GDAH. More generally, see Boles, *Masters and Slaves*, esp. chap. 2; Raboteau, *Slave Religion*, chap. 4; and Mathews, *Religion in the Old South*.

58. Flanders, *Plantation Slavery*, 239–40.

59. Proctor, "Slavery in Southwest Georgia," 10, 5; Flanders, *Plantation Slavery*, 236.

60. Flanders, *Plantation Slavery*, 233–35.

61. Bibb Co. Superior Court, Minutes, July 1850 and July 1851, GDAH.

62. Until 1846, county inferior courts rendered judgment in all cases involving slaves; thereafter, county superior courts heard criminal cases against slaves. Records in the following cases are found in the minutes of the respective courts, GDAH. In Jones County (where the inferior court kept a separate record of the trials of slaves, 1822–46), the following slaves were sentenced to hang: Harry for rape, 4 Jan. 1836; Adam for murdering another slave, 11 Sept. 1835; Charles for rape, 9 Nov. 1836; Claiborne and Shadrack for murdering their master, 17 July 1845. The inferior court of Monroe County sentenced the slave George to death by hanging for insurrection, 10–16 Oct. 1835. The superior court of Crawford County affirmed an earlier judgment of the inferior court sentencing Adam to death by hanging for murder, Aug. 1846. The superior court of Bibb County ordered to death by hanging for the crime of murder the slaves John, May 1855, and Jacob, Nov. 1858; but in the case of Allen, who was originally sentenced to hang for murder (July 1850), the court ordered a new trial at which he was found guilty of voluntary manslaughter and sentenced to whipping and branding (July 1851). The superior court of Houston County sentenced Jerry to hang for murder, Oct. 1853, and found Aggey and Gabriel not guilty of assault with intent to murder, Apr. 1858. A few slaves escaped death sentences, even when found guilty of assaulting a white person with a deadly weapon; see cases of Alfred before the Monroe County inferior court, 12 July 1838; Anthony and John before the Jones County superior court, Apr. 1857 and Apr. 1860, respectively. Other cases for which no court records seem to survive include those of Cain, a slave with "a very bad reputation," sentenced in Bibb County to hang for burglary (*Jnl. & Msgr.*, 18 June 1855), and Emiline, reportedly acquitted by a jury in Crawford County of murder by poison on the grounds that her confession had been "extorted by threats" (*Telegr.*, 13 Mar. 1860).

63. A growing body of work treats the matter of procedural justice in cases involving slave defendants. Important early treatments are Nash, "Fairness and Formalism" and "A

More Equitable Past?"; Flanagan, "Criminal Procedure in Slave Trials"; and Hindus, "Black Justice under White Law." More recently, see Hindus, *Prison and Plantation*; Schwarz, *Twice Condemned*. Important theoretical formulations of the interrelationship between the law and maintenance of planter-class power are Genovese, "The Hegemonic Function of the Law," in *Roll, Jordan, Roll*, 25–49; also Tushnet, *American Law of Slavery*. Overviews of the debate appear in Nash, "Reason of Slavery," and Fox-Genovese and Genovese, *Fruits of Merchant Capital*, chap. 12. The classic reference work on slave trials is Catterall, *Judicial Cases*.

64. Lamar's address to the prisoner in the case of State v. Jacob, published in *Jnl. & Msgr.*, 24 Nov. 1858.

65. See, for example, Central Georgia Genealogical Society, *First Hundred and Ten Years*, chap. 5.

66. Hickson, *Land So Dedicated*, 65–66; see also *Telegr.*, various issues, for advertisements.

67. See, for instance, C. Williams, *History of Jones County*, 19–20.

68. *Jnl. & Msgr.*, 25 Mar. 1857, 30 May 1860.

69. Butler, *Historical Record*, 89–97, 109, 137–67 passim; Young, Gholson, and Hargrove, *History of Macon*, 60–62; Wallenstein, *Slave South to New South*, chaps. 2–3.

70. Estate records of James A. Everett and Daniel Gunn contain numerous notations of such accounts. Houston Co. Court of Ordinary, Inventories and Appraisements, bk. B, pp. 304–8 (Everett); bk. C, pp. 289–98 (Gunn), GDAH.

71. The estates of most decedents, however wealthy or humble, include outstanding notes. See, for instance, annual returns of estates of Joseph Culpepper and William McKenzie, 1847, Houston Co. Court of Ordinary, Annual Returns, GDAH.

72. Ibid., Inventories and Appraisements, bk. B, pp. 286–88, 304–8; Annual Returns, bk. C, pp. 286, 393; bk. D, pp. 341–43, 355.

73. This pattern is especially clear in the cases of smallholders who died intestate. See, for example, inventory of property sold at administrative sale, estate of James Jarrett, 1 Jan. 1835, ibid., bk. A.

74. James Henry Hammond's clients proved especially adept at conveying this message, but his experiences in this regard were not unique. See Faust, *James Henry Hammond*, 131–33; Harris, *Plain Folk and Gentry*, 67.

75. For a general discussion of these matters, see Watson, "Conflict and Collaboration." The paucity of plantation account books makes it impossible to document these trends with precision, but suggestive evidence appears in both annual returns of estates and federal ms. agricultural censuses. For records of labor, see, for example, annual returns of the estates of Appling T. Chambers and J. A. Bryan, 1852, Houston Co. Court of Ordinary, Annual Returns, bk. D, pp. 241, 248, GDAH. For records of sales of provisions by smallholders to plantations, see annual returns of the estates of Curtis Daniel and Cordy D. Stokes, ibid., pp. 478, 578.

76. Wallenstein, *Slave South to New South*, 19–21; Hickson, *Land So Dedicated*, 54–56; Central Georgia Genealogical Society, *First Hundred and Ten Years*, chap. 6. More generally, see Wooster, *People in Power*.

77. For representative actions of a county court regarding roads, see Houston Co. Inferior Court Minute Book, 1851–61, 15, 28, 52, GDAH.

78. For a general treatment of the lower house of the state legislature, see DeBats, "Uncertain Arena." On the legislative service of Hugh Lawson of Houston County, see Hickson, *Land So Dedicated*, 70.

79. On the Georgia context, see esp. Phillips, *Georgia and State Rights*. On Alabama, see Thornton, *Politics and Power*, pt. 1.

80. Wallenstein, *Slave South to New South*, pt. 1.

81. Governor Treutlen Chapter, DAR, *History of Peach County*, 17; estate of James A. Everett, Houston Co. Court of Ordinary, Inventories and Appraisements, bk. B, GDAH.

82. See T. Cobb, *Inquiry*. Planters' estates routinely contained individual volumes, if not entire libraries, of ancient classics. See, for instance, estate of A. C. McBride, Houston Co. Court of Ordinary, Inventories and Appraisements, bk. A, p. 159, GDAH.

83. *Southern Agriculturist* 5 (Nov. 1832): 562; see also ibid. 6 (Dec. 1833): 643. For elaborations of a general defense of slavery, see *Southern Cultivator* 3 (Oct. 1845): 148, and the classic exposition in Fitzhugh, *Cannibals All!* The equally classic historical overview of slave regimes is T. Cobb, *Inquiry*.

84. Quoted in Faust, *James Henry Hammond*, 280.

85. H. Cobb, *Scriptural Examination*, 3 (original emphasis); review of "Capt. Canot; or Twenty Years of an African Slaver," *Jnl. & Msgr.*, 1 Nov. 1854.

86. H. Cobb, *Scriptural Examination*, 3 (original emphasis). Cobb's nephew, Thomas Reed Rootes Cobb, argued that slavery had unquestionably "advanced the negro race." *Inquiry*, 49.

87. The preface to Cobb's *Inquiry*, a book-length "historical sketch of slavery," is perhaps the most comprehensive overview of ancient and modern slavery to be produced in the antebellum South.

88. Ibid., 4.

89. Ibid., xxxv, cli, cxlvii.

90. This "organic" view of society, of course, had an ancient pedigree, but defenders of slavery appropriated the findings of various branches of science to buttress their case. For insight into the scientific side of this phenomenon, see Gould, *The Mismeasure of Man* and *The Flamingo's Smile*, chap. 19. More generally, see Winthrop Jordan, *White over Black*; Fredrickson, *The Black Image in the White Mind*; Horsman, *Race and Manifest Destiny*; Snowden, *Before Color Prejudice*. On the ideological basis of race, see Fields, "Ideology and Race." On Victorian prejudices toward the Irish "race," see Curtis, *Anglo-Saxons and Celts*; Holt, *Problem of Freedom*, 318–36.

91. T. Cobb, *Inquiry*, 22–52.

92. Ibid., clx.

93. Unidentified newspaper clipping dated 3 Nov. 1879 in Junius W. Nisbet scrapbook, Nisbet Family Papers, SHC. In January 1861, Nisbet introduced the resolution to the secession convention of Georgia that carried the state out of the Union. He also served in the Confederate congress.

94. Upholders of the social order also threatened suspected abolitionists with hanging. See *Telegr.*, 16 Nov. 1860.

95. E. A. Nisbet to editors, *Jnl. & Msgr.*, 24 May 1854 (original emphasis); T. Cobb, *Inquiry*, ccix.

96. See esp. Fitzhugh, *Cannibals All!*, and James Henry Hammond, "Letter to an English Abolitionist," in Faust, *Ideology of Slavery*.

97. Quoted in Hickson, *Land So Dedicated*, 105.

98. Augusta *Chronicle & Sentinel*, quoted in *Jnl. & Msgr.*, 1 Oct. 1851; Phillips, *Life of Toombs*, 157.

99. Hammond quoted in Faust, *James Henry Hammond*, 373 (original emphasis); see also Fitzhugh, "Southern Thought," in Faust, *Ideology of Slavery*, esp. 285, 286–87, 289; Phillips, *Life of Toombs*, 161–63; Genovese, *World the Slaveholders Made*, pt. 2, 118.

100. T. Cobb, *Inquiry*, ccxiii.

101. Quoted in Phillips, *Life of Toombs*, 161, 164.

102. T. Cobb, *Inquiry*, ccxvii, ccxiii, ccxiv.

103. Stephens to Voters of 8th Congressional District of Georgia, 14 Aug. 1857, in Phillips, *Correspondence of Toombs, Stephens, and Cobb*, 415.

104. Quoted in Phillips, *Life of Toombs*, 157.

105. T. Cobb, *Inquiry*, ccxiii.

106. Ibid., ccxiii (original emphasis).

107. See, for instance, Ryan, *Cradle of the Middle Class*; C. Clark, *Roots of Rural Capitalism*.

108. Conrad, *Destruction of Brazilian Slavery*; Toplin, *Abolition of Slavery*; Reis, "From Banguê to Usina," esp. 372–80.

CHAPTER 3

1. See, for example, Hickson, *Land So Dedicated*, 83–84.

2. Ball, *Fifty Years in Chains*, 38–39, 68–69, 131–32. Blassingame has concluded that Ball's South Carolina residence was the plantation of Gen. Wade Hampton. See *Slave Testimony*, xxv–xxvi.

3. Ball, *Fifty Years in Chains*, 56, 161, 215–18, 318.

4. Jonas Smith to John B. Lamar, 25 Aug. 1852, in Phillips, *Plantation and Frontier Documents*, 1:310; Smith to Lamar, 25 Sept. 1849, Cobb-Erwin-Lamar Family Papers, UGa. Ball, *Fifty Years in Chains*, 206–7, describes the dangers of pulling fodder in late summer dews. The literature on slave health grows in leaps and bounds. See esp. Savitt, *Medicine and Slavery*; Kiple and King, *Black Diaspora*; and the special issue on "The Biological Past of the Black," *Social Science History* 10 (Winter 1986), ed. Kenneth F. Kiple.

5. For the classic exposition of this theme, see Bauer and Bauer, "Day to Day Resistance"; for a more recent formulation, see J. Scott, "Everyday Forms of Peasant Resistance."

6. Ball, *Fifty Years in Chains*, 276–83, 292–318.

7. Ibid., 223, 230, 233, 262–63, 352–55, makes reference to hunting, as do numerous slave narratives; for instance, see Rawick, Hillegas, and Lawrence, *American Slave*, suppl. ser. 1, 3:27, 77, 221, 226; 4:450, 457, 507, 646. Laws to the contrary notwithstanding, scattered upcountry slaves possessed firearms down to the Civil War. See, for instance,

Ball, *Fifty Years in Chains*, 352, and Hoffmann and Hoffmann, "Limits of Paternalism," 329. Along the coast, rice planters customarily equipped slaves with guns during the rice-bird season, and some slaves had permission to purchase arms and ammunition of their own. See Olmsted, *Cotton Kingdom*, 200.

8. See Ball, *Fifty Years in Chains*, 107, 166–67, 189, 203; Blassingame, *Slave Testimony*, 132; Rawick, Hillegas, and Lawrence, *American Slave*, suppl. ser. 1, 3:27, 72, 121, 201–2, 220, 252; 4:456, 467, 644.

9. Ball, *Fifty Years in Chains*, 45, 188–95.

10. Ibid., 351–52, 273, 186. More generally, see Campbell, "As 'A Kind of Freeman'?," esp. 134–36. By the late antebellum period, the Georgia code mandated a fine of $100 for masters who employed slaves on Sunday—"a day of rest of Divine appointment"—except in "work of absolute necessity and the necessary occasions of the family." Clark, Cobb, and Irwin, *Georgia Code*, 368.

11. Ball, *Fifty Years in Chains*, 273, 187; Olmsted, *Cotton Kingdom*, 83.

12. Ball, *Fifty Years in Chains*, esp. 108, 188; *Southern Agriculturist* 9 (Nov. 1836): 582. Olmsted, *Cotton Kingdom*, 81, noted that slaves in Virginia sometimes traded their rations.

13. Ball, *Fifty Years in Chains*, 190, 194–95, 355; Rawick, *American Slave*, ser. 2, vol. 13, pt. 3, p. 331; Rawick, Hillegas, and Lawrence, *American Slave*, suppl. ser. 1, 3:112–13, 252; annual returns of estates of William Haddock, 1849; William McKenzie, 1850; Jeremiah W. Bunn, 1851; J. A. Bryan, 1852, Houston Co. Court of Ordinary, Annual Returns, GDAH.

14. Medick, "Proto-industrial Family Economy"; Mintz, "Question of Caribbean Peasantries" and *Caribbean Transformations*, pt. 2.

15. The Georgia code expressly prohibited "any boat hand or negro" from engaging in such petty trade. See Clark, Cobb, and Irwin, *Georgia Code*, 310. At various times, the legislature added specific prohibitions against the trade between fishing vessels and slaves, particularly during the 1850s, when legislators especially feared abolitionism. A Mississippi law restricting trade with slaves drew special attention to "slave, negro or mulatto" teamsters. Mississippi General Assembly, *Acts*, 1850, 100–102. It is likely that slave teamsters throughout the South engaged in petty trade.

16. Ms. federal census 1830; ms. census returns of free persons and of slaves, 1850 and 1860, Houston Co., Ga., RG 29. More generally, see Phillips, "Origins and Growth."

17. [Brown], *Slave Life*, 29–39. The punished slave, John Glasgow, is described in n. 51, chap. 2, above.

18. See, for instance, Andrew J. Lamar to John B. Lamar, 21 Dec. 1842; Jonas Smith to John B. Lamar, 5 May 1851; Mrs. Howell Cobb to Howell Cobb, 21 Dec. 1856, Cobb-Erwin-Lamar Family Papers, UGa.

19. Ball, *Fifty Years in Chains*, esp. 144–45; *Southern Cultivator* 11 (Aug. 1853): 227. See also Fox-Genovese, *Within the Plantation Household*, chaps. 3–4.

20. See Jasper Battle's fond recollections of the periodic visits of his father, who lived on another plantation, in Rawick, *American Slave*, ser. 2, vol. 12, pt. 1, p. 63.

21. Although slave narratives rarely mention domestic violence, planter reports frequently do. See, for example, *Southern Cultivator* 11 (Aug. 1853): 227. On slave families generally, see Blassingame, *Slave Community*, chap. 3, and Gutman, *Black Family*, pt. 1.

22. *Jnl. & Msgr.*, 7 May 1856.

23. [Craft], *Running a Thousand Miles*, 10; also Ripley et al., *Black Abolitionist Papers*, 1:272.

24. See the changing apportionment of slaves in the four wills written by Edward Oxford, Edward Oxford Papers, GDAH. See also Biehle, "Edward Oxford," 187–98.

25. See, for instance, the distribution of the estate of Cullen Horne, Houston Co. Court of Ordinary, Inventories and Appraisements, bk. A, GDAH.

26. Records of estates of Everett and others, Houston Co. Court of Ordinary, Inventories and Appraisements, bks. A and B; Annual Returns, bks. C and D, GDAH.

27. Rawick, Hillegas, and Lawrence, *American Slave*, suppl. ser. 1, 3:225.

28. [Craft], *Running a Thousand Miles*, 2; see also Fox-Genovese, *Within the Plantation Household*, esp. 238.

29. On the political significance of slave churches, see Raboteau, *Slave Religion*, pt. 2, and esp. Genovese, *Roll, Jordan, Roll*, 161–84.

30. Statements of Georgia Baker, James Bolton, Alec Bostwick, and Susan Castle in Rawick, *American Slave*, ser. 2, vol. 12, pt. 1, pp. 47, 100, 110, 181; statement of Charlie Hudson in ibid., pt. 2, p. 228; statement of Shade Richards in ibid., vol. 13, pt. 3, p. 202. See also C. Williams, *History of Jones County*, 56.

31. Statements of Martha Colquitt and William McWhorter in Rawick, *American Slave*, ser. 2, vol. 12, pt. 1, pp. 243–44; vol. 13, pt. 3, p. 99.

32. Edgar A. Ross Memoir, SHC; statements of Henry Bland, Wheeler Gresham, Henry Rogers, and Ike Thomas in Rawick, *American Slave*, ser. 2, vol. 12, pt. 1, p. 81, and pt. 2, p. 69; vol. 13, pt. 3, p. 225, and pt. 4, p. 27.

33. *Georgia Messenger*, 11 Sept. 1827.

34. Bibb Co. Superior Court Minutes, 19 Nov. 1858, GDAH. See also *Jnl. & Msgr.*, 29 Sept. and 17 Nov. 1858.

35. See esp. Raboteau, *Slave Religion*, 128–50, 223–24.

36. Statements of Rachel Adams, Jasper Battle, Kizzie Colquitt, Willis Cofer, Mary Colbert, Benny Dillard, Elisha Doc Garey, Wheeler Gresham, Bill Heard, Charlie Hudson, Lina Hunter, Mahala Jewel, Georgia Johnson, Charlie King, Robert Shepherd, Paul Smith, John F. Van Hook, Emma Virgel, and Green Willbanks in Rawick, *American Slave*, ser. 2, vol. 12, pt. 1, pp. 7, 71, 123, 209, 221, 293–94, and pt. 2, pp. 6, 69–70, 142, 228, 266–67, 319–20, 335; vol. 13, pt. 3, pp. 30, 254–55, 334, and pt. 4, pp. 81, 119–20, 144–45.

37. Ball, *Fifty Years in Chains*, 276–77, 293–98.

38. *Acts*, 1831, 214–15 (brackets in original). See also ibid., 1829, 152–53; ibid., 1857, 288–90.

39. Ibid., 1857, 249–50.

40. Ibid., 1831, 214–15.

41. From 1818 onward, Georgia legislators aimed to restrict the interaction between persons on rivercraft and slaves. Early in the period, concern centered around illicit trade in plantation staples and liquor, but by the late antebellum period, fears of commercial fishermen and "incendiary publications" also operated. The preamble to an 1857 law aimed at "preventing obstructions" on several major waterways specifically noted the operations of "companies from the Northern states and others." See ibid., 1849–50, 357–59; ibid., 1857, 289–90.

42. See, for instance, Bibb Co. Superior Court grand jury presentments in *Jnl. & Msgr.*, 21 Dec. 1853. More generally, see Hahn, "Hunting, Fishing, and Foraging," 37–64, and *Roots of Southern Populism*, 58–59.

43. See, for instance, *Acts*, 1855–56, 411–12; ibid., 1857, 249, 252–54; ibid., 1858, 163. Such laws aimed especially at nonresidents of designated counties or of the state.

44. *Southern Agriculturist* 4 (Apr. 1831): 198; ibid. 6 (Aug. 1833): 425; *Southern Cultivator* 3 (Apr. 1845): 58. Northern farmers, no less than southern, suffered the depredations of "sheep-killing cur[s]." See Keller, *Solon Robinson*, 2:438.

45. Urban lawmakers succeeded somewhat in restricting dogs, requiring badges without which a dog would be shot as a stray. The badge fee clearly discriminated against dog-owning slaves. See *Jnl. & Msgr.*, 17 Feb. 1858; *Telegr.*, 9 June 1860.

46. James M. White to Editors, *Jnl. & Msgr.*, 21 Nov. 1860. White referred to the "rule" by way of exculpating his carriage driver, who had been arrested for attempting to pass a counterfeit twenty-dollar bill taken in trade by another of his slaves. The explanation sufficed: the bank whose bill had been counterfeited provided a genuine replacement, and the driver was released from custody.

47. See also Blassingame, *Slave Testimony*, 132. Testimony of Fannie Fulcher in Rawick, Hillegas, and Lawrence, *American Slave*, suppl. ser. 1, 3:250–51. See also Phillips, *Life and Labor*, 272; Rawick, *From Sundown to Sunup*, 70.

48. Ball, *Fifty Years in Chains*, 190; annual returns of estates of William Haddock, 1849, (bk. C, p. 158); William McKenzie, 1850, (bk. C, p. 284); J. A. Bryan, 1852, (bk. D, p. 248), Houston Co. Court of Ordinary, Annual Returns, GDAH. See also Flanders, "Two Plantations and a County," 18–19. For a planter's insightful description of how labor patterns changed according to the season and the weather, see *Southern Cultivator* 8 (Nov. 1850): 162–64. The planter noted his objections to granting garden privileges and his requirement that slaves work after dark on fall and winter nights—the women at spinning or making bed quilts. He also observed that at times he required women to patch clothing "of wet days when they are compelled to be in the house."

49. Estate of Jeremiah W. Bunn, Houston Co. Court of Ordinary, Annual Returns, bk. C, p. 433, GDAH. The 1850 federal census listed Bunn as owning twenty-nine slaves.

50. See Mrs. Howell Cobb to Howell Cobb, 21 Dec. 1856; W. P. Mount to J. B. Lamar, 17 Dec. 1858; Stancil Barwick to Col. Lamar, 23 Jan. 1860; and 1858 list of weights of slaves' cotton, Cobb-Erwin-Lamar Family Papers, UGa. See also Phillips, *American Negro Slavery*, 238, 305. Compare Campbell, "As 'A Kind of Freeman'?," 139–43. Some masters gave their slaves a share of cotton profits; see Phillips, *American Negro Slavery*, 279, and Weymouth Jordan, *Hugh Davis*, 104–5. Still others let slaves cultivate a cotton field, known as a "Christmas Forty," the proceeds of which purchased Christmas presents.

51. Clark, Cobb, and Irwin, *Georgia Code*, 271–72, specifies the requirements of legal fences and the respective rights and liabilities of landowners and animal owners. As Hahn has demonstrated, such common rights provoked intense struggle between landowners and animal owners after the Civil War. See his "Hunting, Fishing, and Foraging" and *Roots of Southern Populism*. But before the war, the supremacy of private rights over common rights was not clearly established. In Georgia as elsewhere, the citizenry at large retained assorted rights to privately owned, but unimproved, land. More than the subsis-

tence rights of gathering firewood and foraging animals, these also included commercial rights. As late as 1857, for instance, persons in certain counties could cut timber for commercial purposes on land they did not own, unless the landowner or his agent posted written notice on the courthouse door specifically "forbidding any person from trespassing on said land or lands" (*Acts*, 1857, 250). Yet the 1850s clearly mark a transitional period in the narrowing of common rights in the interest of private proprietary rights. Proprietors of riparian lands steadily advanced their private rights over river banks and to some extent over the watercourses themselves (ibid., 1855–56, 12–13). And whereas the legislature circumscribed landowners' rights against commercial exploitation in some counties, it extended them in others, for instance, by flatly prohibiting any person from cutting trees for sale "knowing the same to be the property of another" (ibid., 1857, 253; ibid., 1858, 162). It is noteworthy that none of the relevant legislation banned taking wood for home use.

52. Lamar to Howell Cobb, 17 Mar. [1844?], in Phillips, *Plantation and Frontier Documents*, 1:169.

53. Rawick, *American Slave*, ser. 2, vol. 13, pt. 4, pp. 185, 187. Lamar estimated that he had to lay up as much as a ton of bacon for "dodging," which, in addition to "stealage," included such things as mistakes in weighing and appropriations by the overseer to entertain company. Lamar to his sister, 18 Nov. 1849, in Phillips, *Plantation and Frontier Documents*, 1:183. On the social and political dynamics of theft among slaves, see Lichtenstein, "'That Disposition to Theft.'"

54. That "Foby" authorized gardens yet prohibited outside marriages suggests such a trade-off. See *Southern Cultivator* 11 (Aug. 1853): 227.

55. Ball, *Fifty Years in Chains*, 167, 262–63; Olmsted, *Cotton Kingdom*, 372. Although boys served as minders of stock foraging in the woods, girls often minded cows (which they also milked). See Phillips, *Plantation and Frontier Documents*, 1:171. For anthropological perspectives on the sexual division of labor in agricultural settings, see Murdock and Provost, "Factors in the Division of Labor by Sex," and Burton and White, "Sexual Division of Labor in Agriculture."

56. Higman, *Slave Population and Economy*, 208, and *Slave Populations*, 189–91; Craton, *Searching*, 142–43, 146–47; Dunn, "'Dreadful Idlers.'"

57. See, for example, inventory of estate of James A. Everett, Houston Co. Court of Ordinary, Inventories and Appraisements, bk. B, pp. 286–88, 304–8, GDAH. Most of the slave artisans on plantations such as Everett's were carpenters and blacksmiths.

58. See the testimony of Robert Kimbrough and Bob Mobley in Rawick, Hillegas, and Lawrence, *American Slave*, suppl. ser. 1, 4:365, 446; also Ball, *Fifty Years in Chains*, 362–63.

59. *Jnl. & Msgr.*, 13 Feb. 1850. In 1850, the Mississippi legislature prohibited slave teamsters specifically from engaging in petty trade on their own account. See Mississippi General Assembly, *Acts*, 1850, 100–102. Slave teamsters throughout the South no doubt traded on the side, much as merchant seamen did. See Rediker, *Devil and the Deep Blue Sea*, 130–33.

60. [Anderson], *Life of Robert Anderson*, 20–21, 42, 62–63. After the Civil War Anderson distinguished himself as an African Methodist Episcopal minister. Robert Kimbrough described the slaves' perception of wagoning as a "privilege"; see Rawick, Hillegas, and Lawrence, *American Slave*, supp. ser. 1, 4:365.

61. *Jnl. & Msgr.*, 28 Feb. 1833.

62. In the *Jnl. & Msgr.*, see runaway advertisements for Bill (4 May 1837), Isaac (28 Feb. 1833), Jack (29 Sept. 1842), Jacob (20 Sept. 1848), and Caesar (25 July 1849) and the news item noting the escape of an unnamed wagoner, 10 Dec. 1856.

63. *Georgia Messenger*, 20 July 1837.

64. In February 1856, wagoner Sam West was killed. His murderer, a white man, was sentenced to life imprisonment. *Jnl. & Msgr.*, 27 Feb. 1856, 10 June 1857. For evidence of their carrying knives, see the case of the wagoner Allen, accused of murder, in Bibb Co. Superior Court Minutes, 5:267–70, GDAH.

65. *Telegr.*, 11 Mar. 1861, reports a black population closer to 4,000, but the present discussion draws upon the figure of 2,829 in the 1860 federal census. Perhaps another 2,000 resided in towns in the surrounding counties.

66. *Georgia Messenger*, 26 Sept. 1835; Butler, *Historical Record*, 58; Bellamy, "Macon," 301–3.

67. Contrast Goldin, *Urban Slavery*, chaps. 4–5.

68. To simplify the task of tracing slave owners from the slave schedule (where their slaveholdings were enumerated) to the free schedule (where personal data appeared), only slaves belonging to household heads are spotlighted; however, those slaves made up 2,770 of the total slave population of 2,829. See Berlin and Gutman, "Natives and Immigrants," for employment of the same technique.

69. Property list, 1859, Cobb-Erwin-Lamar Family Papers, UGa. More generally, see Bellamy, "Macon," 301–6.

70. Eisterhold, "Commercial, Financial, and Industrial Macon," 438. On such reactions by free white workers against competition from blacks, free and slave, see Berlin and Gutman, "Natives and Immigrants," 1195–96; Johnson and Roark, *Black Masters*, esp. 173–84, 266–70, 276–82; Siegel, "Artisans and Immigrants," 223–24.

71. Ms. federal census returns, free and slave schedules, Bibb Co., Ga., 1860, RG 29.

72. *Georgia Messenger*, 26 Sept. 1835.

73. Iveson L. Brookes Papers, SHC. This collection contains numerous items concerning slaves hired during the 1830s and 1840s.

74. Ms. federal census returns, population schedules, Bibb Co., Ga., 1870, RG 29. See Faust, *James Henry Hammond*, 317–20, for a discussion of such favored treatment.

75. Phillips, *Plantation and Frontier Documents*, 2:38.

76. [Craft], *Running a Thousand Miles*, 10, 31.

77. Some of these men may have acquired their skill butchering hogs and small game on plantations, but early postwar references to their presence in the public market suggests a more formal process of apprenticeship—especially given the growing concern with public health and the consequent proliferation of ordinances governing the market. See the market ordinances published in *Jnl. & Msgr.*, 14 July 1858; on postwar butchers in Macon's public market, see *Telegr.*, 3 and 7 June 1865.

78. That the 1870 census takers enumerated black artisans practicing luxury trades strongly suggests their having served apprenticeships as slaves. In 1860, enumerators listed only one white barber, a German. The mulatto barber Edward Woodliff, who became a prominent political leader after the Civil War, apparently purchased his freedom and that of his wife sometime before the war. See Bellamy, "Macon," 309.

79. [Craft], *Running a Thousand Miles*, 30–31.

80. Historians have neglected white artisans—and white workers generally—in the antebellum South, though an important exception is Berlin and Gutman, "Natives and Immigrants." As a result, the study of artisan culture—both craft and political—lags far behind what has been done on antebellum northern artisans, the best recent example of which is Wilentz, *Chants Democratic*. The relationship between free white and black slave artisanal traditions in the South has yet to be broached, much less studied. On slave artisans, see esp. Starobin, *Industrial Slavery*; Lewis, *Coal, Iron, and Slaves*; Fogel and Engerman, *Time on the Cross*, chap. 2; and Genovese, *Roll, Jordan, Roll*, 388–98.

81. Bellamy, "Macon," 306–7.

82. [Anderson], *Life of Robert Anderson*, 109–11 (quotation on 111). On divisions among slaves, see the remarks of William Craft in Ripley et al., *Black Abolitionist Papers*, 1:272.

83. On similar developments in Richmond, see O'Brien, "Factory, Church, and Community."

84. See Alexander, *Ambiguous Lives*, chaps. 1–3, for a remarkable re-creation of the lives of free people in middle Georgia.

85. Buckingham, *Slave States of America*, 1:211–12; Royall, *Mrs. Royall's Southern Tour*, 2:132–34. See also Butler, *Historical Record*, 209; Bellamy, "Macon," 304.

86. The best brief treatment of the tribulations of free blacks at the hands of Georgia officials is Wallenstein, *Slave South to New South*, 89–95. More extensive is Sweat, "Free Negro in Antebellum Georgia."

87. Bibb Co. Superior Court Minutes, May 1854, GDAH; Wallenstein, *Slave South to New South*, 90; *Jnl. & Msgr.*, 23 Dec. 1857.

88. Local lore, based largely upon an early-twentieth-century account of the Healy family by Samuel Griswold, holds that Mary Eliza moved north before her death. See, for example, C. Williams, *History of Jones County*, 72–74. But Foley, *Bishop Healy*, chaps. 1–4 (esp. 15–16, 43–44), disputes that account on the basis of both Healy family papers and Jones County records.

89. Hickson, *Land So Dedicated*, 80. A photograph of the mansion also appears.

90. C. Williams, *History of Jones County*, 19. On the postwar experience of Jacob Hutchings, see chap. 8, below.

91. Advertisement for Sarah, *Georgia Messenger*, 27 Feb. 1840. Her owner listed four aliases and noted that she had been at large for two and a half years.

92. Berlin, *Slaves without Masters*, chap. 11.

93. U.S. Census Bureau, *Population in 1860*, 58–69.

CHAPTER 4

1. Hobsbawm, *Age of Capital*.

2. *Jnl. & Msgr.*, 20 Jan. 1858.

3. In general, see Wooster, *People in Power*.

4. *Jnl. & Msgr.*, 11 Apr. 1849.

5. U.S. Census Bureau, *Seventh Census*, 377–84, and *Agriculture in 1860*, 22–29; Wallenstein, *Slave South to New South*, 63–68.

6. Ms. federal census returns, free and slave schedules, Houston Co., Ga., 1850 and 1860, RG 29.

7. Ms. federal census returns, population schedules, Houston Co., Ga., 1850 and 1860, RG 29.

8. Calculated from ms. federal census returns, population and slave schedules, Houston Co., Ga., 1850 and 1860, RG 29.

9. The advertising columns in the *Telegraph* and the *Journal & Messenger* clearly illustrate these developments, as do the inventories of the estates of deceased merchants. See, for instance, the estate of Daniel F. Gunn, Houston Co. Court of Ordinary, Inventories and Appraisements, GDAH.

10. Ms. federal census returns, population schedules, for the counties of central Georgia, 1850 and 1860, RG 29, demonstrate the rise of the foreign-born population, especially in the county seats and towns along the railroads.

11. Henry L. Benning to Howell Cobb, 1 July 1849, in Phillips, *Correspondence of Toombs, Stephens, and Cobb*, 171.

12. Cobb to President James Buchanan, 17 June 1849, in ibid., 164; Cooper, *South and the Politics of Slavery*, 287–88. On Calhoun, see Ford, "Republican Ideology in a Slave Society" and *Origins of Southern Radicalism*, 8–192 passim.

13. Generally, see Phillips, *Georgia and State Rights*.

14. Howell Cobb to John B. Lamar, 26 June 1850, and Lamar to Cobb, 5 July 1850 (typescript), Cobb-Erwin-Lamar Family Papers, UGa; Lamar to Cobb, 3 July 1850, in Phillips, *Correspondence of Toombs, Stephens, and Cobb*, 191–92. Other observers concurred with Lamar's assessment. See, for example, Absalom H. Chappell to Cobb, 10 July 1850, in ibid., 193–94. John H. Lumpkin identified those favoring "resistance and . . . disunion" as the "old Nullifiers" of 1832. Lumpkin to Cobb, 21 July 1850, in ibid., 208. Murray, *Whig Party*, 162, describes Herschel V. Johnson as "the most rabid of the fire-eaters in 1850."

15. Murray, *Whig Party*, 152, notes that the public meeting held in Monroe County voted to support the Union even if compromise failed.

16. Ibid., 154. Unlike their counterparts in Monroe County, voters in Jones, Twiggs, and Houston counties strongly favored the Resistance party.

17. *Jnl. & Msgr.*, 21 Aug. 1850.

18. Murray, *Whig Party*, 156; Hahn, *Roots of Southern Populism*, 106.

19. S. T. Chapman to Howell Cobb, 24 Apr. 1851, in Phillips, *Correspondence of Toombs, Stephens, and Cobb*, 232.

20. *Jnl. & Msgr.*, 12 Nov. 1851.

21. Phillips, *Correspondence of Toombs, Stephens, and Cobb*, 241 (original emphasis). Shortly after, Cobb addressed a long letter to a committee of citizens in Macon, expressing his opposition to secession in principle while defending the right of southerners to consider it as a possible option. See ibid., 249–59.

22. *Jnl. & Msgr.*, 21 Nov. 1851.

23. Ibid., 14 Apr. 1852. The same issue also published reports of similar meetings in other counties.

24. Ibid., 9 July 1856.

25. T. W. Thomas to Alexander Stephens, 12 Jan. 1857, in Phillips, *Correspondence of Toombs, Stephens, and Cobb*, 392. Thomas was apparently a former Whig, like Stephens. Thomas continued that if the free-state forces prevailed in Kansas, "there will be no hope for the South but a bloody revolution, and the stake will be worth the contest." Governor Joseph Brown expressed similar sentiments to Stephens, 9 Feb. and 26 Mar. 1858. See ibid., 431–33.

26. *Jnl. & Msgr.*, 25 June 1856.

27. Although young men who had not yet established themselves no doubt led this movement, the planter elite did not stand idly by. In Macon, for instance, prominent planters such as Joseph Bond reorganized the moribund Bibb County Cavalry in 1857. See ibid., 20 May 1857. See also the history of the Macon Volunteers in ibid., 24 Nov. 1858.

28. Ibid., 20 Jan. 1858.

29. Ibid., 20 Jan., 16 Feb., 3 Mar. 1858. By 1860, these proposals included formation of a cotton bank in Europe that would serve as a source of credit. See ibid., 11 Jan. 1860.

30. John B. Lamar to Howell Cobb, 10 Mar. 1858, Cobb-Erwin-Lamar Family Papers, UGa.

31. *Jnl. & Msgr.*, 16 Feb. 1859. Although the editors of the newspaper disagreed with Lee's position, in the same issue they also printed sentiments similar to Lee's, which had originally appeared in the *Cassville Standard*.

32. Quoted in Flanders, *Plantation Slavery*, 193.

33. Takaki, *Pro-Slavery Crusade*; *Jnl. & Msgr.*, every issue, Feb.–Apr. 1859. On 27 Apr. 1859, for instance, the editors of the *Journal & Messenger* regretted "to see so mischievous an issue introduced into the politics and policy of the South." Various cotton planters' conventions also objected to reopening the slave trade. See also ibid., 3 Mar. 1858, 11 Jan. 1860.

34. For an incisive analysis of the relationship between Know-Nothingism and larger social and political developments in an Upper South state, see Fields, *Slavery and Freedom*, chap. 3. For intriguing insights into the simultaneous development of racial Anglo-Saxonism, see Horsman, *Race and Manifest Destiny*, pt. 3.

35. See, for instance, *Jnl. & Msgr.*, 11 Oct., 29 Nov. 1854.

36. A Catholic parish was established in Macon in 1841. Butler, *Historical Record*, 322–25.

37. *Jnl. & Msgr.*, 29 Aug. 1855.

38. Reprinted from the *Charleston Standard* in ibid., 29 Oct. 1851; Young, Gholson, and Hargrove, *History of Macon*, 125.

39. See *Jnl. & Msgr.*, 25 Feb., 29 Sept. 1852, 17 Feb., 5 May 1858; Northen, *Men of Mark*, 3:203–6. After the Civil War, Lochrane championed Cobb's case for a pardon before President Andrew Johnson. Howell Cobb to his wife, 28 Oct. 1865, Cobb-Erwin-Lamar Family Papers, UGa. The brothers E. D. and Philemon Tracy, who like Lochrane had studied law, also brokered the interests of traditional party regulars and Irish immigrants. Both held public office: E. D. as city surveyor and Philemon as state senator. See *Jnl. & Msgr.*, 26 Apr., 13 Dec. 1854, 5 Oct. 1859; Young, Gholson, and Hargrove, *History of Macon*, 188. In 1858, Philemon Tracy used his position of public trust to denounce the

disenterment of a slave named Essex, presumably by students of the Medical Reform College. "Such outrages" cause general "insecurity," he claimed, but "foster a spirit of discontent among negroes, in particular, who, by reason of their superstitious fancies, are peculiarly excited by such events." He averred that faithful slaves "ought at least to be assured of a quiet grave." See *Jnl. & Msgr.*, 27 Jan. 1858.

40. Know-Nothing sentiment in central Georgia peaked in 1855 with triumphs in Bibb, Monroe, and Houston counties in state elections and a sweep of the mayor's office and all eight aldermanic seats in the municipal elections in Macon. *Jnl. & Msgr.*, 28 Nov., 12 Dec. 1855. In 1856, Know-Nothings repeated only in Monroe County; Democrats prevailed in Bibb and Houston counties and in the city of Macon. Ibid., 12 Nov., 17 Dec. 1856.

41. Thomas Dougherty won a seat as city alderman on the opposition ticket. Ibid., 8 and 15 Dec. 1858, 14 Dec. 1859.

42. The quotation appears in ibid., 18 Mar. 1857.

43. Quoted in Hahn, *Roots of Southern Populism*, 105.

44. *Jnl. & Msgr.*, 1 July 1857.

45. On northern debates regarding schools and asylums, see, respectively, Kaestle, *Pillars of the Republic*, esp. chaps. 3–4, and Rothman, *Discovery of the Asylum*, esp. chaps. 3, 7–9.

46. Wallenstein, *Slave South to New South*, pt. 1.

47. Compare Dawley, *Class and Community*, chap. 4. Insurance companies also had a heavy hand in promoting these improvements. See *Jnl. & Msgr.*, 26 Oct. 1853, for the notice that the Hartford Insurance Company had opened an agency in Macon "prepared to issue Insurance upon the lives of both whites and servants."

48. *Jnl. & Msgr.*, 17 Dec. 1851, 15, 22, and 29 Dec. 1852, 2 Mar. 1853.

49. Ibid., 2 Mar. 1853.

50. Ibid., 24 May 1854. Rivalry between fire companies was a staple of antebellum America. Fires often raged out of control as the companies fought over which had arrived first and consequently had the right to extinguish the flames.

51. Ibid., 3 Nov. 1858.

52. Ibid., 15 July 1857, 21 Apr., 5 and 19 May 1857, 19 Jan. 1859.

53. Houston Co. Superior Court Minutes, Apr. 1853, GDAH.

54. Ms. federal census returns, free and slave schedules, Houston Co., Ga., 1850, RG 29.

55. Houston Co. Superior Court Minutes, Apr. 1858, GDAH.

56. *Jnl. & Msgr.*, 16 Mar. 1859.

57. See Wallenstein, *Slave South to New South*, 65–68.

58. See *Jnl. & Msgr.*, 19 May, 7 July 1852, for the statements of grand juries from Upson and Bibb counties.

59. Ibid., 22 Mar., 14 June 1854.

60. Bibb Co. Superior Court grand jury presentments, May 1858, in *Jnl. & Msgr.*, 7 June 1858; Houston Co. Superior Court grand jury presentments, Oct. 1853 and Oct. 1857, Houston Co. Superior Court Minutes, GDAH. For similar sentiments, see Monroe Co. Superior Court grand jury presentments, Aug. 1852, in *Jnl. & Msgr.*, 22 Sept. 1852.

61. The quotations come, respectively, from Houston Co. Superior Court grand jury presentments, Oct. 1857, Houston Co. Superior Court Minutes, GDAH; Monroe Co. Superior Court grand jury presentments, Feb. 1853, in *Jnl. & Msgr.*, 23 Mar. 1853; and Bibb Co. Superior Court grand jury presentments, May 1860, in ibid., 6 June 1860. On proposed efforts to control the distribution of liquor, at times by local option, see ibid., 2 Feb. 1853; Houston Co. Superior Court grand jury presentments, Apr. 1853, in ibid., 11 May 1853; Houston Co. Superior Court grand jury presentments, Apr. 1854, Houston Co. Superior Court Minutes, GDAH. In 1858, Macon enacted a perfectly ineffective liquor licensing ordinance. See *Jnl. & Msgr.*, 17 Feb. 1858.

62. Bibb Co. Superior Court grand jury presentments, in *Jnl. & Msgr.*, 19 Dec. 1855, 7 June 1858; Ayers, *Vengeance and Justice*, 113.

63. *Jnl. & Msgr.*, 14 June 1854.

64. Ibid., 22 Mar. 1854.

65. Ibid., 20 May 1857.

66. Ibid., 20 Dec. 1854.

67. Ibid., 22 Mar. 1854, 26 May 1858; Houston Co. Superior Court grand jury presentments, Apr. 1854, Houston Co. Superior Court Minutes, GDAH.

68. *Jnl. & Msgr.*, 31 July, 18 Aug., 25 Aug., 15 Sept. 1858, 19 Jan., 13 Apr. 1859.

69. More recent formulations of this mythical theme abound. For one example, see C. Williams, *History of Jones County*, 63–64.

70. *Jnl. & Msgr.*, 20 Feb. 1856.

71. Ibid., 26 May, 7 June 1858.

72. Quoted in Wallenstein, *Slave South to New South*, 66.

73. Quoted in ibid., 67.

74. Clark, Cobb, and Irwin, *Georgia Code*, 368–69.

75. Olmsted, *Cotton Kingdom*, 257–58.

76. For opposition to trafficking, see *Southern Agriculturist* 5 (Apr. 1832): 183, and 6 (June 1833): 285–86. For opposition to gardening and other productive activity, see ibid. 9 (May 1836): 230, and 9 (Oct. 1836): 518–20; also *Southern Cultivator* 8 (Nov. 1850): 163. Campbell, "As 'A Kind of Freeman'?," 137–44, treats similar developments in the South Carolina upcountry.

77. Gaspar, "Slavery, Amelioration, and Sunday Markets."

78. Rawick, Hillegas, and Lawrence, *American Slave*, suppl. ser. 1, vol. 5 (Indiana and Ohio narratives), p. 334. (Thanks to Leslie S. Rowland for this reference.) Doubtless the slaves of James A. Everett, one of the chief financial backers of the Southwestern Railroad running from Macon to southwest Georgia, did the same.

79. See Capt. J. W. Mallet to A. G. Rogers et al., 31 Jan. 1863, Macon Ordnance Laboratory, Letters Received, 28:207, RG 109.

80. *Jnl. & Msgr.*, 3 Nov. 1858.

81. Advertisements in ibid., for Charles, 3 July 1850, and Paul, 8 Dec. 1852.

82. Charles Ball even received such assistance from a slaveholder. See *Fifty Years in Chains*, 362–69, 404–8.

83. *Jnl. & Msgr.*, 31 May 1854.

84. Blassingame, *Slave Testimony*, 500–501.

85. Jones Co. Superior Court grand jury presentments, Apr. 1853, quoted in *Jnl. &*

Msgr., 27 Apr. 1853. Legislative action against such slaves had a long pedigree; see, for instance, *Acts*, 1831, 223–24, 226–27; ibid., 1857, 320–21.

86. A postwar controversy over market regulations hints at the participation of blacks in such provisioning, a pattern that most likely originated during slavery. See n. 38, chap. 6, below.

87. *Jnl. & Msgr.*, 6 July 1853. The ban also included buying and selling cotton for the purpose of making mattresses.

88. Houston Co. Superior Court grand jury presentments, Oct. 1852, Houston Co. Superior Court Minutes, GDAH. More generally, see Wade, *Slavery in the Cities*, esp. chaps. 6, 9.

89. *Jnl. & Msgr.*, 11 Oct., 15 Nov. 1854.

90. [Craft], *Running a Thousand Miles*, 29–31; Ripley et al., *Black Abolitionist Papers*, 1:273–74.

91. Account of the funeral of Jim Danielly in *Jnl. & Msgr.*, 8 July 1857.

92. Bibb Co. Superior Court grand jury presentments, quoted in *Jnl. & Msgr.*, 7 July 1852.

93. Thos. A. Jones to [Marcus Johnston], 10 Jan. 1856, Marcus Johnston Family Papers, UGa. Unlike the similar case of Denmark Vesey in 1800, it is almost certain that John did not collect the prize; it is not clear whether his master did.

94. *Jnl. & Msgr.*, 2 Feb., 23 Mar. 1859. I am grateful to Susan E. O'Donovan, of the University of California at San Diego, for sharing with me information about Joseph Bond's death.

95. Houston Co. Superior Court grand jury presentments, Oct. 1852, Houston Co. Superior Court Minutes, GDAH.

96. Quoted in Phillips, *Life of Toombs*, 164. See also T. Cobb, *Inquiry*, xlvii.

97. H. Cobb, *Scriptural Examination*, 24 (original emphasis).

CHAPTER 5

1. Cleveland, *Alexander H. Stephens*, 721–23.

2. Lincoln to border state representatives, 12 July 1862, Lincoln, *Collected Works*, 5:318.

3. See esp. Thomas, *Confederacy as a Revolutionary Experience*; Bensel, *Yankee Leviathan*, chaps. 2–3.

4. Cohen and Greene, *Neither Slave Nor Free*, app.; D. Davis, *Slavery and Human Progress*, 107–279; Genovese, *World the Slaveholders Made*, pt. 1; Woodward, "Emancipations and Reconstructions," 144–66; Blum, *Noble Landowners*, esp. chap. 1.

5. R. Scott, *Slave Emancipation in Cuba*, pt. 1.

6. On secession in Georgia, see esp. M. Johnson, *Patriarchal Republic*, which supersedes Phillips, *Georgia and State Rights*. Accounts of the secession crisis in neighboring states include (for South Carolina) Channing, *Crisis of Fear*, and Ford, *Origins of Southern Radicalism*, chap. 10; and (for Alabama) Barney, *Secessionist Impulse*, and Thornton, *Politics and Power*, chap. 6. For an insightful analysis of the upcountry yeomen's perspective on this contest, see Hahn, *Roots of Southern Populism*, chap. 3.

7. The vote of the secession convention is reported in *Telegr.*, 4, 5 Jan. 1861, and *Jnl. &*
Msgr., 23 Jan. 1861. Bibb County's delegation was led by the longtime firebrand Eugenius
A. Nisbet—memorable for having earlier placed a price on the head of William Lloyd
Garrison—who introduced the resolution that ultimately led Georgia out of the Union.
Every issue of the two papers in November and December 1860 reports upon the local
meetings wherein citizens debated the appropriate response to Lincoln's election.

8. Johnson clearly identifies Cobb's essentially political assessment of the situation:
unless the slave states seceded, Lincoln would use the patronage system to seed abolitionists throughout the South and ultimately destroy slavery. *Patriarchal Republic*, esp. 44.
Alexander H. Stephens epitomized the reluctant secessionism of the old-line Whigs. In
addition to ibid., pts. 1 and 2 passim, see Phillips, *Correspondence of Toombs, Stephens, and*
Cobb, 502–5.

9. M. Johnson, *Patriarchal Republic*, esp. chaps. 7–9.

10. Johnson, in ibid., 29–30, sees this invocation of the Spirit of '76 as a carefully
devised alternative to claiming slaveholders' rights as the rationale for revolution. Within
central Georgia—and the plantation belt more generally—this distinction is somewhat
artificial. Even lukewarm secessionists blamed the sectional troubles upon Republican
declarations in favor of "an 'irrepressible conflict' against the domestic slavery of the
Southern States" and of "the universal equality and community of political privileges"
between the races. See *Jnl. & Msgr.*, 28 Nov. 1860.

11. A group of eighty "sons of the Emerald Isle" formed the Lochrane Guards in honor
of their distinguished fellow countryman O. A. Lochrane. See *Jnl. & Msgr.*, 4 Sept. 1861.

12. See, for example, ibid., 31 July 1861; Governor Treutlen Chapter, DAR, *History of*
Peach County, 81.

13. Testimony of George Carter in Rawick, Hillegas, and Lawrence, *American Slave*,
suppl. ser. 1, 3:160–63. Railroads perennially advertised for slaves. See, for example, *Jnl.*
& Msgr., 28 Nov. 1848, 22 Dec. 1852, and 23 Nov. 1859; *Telegr.*, 1 Jan. 1861. In the
advertisement of 23 Nov. 1859, the Southwestern Railroad sought 200 men and 40 to 50
women "as Cooks and Shovel Hands." More generally, see Mohr, *Threshold of Freedom*,
136–42.

14. *Southern Cultivator* 19 (May 1861): 138.

15. John J. Cheatham to Hon. L. P. Walker, 4 May 1861, in Berlin, Reidy, and Rowland,
Black Military Experience, doc. 114. To sweeten the deal for the owners, the planter
proposed that slaves under arms "be valued as you would a horse or other property, and
let the government pay for them provided they was killed in battle." To sweeten the deal
for the slaves he proposed "that if they distinguished themselves by good conduct in
battle, they should be rewarded." The "frollick" reference is from O. G. Eiland to
President Davis, 20 July 1863, in ibid., doc. 116.

16. *Southern Cultivator* 18 (Sept. 1860): 289.

17. Ibid. 20 (Jan. 1862): 13.

18. S. T. Bailey to Howell Cobb, 4 May 1861, Cobb-Erwin-Lamar Family Papers,
UGa.

19. Mohr, *Threshold of Freedom*, chaps. 1–2, treats antinorthern sentiment generally; for
particular instances, see *Telegr.*, 15 Oct. 1860, and Flanders, *Plantation Slavery*, 225–26.

20. *Telegr.*, 22 Feb., 1 and 24 May 1861; *Acts*, 1861, 68; ibid., 1863, 61–62.

21. For general discussions of the transformation of slavery during the war, see Thomas, *Confederacy as a Revolutionary Experience*, and Luraghi, *Rise and Fall of the Planter Class*. The best specific treatment of events in Georgia is Mohr, *Threshold of Freedom*, which supersedes Bryan, *Confederate Georgia*, chap. 8. The best account of comparable developments in the other slave states is Fields, *Slavery and Freedom*, chap. 5.

22. The soil and climate above the fall line favored grain production, and, even before the war, Monroe County was one of the leading wheat-producing counties in the state. See *Southern Cultivator* 18 (Apr. 1860): 125–26.

23. For a sampling of views on this issue, see *Telegr.*, 25 Jan., 4 May, 15 and 17 June, 6, 8, and 10 July 1861; *Southern Cultivator* 20 (May–June 1862): 104; Phillips, *Correspondence of Toombs, Stephens, and Cobb*, 595, 613–14.

24. *Telegr.*, 15, 17 June, 6, 8, 10 July, 15–18 Oct. 1861; *De Bow's Review*, n.s. 6 (Oct.–Nov. 1861): 462–63.

25. See, for instance, *Jnl. & Msgr.*, 30 Oct., 6, 13 Nov. 1861.

26. See E. Foner, *Tom Paine*, chap. 5.

27. On the impact of the war in areas where yeomen predominated, see Hahn, *Roots of Southern Populism*, chap. 3. Although fewer in number than their counterparts in the upper Piedmont, yeomen in the black belt experienced the war similarly.

28. *Southern Cultivator* 20 (July–Aug. 1862): 132, and 20 (Nov.–Dec. 1862): 204.

29. Ibid. 19 (Oct. 1861): 266.

30. Ibid. 19 (Mar. 1861): 73–75.

31. Ibid. 19 (July 1861): 201; 19 (Nov. 1861): 285–86; 19 (Dec. 1861): 298; 20 (Nov.–Dec. 1862): 210, 212; 21 (May–June 1863): 81; 21 (Nov.–Dec. 1863): 136. See also ibid. 22 (Feb. 1864): 37. Dogs killed an estimated 31,000 sheep per year. See Range, *Century of Georgia Agriculture*, 42.

32. *Southern Cultivator* 20 (July–Aug. 1862): 132.

33. Quoted in ibid. 20 (Jan. 1862): 11 (original emphasis).

34. Ibid. 22 (Jan. 1864): 10.

35. That the freedpeople worked considerably less than they had as slaves is now a commonplace of historical understanding regarding the postbellum South. Although no one has undertaken a quantitative study of this phenomenon during the war, impressionistic evidence suggests that the reduction in labor began then, and the trend continued into the postwar years.

36. A. Moore, *Conscription and Conflict*, 53, 67–68.

37. Statement of Rebecca Bryan, 3 Nov. 1862, M-2754 1862, Letters Received, Adjutant and Inspector General, RG 109; A. Moore, *Conscription and Conflict*, 107–8. For a wider discussion of women's difficulties managing slaves, see Bryan, *Confederate Georgia*, 125 and chap. 11 passim; Robinson, "Bitter Fruits of Bondage." Early in 1864, the Confederate congress authorized an exemption for every fifteen slaves, which intensified the sense that it was a rich man's war but a poor man's fight without materially affecting the number of men who claimed exemption.

38. Mohr, *Threshold of Freedom*, 212.

39. *Southern Cultivator* 22 (Jan. 1864): 20.

40. During the war, the state legislature enacted restrictions upon the rights of nonresidents to pasture sheep and cattle in selected counties. See *Acts*, 1861, 104–5.

41. *Southern Cultivator* 21 (May–June 1863): 75.

42. Ibid. 18 (Sept. 1860): 289 (original emphasis).

43. Ibid. 19 (May 1861): 138.

44. Ibid. 21 (Nov.–Dec. 1863): 133; ibid. 22 (Feb. 1864): 32.

45. *Telegr.*, 7 Jan. 1863.

46. Ibid., 19 Aug. 1864; Augusta *Chronicle and Sentinel*, 21 July 1864, cited in J. Owens, "Negro in Georgia," 8. Runaway advertisements confirm this allegation. See, for example, advertisements for Mary, 27 Feb. 1864, and Tisha, 23 Oct. 1864, in the *Telegraph*.

47. Mohr, *Threshold of Freedom*, 22–23, 30–31; *Telegr.*, 14 Feb. 1861, 18 Mar. 1863; *Jnl. & Msgr.*, 18 Dec. 1861, 18 Mar., 15 July, 16 and 29 Sept. 1863, 11 May 1864, 8 Feb. 1865.

48. See Franklin, *Emancipation Proclamation*, 136–41; Berlin et al., *Destruction of Slavery*, 36–39.

49. *Telegr.*, 4 June 1863.

50. Berlin et al., *Destruction of Slavery*, chap. 9.

51. For explicit mention of runaways' desires to rejoin family members, see notices in the *Telegraph* for Mary Jane, 9 July 1863; Henry, 11 Aug. 1864; and Daniel, 27 Aug. 1864.

52. Railroads advertised for runaways regularly in ibid.: the Macon and Western for Mathews, 21 Jan. 1863; Mark, Angus, Hardy, and George, 26 Jan. 1863; and Mark and Cato, 23 Sept. 1864; the Macon and Brunswick for Albert, 12 Sept. 1863; and the Western and Atlantic for Pinckney, 20 July 1864. A notice appearing on 8 October 1864 advertised the disappearance of Jim, raised in Crawford County, Georgia, from his master, a lieutenant in an Alabama regiment. On 15 June 1864 the Confederate quartermaster's depot at Macon advertised for Hester, and on 24 September 1864 the Confederate Naval Iron Works at Columbus, Georgia, advertised for William Kuhn, suspected of heading for Etowah, Georgia, where he had formerly worked at the iron works.

53. For a more general discussion of the Confederate mobilization in Georgia, see DeCredico, *Patriotism for Profit*, chaps. 2–3.

54. For accounts of similar developments in Virginia, see Brewer, *Confederate Negro*; Dew, *Ironmaker to the Confederacy*, chaps. 5–13.

55. Findlay to Cuyler, 28 Apr. 1862, Macon Arsenal Letters Received, 36:2, RG 109.

56. N. A. Harvey to Cuyler, [June 1862], in ibid., p. 213.

57. Jared I. Irwin to Cuyler, 8 June 1862, in ibid., p. 176.

58. R. Habersham to Cuyler, 15 July 1862, with Cuyler endorsement, in ibid., p. 213.

59. On Mallet, see Vandiver, *Plowshares into Swords*, 112–14.

60. See Berlin et al., *Destruction of Slavery*, chaps. 5, 9, and *Wartime Genesis of Free Labor*, chap. 3, on the phenomenon of refugeeing from the Tennessee and Mississippi river valleys.

61. F. O. Rogers to Mallet, 23 Dec. 1862, Supt. of Laboratories Letters Received, 5:137; Henry to Mallet, 17, 28 Jan. and 8 Feb. 1863, in ibid., pp. 198, 227, 245A; and Mallet to Henry, 26 Feb. 1863, Supt. of Laboratories Letters Sent, 28:244, RG 109.

62. *Southern Cultivator* 19 (May 1861): 164–65.

63. Mallet to J. C. Barnett, 12 Nov. 1863, Supt. of Laboratories Letters Sent, 24:459, RG 109.

64. E. H. Walker to [Mallet], 1 July 1863, Supt. of Laboratories Letters Received, 38:121, RG 109.

65. Mallet to Rogers (and others), 31 Jan. 1863, Supt. of Laboratories Letters Sent, 28:207, RG 109.

66. Mallet to W. R. Phillips, 11 June 1863, ibid., 24:142.

67. Mallet to Rogers, 16, 20 Dec. 1862, ibid., 28:91, 103; Rogers to Mallet, 18, 26 Dec. 1862, Supt. of Laboratories Letters Received, 5:134, 145, RG 109. See also Manuscript Roll #6293 (Hired Slaves of the Macon Ordnance Laboratory for Feb. 1863), RG 109, which indicates that Rogers leased twelve slaves to the laboratory. The names of the carpenter and his helper do not appear; all of Rogers's slaves are listed as laborers. Genovese, *Roll, Jordan, Roll*, 648–57, analyzes the kind of running away that Rogers describes.

68. For related complications of a changed diet upon black federal soldiers later in the war, see Berlin, Reidy, and Rowland, *Black Military Experience*, chap. 15.

69. Rogers to Mallet, 9, 15, 19, 23 Feb. 1863, Supt. of Laboratories Letters Received, 5:246, 254–254A, 261–261A, 268; Mallet to Rogers, 17, 20, 24 Feb. 1863, Supt. of Laboratories Letters Sent, 28:222, 227, 235, RG 109. In January 1863, Macon physicians decided not to perform any more contract work—for the Confederate government or anyone. Mallet faced three alternatives: ending medical care for his large slave force, paying for care on a patient by patient basis, or assigning a Confederate medical officer to the slaves. He preferred the latter alternative, but it does not appear that he got his wish. As a result, the health of the slaves declined precipitously. Mallet to Dr. H. V. M. Miller, Chief Surgeon, 13 Jan. 1863, ibid., 28:184.

70. Rogers to Mallet, 4, 25 Mar., 6 Apr. 1863, Supt. of Laboratories Letters Received, 5:289A, 342A–342B, 372, RG 109.

71. Lt. George Little to Rogers, 9 June, 8 July 1863, Supt. of Laboratories Letters Sent, 24:124, 172; Rogers to Little, 23 May, 16 June 1863, Supt. of Laboratories Letters Received, 38:91A; Rogers to Mallet, 20 May, 1 June, 13 Sept. 1863, ibid., 38:25, 42A, 30 (original emphasis), 333; Mallet to Rogers, 15 Sept. 1863, Supt. of Laboratories Letters Sent, 24:330–31, RG 109.

72. A. Moore, *Conscription and Conflict*, 53, 67–68; Vandiver, *Plowshares into Swords*, chap. 13.

73. See esp. Dew, *Ironmaker to the Confederacy*, chaps. 12–13; Brewer, *Confederate Negro*, 20, 60–61, 101.

74. See Burton to Maj. Gen. Benjamin Huger, Inspector General of Ordnance and Artillery, Jan. 1863, Macon Armory Letters Sent, 20:367–69, RG 109.

75. DeCredico, *Patriotism for Profit*, 61, notes that in Columbus, wages tended to keep pace with the rising cost of living, but this pattern reflected local circumstances rather than a statewide trend.

76. Burton to J. Gorgas, 17 Mar. 1863, Macon Armory Letters Sent, 20:461–62; Burton to Gorgas, 1 May 1863, ibid., 31:24; R. M. Cuyler to Gorgas, 17 Aug. 1863, ibid., 31:94, RG 109. On the parity question, see also J. Fuss, master armorer, to F. B. DuBarry, 29 May 1863, Master Armorer's Letters Sent, 30:18, RG 109. Fuss recommended parity with Richmond. See advertisements dating from May 1863 to June 1864 in Macon Armory Letters Sent, 31:31, 99–102, 106, 231, 235, 369, 382, 451, 455, RG 109. See also *Telegr.*, 7 July 1863. Foreigners figured prominently among the deserters thus advertised. See Lonn, *Foreigners in the Confederacy*, chap. 10. On the similarly remarkable

likeness in advertisements for runaway slaves and runaway servants in the eighteenth century, see Prude, "To Look Upon the 'Lower Sort.'"

77. *Jnl. & Msgr.*, 6 and 13 Nov. 1861. Others also called for "retributive justice" against "extortioners." See ibid., 30 Oct. 1861.

78. See *Telegr.*, 10 Mar. 1863, 13 Jan. 1864.

79. Burton to Gorgas, 8 Mar. 1864, Macon Armory Letters Sent, 31:287–88; Burton to [?], [Nov.–Dec. 1864], Master Armorer's Letters Sent, 30:60, RG 109. The strike of the women operatives is reported in the *Telegraph*, 19 Oct. 1864, which also carried an advertisement seeking new employees. The outcome of the strike is unclear; Superintendent Mallet's letters sent (vol. 24) survive only to April 1864, and his letters received (vol. 37) make no mention of the strike.

80. Mohr, *Threshold of Freedom*, 93–95; Drago, "Sherman's March"; Escott, "Context of Freedom," 90–95; Glatthaar, *March to the Sea*, chap. 3; Bryan, *Confederate Georgia*, 128.

81. *Southern Cultivator* 22 (Mar. 1864): 52.

82. Statement of Bob Mobley in Rawick, Hillegas, and Lawrence, *American Slave*, suppl. ser. 1, vol. 4, pt. 2, pp. 451–52; statement of Sara Crocker in ibid., vol. 3, pt. 1, p. 227.

83. Statement of George Womble in Rawick, *American Slave*, ser. 2, vol. 13, pt. 4, p. 193.

84. See runaway advertisements in the *Telegraph* for Andrew, 27 May 1864; Nelson and John Sparrow, 13 June 1864; Pinkney, 20 July 1864; Elias, 23 Aug. 1864; Ed, 15 Oct. 1864; Claiborne and wife, 1 Nov. 1864.

85. Testimony of George Carter in Rawick, Hillegas, and Lawrence, *American Slave*, suppl. ser. 1, 3:160–63.

86. See runaway advertisements in the *Telegraph* for Henry, 11 Aug. 1864; Daniel, 27 Aug. 1864; Bill, 4 Oct. 1864; Bill, 15 Oct. 1864.

87. Runaway advertisement for John Sparrow in ibid., 13 June 1864; C. Williams, *History of Jones County*, 147.

88. Ell Robinson to Col. C. C. Sibley, 17 Aug. 1868, #2060 1868, Letters Received, Ga. Asst. Comr., RG 105. The Freedmen's Bureau granted Robinson's request for transportation back to Virginia.

89. *Southern Cultivator* 22 (Mar. 1864): 52.

90. Mallet to A. M. Lockett, Supt. of Laboratories Letters Sent, 24:493; Burton to Gorgas, 10 Mar, 12, 20 Apr. 1864, Macon Armory Letters Sent, 31:291, 349, 360, RG 109. See also Burton to D. Whitaker, 15 Mar. 1864, ibid., pp. 298–99; Burton to J. C. Plant, 23 Jan. 1864, ibid., p. 199; and Burton to Maj. Gen. Sam Jones, Commanding Department of South Carolina, Georgia, and Florida, 16 June 1864, ibid., p. 444. On the effects of Confederate impressment in Georgia, see Mohr, *Threshold of Freedom*, 162–63; in other areas of the South, Berlin et al., *Destruction of Slavery*, chap. 9; Brewer, *Confederate Negro*, chap. 1; Dew, *Ironmaker to the Confederacy*, chap. 12.

91. As early as August 1863, the Bibb County enrolling officer notified slave owners to present one-quarter of their able-bodied men (complete with adequate clothing and three days' rations) for work on the fortifications at Macon. *Telegr.*, 10 Aug. 1863.

92. Burton to Aiken, 23 June 1864, Burton to Gorgas, 1, 4 July 1864, Macon Armory Letters Sent, 31:457, 471–72, 476, RG 109; see also Vandiver, *Plowshares into Swords*,

chap. 17. Complicating this affair was the fact that Burton's superior, Josiah Gorgas, was the brother-in-law of the post commander, T. Wyatt Aiken.

93. Burton to Gorgas, 8 Mar., 13 May 1864, Macon Armory Letters Sent, 31:287, 398, RG 109.

94. See Burton to Gen. J. B. Hood, 3 Aug. 1864, Macon Armory Letters Sent, 31:519; Burton to Gorgas, 24 Aug. 1864, ibid., pp. 540–41; Burton to Editor, *Macon Daily Telegraph*, 3 Sept. 1864, ibid., 29:172; Burton to Gen. Howell Cobb, commanding Military District of Georgia, 7 Oct. 1864, ibid., p. 89, RG 109.

95. See Burton to Lt. N. G. Clarkson, engineer of defenses at Atlanta, 18 Aug. 1864, Macon Armory Letters Sent, 31:535; also Burton to A. Cobb, 13 Dec. 1864, ibid., 29:172, RG 109.

96. Lt. N. B. Clarkson, supervising black laborers in Macon, to Mallet, 23 Sept. 1864, Supt. of Laboratories Letters Received, vol. 37, pt. 2, sheets 209–209A, 216; L. A. Pynchon to [Mallet], 3 Oct. 1864, ibid., sheets 241, 307; and R. G. Lawton to James C. Caborn, 30 Oct. 1864, ibid., pt. 3, p. 408, RG 109. The correspondence between Mallet, on the one hand, and A. M. Rowland, commander of the Camp of Instruction, and R. S. Lanier, his adjutant, on the other, dated December 1864 to March 1865, indicated the magnitude of the runaway problem. Supt. of Laboratories Letters Received, vol. 37, sheets 385–608 passim, RG 109. See also the advertisement in the *Telegraph*, 24 Nov. 1864, for five free black men who had run away from the medical purveyor's office.

97. C. Williams, *History of Jones County*, chap. 10.

98. Cobb's conscription order appears in the *Telegraph*, 23 Sept. 1864.

99. Nichols, *Story of the Great March*, 63–64; Glatthaar, *March to the Sea*, 161; C. Williams, *History of Jones County*, 149–62. For the official report of events in the vicinity of Macon by Gen. O. O. Howard, one of Sherman's corps commanders, see U.S. War Department, *Official Records*, ser. 1, 44:66.

100. C. Williams, *History of Jones County*, 159–60.

101. Both quotations from Bryan, *Confederate Georgia*, 169.

102. U.S. War Department, *Official Records*, ser. 1, 44:75.

103. Nichols, *Story of the Great March*, 58–59.

104. Ibid., 59.

105. Burton to E. V. Johnson, 31 Dec. 1864, Macon Armory Letters Sent, 29:194, RG 109.

106. Burton to O. Porter, 31 Dec. 1864, ibid., 29:192.

107. See, for example, A. Fuss to T. A. Brewer, 15 Jan. 1865; Fuss to J. Branham, 3 Feb. 1865; Fuss to Col. W. W. Hollard, 7 Feb. 1865; Fuss to A. J. Wellmaker, 8 Mar. 1865; Fuss to Branham, 9 Mar. 1865; Fuss to Brewer, 15 Mar. 1865; and Fuss to Wellmaker, 4 Apr. 1865, in ibid., 29:201, 210, 211, 221, 223, 252.

108. Fuss to Wm. A. Fort, 13 Mar., 10 Apr. 1865, in ibid., 29:222, 270.

CHAPTER 6

1. DeCredico traces the antebellum and wartime history of these businessmen in *Patriotism for Profit*, esp. chap. 1.

2. The classic studies of northern agriculture are Gates, *Farmer's Age*, and Danhof, *Change in Agriculture*. On tenants and farm laborers, see M. Bogue, *Patterns from the Sod*; A. Bogue, *From Prairie to Cornbelt*; Gates, *Landlords and Tenants*; Winters, *Farmers without Farms*; and Schob, *Hired Hands and Plowboys*. For a recent overview that takes in northern and southern developments, see Ferleger, *Agriculture and National Development*.

3. See McPherson, "West Indian Emancipation"; Holt, *Problem of Freedom*; E. Foner, *Nothing But Freedom*, 8–38, 41–43; D. Davis, *Slavery and Human Progress*, pt. 2; Genovese, *World the Slaveholders Made*, pt. 1. On revolutionary-era emancipation in the North, another phenomenon with ambiguous lessons for the postbellum South, see Zilversmit, *First Emancipation*, as well as D. Davis, *Problem of Slavery*.

4. See E. Foner, *Reconstruction*, chaps. 3–4, which elaborates themes earlier addressed in his *Politics and Ideology*, chap. 6, "Reconstruction and the Crisis of Free Labor," and *Nothing But Freedom*.

5. The vast literature examining the transition from one social system to another is relevant in this regard. Apart from that which treats slave emancipation per se, see Marx, *Capital*, vol. 1; Dobb, *Development of Capitalism*; Hilton, *Feudalism to Capitalism*; Aston and Philpin, *Brenner Debate*.

6. See esp. Litwack, *Been in the Storm*.

7. Rawick, *American Slave*, ser. 2, vol. 13, pt. 3, p. 176; testimony of Robert Sheets, U.S. Congress, House, *Affairs in the Late Insurrectionary States*, 652–53. For more general discussion of these points, see Gutman, *Black Family*; Litwack, *Been in the Storm*; Mann, "Slavery, Sharecropping, and Sexual Inequality."

8. For general treatment of these interrelated points, see Glymph, "Freedpeople and Ex-Masters"; Woodman, "Reconstruction of the Cotton Plantation"; Wayne, *Reshaping of Plantation Society*, chap. 2; and Flynn, *White Land, Black Labor*, esp. chaps. 1–3; R. Davis, *Good and Faithful Labor*; Robinson, "Beyond the Realm of Social Consensus."

9. Andrews, *South since the War*, 398.

10. T. W. Brock to J. D. Havis, 22 May 1866, Unregistered Letters Received, Ga. Asst. Comr., RG 105.

11. Regarding English's case, Freedmen's Bureau subassistant commissioner N. Sellers Hill despairingly observed, "Owing to the feeling existing . . . against the negro . . . arresting the party will be useless." Affidavit of Ben English, 11 July 1866 (with endorsement by Hill), filed under letter "B," Unregistered Letters Received, Ga. Asst. Comr., RG 105. See also testimony of Henry M. Turner, U.S. Congress, House, *Affairs in the Late Insurrectionary States*, 1041.

12. Woodfolk statement, 1867, W-25 1867, Registered Letters Received, Macon Subasst. Comr., RG 105.

13. See U.S. Congress, House, *Condition of Affairs in Georgia*, 132–33, for a sample catalog of the violence perpetrated upon freedpeople in the bureau's subdistrict of Macon. See also the testimony of Henry M. Turner, U.S. Congress, House, *Affairs in the Late Insurrectionary States*, 1042, wherein he estimated that some 1,500 to 1,600 freedmen had been murdered in Georgia between 1867 and 1871. The records of the Freedmen's Bureau and other military officials are replete with additional testimony from freedpeople and reports of investigations. See, in particular, series of letters received, statements and affidavits, and reports of outrages of the respective offices in central Georgia, RG 105 and

RG 393. Also see the testimony in U.S. Congress, House, *Affairs in the Late Insurrectionary States*.

14. Quoted in C. M. Thompson, *Reconstruction in Georgia*, 42. Cobb had good reason to be nostalgic for the good old days: his brother Thomas and his brother-in-law and business agent, John B. Lamar, were killed during the war; with his political career in shambles, he settled in Macon, where he established a law practice and attempted to manage his plantations with the assistance of his sons.

15. Chappell, *Miscellanies of Georgia*, 13–17 (quotation on 16).

16. Quoted in C. M. Thompson, *Reconstruction in Georgia*, 55–56. See also Andrews, *South since the War*, 364.

17. *Telegr.*, 31 May, 7 June 1865; *Southern Cultivator*, July 1865, quoted in C. M. Thompson, *Reconstruction in Georgia*, 38. The most insightful treatment of the transformation of planter paternalism after the Civil War is Roark, *Masters without Slaves*, esp. 144–47, 198–203.

18. *Telegr.*, 8 June, 31 May 1865. See also E. Foner, *Politics and Ideology*, chap. 6, "Reconstruction and the Crisis of Free Labor," and *Nothing But Freedom*, 42–43; and D. Davis, *Slavery and Human Progress*, 214–20.

19. Andrews, *South since the War*, 398. See also U.S. War Department, *Official Records*, ser. 1, vol. 49, pt. 2, pp. 1041–42. More generally, see E. Foner, *Nothing But Freedom*, chap. 1; Jaynes, *Branches without Roots*, esp. chap. 4.

20. Anonymous to A. P. Ketchum, 20 Aug. 1865, Letters Received by Capt. A. P. Ketchum re Restoration of Property, Savannah Subasst. Comr., RG 105. During the Civil War, northern architects of the free-labor system—particularly Gen. Nathaniel P. Banks in Louisiana—instituted pass systems that military authorities replicated throughout the South at the end of the war. In June 1865, Secretary of War Edwin M. Stanton put an end to all such practices. See C. M. Thompson, *Reconstruction in Georgia*, 39; Carter, *When the War Was Over*, 180.

21. The work of J. Scott, esp. *Moral Economy of the Peasant* and *Weapons of the Weak*, is peerless with regard to these themes. Other general treatments include Paige, *Agrarian Revolution*. On the specific context of the plantation societies of the Americas, see Mintz, "Slavery and the Rise of Peasantries."

22. Collins to Cobb, 31 July 1865; Howell Cobb to his wife, Dec. 1866, Cobb-Erwin-Lamar Family Papers, UGa; also printed in Phillips, *Correspondence of Toombs, Stephens, and Cobb*, 665, 684; Brooks, *Agrarian Revolution in Georgia*, 20, 22; and C. M. Thompson, *Reconstruction in Georgia*, 60–61.

23. On the paucity of cash, see *Telegr.*, 29 June 1865, and *New York Times*, 14 Oct. 1865.

24. See Magdol, *Right to the Land*; Oubre, *Forty Acres and a Mule*; E. Foner, *Politics and Ideology*, esp. 128–49. On the quest for land among emancipated serfs and slaves, see Hobsbawm, *Age of Capital*, chap. 10; Blum, *End of the Old Order*; Green, *British Slave Emancipation*, esp. 296–304; and esp. Mintz, "Slavery and the Rise of Peasantries." Without addressing the question directly, Kolchin, *Unfree Labor*, pt. 2, provides evidence that the Russian serfs' concerns over land centered around use rights rather than ownership per se.

25. See, for example, *Telegr.*, 22 Aug. 1865; Gottlieb, "Land Question"; Oubre, *Forty Acres and a Mule*, chap. 3.

26. For the fullest elaboration of this view of the freedpeople's sensibilities regarding the use of land, see Saville, *Work of Reconstruction*. Although individual freedpeople did adopt more properly bourgeois approaches to the land in response to openings created by developing markets in land and labor power, Kolchin, *Unfree Labor*, chaps. 5 and 6, and Fogel and Engerman, *Time on the Cross*, esp. chap. 4, seem to overstate the degree of possessive individualism among black southerners.

27. See *Telegr.*, 29 Aug. 1865; Fred. A. Poomer et al. to Brig. Gen. Craxton, 4 Aug. 1865, AMA. The petition's twenty-three signers, all residents of Perry, included virtually all the town's planter elite. The petition was endorsed by the Reverend Mansfield French of the Freedmen's Bureau, indicating that he "responded to this call." On the larger context of the insurrection scare, see Berlin, Reidy, and Rowland, *Black Military Experience*, doc. 325 and chap. 17, and, from a different perspective, Carter, "Anatomy of Fear." The Union army had begun recruiting a regiment of black soldiers in Macon after occupying the city, but the effort soon ended and the recruits dispatched with other black regiments to the Mexican border. See records of the 136th United States Colored Infantry, Colored Troops Division, RG 94.

28. See chap. 8, below.

29. J. H. Wilson to W. D. Whipple, 15 June 1865, vol. 13/22 CCMDM, pp. 121–27, Letters Sent, Cavalry Corps, Mil. Div. of the Miss., RG 393, pt. 2, no. 151; C. M. Thompson, *Reconstruction in Georgia*, 71.

30. U.S. War Department, *Official Records*, ser. 1, vol. 49, pt. 2, p. 1068; *Telegr.*, 8 July 1865; *New York Times*, 21 July 1865. Wilson's orders reflected the prevailing guidelines for organizing plantation labor that federal military officials in the Mississippi Valley had devised during the war. In contrast to E. Foner, *Reconstruction*, chap. 2, and esp. Berlin et al., *Wartime Genesis of Free Labor*, chaps. 2 and 3, see Gerteis, *From Contraband to Freedman*, and R. Davis, *Good and Faithful Labor*, who treat wartime labor arrangements as important precedents for postwar sharecropping arrangements.

31. Hobsbawm, *Age of Capital*, 218–19, properly points out that even in England, the original home of "free labor," a variety of noneconomic compulsions to work, such as the Master and Servant Act that prescribed jail for breach of contract, survived until the 1860s. On coercion in the postbellum South, see Daniel, *Shadow of Slavery*; Novak, *Wheel of Servitude*; and Cohen, "Negro Involuntary Servitude."

32. *Telegr.*, 13, 26, 28, and 30 May, 1 June, 19 and 25 Sept. 1865. At the beginning of June, the provost marshal employed a sixty-man detail to round up all black persons who did not reside in the city when Union forces arrived.

33. Ibid., 5 Oct. 1865, notes the predicament of the families of absent laborers. On the government's effort to provide transportation home for refugeed former slaves, see ibid., 19, 20, 21 July, 4 Aug. 1865. Descriptions of the shanties on the outskirts of Macon are in ibid., 23 June 1865; in Andrews, *South since the War*, quoted in C. M. Thompson, *Reconstruction in Georgia*, 34–35; and also in Litwack, *Been in the Storm*, 310–11, from which the quotation of the freedman comes. On other such communities of squatters (for instance, Old Field and New Hope on the outskirts of Perry), see Hickson, *Land So Dedicated*, 120–21; C. M. Thompson, *Reconstruction in Georgia*, 46.

34. *Telegr.*, 24 and 30 May, 23 June 1865.

35. Ibid., 15 June, 19, 25 Sept. 1865. On the role of military authorities in establishing

the mayor's court, see Carter, *When the War Was Over*, 180–81. Like their counterparts throughout the South, local authorities in other Georgia cities established similar courts during the early days of freedom. See C. M. Thompson, *Reconstruction in Georgia*, 36, 39. Authorities in Columbus, Georgia, acted with an even heavier hand, violently destroying a shantytown in order to force freedpeople back to the plantations. See *Columbus Sun*, 21 Dec. 1865, quoted in Wilson, *Black Codes of the South*, 52–53.

36. *Telegr.*, 24 June 1865. In Houston County, for example, the white citizenry favored generous aid to the disabled and destitute "heroes of our 'lost cause'" and their families. When it was evident that the occupants of the county poorhouse were objects of charity rather than fugitives from labor, grand jurors recommended "discontinuance of the farming operation heretofore carried on" and provision of a cart and mule to facilitate hauling firewood. See Houston Co. grand jury presentments, August adjourned term 1866, August adjourned term 1867, Houston Co. Superior Court Minutes, GDAH. For the larger context of post–Civil War relief, see Bremner, *Public Good*, pt. 2.

37. J. G. Barney to Davis Tillson, 1 Nov. 1865, Unregistered Letters Received, Ga. Asst. Comr., RG 105. Trowbridge, *The South*, 462. Trowbridge reports the results of a census taken by the Freedmen's Bureau, but the census itself no longer survives.

38. See ms. federal census, population returns, 1870, Bibb Co., RG 29; *Haddock's Directory*, 1872. During the spring of 1865, Macon's officials began enforcing the lapsed market ordinances, in part to regulate butchering and to remove hucksters from the public streets. See *Telegr.*, 30 May, 1–3, 6, 7, 9, 10, 18, 23 June, 2, 22 July 1865. The reference to "chicken pies and goober peas" appears in ibid., 1 June 1865.

39. Louis Lambert to W. W. Deane, 12 Dec. 1865, 296:3–4, Letters Sent, Macon Subasst. Comr., RG 105.

40. The bureau's point man in upcountry Georgia was John Emory Bryant, a former captain in a black regiment who would later play a prominent role in Reconstruction politics in the state. Bryant advocated minimum wages of $7 per month for first-class men and $6 for first-class women, but neither General Wilson nor bureau commissioner O. O. Howard countenanced the plan. See *Telegr.*, 16 July 1865, for Bryant's order and reports of his superiors' reactions to it. For additional details on Bryant, see chaps. 7–9, below, and, more generally, Currie-McDaniel, *Carpetbagger of Conscience*, chaps. 3–6; Shadgett, *Republican Party in Georgia*.

41. Charles H. Howard to O. O. Howard, 30 Dec. 1865, U.S. Congress, House, *Report of the Joint Committee*, pt. 3, pp. 45–46; Henry M. Loyless to Davis Tillson, 13 Aug., 2 Dec. 1866, Unregistered Letters Received, Ga. Asst. Comr., RG 105. The assistant commissioner's correspondence contains countless such reports from all over the state following the harvest.

42. Under cover of the stay law enacted early in 1866, employers claimed relief from their obligations for 1865 wages. See, for example, T. W. White to Geo. H. Pratt, 22 Mar. 1866, Unregistered Letters Received, Ga. Asst. Comr., RG 105.

43. Circular No. 2, 3 Oct. 1865, vol. 26, General Orders, Special Orders and Circulars, Ga. Asst. Comr., RG 105; Kennaway, *On Sherman's Track*, 49; Tillson to John B. Walker, 20 Nov. 1865, 11:170–73, Press Copies of Letters Sent, Ga. Asst. Comr., RG 105. See also Cimbala, "'Talisman Power'"; Fields and Rowland, "Free Labor Ideology." The most accommodating southerners also learned to mouth the same shibboleths;

one testified before Congress that through the combination of the friendliness of the "better classes" of whites "and the laws of capital and labor, the relations of the classes will settle down together on terms equitable and just to both." Quoted in C. M. Thompson, *Reconstruction in Georgia*, pp. 121–22. A remarkable editorial in the *Telegraph*, 27 Aug. 1866, outlined the new relations between capital and labor and the role of the "market overt" in mediating differences.

44. Tillson's Circular No. 5, 22 Dec. 1865, established the wage rates, and Circulars No. 1 (5 Jan. 1866), 2 (16 Jan. 1866), and 3 (1 Feb. 1866) required planters to pay the stipulated rates. Vol. 26, General Orders, Special Orders, and Circulars, Ga. Asst. Comr., RG 105. Despite their fondness for the principle of noninterference, both Tillson and his successor, Col. Caleb C. Sibley, kept the wage standards in effect until 1868, when Sibley judged them no longer operable in the face of perennial crop failures. In acknowledging the need to remove the guidelines, Sibley instructed all agents to "seek by every means in their power to secure the largest remuneration for labor, consistent with the circumstances." On the bureau under Tillson, see C. M. Thompson, "Freedmen's Bureau" and *Reconstruction in Georgia*, 50–55; Conway, *Reconstruction of Georgia*, 75–84; McFeely, *Yankee Stepfather*, 121–22, 132, and esp. 202; and Cimbala, "Talisman Power." Many historians have attempted to decide whether the bureau primarily served the interests of the planters or those of the freedpeople. For an extreme recent formulation, see Wiener, *Social Origins*, 47–58. The best correctives of those views shift the terms of the discussion away from this false dichotomy and situate the bureau and its functionaries in the context of northern free-labor ideology. See E. Foner, *Politics and Ideology*, chap. 6, "Reconstruction and the Crisis of Free Labor," and *Reconstruction*, esp. 153–70; and Fields and Rowland, "Free Labor Ideology."

45. In this respect, Tillson's support for President Johnson's program of reconstruction is significant. Tillson's appointment of Whiggish civilian agents complemented Johnson's appointment of Whiggish provisional governors. See E. Foner, *Reconstruction*, 193–95.

46. Lambert to W. W. Deane, 12 Dec. 1865, 16 Jan. 1866, and Lambert to N. S. Glover, 28 Dec. 1865, 296:3–4, 22, 11, Letters Sent, Macon Subasst. Comr., RG 105. For the full statement of the quoted planter, see "Houston" to editors, *Jnl. & Msgr.*, 17 Jan. 1866. Reports from elsewhere in the Macon area concur in these assessments of the behavior of landholders and laborers; see, for instance, J. D. Havis to Davis Tillson, 22 Dec. 1865, Unregistered Letters Received, Ga. Asst. Comr.; and Henry C. Loyless to Lambert, 17 Jan. 1866, Letters Received, Marion Agent, RG 105.

47. Howell Cobb, Jr., to his father, 3 Jan. 1866, Cobb-Erwin-Lamar Family Papers, UGa (original emphasis); *Telegr.*, 22, 29 Aug. 1865.

48. See, for examples, Contracts, Perry Agent, RG 105. See esp. Glymph, "Freedpeople and Ex-Masters," 52–54; Shlomowitz, "Squad System"; Jaynes, *Branches without Roots*, chap. 10.

49. For trends in Monroe County, see *Telegr.*, 7 Apr. 1866. The respective preferences of freedpeople and planters in Houston County are noted in ibid., 29 June 1865, 7 Apr. 1866. Surviving contracts in the records of the Freedmen's Bureau further document these preferences. See, for instance, Contracts, Perry Agent, RG 105.

50. The series of letters received by the Macon subassistant commissioner, RG 105, contains numerous references to contract terms and contract disputes that illustrate these points.

51. See McQueen McIntosh to Davis Tillson, 4 Dec. 1865 (with enclosures), Unregistered Letters Received, Ga. Asst. Comr., RG 105. As noted earlier, former masters quickly realized their "emancipation" from such responsibilities, but this freedom was short-lived. Tillson seconded Wilson's directive, ordering that former masters support elderly freedpeople. Circular No. 5, 22 Dec. 1865, vol. 26, General Orders, Special Orders, and Circulars, Ga. Asst. Comr., RG 105.

52. See the summary report on conditions in the state of J. R. Lewis to O. O. Howard, 9 Oct. 1867, Reports, Office of the Comr., RG 105. Such a system, typical of peasant forms of agriculture, in essence shifts capital costs from the landowners to the laborers.

53. For the case of a Bibb County middleman who rented 150 acres and employed twelve freedmen, see Wm. Mathews to O. O. Howard, 4 Apr. 1867, M-0 1867, Registered Letters Received, Macon Subasst. Comr., RG 105. Similarly, see Jerry Lyons to C. C. Sibley, 19 Dec. 1868, #498 1868, Registered Letters Received, Ga. Asst. Comr., RG 105. For the experiences of other renters, see Wm. F. Martins to Eugene Pickett, 12 Jan. 1867, Unregistered Letters Received, Ga. Asst. Comr.; Picket to Martins, 21 Jan. 1867, Letters Received, Waynesboro Agent, RG 105. See also Jos. H. Taylor to W. W. Deane, 24 May 1866, T-480 1866, Registered Letters Received, and H. L. O'Neal to Davis Tillson, 25 Jan. 1867, Unregistered Letters Received, Ga. Asst. Comr., RG 105.

54. Jaynes, *Branches without Roots*, chaps. 3 and 9; Wright, *Old South, New South*, 87, 89; Ransom and Sutch, *One Kind of Freedom*, chap. 6.

55. In 1866, the Georgia legislature facilitated these developments by granting a lien on crops to merchants. See *Acts*, 1866, 141; on the importance of these changes, see Banks, *Economics of Land Tenure*, 46; Brooks, *Agrarian Revolution in Georgia*, 32–36; Conway, *Reconstruction of Georgia*, 123–25; Flynn, *White Land, Black Labor*, 87, 91–92; Hahn, *Roots of Southern Populism*, 174–76. Regardless of state law granting first liens to landlords and merchants, bureau officials held the common-law laborers' lien superior to all others. See Geo. Wagner to Frank Gallagher, 5 Nov. 1867, enclosing petitions of L. Pitts to C. C. Sibley and O. O. Howard; also Jos. E. Walker to U. S. Grant, 26 Nov. 1867, Unregistered Letters Received, Ga. Asst. Comr., RG 105. On 4 December 1867, Commissioner O. O. Howard endorsed the policy of recognizing the laborers' lien.

56. Two classic expositions of the connection between "free labor" and control over the means of subsistence are Marx, *Capital*, vol. 1, and E. Thompson, *Whigs and Hunters*.

57. *Acts*, 1865–66, 239–41 (Title XXXI, Persons of Color). For fuller discussion of its provisions, see below, chap. 7.

58. Ibid., 1866, 153–54, 164–66. For an 1865 enticement act that apparently failed to pass, see (Augusta) *Colored American*, 30 Dec. 1865. At times counties assessed additional poll taxes of one dollar and permitted collectors to add a fifty-cent charge for collecting delinquent taxes. See W. F. White to M. Frank Gallagher, 21 Oct. 1867, W-154 1867; and H. Catley to Max Marbach, 26 Mar. 1868, and Marbach's reply, 2 Apr. 1868, #945 1868, Registered Letters Received, Ga. Asst. Comr., RG 105.

59. *Acts*, 1865–66, 234–35, 237–38; ibid., 1866, 39, 160–62, 154–55.

60. *Telegr.*, 16 May 1865; testimony of Charles Stearns in U.S. Congress, House, *Condition of Affairs in Georgia*, 110; Carter, *When the War Was Over*, 177. Such language was not peculiar; Britons employed it in reference to emancipation in the West Indies. See quotation of Henry G. G. Howick in D. Davis, *Slavery and Human Progress*, 218.

61. See Horwitz, *Transformation of American Law*; Kulik, "Dams, Fish, and Farmers"; Fox-Genovese and Genovese, *Fruits of Merchant Capital*. Of course, England had experienced a similar transformation earlier (see E. Thompson, *Whigs and Hunters*), and upcountry Georgia would experience it later (see Hahn, *Roots of Southern Populism*).

62. See Hahn, "Hunting, Fishing, and Foraging"; Flynn, *White Land, Black Labor*, 115–24.

63. For details of the contract (and an ensuing dispute) between W. I. Tooke and the freedmen, see N. Sellers Hill to Eugene Pickett, 27 Dec. 1866, 296:71–72, Letters Sent, Macon Subasst. Comr., RG 105.

64. Cobb to his wife, Dec. 1866, Cobb-Erwin-Lamar Family Papers, UGa.

65. N. Sellers Hill to Eugene Pickett, 27 Dec. 1866, 296:71–72, Letters Sent, Macon Subasst. Comr.; contract between Biney and Stephen Hornee, filed under date 3 July 1867, and contract between Aaron Bowman and Bennett Jones, filed under date 4 May 1866, Unregistered Letters Received, Macon Subasst. Comr.; contract between G. W. Singleton and freedpeople, 1 Jan. 1867, Contracts, Perry Agent, RG 105. In 1850, Singleton was an overseer with no real property, but two slaves; in 1860 he was a farmer with $8,000 in real property and ten slaves. Ms. federal census records, free and slave schedules, Houston Co., Ga., 1850 and 1860, RG 29.

66. John A. Steele to Davis Tillson, 16 Jan. 1866, Unregistered Letters Received, Ga. Asst. Comr., RG 105.

67. Thaddeus S. Stoy to John Pope, 21 Apr. 1867, A-217, Letters Received, Bureau of Civil Affairs, 3d Mil. Dist., RG 393, pt. 1.

68. See Gutman, *Black Family*, esp. 222, 226–28.

69. Circular No. 3, 14 Oct. 1865, General Orders, Special Orders, and Circulars, vol. 26, Ga. Asst. Comr., RG 105.

70. *Acts*, 1865–66, 6–8. Apprenticeship played a crucial part in the transition from slavery to freedom in both the British West Indies, where slavery ended in 1833, and Maryland, where a new state constitution abolished slavery in 1864. See Green, *British Slave Emancipation*, 129–61; Fields, *Slavery and Freedom*, chap. 6.

71. Edwin Belcher to C. C. Sibley, 23 Sept. 1867, 367:11–12, Letters Sent, Forsyth Agent, RG 105. One John Lester of Jones County bound his nineteen-year-old mulatto son to himself in 1872 and again in 1873. In return for paying the mother forty dollars per year, Lester assumed "full power and authority to control Said minor in reason and according to law." See Jones Co. Court of Ordinary, Minutes, 1868–73, p. 187, GDAH. Belcher was the son of a South Carolina planter and slave woman who, with his mother and other siblings, had settled in Philadelphia before the Civil War. He served in a Pennsylvania volunteer regiment during the war and achieved the rank of captain. After the war he settled in Georgia and commenced work with the bureau, later becoming a mainstay in the Republican party of the state.

72. Belcher to Sibley, 23 Sept. 1867, 367:11–12, Letters Sent, Forsyth Agent, RG 105. Jack Gill (per E. B. Rucker) to J. R. Lewis, 21 Sept. 1867, Letters Received, Marietta Agent, RG 105. Rucker was a black Baptist minister who served as a scribe for freedpeople in Cobb County. Numerous letters in his handwriting survive in the Georgia Freedmen's Bureau papers.

73. Houston Co. Court of Ordinary, Indentures of Apprenticeship, GDAH.

74. Of the seventy-seven black children listed on the postwar apprenticeship rolls of Houston County, three were bound to relatives. See Houston Co. Court of Ordinary, Indentures of Apprenticeship, GDAH.

75. Ibid.; Hill to Jesse Aycock, 24 May 1867, and Hill to J. P. Culverhouse, 16 July 1868, 297:44, 125, Letters Sent, Macon Subasst. Comr., RG 105. See also 296:12, Letters Sent, Macon Subasst. Comr.; and James Chapman to Davis Tillson, 30 Jan. 1866, Unregistered Letters Received, Ga. Asst. Comr., RG 105.

76. Deposition of Gracie Brown, 23 July 1866, #79 1866, Registered Letters Received, Macon Subasst. Comr., RG 105. Daniel apparently went unpunished. For a case involving prosecution for enticement, see J. H. Kulbfleisch to Jacob R. Davis, 10 Mar. 1868; Edwin Belcher to C. T. Watson, 7 Mar. 1868; and Belcher to John Colflash, 7 Mar. 1868, #637 1868, Registered Letters Received, Ga. Asst. Comr., RG 105.

77. Where landowners in mixed farming regions such as Maryland might conceivably rely upon a bound laborer or two, apprenticeship enjoyed some vitality. See Fields, *Slavery and Freedom*, chap. 6. But it failed miserably in large plantation regions such as the South and the British West Indies. See Green, *British Slave Emancipation*.

78. Louis Lambert to W. W. Deane, 4 and 16 Jan. 1866, 296:16–17, 22, Letters Sent, Macon Subasst. Comr., RG 105.

79. J. D. Havis to Davis Tillson, 23 July 1866, Unregistered Letters Received, Ga. Asst. Comr., RG 105. The *Telegraph*, 7 Apr. 1866, reported the withdrawal of black women from field work in Monroe County. See also C. M. Thompson, *Reconstruction in Georgia*, 44; Flynn, *White Land, Black Labor*, 60–62; Wiener, *Social Origins*, 47; Litwack, *Been in the Storm*, 244–46.

80. Bowman and Jones contract cited in n. 65, above. On domestic patriarchy, see Mann, "Slavery, Sharecropping, and Sexual Inequality" and *Agrarian Capitalism*, esp. 83–84, although she may paint too one-dimensional a portrait of patriarchy in southern black households. Contrast Ned Cobb's description of his household with that of his father in Rosengarten, *All God's Dangers*, pt. 1. See also Jones, *Labor of Love, Labor of Sorrow*, chap. 2; Burton, *My Father's House*, chap. 6.

81. Although they generally discouraged movement from the countryside to the city, bureau authorities actively promoted relocation to areas of labor scarcity, particularly the newly developing regions of the Mississippi Valley, and often provided transportation to prospective migrants. See, for instance, Davis Tillson's endorsement on letter of R. F. Johnston, 28 Jan. 1866, 20:96, Endorsements; and H. Sweeney to Adjutant General of the Ga. Freedmen's Bureau, 28 Jan. 1867, S-432, 1867, Letters Received, Ga. Asst. Comr., RG 105. Figures on hands employed come from C. M. Thompson, *Reconstruction in Georgia*, 264. The reductions contrast sharply with the dramatic increases in the black populations of Houston and Monroe counties after the war (see Appendix). In southwest Georgia, the trend was similar: in Dougherty County, the number of black laborers dropped from 3,140 in 1867 to 1,669 in 1872. In the older sections of Georgia's cotton belt, not all counties experienced a net loss of laborers, though two along the Savannah River lost dramatically: Burke, from 4,595 to 1,462, and Columbia, from 2,789 to 1,090. Ibid., 265. In Columbia County, Ku Klux terror contributed substantially to the reduction in hands. See Stearns, *Black Man*.

82. Wives of men working for wages or shares often rented small patches on their own,

the *Telegraph* observed in 1870. See *Telegr. & Msgr.*, 25 Jan., 1 Feb. 1870. See the cases of Biney and the wife of Aaron Bowman cited in n. 65, above.

83. Entry for complaint by Mary Flower, 4 Apr. 1866, 1:146, Register of Letters Received, Ga. Asst. Comr., RG 105. Although Mary Flower did state her case before the bureau, it does not appear that Jess Flower carried through his threat.

84. Complaint of Mary Ann Gibson, 27 Aug. 1866, 291:61, Register of Letters Received, Macon Subasst. Comr., RG 105.

85. See "Houston Factory" to editors, *Jnl. & Msgr.*, 26 June 1867; the reference to "freed Friends" appears in contract between E. R. Lewis and freedpeople, 18 Mar. 1867, Contracts, Perry Agent, RG 105. Other contracts in this and similar series of records from other bureau offices document the variety of restrictions imposed upon plantation workers.

86. *Southern Cultivator* 25 (1867): 69, quoted in Conway, *Reconstruction of Georgia*, 108.

87. See Contracts, Perry Agent, RG 105.

88. Contract between Barrington and Miller, 11 Jan. 1866, filed with Thos. J. Williams to J. Ross, 18 July 1866, Unregistered Letters Received, Macon Subasst. Comr., RG 105.

89. Ibid.

90. Charles Raushenberg to O. H. Howard, 14 Nov. 1867, Letters Received, Cuthbert Subasst. Comr.; general remarks, report of contracts filed, Nov. 1867, Perry Agent, RG 105.

91. L. C. Warren to Davis Tillson, 15 Dec. 1866, Unregistered Letters Received, Ga. Asst. Comr.; N. Sellers Hill to W. W. Deane, 17 May 1866, 296:53–54, Letters Sent, Macon Subasst. Comr., RG 105; entry for letter from J. D. Havis, [May 1866], and endorsement by Hill, 19 May 1866, 1:197–98, Register of Letters Received, Ga. Asst. Comr., RG 105. Bureau agents often sided with the employers on the matter of routine maintenance work. See, for example, F. A. H. Gaebel to W. W. Deane, 27 Aug. 1866, Letters Received, Cuthbert Agent, RG 105.

92. Allen, *Reconstruction*, chaps. 3–4; E. Foner, *Nothing But Freedom*, chap. 2, and *Reconstruction*, chap. 7.

93. See Anonymous to John Pope, 9 June 1867, with enclosed newspaper clipping, A-601, Letters Received, Bureau of Civil Affairs, 3d Mil. Dist., RG 393, pt. 1.

94. E. Foner, *Nothing But Freedom*, esp. chap. 2.

95. See the several contracts between J. G. Davis and J. A. Spivey and freedpeople, 2 and 18 Apr. 1867, Contracts, Perry Agent, RG 105. Complaints about armed freedmen filled the correspondence of military authorities. See, for instance, John P. Duncan to John Pope, 3 June 1867, A-539, Letters Received, Bureau of Civil Affairs, 3d Mil. Dist., RG 393, pt. 1.

96. For a sampling of evidence from a vast body of testimony to this effect, see George Clower to J. R. Lewis, 19, 26 Nov. 1867, C-154 and C-156 1867, Registered Letters Received, Ga. Asst. Comr.; and proceedings in the case of B. F. Tharpe v. B. Jackson, 20 Feb. 1868, Settlements, Perry Agent, RG 105.

97. Barrow, "Georgia Plantation," 830–36, esp. 833. As early as December 1865, a bureau agent had reported the reluctance of freedpeople to make contracts because wives wanted homes of their own. Joel Mathews to Davis Tillson, 6 Dec. 1865, Unregistered Letters Received, Ga. Asst. Comr., RG 105.

98. See, for instance, *Jnl. & Msgr.*, 5 Apr. 1854. The implication—often noted explicitly—was an equal partnership, with each partner owning half the business.

99. Ibid., 8 Dec. 1868; *Southern Cultivator* 26 (May 1868): 133, 135. See also ibid. 26 (Feb. 1868): 61, and 29 (Jan. 1871): 10. For subsequent reflections on these changes, see Stone, *American Race Problem*; Percy, *Lanterns on the Levee*; and, from a much different perspective, Du Bois, *Souls of Black Folk*.

100. *Southern Cultivator* 26 (May 1868): 133; *Telegr.*, 9 Oct. 1868.

101. See, for example, A. C. Walker to O. O. Howard, 8 Feb. 1868 (with endorsements), #522 1868, and Walker to H. Catley, 8 Aug. 1868, filed with #2023 1868, Registered Letters Received, Ga. Asst. Comr., RG 105.

102. *Jnl. & Msgr.*, 8 Dec. 1868; *Southern Cultivator* 26 (May 1868): 135.

103. Economic historians have described a complementary sense of frustration with share wages on the part of freedpeople and held it up as an example of the "free-rider problem." See esp. Jaynes, *Branches without Roots*, esp. 162–74; Wright, *Old South, New South*, 89–90. Apart from the fact that it presumes a particular variety of behavior to be a universal trait in the social psychology of Homo sapiens, this formulation oversimplifies the complex layers of economic, social, and cultural struggle that co-partnership addressed.

104. General remarks, report of contracts filed, Dec. 1868, Contracts, Perry Agent, RG 105; R. C. Anthony to J. R. Lewis, 25 Aug. 1868, #2180 1868; R. Ballou to O. H. Howard, 2 Nov. 1868, #231 1868, Registered Letters Received, Ga. Asst. Comr., RG 105; Squire A. Cobb and Crawford Jones to Col. C. C. Sibley, 22 Aug. 1867, C-66 1867, Letters Received, Ga. Asst. Comr., RG 105.

CHAPTER 7

1. R. Scott, *Slave Emancipation in Cuba*, esp. chap. 2.

2. The specific wording quoted here is that of Cabaniss, but it is typical of this group of men. See C. M. Thompson, *Reconstruction in Georgia*, 183.

3. General assessments of this new political constellation appear in ibid., chap. 6; Conway, *Reconstruction of Georgia*, chap. 3; Nathans, *Losing the Peace*, chaps. 1–2, esp. 44 on Brown.

4. See C. M. Thompson, *Reconstruction in Georgia*, 131–39; Conway, *Reconstruction of Georgia*, 42–50; Nathans, *Losing the Peace*, 6–11. Thompson, 133, notes that O. A. Lochrane had persuaded the president to appoint James Johnson as provisional governor in lieu of Joshua Hill, whose upcountry unionism was considered too radical.

5. *Acts*, 1865–1866, 239–41; ibid., 1866, 222. "Persons of color" subject to the provisions of these laws were those with "one-eighth negro, or African blood, in their veins." See also Wilson, *Black Codes*, 102–5.

6. E. Foner, *Reconstruction*, 239–51; Belz, *Emancipation and Equal Rights*, 114–24; Benedict, *Compromise of Principle*, 147–50, esp. 148; Nieman, *To Set the Law in Motion*, chap. 3, esp. 94–96.

7. *Telegr.*, 7 June 1865.

8. Ibid., 8 June 1865.

9. Roark, *Masters without Slaves*, 121–31, describes those who emigrated from the South rather than submit to a loss of mastership.

10. See Curtis, *Anglo-Saxons and Celts*; Montgomery, *Fall of the House of Labor*, 68, 81–87; and in particular Holt, *Problem of Freedom*, esp. 318–36.

11. For a keen assessment of the historical career of racial ideology in the United States, see Fields, "Ideology and Race."

12. Carter, *When the War Was Over*, 136.

13. Wallenstein, *Slave South to New South*, 137–38.

14. Carter, *When the War Was Over*, 111–12, notes such a commercial orientation, coupled with a mild indictment of slavery as detrimental to economic improvement, on the part of the *Macon Telegraph*.

15. For sensitive recent evocations of this combination of unity and diversity, see E. Foner, *Reconstruction*, esp. chaps. 3–4; Litwack, *Been in the Storm*; Holt, *Black over White*; Williamson, *After Slavery*. See also the three pioneering studies of A. A. Taylor: *Negro in South Carolina*, *Negro in Tennessee*, and *Negro in the Reconstruction of Virginia*.

16. Proceedings of the Georgia Education Association convention, *Telegr.*, 10 May 1867; William J. White to G. L. Eberhart, 4 June 1867, #385 1867, Ga. Supt. of Educ., RG 105. Delegates to the GEA convention documented a similar paucity of church and school buildings throughout the state.

17. Berlin, Reidy, and Rowland, *Black Military Experience*, chap. 16, esp. doc. 276A.

18. See the records of the Supt. of Educ., RG 105, and of the AMA for Georgia. For a vivid representation of how the geography of postbellum plantations transformed antebellum communities, see Barrow, "Georgia Plantation," 832–33.

19. See, for instance, *Telegr.*, 20 Aug. 1866.

20. Minutes of the Smyrna Baptist Church (28 May, 22 July 1865), Houston Factory Baptist Church (20 Aug. 1865), GDAH.

21. It is beyond the scope of this study to address the development and larger significance of segregated Christian churches except in passing. Suffice it to say that in central Georgia and across the entire plantation belt, the matter was complicated by changing power relationships among different groups of Christians. Before the Civil War, when slaves were legally powerless, masters often insisted upon integrated worship services. But after the war and the end of the masters' ownership over slaves, both parties exercised varying degrees of choice in the matter. It is therefore striking that within the first five years of the Civil War, virtually every Protestant congregation in central Georgia split along racial lines. For fuller treatment, see Rabinowitz, *Race Relations*, chap. 9. For a recent general survey of the racial dimensions of American Christianity, see F. Wood, *Arrogance of Faith*.

22. See minutes of Perry Baptist Church (22 July, 22 Aug. 1865), Midway Missionary Baptist Church (May–June 1866), Jeffersonville Baptist Church (7 Apr. and 10 Nov. 1866, 18 Aug. 1867, 13 Feb. 1868, 11 Sept. 1869), GDAH.

23. H. Eddy to E. A. Strieby, 9 Jan. 1866; E. P. Smith to Strieby, 28 Apr. 1866, AMA; *Telegr.*, 4 May, 7 May 1866; *New York Times*, 21 May 1866. During the Civil War, Carter reportedly led his congregation in prayer that "the Lion" would "conquer" and that "all her foes might be smitten and confounded, and her starry banner wave in triumph over all the land." See J. Owens, "Negro in Georgia," 143. Carter laid the cornerstone for a new

Presbyterian church in Macon on New Year's Day, 1869, but seems to have identified with the Congregationalists of the AMA shortly thereafter and moved to Savannah. See *Jnl. & Msgr.*, 5 Jan. 1869.

24. The travails of southern black Methodists, including struggles similar to the ones in Macon described below, are chronicled in detail in the columns of the African Methodist Episcopal church organ, the *Christian Recorder*. More generally, see Walker, *Rock in a Weary Land*, chap. 4.

25. Pierce, *History of Methodism in Georgia*, 141.

26. The *Christian Recorder* documents the church property struggle throughout the South. See, for example, the letter from Richard H. Cain, Charleston, S.C., 3 June 1865. A resolution of the January 1866 freedmen's convention of Georgia pointedly denounced such practices. *Proceedings of the Freedmen's Convention*, 30.

27. Louis Lambert to W. W. Deane, 19 Dec. 1865, enclosing resolutions of the black Methodist congregation, 19 Nov. 1865, with endorsement by Davis Tillson, 25 Dec. 1865, Unregistered Letters Received, Macon Subasst. Comr., RG 105.

28. *Telegr.*, 25 Feb. 1869. Although Campbell's politics remain unknown, Steward's congregation was a hotbed of radical political sentiment and activity. Steward himself served as cashier at the branch of the Freedman's Bank in Macon and took a spirited part in Republican politics. Henry M. Turner, presiding elder of the North Georgia Conference of the AME church, former member of both the 1867–68 state constitutional convention and the 1868 state legislature, and probably the leading black Republican in the state, supported Steward. Jefferson F. Long, kingpin of the Bibb County Republican party and eventually Georgia's first black congressman, was treasurer of Steward's congregation. Campbell's faction included no such politically prominent members.

29. See *Christian Recorder*, 22 May 1869; *Telegr.*, 26 Feb. 1869; Steward, *Fifty Years*, 116–23; Bibb Co. Superior Court Minutes, Adjourned Term 1870, GDAH, each of which differs from the other accounts in minor details. The subsequent separation of the Colored Methodist Episcopal (CME) church from the African Methodist Episcopal church reflected the continuing efforts of former masters to influence the religious lives of former slaves. In 1870, a group of approximately 100 persons left the AME congregation in Macon to affiliate with the CME church. When, two years later, they undertook to raise money for a church, they bypassed the traditional route of soliciting subscriptions from communicants. Instead, they petitioned the Bibb County Superior Court for permission to borrow $2,000 from the Macon Building and Loan Association; as they no doubt knew it would be, the loan was granted. See J. Owens, "Negro in Georgia," 129–30; Bibb Co. Superior Court Minutes, 24 June 1872, GDAH. See also *Christian Recorder*, 22 May 1869.

30. See Drago, *Black Politicians*, chap. 4 and app.; Robinson, "Plans Dat Comed from God."

31. On Turner, see Redkey, *Black Exodus* and *Respect Black!*; on Steward, see Steward, *Fifty Years*.

32. Steward, *Fifty Years*, 92.

33. Although Macon hosted a thriving branch of the Freedman's Bank, its records have disappeared; hence it is impossible to examine depositors' accounts for insight into the associational life of Macon freedpeople, which surviving records of this kind make

possible. The definitive history of the bank indicates that the branch was exceptionally vibrant, with an active advisory board and over 700 depositors in 1870. See Osthaus, *Freedmen, Philanthropy, and Fraud*, 96, 110, and, more generally, Rabinowitz, *Race Relations*, chap. 10. See Rachleff, *Black Labor in the South*, chap. 2, for a perceptive analysis of the freedpeople's community in Richmond, Virginia, based upon a careful and imaginative reading of surviving bank deposit records.

34. Turner's periodic reports to the Freedmen's Bureau document his nearly boundless energy, as does his testimony before the joint committee of Congress investigating Ku Klux violence. See Turner to Davis Tillson, Letters Received, Ga. Asst. Comr., RG 105; testimony of Henry M. Turner, U.S. Congress, House, *Affairs in the Late Insurrectionary States*, 1034–42.

35. Ponton, *Henry M. Turner*; Redkey, *Respect Black!*

36. See [Anderson], *Life of Robert Anderson*; Steward, *Fifty Years*, 91–100. Even as they vied for new members, ministers of the various churches cooperated. When African Methodist Episcopal elder Henry M. Turner organized a congregation in Perry, Houston County, for example, Isaac L. Primus, a black carpenter and Baptist minister formerly from Macon, offered his church building as a meeting place and even rescheduled his own congregation's services to accommodate the Methodists. See Turner to Editors, *Christian Recorder*, 3 June 1871.

37. See the testimony of Henry M. Turner in U.S. Congress, House, *Affairs in the Late Insurrectionary States*, esp. 1035–37.

38. *Telegr.*, 10 May 1867.

39. Trowbridge, *The South*, 465–66.

40. Deveaux to Lewis, 3 June 1869, #35 1869, Letters Received, Ga. Supt. of Educ., RG 105. Deveaux is the brother of the man who founded the *Savannah Tribune*.

41. See, for example, George H. Clower to E. A. Ware, 26 Nov. 1867, #448 1867, Letters Received, Ga. Supt. of Educ., RG 105; Steward, *Fifty Years*, 93–97, explains in even greater detail the erection of a church building in this fashion.

42. Mitchell to G. L. Eberhart, 23 Oct. 1865, #12 1865; W. H. Robert to Eberhart, 25 Oct. 1865, enclosing Report of Freedmen's Schools for the City of Macon; Robert to Eberhart, 30 Oct. and 2 Nov. 1865; Lewis Smith et al. to Eberhart, 18 Oct. 1865, #9 1865, #10 1865, #14 1865, #15 1865, Letters Received, Ga. Supt. of Educ., RG 105; E. M. Cravath to Hunt, 15 Dec. 1865, AMA.

43. For the general picture, see the proceedings of the conventions of the Georgia Education Association, *Telegr.*, 10 May, 11 and 18 Oct. 1867. On developments in central Georgia, see the following letters from African American school organizers in Letters Received, Ga. Supt. of Educ., RG 105: W. J. White to G. L. Eberhart, 4 June 1867, #385 1867; G. H. Clower to E. A. Ware, 3 and 26 Nov. 1867, #448 1867; Jas. B. Deveaux to J. R. Lewis, 31 Mar. 1869, and resolutions of Thomas Crayton et al., 28 Mar. 1869, #331 1869. See also Edwin Belcher to J. R. Lewis, 26 Sept. 1867, Unregistered Letters Received, Ga. Asst. Comr., RG 105. The quoted passages occur in the resolutions of Crayton et al. and in the letter of Deveaux.

44. Laura Holt to Col. Lewis, 19 Aug. 1869, #370 1869, Letters Received, Ga. Supt. of Educ., RG 105.

45. Letters from black teachers, school committees, and Freedmen's Bureau agents

describe organizing and financing black schools in detail. See, for instance, Edwin Belcher to J. R. Lewis, 26 Sept. 1867, Unregistered Letters Received, Ga. Asst. Comr.; George H. Clower to E. A. Ware, 3 and 26 Nov. 1867, #448 1867, Letters Received, Ga. Supt. of Educ.; Daniel Losey to Ware, 14 Sept. 1868, 332:124–25, Letters Sent, Perry Agent; E. S. Kydd to Ware, 26 Nov. 1868, #365 1868, Letters Received, Ga. Supt. of Educ., RG 105; S. Ashley to Wm. Coppinger, [Mar. 1868], 190:283, series 1-A, ACS.

46. Subscription statements of Jerry Williams et al., 24 Aug. 1867, and of Ruben Pickets et al., 26 Aug. 1867, Letters Received, Macon Subasst. Comr., RG 105.

47. See, for instance, J. P. Hutchings to J. R. Lewis, 12 Aug. 1867, #139 1867, Letters Received, Ga. Supt. of Educ., RG 105.

48. *Telegr.*, 5 Sept. 1865; Daniel Hough to John Ogden, 29 Sept. 1865; W. H. Robert to Ogden, 29 Sept. 1865, AMA.

49. See *Telegr.*, 5 Sept. 1865; Daniel Hough to John Ogden, 29 Sept. 1865, and W. H. Robert to John Ogden, 29 Sept. 1865, both in AMA; G. L. Eberhart, report for 1 Oct. 1865 to 1 Oct. 1866, Reports, Ga. Asst. Comr., RG 105; Lewis Smith et al. to G. L. Eberhart, 18 Oct. 1865, #5 1865; R. M. Mitchell to G. L. Eberhart, 23 Oct. 1865, #12 1865, Letters Received, Ga. Supt. of Educ., RG 105.

50. See, for instance, William Travis and Benjamin Curry to E. A. Ware, 5 Nov. 1868, #299 1868, Letters Received, Ga. Supt. of Educ., RG 105. Travis had served as a registrar in the enrollment of new voters following passage of the Reconstruction Acts in 1867.

51. Printed prospectus, "The Georgia Educational Association: A New Plan for Educating the Freedmen of the South," [Jan. or Feb. 1867], Letters Received, Ga. Supt. of Educ., RG 105.

52. Freedmen's Bureau school superintendent George L. Eberhart pronounced the schools organized by the Western Freedmen's Aid Society "inefficient" by virtue of the fact that the schools "were all under the tuition of resident colored teachers," but he did not similarly describe the bureau's schools that were being taught by freedpeople. Annual School Report of G. L. Eberhart, Supt. of Educ., for 1 Oct. 1865 to 1 Oct. 1866, Reports, Ga. Asst. Comr., RG 105.

53. Printed prospectus, "The Georgia Educational Association: A New Plan for Educating the Freedmen of the South," [Jan. or Feb. 1867], Letters Received, Ga. Supt. of Educ., RG 105; Currie-McDaniel, *Carpetbagger of Conscience*, chap. 3.

54. *Telegr.*, 10 May 1867.

55. Jones, *Soldiers of Light and Love*, esp. 69–70, 182–83.

56. J. A. Rockwell to E. A. Hunt, 7 May 1866, AMA.

57. Frank Haley to E. P. Smith, 1 Dec. 1867, AMA.

58. E. M. Cravath to Hunt, 15 Dec. 1865; H. Eddy to M. E. Strieby, 22 Dec. 1865, AMA; *New York Times*, 18 Feb. 1866; *Telegr.*, 7 Mar. 1866; Eberhart to O. O. Howard, 14 Mar. 1866, School Reports, Ga. Supt. of Educ., RG 105; Trowbridge, *The South*, 465–66. See also the tabular monthly school reports in the records of the AMA and the Macon Subasst. Comr., RG 105.

59. In general, see Wallenstein, *Slave South to New South*, 152–53; Rabinowitz, *Race Relations*, chap. 7. The report of the committee of Macon's white leaders appears in *Telegr.*, 20 Aug. 1866. For a small sampling of the voluminous testimony regarding

opposition against northern teachers—including physical assaults and other species of violence and intimidation—see W. J. White to G. L. Eberhart, 4 June 1867, #385 1867, Letters Received, Ga. Supt. of Educ.; J. R. Lewis to Eugene Pickett, 28 July 1867, L-21 1867, Letters Received, Ga. Asst. Comr., RG 105.

60. *Loyal Georgian*, 9 May 1867; *Telegr.*, 10 May 1867.

61. See J. Anderson, *Education of Blacks in the South*.

62. See the statements of Howell Cobb and A. H. Chappell, quoted in chap. 6, above, for similar retrospective justifications of slavery by paternalists adjusting to a world without slaves.

63. *Telegr.*, 20 Aug. 1866. In addition to the mayor, ministers of the leading churches, and other luminaries, the committee included representatives from the AMA and the Freedmen's Bureau.

64. See W. J. White to G. L. Eberhart, 4 June 1867, #385 1867, Letters Received, Ga. Supt. of Educ.; petition of Jas. S. Pincard et al., 3 Aug. 1867, entry P-12 1867, Register of Letters Received, Ga. Asst. Comr.; *Telegr.*, 10 May, 2 Aug., and 18 Oct. 1867; Edwin Belcher to J. R. Lewis, 26 Sept. 1867, Unregistered Letters Received, Ga. Asst. Comr., RG 105.

65. Printed prospectus, "The Georgia Educational Association: A New Plan for Educating the Freedmen of the South," [Jan. or Feb. 1867], Letters Received, Ga. Supt. of Educ., RG 105; Currie-McDaniel, *Carpetbagger of Conscience*, 57–60.

66. *Loyal Georgian*, 9 May 1867; *Telegr.*, 10 May, 11 and 18 Oct. 1867; White to G. L. Eberhart, 4 June 1867, #385 1867, Letters Received, Ga. Supt. of Educ., RG 105; Ashley to William Coppinger, 5 Mar. 1868, vol. 190, #283, series 1-A, ACS. In addition to the letters of White cited here and elsewhere, see his protest against being ousted from a first-class car on the Macon and Western Railroad. White to C. C. Sibley, 29 June 1867, W-15 1867, Letters Received, Ga. Asst. Comr., RG 105.

67. *Telegr.*, 10 May, 18 Oct. 1867.

68. See below, chap. 9.

69. Anonymous to A. P. Ketchum, 20 Aug. 1865, Letters Received by Capt. A. P. Ketchum re: Restoration of Property, Savannah Subasst. Comr., RG 105.

70. "Foby's" antebellum guidelines for the "Management of Servants" stipulated that "On Sunday, two and only two boys are permitted to visit town for the purpose of trading." *Southern Cultivator* 11 (Aug. 1853): 227.

71. The literature demonstrating this point is immense and still growing. For a sample of the best, see E. Thompson, *Making of the English Working Class*; Hobsbawm, *Workers*, esp. chap. 14; Wilentz, *Chants Democratic*; Montgomery, *Fall of the House of Labor*, esp. chap. 1; Magdol, "Local Black Leaders."

72. For accounts of such gatherings, see *Telegr.*, 5 July 1865, 3 Apr. 1868; *Jnl. & Msgr.*, 3 Apr. 1867, 1 Apr. 1868; *Christian Recorder*, 13 Apr. 1867.

73. *Proceedings of the Freedmen's Convention*; Cason, "Loyal League"; Currie-McDaniel, *Carpetbagger of Conscience*, 61–62. On the Loyal Leagues in Alabama and Mississippi, see Fitzgerald, *Union League Movement*, esp. chaps. 1–2, which deal with the origins and organizing tactics of the leagues.

74. Except for the ministers associated with the AME church and the northern Congregationalists' American Missionary Association, who devoted full time to the

ministry, virtually every black minister active in central Georgia (and, for that matter, the entire state) between 1865 and 1880 preached as a sideline, earning a living in a skilled trade or in farming. See Drago, *Black Politicians*, app.

75. See ibid.; Magdol, "Local Black Leaders" and *Right to the Land.*

76. The press attributed the agitation to white northerners and, railing against what it termed "ill timed and inappropriate" speeches, advised the freedmen to go to work and leave political meetings alone. *Telegr.*, 5, 12 July 1865.

77. Unlike its opposition to the league, the Macon press heartily endorsed Banks's "eminently conservative" proposition. See ibid., 10 Sept. 1865.

78. The comparison to Booker T. Washington's repudiation of political agitation in favor of industrious labor is evident.

79. See Banks's advertisement for carriage work in *Telegr.*, 15 Aug. 1865, and Macon *Daily Evening Mirror*, 11 Feb. 1866. The endorsement appeared in ibid., 17 Mar. 1866.

80. See *Proceedings of the Freedmen's Convention.* Universal male suffrage implied the unqualified right to vote of all men over a certain age, usually twenty-one. Impartial suffrage sanctioned voter eligibility requirements, such as property ownership or ability to read and write, provided they were imposed impartially on all prospective voters, white and black alike. The best introduction to the land question is Oubre, *Forty Acres and a Mule.*

81. Thomas Beard, a black man from Augusta who with Maine carpetbagger John E. Bryant edited the *Loyal Georgian*, responded to such charges in *Loyal Georgian*, 17 Feb. 1866.

82. Letter from George Macon in ibid., 24 Feb. 1866.

83. *Telegr.*, 24 Mar. 1866; *Jnl. & Msgr.*, 28 Mar. 1866. If this tally is correct, assuming Macon's black population to number something between 4,000 and 5,000, it is likely that every black man in the city cast a vote. Banks appealed his defeat to the executive council of the GERA, but without success. See *Proceedings of the Council of the Georgia Equal Rights Association*, esp. 8.

84. For treatment of similar developments in Memphis, see Robinson, "Plans Dat Comed from God."

85. This account was pieced together from the following sources: Jones County Superior Court Minutes, April and October terms 1866, and April term 1867, GDAH; *Telegr.*, 18, 20, 21, 22 Apr. 1866; Capt. N. Sellers Hill to Capt. W. W. Deane, 21 Apr. 1866, 296:50, Letters Sent, Macon Subasst. Comr.; Hill to Deane, 25 Apr. 1866, Unregistered Letters Received, Ga. Asst. Comr.; Lewis Smith to Davis Tillson, 24 June 1866, #93 1866, Registered Letters Received, Macon Subasst. Comr., RG 105; M. A. Cochran to [?], 25 Apr. 1866, M-61 1866, Letters Received, Mil. Dist. of Ga., Records of the U.S. Army Continental Commands, RG 393, pt. 1.

86. Besides Smith, Lewis Sherman, a painter, and Moses Pollock, a watchmaker, took part. Both were leading spirits in a later African emigration movement in Macon, described below.

87. *Telegr.*, 5 May, 24 Sept. 1866.

88. On the tactical shift, see *Proceedings of the Convention of the Equal Rights and Educational Association of Georgia.* Because he served as a vice-president in the GERA, Smith may well have known of this tactical shift before the convention made its official stand.

89. ACS, ser. 1-A, 184:18–19, 43, 55, 87.

90. Ibid., pp. 87, 118, 129.

91. Ibid., p. 255; *Telegr.*, 28, 30 Oct., 2 Nov. 1866; *African Repository* 42 (Dec. 1866): 372–74; 43 (Jan. 1867): 11–14. Among the featured speakers at meetings of the emigration association were Henry M. Turner and Jefferson F. Long, both of whom later achieved national stature as political leaders among Georgia freedmen.

92. *African Repository* 43 (Jan. 1867): 11–14. Names appeared in family groups; occupations were given for 54 of the total of 194 migrants.

93. Compare ibid. 43 (Jan. 1867): 14–23; 45 (Dec. 1869): 366–69, 373–74; 46 (Dec. 1870): 353–54, 373–77; 47 (Dec. 1871): 353–60; 48 (Dec. 1872): 353–58.

94. ACS, ser. 1-B, 14:5/2. Even after the second departure, interest in African emigration lingered on, especially in rural areas. A third group of emigrants, based in Twiggs County, eventually departed for Africa.

95. Liberian emigrants both before and after the Civil War made standard reference to republican precepts. In virtually every surviving expression of their aspirations, they fault the United States for failing to extend the benefits of republican government to blacks and anticipate full realization of those rights in Liberia. See the *African Repository*, issues for the antebellum years, and Berlin, *Slaves without Masters*, 356, for typical expressions.

96. *Christian Recorder*, 2 Nov. 1867. Another person from Macon declared that without "rights before the law in every respect," freedpeople might as well migrate to Liberia. See ibid., 11 Jan. 1868.

97. ACS, ser. 1-B, 14:77; *Jnl. & Msgr.*, 8 Sept. 1868.

98. Bracey, Meier, and Rudwick, *Black Nationalism*, esp. xxxviii–xl, lvi–lix. Henry M. Turner's emergence as a proponent of African emigration during the late nineteenth century related directly to his experience in Georgia during Reconstruction.

99. Testimony of B. H. Hill, U.S. Congress, House, *Affairs in the Late Insurrectionary States*, 763. See also the testimony of Cabaniss in U.S. Congress, House, *Condition of Affairs in Georgia*, 162–63.

100. Henry M. Loyless to John Pope, 27 July 1867, A-1048, Letters Received, Bureau of Civil Affairs, 3d Mil. Dist., RG 393, pt. 1; *New York Times*, 2 Sept. 1867.

CHAPTER 8

1. Du Bois, *Black Reconstruction*, esp. chap. 9. See also E. Foner, *Nothing But Freedom*, chap. 2, and *Reconstruction*.

2. E. Foner, *Nothing But Freedom*, chap. 2; Woodward, "Emancipations and Reconstructions."

3. Holt, *Black over White*, chap. 5, esp. 95–98.

4. Bensel, *Yankee Leviathan*, chaps. 4–5.

5. Currie-McDaniel, *Carpetbagger of Conscience*; Nathans, *Losing the Peace*, 25–26, 36; Conway, *Reconstruction of Georgia*, 150; C. M. Thompson, *Reconstruction in Georgia*, 174–76.

6. Republican agents included Capt. N. Sellers Hill in Macon, Daniel Losey in Houston County, and Henry Loyless in Twiggs County.

7. The names of white Republicans appear in scattered contemporary newspaper reports of Republican meetings. On Griffin's background and experience, see esp. his printed "Personal and Political Defence" (21 Dec. 1869), filed with G-9 1870, Letters Received, Dept. of the South, RG 393, pt. 1. In the same file is one of the innumerable affidavits of a freedman (in this instance, John Royals) taken by Griffin in his capacity as justice of the peace and submitted to military authorities for action.

8. Stephens to J. Barrett Cohen, 25 May 1867, and Cobb to J. D. Hoover, 4 Jan. 1868, in Phillips, *Correspondence of Toombs, Stephens, and Cobb*, 686, 692.

9. Nathans, *Losing the Peace*, 45–48.

10. Ibid., 48–50; Conway, *Reconstruction of Georgia*, 141–42, 144; C. M. Thompson, *Reconstruction in Georgia*, 158–59.

11. Statement of E. G. Cabaniss in U.S. Congress, House, *Condition of Affairs in Georgia*, 162–63.

12. Nathans, *Losing the Peace*, 49.

13. *Telegr.*, 13 Sept. 1867.

14. For an excellent discussion of how the Confederate mobilization affected these groups, see DeCredico, *Patriotism for Profit*.

15. *Jnl. & Msgr.*, 3 Apr. 1867.

16. Cobb to Gen. John Pope, [Apr. 1867], A-48, Letters Received, Bureau of Civil Affairs, 3d Mil. Dist., RG 393, pt. 1. Cobb appears to be the same person as the Samuel A. Cobb who later served as a delegate from Houston County to the constitutional convention and the state legislature. Cox had taken part in a meeting of "Constitutional Resistance Men" from Houston County in December 1860; these men were (at best) reluctant secessionists. Like other cooperationists, they grasped for straws, opposing the immediate secession of Georgia without similar action by other southern states. See *Jnl. & Msgr.*, 26 Dec. 1860. On Cox's antebellum holdings, see ms. federal census returns, free and slave schedules, Houston Co., 1860, RG 29.

17. *Loyal Georgian*, 9 May 1867.

18. See, for example, Peter Lamar to N. Sellers Hill, 22 Aug. 1867, L-21 1867, Letters Received, Macon Subasst. Comr., RG 105.

19. A shady character at best, Brock had been embroiled in a bitter controversy over his treatment of a black employee during the spring of 1867. Brock chained the man by the neck to the axle of his buggy and trotted him eight miles for allegedly refusing to follow directions. See George L. Eberhart to N. Sellers Hill, 28 May 1867, E-55 1867, Letters Received, Ga. Asst. Comr., RG 105; Lt. Jas. M. Ingalls to Lt. A. McIntyre, 28 Mar. 1868, enclosing Moses Hughs to Maj. Gen. George Mead, 25 Jan. 1868, filed with T-19 1868, Letters Received, 3d Mil. Dist., RG 393, pt. 1. Military authorities eventually removed Brock from office.

20. Daniel Losey to Col. J. R. Lewis, 3 Nov. 1867, 322:40–42, Letters Sent, Perry, Ga., Agent, RG 105. Losey's later reports painted a similarly dim picture of the administration of justice in Houston County: Losey to Lewis, 5 Nov. 1867, and Losey to Col. C. C. Sibley, 25 Nov. 1867 and 17 Feb. 1868, 322:43, 47–48, 69–70, Letters Sent, Perry, Ga., Agent, RG 105.

21. *Telegr.*, 30 Aug. 1867.

22. Ibid. For the report of a speech wherein John T. Costin accused the "hereditary

lords of Georgia" of desiring to restrict the ballot from the freedman and "the honest white man," see *Telegr.*, 27 Mar. 1868.

23. Ibid., 13 Sept. 1867.

24. Ibid., 20 Sept. 1867.

25. Ibid.

26. Ibid.

27. Drago, *Black Politicians*, 36, app.; Hume, "Negro Delegates," 133; Nathans, *Losing the Peace*, 56–57; Currie-McDaniel, *Carpetbagger of Conscience*, 82; C. M. Thompson, *Reconstruction in Georgia*, 173; E. Foner, *Reconstruction*, 318, all report slightly different figures.

28. Hume, "Negro Delegates," 133; E. Foner, *Reconstruction*, 318.

29. On Bradley's career, see my "Aaron A. Bradley," which counters the interpretive biases of Coulter, *Negro Legislators*, chap. 2.

30. In an August 1867 speech, for instance, Turner advocated interracial cooperation to steady the "ship of State" tossing "amid the mad billows." Insisting that "all we want is our rights—without them freedom amounts to nothing," Turner discouraged the freed-people's hope for land, saying he did not want to see whites lose their property. See *Telegr.*, 30 Aug. 1867. Reports of similar meetings appeared routinely in the press during the summer of 1867. On the practice of "deference" among Georgia black leaders, see Drago, *Black Politicians*, 44–46. Regarding his performance at the constitutional convention, an analysis of eleven key votes reveals that Turner voted "conservatively" more often than all but three of the thirty-three blacks in attendance. See Hume, "Black and Tan Constitutional Conventions," 236–49.

31. Nine other black delegates shared Turner's opposition to the homestead exemption, a mistaken stand that Turner later attributed to his political "inexperience." Quoted in Drago, *Black Politicians*, 45.

32. Every account of Georgia Reconstruction addresses the convention and the document it produced: C. M. Thompson, *Reconstruction in Georgia*, chap. 7; Conway, *Reconstruction of Georgia*, chap. 6; and esp. Nathans, *Losing the Peace*, chap. 3.

33. See C. M. Thompson, *Reconstruction in Georgia*, 175–81; Conway, *Reconstruction of Georgia*, 154–55; Nathans, *Losing the Peace*, 66–68; Drago, *Black Politicians*, 44–45.

34. *Jnl. & Msgr.*, 25 Mar. 1868; *Telegr.*, 27 Mar. 1868.

35. Chas. R. Holcombe to C. C. Sibley, 25 Mar. 1868, #98 1868, Letters Received, Ga. Asst. Comr., RG 105; U.S. Congress, House, *Affairs in the Late Insurrectionary States*, 272; *New York Times*, 6 Jan. 1868. Tunis G. Campbell, a black leader in McIntosh County along the coast, expressed the sentiment succinctly: "[T]he great cry of our people is for land. . . . They want to be free-holders, land-holders, and to hold office like white men." See U.S. Congress, House, *Affairs in the Late Insurrectionary States*, 861. More generally, see Oubre, *Forty Acres and a Mule*; Magdol, *A Right to the Land*.

36. *Telegr.*, 4 Oct. 1867. For other similar statements from black Conservatives, see ibid., 30 Aug., 18 Oct. 1867.

37. Ibid., 23 Oct. 1868.

38. Ibid., 24 July 1868.

39. Ibid., 2 Oct. 1868.

40. For Dupree's activities, see ibid., 24 July, 7 Aug. 1868.

41. Ibid., 23 Oct. 1868.

42. Regarding the threat upon Long, see *Jnl. & Msgr.*, 15 Sept. 1868. For Smith's appeal, see Smith to Pope, 12 June 1867, A-618, Letters Received, Bureau of Civil Affairs, 3d Mil. Dist., RG 393, pt. 1.

43. Cupid to Pope, 12 June 1867, A-651, Letters Received, Bureau of Civil Affairs, 3d Mil. Dist., RG 393, pt. 1. Cupid's letter appears to be in the handwriting of Joel R. Griffin, the Houston County planter and lawyer who identified with the Republican party.

44. *Telegr.*, 3 Apr. 1868.

45. See Nathans, *Losing the Peace*, 79–88, esp. 86; also C. M. Thompson, *Reconstruction in Georgia*, chap. 8, where the quotes appear on 183 and 186. More generally on the planters' opposition to Radical Reconstruction, see Roark, *Masters without Slaves*, pt. 3.

46. *Jnl. & Msgr.*, 1 Apr. 1868; *Telegr.*, 3 Apr. 1868.

47. *Jnl. & Msgr.*, 1 Apr. 1868; *Telegr.*, 3 Apr. 1868.

48. *Jnl. & Msgr.*, 7 Apr. 1868; *Telegr.*, 10 Apr. 1868. Persons in attendance included the mayor in the chair, such business leaders as J. W. Burke, and such planters as T. G. Holt and even the old firebrand E. A. Nisbet.

49. Turner's testimony in U.S. Congress, House, *Condition of Affairs in Georgia*, 11. Turner expressed substantially the same views two years later; see U.S. Congress, House, *Affairs in the Late Insurrectionary States*, 1036.

50. "Houston" to the Editors, *Telegr.*, 8 May 1868. For a list of the Houston County Democrats' candidates for office, see *Telegr.*, 10 Apr. 1868. Swift won election, though Jackson did not.

51. "Houston" to the Editors, *Telegr.*, 8 May 1868.

52. By his characteristically convoluted logic, Joseph Brown also endorsed this view. "It is precisely for the reason that they [the freedmen] can be so easily coaxed into voting for us [the Republicans] that I opposed negro suffrage," he testified before Congress. "Men so easily influenced ought not to have any political power." See U.S. Congress, House, *Affairs in the Late Insurrectionary States*, 818.

53. *Telegr.*, 21 Aug. 1868.

54. Edwin Belcher, who had earlier served as a Freedmen's Bureau agent in Monroe County, was elected state representative from Wilkes County in middle Georgia.

55. Nathans, *Losing the Peace*, 93–96; Hahn, *Roots of Southern Populism*, 211–12, 214–15. Nathans, *Losing the Peace*, 66–69, and C. M. Thompson, *Reconstruction in Georgia*, 180, describe Joseph Brown's role in setting up the inevitable controversy over the freedmen's right to hold elected office.

56. Nathans, *Losing the Peace*, 121–25; Conway, *Reconstruction of Georgia*, 165–68; C. M. Thompson, *Reconstruction in Georgia*, 193–98; Drago, *Black Politicians*, chaps. 3–4 passim. Shortly after the vote, state representative John A. Cobb explained to his father the legislators' continuing effort to expel three men whose complexions were indistinguishable from white: "We have not been able as yet to get the testimony to prove that they have more than one eighth negro blood, and until we do prove it we will not turn them out, although we are satisfied that they are negroes." John A. Cobb to Howell Cobb, 26 Sept. 1868, Cobb-Erwin-Lamar Family Papers, UGa. Eventually, four men were allowed to retain their seats, among them Edwin Belcher, the former Freedmen's Bureau

agent in Monroe County, and F. H. Fyall, representative from Macon County, lying just west of Houston County.

57. *Congressional Globe*, 7 Dec. 1868, prints the address. For accounts of the convention, see *Telegr.*, 18, 25 Sept., 9 Oct. 1868; *Appleton's Annual Cyclopedia* 8 (1868): 318; *Christian Recorder*, 26 Sept. 1868; Avery, *History of Georgia*, 405–6.

58. Redkey, *Black Exodus* and *Respect Black!*

59. Powell, "Politics of Livelihood," esp. 316–18.

60. *Telegr.*, 18 Sept. 1868; *Jnl. & Msgr.*, 15 Sept. 1868.

61. *Telegr.*, 18 Sept. 1868.

62. For representative accounts of such intimidation, see Henry Keating et al. to John Pope, 3 Nov. 1867, A-2023, and Joel Johnson to E. Hulbert, 5 Nov. 1867, A-2061, Letters Received, Bureau of Civil Affairs, 3d Mil. Dist., RG 393, pt. 1; Bill Jackson to [?], 7 July 1868, J-137 1868, Letters Received, 3d Mil. Dist., RG 393, pt. 1; John H. Sullivan to H. Catley, 10 Sept. 1868, enclosed in Catley to M. Frank Gallagher, 26 Sept. 1868, #101 1868; and H. deF. Young to Gallagher, 16 Oct. 1868, #127 1868, Registered Letters Received, Ga. Asst. Comr., RG 105.

63. General remarks, reports of contracts filed for March, May, and July 1868, Contracts, Perry Agent, RG 105; *Telegr.*, 14 Aug. 1868; H. deF. Young to N. Sellers Hill, 11 Nov. 1868, enclosed in Hill to J. R. Lewis, 18 Nov. 1868, #296 1868, Registered Letters Received, Ga. Asst. Comr., RG 105.

64. Turner to the Editors, *Christian Recorder*, 17 Aug. 1867.

65. The pattern of Klan violence against black political leaders has been known to historians from early in this century, but for the most comprehensive treatment of the subject, see Trelease, *White Terror*, esp. chaps. 4 and 14, which treat developments in Georgia.

66. For a pioneering statement of the striking degree of political activity among black artisans and the resulting oppression they suffered, see Magdol, "Local Black Leaders."

67. C. M. Thompson, *Reconstruction in Georgia*, 363; Cason, "Loyal League," 140.

68. T. W. M. Cox to [Gen. John Pope?], 1 July 1868, entry C-308 1868, Register of Letters Received, 3d Mil. Dist., RG 393, pt. 1. In one instance authorities responded by invoking General Pope's orders requiring prior notification of planned mass meetings and forbidding attendance with arms.

69. Ormond and Primus to Capt. Hill, 21 July 1868, Correspondence of Governor Rufus B. Bullock, GDAH. For a different perspective, see "Houston" to Editor, *Telegr.*, 21 Aug. 1868. "Houston" noted that "prudent counsels of the calmest men of both races happily prevailed," but in the aftermath of the incident freedmen paraded in triumph, some bragging "they had backed out the whites."

70. Daniel Losey to N. Sellers Hill, 28 July 1868, L-56 1868, Letters Received, and Hill to Col. Caleb Sibley, 22 July 1868, vol. 127, #297, Letters Sent, Macon Subasst. Comr., RG 105.

71. See, for instance, Hutchings's affidavit, 28 Nov. 1868, in U.S. Congress, House, *Condition of Affairs in Georgia*, 83–84.

72. In this context it is relevant to recall the movement of skilled slaves to Macon during the Civil War. No doubt many stayed in the city after the war, bolstering the artisan community there but at the same time weakening it in their hometowns.

73. The names of four such captains of Twiggs County clubs survive: Charles Bell, Alfred Flemming, Berry Hill (mentioned above), and Captain Jones.

74. The account is summarized from evidence in Henry M. Loyless to N. S. Hill, 13 Apr. 1868, and Lt. Wm. Conway to Lt. J. Ulie, 10 May 1868, L-53 1868, Letters Received, 3d Mil. Dist., RG 393, pt. 1.

75. The affair described in this and the following two paragraphs has been reconstructed from the following: file #2092 1868, Letters Received, Ga. Asst. Comr., RG 105; *Telegr.*, 28 Aug., 4 Sept. 1868; and *Jnl. & Msgr.*, 1 Sept., 6 Oct. 1868.

76. N. Sellers Hill to Bvt. Col. J. R. Lewis, 18 Nov. 1868, #206 1868, Letters Received, Georgia Asst. Comr., RG 105.

77. See Nathans, *Losing the Peace*, 141–42.

78. Daniel Losey to N. Sellers Hill, 22 Nov. 1868, L-182 1868, Letters Received, Macon Subasst. Comr., RG 105; Walker Ellison to [Gen. John Pope?], 5 May 1868, entry E-43 1868, Register of Letters Received, 3d Mil. Dist., RG 393, pt. 1.

79. Affidavit of A. A. Gaulding, 26 Nov. 1868, in U.S. Congress, House, *Condition of Affairs in Georgia*, 62–63.

80. See Hutchings's affidavit, 28 Nov. 1868, in ibid., 83–84; N. Sellers Hill to Col. J. R. Lewis, 30 Nov. 1868, 297:181–82, Letters Sent, Macon Subasst. Comr., RG 105; *Telegr.*, 13 Nov. 1868.

81. C. M. Thompson, *Reconstruction in Georgia*, map on 188. Republicans had carried Monroe in the April election.

82. See, for example, Belcher to Charles Sumner, 5 Apr. 1869, Sumner Papers, Harvard University; Reidy, "Aaron A. Bradley," 298–99. More generally, see Powell, "Politics of Livelihood."

83. Matthews, "Jefferson Franklin Long," 146–47, views Long's involvement in the labor convention as indicative of his growing disenchantment with Republican party politics, a tendency that became more pronounced during the 1870s.

84. Both the *Telegraph* and the *Journal & Messenger* reported extensively on the convention. These and other reports have been republished in P. Foner and Lewis, *Black Worker*, 2:4–18.

85. *Acts*, 1869, 178; ibid., 1870, 458.

86. Georgia General Assembly, *House Journal, 1870*, 1:184, 239, 247, 306–7.

87. Turner's testimony appears in U.S. Congress, House, *Affairs in the Late Insurrectionary States*, 1040. Republican state treasurer Needom L. Angier corroborated Turner's impressions with statistics in ibid., 153, 156. See also the book of Executive Pardons Granted and Refused, 1868–82, GDAH.

88. See, for example, *Telegr.*, 21 May 1869.

89. *Telegr. & Msgr.*, 20 Sept. 1870.

90. The question of black candidates produced tension in Republican ranks throughout the South. See, for instance, the revealing exchange between Albion W. Tourgée and James E. O'Hara reported in E. Anderson, *Race and Politics in North Carolina*, 51–52.

91. *Telegr. & Msgr.*, 11, 18 Oct. 1870. Similar comments are quoted in Matthews, "Jefferson Franklin Long," 147. The newspaper also noted that mulatto barber Aleck H. Gaston planned to oppose Long, but nothing appears to have come of the challenge.

92. Testimony of Turner in U.S. Congress, House, *Affairs in the Late Insurrectionary*

States, 1037–38. White Democrats applied a similar line of reasoning to differentiate between black men who served in the state legislature in Atlanta and those who occupied local offices. See the remarks of Howell Cobb, Jr., quoted in Drago, *Black Politicians*, 78–79.

93. Testimony of Judge C. B. Cole in U.S. Congress, House, *Affairs in the Late Insurrectionary States*, 1183–84.

94. Testimony of Henry M. Turner in ibid., 1037–39.

95. *Telegr. & Msgr.*, 4 Oct., 15 Nov., 20 Dec. 1870. Following the end of Reconstruction in Georgia a year later, Clower reportedly moved west.

96. Ibid., 24 Jan. 1871.

97. *Telegr. & Msgr.*, 3 Jan. 1871.

98. See, for instance, William J. White to G. L. Eberhart, 4 June 1867, #385 1867, Letters Received, Ga. Supt. of Educ., RG 105.

99. Ibid., 12 Sept. 1871. See also ibid., 14 May 1872.

100. Du Bois, *Black Reconstruction*, esp. chap. 12; Conway, *Reconstruction of Georgia*; Nathans, *Losing the Peace*.

101. Olsen, "Introduction," in *Reconstruction and Redemption*.

CHAPTER 9

1. Bensel, *Yankee Leviathan*, chaps. 4–5; Sharkey, *Money, Class, and Party*, esp. chaps. 4, 6.

2. U.S. Census Bureau, *Manufactures in 1860*, 61, and *Statistics of Wealth and Industry*, 646.

3. U.S. Census Bureau, *Report on the Manufactures*.

4. This description is based upon an analysis of the occupation of every household head listed in the ms. federal census returns for the city of Macon (Bibb County), 1870 and 1880, RG 29.

5. The most important studies of mill towns are Carlton, *Mill and Town*, and Billings, *Making of a "New South."*

6. See Wynne, *Continuity of Cotton*, 94–95; Russell, *Atlanta*, 128.

7. *Telegr. & Msgr.*, 24 Dec. 1872.

8. N. D. Sneed, Frank Disroon, Tilmon Lowe, and George Fraction to Gov. James M. Smith, 18 Apr. 1872, Correspondence of Governor James M. Smith, GDAH.

9. Sneed to Smith, 5, 9, 17, 19 Sept. 1873 (quote from 19 Sept., original emphasis), and Disroon to Smith, 3 Oct. 1873, in ibid.

10. A. O. Bacon et al. to Smith, 9 June 1874, in ibid.

11. Scarborough, "Echoes from the South," dated 12 June 1876, *Christian Recorder*, 29 June 1876.

12. *Telegr. & Msgr.*, 24 Sept. 1872.

13. Ibid., 8 Oct., 22 Nov. and 17 Dec. 1872; Young, Gholson, and Hargrove, *History of Macon*, 314, 317. In central Georgia, Isaac H. Anderson of Houston County and James B. Deveaux of Jones County won seats in the state senate. No black men entered the state house of representatives from the Macon area, and only six throughout the rest of the

state did: two each from Greene County in the old black belt and Thomas County in the
southwest, and one each from Glynn and McIntosh counties along the coast. In the
municipal elections in Macon, barber Edward Woodliff ran for reelection as alderman but
lost miserably.

14. *Telegr. & Msgr.*, 12 Nov. 1872.

15. *Savannah Republican*, 24 Apr. 1873; *New York Times*, 12 May 1873.

16. *Telegr. & Msgr.*, 25 Aug., 22 and 29 Sept., 6 and 12 Oct., 10 Nov. 1874; Mary E.
Sands to E. A. Cravath, 7 Oct. 1874, AMA; Young, Gholson, and Hargrove, *History of
Macon*, 319. Symptomatic of the Republican drubbing, white congressman Samuel F.
Gove, who had won the Fourth Congressional District nomination in 1872, lost to a
Democrat in 1874. The quote from the *Telegraph & Messenger* comes from the issue of 10
October 1874.

17. *Telegr. & Msgr.*, 22 Aug. 1876; Currie-McDaniel, *Carpetbagger of Conscience*, 135–
36; Shadgett, *Republican Party in Georgia*, chaps. 5 and 6. As a young house servant during
the Civil War, Harrison was implicated in a slave conspiracy but was acquitted of the
charge.

18. *Savannah Tribune*, 12 Aug. 1876. The *Tribune*, soon to be one of the leading black
newspapers in the South, was edited by Deveaux's brother, John H. Deveaux.

19. *New York Times*, 11 Oct. 1876.

20. *Telegr. & Msgr.*, 7 Nov. 1876.

21. Ibid., 14 Nov. 1876.

22. Ibid., 7 Mar. 1876.

23. *Southern Cultivator* 33 (Nov. 1875): 423–24.

24. *Telegr. & Msgr.*, 25 Apr., 30 May 1871.

25. *Acts*, 1872, 34–36.

26. Ibid., 1865–66, 52–53. Similar controversies over fences had erupted in the
Midwest before the Civil War and in the Trans-Mississippi West after it. In those areas,
the struggle for the most part pitted cattle raisers favoring open ranging and droving rights
against sedentary farmers favoring protection of private holdings of range and water. The
southern agitation contained similar shades, with sheep raisers favoring the open range.
See King, "Closing of the Southern Range."

27. Houston Co. Court of Ordinary, Minutes, 13 Feb. 1873, GDAH; ms. federal
census returns, free and slave schedules, 1860, population schedule, 1870, Houston Co.,
RG 29.

28. Houston Co. Court of Ordinary, Minutes, 28 Feb. 1873, GDAH; ms. federal
census returns, free and slave schedules, 1860, population schedule, 1870, Houston Co.,
RG 29.

29. See Flynn, *White Land, Black Labor*, 131–36, esp. 135–36.

30. Houston Co. Court of Ordinary, Minutes, 8 July 1873, GDAH. On the importance
of this struggle over fences, see Hahn, "Common Right and Commonwealth," "Hunting,
Fishing, and Foraging," and *Roots of Southern Populism*, esp. chap. 7.

31. *Acts*, 1870, 458; ibid., 1872, 484–85; ibid., 1880–81, 653–54. For objections of
various legislators to these bills, see Georgia General Assembly, *House Journal, 1871*, 20,
61, 338. As late as the summer of 1879, the Twiggs County Agricultural Society was

equally divided on the fence question. See *Telegr. & Msgr.*, 15 July 1879. More generally, see Woodman, "Post–Civil War Southern Agriculture"; E. Foner, *Reconstruction*, 593.

32. Flynn, *White Land, Black Labor*, 87–92; Conway, *Reconstruction of Georgia*, 124–25; Brooks, *Agrarian Revolution*, 32–34; Banks, *Economics of Land Tenure*, 46–50.

33. See Houston Co. Superior Court grand jury presentments, May 1878, Houston Co. Superior Court Minutes, GDAH. For a map of the counties affected by such legislation, see *Atlanta Constitution*, 11 Nov. 1883.

34. The 1866 laws on vagrancy, enticement, Sunday hunting, and insurrection appear in *Acts*, 1866, 153–55, 234–35. The 1871 amendment to the insurrection law and the new definition of arson appear in ibid., 1871–72, 19–20, 72–73. The "holocaust" characterization comes from the *Telegr. & Msgr.*, 3 Nov. 1873; other notices of gin-house arson appear in the issues of 4 Oct. 1870, 10, 17, and 24 Dec. 1872, 25 Jan. 1876, and 8 Oct. 1878.

35. *Acts*, 1875, 26. The 1868 Republican legislature fixed the punishment for stealing a horse or a mule at two to four years as a substitute for the 1866 law that had made it a capital crime. Ibid., 1868, 16–17; ibid., 1865–66, 235.

36. Ibid., 1876, 112; ibid., 1878–79, 183–84; ibid., 1880–81, 247, 318.

37. Ibid., 1880–81, 167.

38. Jones Co. Superior Court grand jury presentments, Apr. 1877 and Apr. 1878, Jones Co. Superior Court Minutes, GDAH.

39. See esp. Ayers, *Vengeance and Justice*, pt. 2.

40. Appling v. Odum and Mercier, 46 Ga. 583 (1872); Brooks, *Agrarian Revolution*, 67–68; Banks, *Economics of Land Tenure*, 80–82; E. Foner, *Reconstruction*, 594–95.

41. See esp. Woodman, "Post–Civil War Southern Agriculture."

42. During the December 1871 election wherein Democrats regained the governorship, black schoolteacher and political leader George Ormond in Houston County correctly predicted that legislation to restrict fishing rights would follow shortly. *Telegr. & Msgr.*, 2 Jan. 1872. The definitive treatment of this legal transformation as it applies to postbellum Georgia is Hahn, "Hunting, Fishing, and Foraging," "Common Right and Commonwealth," and *Roots of Southern Populism*. For related discussions, see Kulik, "Dams, Fish, and Farmers," and more broadly, Horwitz, *Transformation of American Law*.

43. *Acts*, 1865–66, 237–38.

44. See, for example, ibid., 1873, 21–22, 400; ibid., 1875, 295; Jones Co. Superior Court grand jury presentments, Apr. 1879, Jones Co. Superior Court Minutes, GDAH. By the end of the century, this prohibition extended to unenclosed as well as enclosed land; see *Acts*, 1897, 36.

45. *Acts*, 1875, 302–3. See also Hahn, "Hunting, Fishing, and Foraging"; Flynn, *White Land, Black Labor*, 124–25.

46. *Acts*, 1890–91, 218–19. As of 1881, game legislation appeared in a separate section of the annual session laws. Ibid., 1881, Title V.

47. See J. Anderson, *Education of Blacks*, intro. and chap. 1, for a cogent exposition of the stakes involved in freedpeople's education. See also Rabinowitz, *Race Relations*, chap. 7.

48. *Acts*, 1871–72, 279–83; ibid., 1872, 64–75; *Telegr. & Msgr.*, 2 Jan. 1872.

49. *Telegr.*, 3 Apr. 1868.

50. Williams to E. A. Cravath, 10 May 1871; M. E. Sands to Cravath, 3 Nov. 1871, AMA; *Telegr. & Msgr.*, 9 May 1871.

51. *Haddock's Macon, Ga., Directory and General Advertiser*, 15.

52. M. E. Sands to E. A. Cravath, 24 May 1873; Williams to Cravath, 4 June 1873, AMA.

53. *Telegr. & Msgr.*, 22 July 1873, 3 July 1874. In 1867, approximately 1,200 black students attended classes.

54. Petition dated 31 July 1874; Haley to Cravath, 31 July, 9 Sept. 1874, AMA.

55. *Telegr. & Msgr.*, 30 Mar. 1875.

56. Ibid., 13 and 20 July 1875; W. A. L. Campbell to Strieby, 30 June, 1, 2, 12, 15, 21, and 28 July, 3 and 20 Sept. 1875; C. W. Francis to Wm. Whipple, 14 July 1875; Willis Epps to Francis, 16 July 1875; Zettler to the AMA, 24 Sept. 1875, AMA.

57. M. B. Pollock, G. Smith, and W. S. Scarborough to Strieby, 10 Dec. 1875; T. N. M. Sellers to Strieby, 22 Dec. 1875; Ashley to Strieby, 4 Jan. 1876, AMA. Although AMA officials refused to cede control over the school to the former slaves, they did at times agree to appoint black teachers recommended by the black school boards. William S. Scarborough met the association's test of acceptability. See Annetta Lynch to [M. E.] Emerson, 15 Oct. 1875; Lynch to Strieby, 25 and 26 Oct. 1875, AMA. For a brief biography of Scarborough's later distinguished career, see Simmons, *Men of Mark*, 410–18.

58. Scarborough, "Echoes from the South," *Christian Recorder*, 29 June 1876; *Telegr. & Msgr.*, 15 Aug. 1876.

59. S. C. Bierce to Strieby, 15 Sept. 1876, AMA. Shortly after the board took control of Lewis High School it burnt to the ground, touching off a storm of controversy. Black residents of the city accused the fire companies of exerting insufficient effort, and in turn a black man was accused of arson and committed to the insane asylum. By the end of the decade, the building had been reconstructed. See G. J. Webster to Strieby, 19 Oct. 1876; Webster to D. E. Emerson, 18 Dec. 1876, AMA. See also *Telegr. & Msgr.*, 27 Mar. 1877, 3 June 1879; P. M. Webster to Emerson, 1 Jan. 1877; Thos. N. Chase to Strieby, 16 Oct. 1877, AMA.

60. Jefferson F. Long provided half-hearted direction to the group in Macon, whose interest never reached the point of emigrating. Northeast of Macon in Clarke County, however, William Pledger, a promising young black newspaperman and Republican party organizer, arranged a successful migration to Jefferson County, Mississippi, through the assistance of Merryman Howard, a black man who held the post of sheriff in Jefferson County. See the correspondence in Pledger's letterbook, John E. Bryant Papers, DU. On the general contours of such migration, see Cohen, *At Freedom's Edge*, esp. pt. 1.

61. P. Foner and Lewis, *Black Worker*, 2:4–18, esp. 14; *Proceedings of the Southern States Convention of Colored Men*, 65–66. Turner's emigrationism emerged from the crucible of Georgia politics. During the African emigration movement of 1866–67, he stood on the sidelines, and from then through the mid-1870s, he became increasingly convinced of the viability of migration—both to the western United States and to Africa—as a strategy for southern plantation laborers. At a state convention of Georgia freedmen in 1874, for instance, he urged the federal government to provide transportation and six months' rations so that freedpeople could settle in New Mexico territory. Thereafter, his attention turned increasingly to Africa. See *Atlanta Constitution*, 1–3 Dec. 1874; Redkey, *Respect Black!*

62. *Atlanta Constitution*, 1–3 Dec. 1874.

63. Ibid. In their speeches before the convention, delegates cited case after case of fraud, violence, and official intransigence. They memorialized Congress for redress, laying special emphasis on the importance of the pending civil rights bill sponsored by Senator Charles Sumner. The memorial is printed in Aptheker, *Documentary History*, 1:604–6. For more on Governor Smith's exchange with the delegates, see the *Atlanta Herald*, 4 Dec. 1874.

64. The account of the 1875 unrest was pieced together from the following: Herschel V. Johnson to James M. Smith, 19 Aug. 1875; M. I. Mason to Smith, 5 Aug. 1875; John W. Robison to Smith, 23 Aug. 1875; Samuel D. Killen to Smith, 1 and 4 Sept. 1875; and S. C. Williams to Smith, 6 Sept. 1875; all in Correspondence of Governor James M. Smith, GDAH; *Telegr. & Msgr.*, 27 July and 3, 24, and 31 Aug. 1875; *New York Times*, 19, 20, 21, 24, 26, 30, 31 Aug. and 10 and 21 Sept. 1875.

65. Johnson to Turner, 1 Feb. 1876, Herschel V. Johnson Papers, DU.

66. The *Augusta Chronicle & Sentinel*, 8–9 Oct. 1875, published the proceedings of the convention. For more on Turner's views of Africa, see Redkey, *Respect Black!*

67. *Augusta Chronicle & Sentinel*, 8–9 Oct. 1875.

68. Wright, *Old South, New South*, esp. 7–10, 64–70; Cohen, *At Freedom's Edge*, 109–97.

69. Much of the discussion of development of labor markets in the postbellum South seems to rest upon an erroneous assumption that free labor systems employ atomized labor power as opposed to commodified labor power. As the recent experience of industrial communities makes clear, even though workers are legally entitled to dispose of their labor power at their discretion, they rarely do so as individual atoms devoid of ties to family and community. Even in urban, industrial settings, where market relations embrace every facet of the workers' lives, it is erroneous to presume that their refusal to follow the dictates of labor markets indicates the absence of capitalist relations of production. Hence the need for caution in viewing the freedpeople's behavior as evidence against the presence of capitalist relations of production. For the latter-day comparison, see Lynd, "Genesis of the Idea."

70. Wynne, *Continuity of Cotton*, 101–17, esp. 114. Wiener, *Social Origins of the New South*, 3–4 and 71–73, popularized the term "Prussian Road," which he derived from B. Moore, *Social Origins of Dictatorship and Democracy*.

71. For stunning criticisms of the "Prussian Road" depiction of the postbellum South, see esp. Powell, "The Prussians Are Coming," and Hahn, "Class and State."

72. Robert Toombs to L. N. Trammell, 26 Apr. 1877, in Phillips, *Correspondence of Toombs, Stephens, and Cobb*, 730–31. See also Shaw, *Wool Hat Boys*, 17–19.

73. Ibid., 728–29.

74. Ibid., 728.

75. *Telegr. & Msgr.*, 22 Aug. 1876.

76. Georgia Constitutional Convention, 1877, *Journal of the Constitutional Convention* and *Stenographic Report of the Proceedings of the Constitutional Convention*. See also *Acts*, 1878–79, 99–102, for supplemental homestead legislation. Kousser, *Shaping of Southern Politics*, 65–68, describes the drastic effect of the cumulative poll tax upon freedmen's voting in Georgia.

77. *Telegr. & Msgr.*, 1 Jan. 1878. The new poll tax requirement effectively disfranchised

many poor whites too, but election managers did not have the same incentive for applying
it against political insurgency as they would later in the century. In the meantime, poor
blacks suffered most. Kousser, *Shaping of Southern Politics*, 67–68, 71–72, and esp. 211–
13, discusses the effect of the cumulative poll tax on black voting. The graph on 212
makes the point vividly.

78. See Houston Co. Superior Court, Deed Books, GDAH.

79. For one of the more vivid descriptions of how this system functioned, see Rosengarten, *All God's Dangers*. Surviving mortgage books from the counties of central Georgia
document the changes wrought by the new constitution. After it was approved, all but a
handful of borrowers waived their homestead exemptions as a precondition to their
getting advances from merchants. See, for instance, Houston Co. Mortgages, GDAH.

80. *Telegr. & Msgr.*, 5 Nov. 1880. See also Kousser, *Shaping of Southern Politics*, 63–72.

81. Rosengarten, *All God's Dangers*, 21–22, 83–91, 113, 173–77, 193–97.

82. These figures derive from a stratified random sample of approximately 400 household heads drawn from the ms. federal census returns, population, Bibb, Crawford,
Houston, Jones, Monroe, and Twiggs counties, 1870 and 1880, RG 29. For each
individual selected, information from the ms. federal census returns, agriculture, SHC,
was matched with that from the population returns. The names were selected by means of
a table of random numbers to obtain a confidence level of 95 percent and a confidence
interval of plus or minus 5 percent; the data were processed by means of the Statistical
Package for the Social Sciences computer program. In the following discussion, figures
derived from these data will be cited to the appropriate census sample: 1870 or 1880.

83. Du Bois, "Negro Landholder." The experience of Ned Cobb and his literate wife is
also instructive in this regard. See Rosengarten, *All God's Dangers*, 266–68, for the
account of an incident in which she advised him not to sign a contract that would have
jeopardized all their property in exchange for a loan on a piece of land.

84. This portrait derives from information on the ms. federal census returns of
population, RG 29, and of agriculture, SHC.

85. For discussions of patterns of tenure, see esp. Banks, *Economics of Land Tenure*,
chap. 5; Brooks, *Agrarian Revolution*, chaps 3–4; Higgs, "Patterns of Farm Rental";
Woodman, "Post–Civil War Southern Agriculture"; and Edwards, "Tenant System and
Some Changes."

86. Ms. federal census returns, population, 1870, and population and agriculture,
1880, for Bibb, Crawford, Houston, Jones, Monroe, and Twiggs counties, RG 29 and
SHC.

87. This pattern contradicts the picture that some recent analyses have painted for the
entire cotton South. Ransom and Sutch, *One Kind of Freedom*, 99–103, for instance,
suggest that planters located share tenants on the best tracts and cash renters on inferior
ones.

88. The baldest expression of this view is Stone, "A Plantation Experiment," in his
Studies in the American Race Problem, 125–47. See also Brooks, *Agrarian Revolution*, 60–
61.

89. See Fields, "Ideology and Race."

90. Ms. federal census returns, population, RG 29, and agriculture, SHC, for Houston
Co., 1880.

91. Census sample, 1880.

92. Ms. federal census returns, population, RG 29, and agriculture, SHC, for Houston Co., 1880.

93. Brooks, *Agrarian Revolution*, 96–98.

94. Georgia Department of Agriculture, "Statistical Farm Reports," 15.

95. See *Telegr. & Msgr.*, 2 Apr. 1872; ms. federal census returns, population, 1880, for Macon and Perry, RG 29. Powdermaker, *After Freedom*, 83, 92–94.

96. Superior court grand juries repeatedly exhorted legislators to require penning of stock "to meet the emergency of the Country," as Monroe County jurors described the situation. See grand jury presentments, Aug. 1878, Monroe Co. Superior Court Minutes, GDAH.

97. *Atlanta Constitution*, 11 Nov. 1883.

98. See in particular the work of Hahn, "Hunting, Fishing, and Foraging," "Common Right and Commonwealth," and esp. *Roots of Southern Populism*, chap. 7.

99. For a brilliant fictional account of what followed from these changes, see William Faulkner's tale of Mink Snopes in *The Mansion*, pt. 1.

CONCLUSION

1. Eugene D. Genovese and Elizabeth Fox-Genovese have examined this theme in great detail. See esp. Genovese, *Political Economy of Slavery*; Fox-Genovese and Genovese, *Fruits of Merchant Capital*; and Fox-Genovese, *Within the Plantation Household*.

2. See Gallay, *Formation of a Planter Elite*; Klein, *Unification of a Slave State*; Gross, *Minutemen and Their World*; C. Clark, *Roots of Rural Capitalism*; Slaughter, *Whiskey Rebellion*; Faragher, *Sugar Creek*.

3. See E. Foner, *Tom Paine*; Dawley, *Class and Community*; Prude, *Coming of Industrial Order*; Dublin, *Women at Work*; Hahn and Prude, *Countryside*; Wilentz, *Chants Democratic*; Stansell, *City of Women*.

4. C. Clark, *Roots of Rural Capitalism*; Prude, *Coming of Industrial Order*; Hahn and Prude, *Countryside*; Kulikoff, "Transition to Capitalism."

5. For assorted dimensions of this process, see P. Johnson, *Shopkeeper's Millennium*; Ryan, *Cradle of the Middle Class*.

6. Genovese, *Political Economy of Slavery*; Fox-Genovese and Genovese, *Fruits of Merchant Capital*; Hahn, *Roots of Southern Populism*; Watson, "Conflict and Collaboration."

7. Fox-Genovese, *Within the Plantation Household*; Hahn, *Roots of Southern Populism*.

8. See esp. Cooper, *South and the Politics of Slavery* and *Liberty and Slavery*; Thornton, *Politics and Power*; Barney, *Secessionist Impulse*.

9. See esp. Fields, *Slavery and Freedom*.

10. For a good general overview, see Laurie, *Artisans into Workers*.

11. The literature on West Indian slavery is enormous. See esp. Craton, *Searching*; Higman, *Slave Population*; Mintz, *Caribbean Transformations*; Knight, *Slave Society in Cuba*; Tomich, *Slavery in the Circuit of Sugar*. On eastern European serfdom, see esp. Kolchin, *Unfree Labor*.

12. Toplin, *Abolition of Slavery in Brazil*; R. Scott, *Slave Emancipation in Cuba*; Moreno Fraginals, Moya Pons, and Engerman, *Between Slavery and Free Labor*; Green, *British Slave Emancipation*; Adamson, *Sugar without Slaves*; Rodney, *Guyanese Working People*; Holt, *Problem of Freedom*.

13. See Green, *British Slave Emancipation*; Rodney, *Guyanese Working People*; Holt, *Problem of Freedom*; Mintz, "Slavery and the Rise of Peasantries"; Engerman, "Economic Adjustments to Emancipation." The process of emancipation in the Spanish islands of the Caribbean and in Brazil has certain formal similarities but many historical differences too numerous to examine in detail here. Suffice it to say that the world of the late 1880s was a much different place from that of the mid-1860s. See esp. Toplin, *Abolition of Slavery in Brazil*; R. Scott, *Slave Emancipation in Cuba*; Moreno Fraginals, Moya Pons, and Engerman, *Between Slavery and Free Labor*.

14. See Kerridge, *Farmers of Old England*; Fields, "Nineteenth-Century American South" and "Advent of Capitalist Agriculture." For a different perspective on developments in the U.S. South, see Mandle, *Roots of Black Poverty*, and Wiener, "Class Structure and Economic Development."

15. See Berlin et al., *Wartime Genesis of Free Labor*, for extended treatment of this theme. Also helpful is Rose, *Rehearsal for Reconstruction*, and Powell, *New Masters*. These issues were far from resolved within the framework of northern politics during the Civil War and Reconstruction. See Montgomery, *Beyond Equality*.

16. See E. Foner, *Nothing But Freedom*, esp. chaps. 1 and 2.

17. Hahn, *Roots of Southern Populism*; Shaw, *Wool Hat Boys*.

18. Maddox, "Virginia," 149–50.

BIBLIOGRAPHY

. . . .

MANUSCRIPTS

Athens, Georgia

Special Collections Division, University of Georgia Library
  Robert P. Brooks Papers
  Cobb-Erwin-Lamar Family Papers
  Marcus Johnston Family Papers

Atlanta, Georgia

Atlanta University Library
  Henry P. Slaughter Collection
Georgia Department of Archives and History
  Anderson Family Records
  Barnett Bell Collection
  Governor Joseph E. Brown Collection
  Tunis G. Campbell Papers
  Church Records
    Houston Factory Baptist Church, Houston County
    Perry Baptist Church, Houston County
    Richland Baptist Church, Twiggs County
    Sharon Primitive Baptist Church, Monroe County
    Smyrna Baptist Church, Monroe County
  Walter Henry Cook, "Secret Political Societies in the South during the Period of Reconstruction," Leon Thomas Collection
  County Records
    Annual Returns of Estates
    Indentures of Apprenticeship
    Inferior Court Minute Books
    Inventories and Appraisals of Estates
    Ordinary Court Minute Books
    Superior Court Minute Books
    Tax Digests

Mrs. H. P. Dobbins and Mrs. C. B. Andrews, comps., "A History of Houston
   County, Georgia," edited by W. Grice, [1934], (microfilm)
Executive Pardons Granted and Refused, 1868–82
Governors' Correspondence
   Rufus B. Bullock, 1868–71
   Alfred H. Colquitt, 1877–82
   Benjamin Conley, 1871–72
   Charles J. Jenkins, 1865–68
   James Johnson, 1865
   Gen. Thomas H. Ruger, 1868
   James M. Smith, 1872–77
Ku Klux Klan File
McSwain-Jones Collection
Edward Oxford Papers
Penitentiary Committee, Journal, May–July 1870
Pope Family Papers
Reconstruction File
Shelton Palmer Sanford Diary, 1878
Hiram Warner Collection
Maj. Joseph M. White Journal

Cambridge, Massachusetts

Houghton Library, Harvard University
   Charles Sumner Papers

Chapel Hill, North Carolina

Southern Historical Collection, University of North Carolina
   Edward C. Anderson Diaries
   Octavius A. Bacon Papers
   Iveson L. Brookes Papers
   Hamilton Brown Papers
   Nisbet Family Papers
   Edgar A. Ross Memoir
   U.S. Agricultural Census Returns, 1850–80 (microfilm)
   Hermione (Ross) Walker Collection
   Lewis N. Whittle Papers

Durham, North Carolina

Perkins Library, Duke University
   Trueman G. Avery Diary
   Abbie M. Brooks Diary
   John E. Bryant Papers
   James R. Coombs Recollections

Charles J. Harris Papers
Andrew Johnson Papers
Herschel V. Johnson Papers
Eugenius A. Nisbet Papers
John W. Nisbet Diary

New Orleans, Louisiana

Amistad Research Center, Tulane University
American Missionary Association Papers (microfilm)

Washington, D.C.

Library of Congress
American Colonization Society Papers
National Archives
Records of the Adjutant General's Office, Record Group 94
Records of the Bureau of the Census, Record Group 29
Records of the Bureau of Refugees, Freedmen, and Abandoned Lands, Record
  Group 105
Records of the Department of Justice, Record Group 60
Records of the Secretary of War, Record Group 107
Records of U.S. Army Continental Commands, Record Group 393
War Department Collection of Confederate Records, Chapter 4, Ordnance Depart-
  ment, Record Group 109

GOVERNMENT PUBLICATIONS

Clark, R. H., T. R. R. Cobb, and D. Irwin, comps. *The Code of the State of Georgia.* At-
  lanta: Franklin Steam Printing House, 1861.
Georgia Comptroller General. *Annual Report,* 1873–1910.
Georgia Constitutional Convention, 1867–68. *Journal of the Proceedings of the Constitu-
  tional Convention of the People of Georgia, Held in the City of Atlanta in the Months of
  December, 1867, and January, February, and March, 1868.* Augusta, Ga.: E. H. Pughe,
  1868.
Georgia Constitutional Convention, 1877. *Journal of the Constitutional Convention of the
  People of Georgia . . . 1877.* Atlanta: State Printer, 1877.
————. *A Stenographic Report of the Proceedings of the Constitutional Convention . . . 1877.*
  Atlanta: Constitution Publishing Co., 1877.
Georgia Department of Agriculture. "Statistical Farm Reports. Circular No. 10." *Pub-
  lications of the Georgia State Department of Agriculture for the Year 1875.* Atlanta, 1876.
Georgia General Assembly. *Acts,* 1820–80.
————. *House Journal,* 1865–80.
Mississippi General Assembly. *Acts,* 1850.
Statutes at Large, Treaties, and Proclamations of the United States. Vol. 12. Boston, 1863.

U.S. Census Bureau. *Aggregate Amount of Each Description of Persons within the United States of America . . . in the Year 1810.* Washington: n.p., 1811.

———. *Agriculture of the United States in 1860.* Washington: Government Printing Office, 1864.

———. *Census for 1820.* Washington: Gales & Seaton, 1821.

———. *Compendium of the Enumeration of the Inhabitants and Statistics of the United States . . . from the Returns of the Sixth Census.* Washington: Thomas Allen, 1841.

———. *Compendium of the Ninth Census.* Washington: Government Printing Office, 1872.

———. *Fifth Census; or, Enumeration of the Inhabitants of the United States, 1830.* Washington: Duff Green, 1832.

———. *Manufactures of the United States in 1860.* Washington: Government Printing Office, 1865.

———. *Negro Population, 1790–1915.* Washington: Government Printing Office, 1918.

———. *Population of the United States in 1860.* Washington: Government Printing Office, 1864.

———. *Report on the Manufactures of the United States.* Washington: Government Printing Office, 1883.

———. *Report on the Production of Agriculture in the United States.* Washington: Government Printing Office, 1883.

———. *Seventh Census of the United States: 1850.* Washington: Robert Armstrong, Public Printer, 1853.

———. *Sixth Census, or Enumeration of the Inhabitants of the United States . . . in 1840.* Washington: Blair and Rives, 1841.

———. *The Statistics of the Population of the United States.* Washington: Government Printing Office, 1872.

———. *Statistics of the Population of the United States.* Washington: Government Printing Office, 1883.

———. *The Statistics of the Wealth and Industry of the United States.* Washington: Government Printing Office, 1872.

U.S. Congress. House. *Condition of Affairs in Georgia.* 40th Cong., 3d sess., 1868. H. Misc. Doc. 52.

———. *Report of the Joint Committee on Reconstruction.* 39th Cong., 1st sess., 1866. H. Rept. 30.

———. *Report of the Joint Select Committee to Inquire into the Condition of Affairs in the Late Insurrectionary States.* Georgia Reports. 42d Cong., 2d sess., 1872. H. Rept. 22.

U.S. War Department. *The War of the Rebellion: A Compilation of the Official Records of the Union and Confederate Armies.* 128 vols. Washington: Government Printing Office, 1880–1901.

NEWSPAPERS AND PERIODICALS

African Repository, 1849–80
Appleton's Annual Cyclopedia, 1868

Atlanta *Constitution*, 1867–68, 1883, 1890
Atlanta *Daily Intelligencer*, 1866
Atlanta *Daily New Era*, 1867–68
Augusta *Colored American*, 1865, 1866
Christian Recorder, 1859–80
De Bow's Review, 1861
Georgia Journal & Messenger, 1823–69
Georgia Messenger, 1823–49
Loyal Georgian, 1866, 1867
Macon Telegraph, 1826–69
Macon *Telegraph & Messenger*, 1869–80
New York Times, 1865–80
New York Tribune, 1867–68
Savannah Republican, 1865–68
Southern Agriculturist, 1828–38
Southern Cultivator, 1842–80

PUBLISHED PRIMARY SOURCES

Alvord, John W. *Letters from the South, Relating to the Condition of Freedmen*. Washington: Howard University, 1870.
[Anderson, Robert.] *The Life of Rev. Robert Anderson*. 2d ed. Macon: Privately printed, 1892.
Andrews, Sidney. *The South since the War, as Shown by Fourteen Weeks of Travel and Observation in Georgia and the Carolinas*. Boston: Ticknor and Fields, 1866.
Aptheker, Herbert. *A Documentary History of the Negro People in the United States*. 3 vols. New York: Citadel Press, 1951–76.
Avery, Isaac W. *The History of the State of Georgia from 1850 to 1881*. New York: Brown and Derby, 1881.
Ball, Charles. *Fifty Years in Chains*. 1837. Reprint. New York: Dover, 1970.
Barrow, David C., Jr. "A Georgia Plantation." *Scribner's Monthly* 21 (Apr. 1881): 830–36.
Berlin, Ira, Barbara J. Fields, Thavolia Glymph, Joseph P. Reidy, and Leslie S. Rowland, eds. *The Destruction of Slavery*. Ser. 1, vol. 1 of *Freedom: A Documentary History of Emancipation, 1861–1867*. Cambridge: Cambridge University Press, 1985.
Berlin, Ira, Thavolia Glymph, Steven F. Miller, Joseph P. Reidy, Leslie S. Rowland, and Julie Saville, eds. *The Wartime Genesis of Free Labor: The Lower South*. Ser. 1, vol. 3 of *Freedom: A Documentary History of Emancipation, 1861–1867*. Cambridge: Cambridge University Press, 1990.
Berlin, Ira, Joseph P. Reidy, and Leslie S. Rowland, eds. *The Black Military Experience*. Ser. 2 of *Freedom: A Documentary History of Emancipation, 1861–1867*. Cambridge: Cambridge University Press, 1982.
Blassingame, John W., ed. *Slave Testimony: Two Centuries of Letters, Speeches, Interviews, and Autobiographies*. Baton Rouge: Louisiana State University Press, 1977.

Botume, Elizabeth H. *First Days amongst the Contrabands.* 1893. Reprint. New York: Arno Press and the New York Times, 1968.

Breeden, James O., ed. *Advice among Masters: The Ideal in Slave Management in the Old South.* Westport, Conn.: Greenwood Press, 1980.

[Brown, John.] *Slave Life in Georgia: A Narrative of the Life, Sufferings, and Escape of John Brown, a Fugitive Slave.* Edited by F. N. Boney. Savannah: Beehive Press, 1972.

Bruce, Philip A. *The Plantation Negro as a Freeman.* New York: G. P. Putnam's Sons, 1889.

Buckingham, James S. *The Slave States of America.* 2 vols. London: Fisher, Son & Co., 1842.

Butler, John C. *Historical Record of Macon and Central Georgia.* Macon: J. W. Burke & Co., 1879.

Campbell, Sir George. *White and Black: The Outcome of a Visit to the United States.* New York: R. Worthington, 1879.

Catterall, Helen T., ed. *Judicial Cases Concerning American Slavery and the Negro.* 5 vols. Washington, D.C.: Carnegie Institution, 1936.

Cauthen, Charles E., ed. *Family Letters of the Three Wade Hamptons, 1782–1901.* Columbia: University of South Carolina Press, 1953.

Chappell, Absalom H. *Miscellanies of Georgia: Historical, Biographical, Descriptive, Etc.* Atlanta: James F. Meegan, 1874.

Cleveland, Henry. *Alexander H. Stephens, in Public and Private; with Letters and Speeches Before, During, and Since the War.* Philadelphia: National Publishing Co., 1866.

Cobb, Howell. *A Scriptural Examination of the Institution of Slavery in the United States; with Its Objects and Purposes.* [Perry,] Ga.: Printed for the author, 1856.

Cobb, Thomas R. R. *An Inquiry into the Law of Negro Slavery in the United States of America.* 1858. Reprint. New York: Arno Press and the New York Times, 1968.

[Craft, William.] *Running a Thousand Miles for Freedom; or, The Escape of William and Ellen Craft from Slavery.* London: William Tweedie, 1860.

Dennett, John Richard. *The South as It Is: 1865–1866.* Edited by Henry M. Christman. New York: Viking Press, 1965.

Dickson, David. *David Dickson's System of Farming.* Atlanta: Cultivator Publishing Co., 1906.

Felton, Mrs. William H. [Rebecca Latimer]. *My Memoirs of Georgia Politics.* Atlanta: Index Printing Co., 1911.

Fitzhugh, George. *Cannibals All! or, Slaves without Masters.* 1858. Reprint, edited by C. Vann Woodward. Cambridge: Belknap Press of Harvard University Press, 1960.

Foner, Philip S., and Ronald L. Lewis, eds. *The Black Worker: A Documentary History from Colonial Times to the Present.* 6 vols. Philadelphia: Temple University Press, 1978–84.

Gaines, Wesley J. *African Methodism in the South; or, Twenty-five Years of Freedom.* Atlanta: Franklin Publishing House, 1890.

———. *The Negro and the White Man.* Philadelphia: A.M.E. Publishing House, 1897.

Haddock's Macon, Ga., Directory and General Advertiser. Macon, 1872.

Hall, Basil. *Travels in North America in the Years 1827–1828.* 2 vols. Philadelphia: Carey, Lea & Carey, 1829.

[Hall, Mrs. Basil.] *The Aristocratic Journey . . . Letters of Mrs. Basil Hall . . . 1827–1828*. Edited by Una Pope-Hennessy. New York: G. P. Putnam's Sons, 1931.

[Hamilton, Thomas.] *Men and Manners in America*. Edinburgh: William Blackwood, 1833.

Harrison, William Pope. *The Gospel among the Slaves*. Nashville: Publishing House of the M.E. Church, South, 1893.

Haygood, Atticus G. *Our Brother in Black: His Freedom and His Future*. New York: Phillips & Hunt, 1881.

Hodgson, Adam. *Letters from North America, Written during a Tour in the United States and Canada*. 2 vols. London: Printed for Hurst, Robinson & Co., 1824.

Holsey, Lucius H. *Autobiography*. Atlanta: Franklin Printing & Publishing Co., 1898.

Jordan, Rev. Lewis G. *Negro Baptist History, U.S.A., 1750, 1930*. Nashville: Sunday School Publishing Board, N.B.C., 1930.

Keller, Herbert Anthony, ed. *Solon Robinson: Pioneer and Agriculturist*. 2 vols. Indianapolis: Bobbs-Merrill, 1936.

Kelsey, Carl. *The Negro Farmer*. Chicago: Jennings & Pye, 1903.

Kennaway, John H. *On Sherman's Track; or, The South after the War*. London: Seeley, Jackson, and Halliday, 1867.

King, Edward. *The Southern States of North America*. London: Blackie and Son, 1875.

Latham, Henry. *Black and White: A Journal of a Three Months' Tour in the United States*. Philadelphia: J. B. Lippincott, 1867.

Latrobe, Charles J. *The Rambler in North America*. 2 vols. London: R. B. Seeley & W. Burnside, 1835.

Lincoln, Abraham. *The Collected Works of Abraham Lincoln*. Edited by Roy P. Basler, Marion Dolores Pratt, and Lloyd A. Dunlap. New Brunswick: Rutgers University Press, 1953.

Lyell, Sir Charles. *A Second Visit to the United States of North America*. 2 vols. New York: Harper & Brothers, 1849.

Mackay, Alex[ander]. *The Western World; or, Travels in the United States in 1846–47*. 2d ed. Philadelphia: Lea & Blanchard, 1849.

Mackay, Charles. *Life and Liberty in America; or, Sketches of a Tour in the United States and Canada in 1857–58*. New York: Harper & Brothers, 1859.

McKaye, James. *The Mastership and Its Fruits*. New York: Loyal Publication Society, 1864.

Martineau, Harriet. *Society in America*. 4th ed. 2 vols. New York: Saunders and Otley, 1837.

Mullin, Michael, ed. *American Negro Slavery: A Documentary History*. New York: Harper & Row, 1976.

Murray, Amelia M. *Letters from the United States, Cuba, and Canada*. New York: G. P. Putnam & Co., 1856.

Nichols, George Ward. *The Story of the Great March from the Diary of a Staff Officer*. 24th ed. New York: Harper & Brothers, 1866.

Nordhoff, Charles. *The Cotton States in the Spring and Summer of 1875*. New York: D. Appleton & Co., 1876.

Olmsted, Frederick Law. *The Cotton Kingdom: A Traveller's Observations on Cotton and Slavery in the American Slave States*. 2 vols. New York: Mason Brothers, 1861.

———. *A Journey in the Back Country*. New York: Mason Brothers, 1860.

———. *A Journey in the Seaboard Slave States, with Remarks on Their Economy*. New York: Mason Brothers, 1859.

Pearson, Elizabeth Ware, ed. *Letters from Port Royal Written at the Time of the Civil War*. Boston: W. B. Clarke Co., 1906.

Percy, William Alexander. *Lanterns on the Levee: Recollections of a Planter's Son*. New York: Alfred A. Knopf, 1941.

Phillips, Ulrich Bonnell, ed. *The Correspondence of Robert Toombs, Alexander H. Stephens, and Howell Cobb*. Washington, D.C.: American Historical Association, 1913.

———, ed. *Plantation and Frontier Documents, 1649–1863*. Cleveland: A. H. Clark Co., 1909.

Pierce, Alfred M. *A History of Methodism in Georgia, February 5, 1736–June 24, 1955*. N.p., 1956.

Pierson, Hamilton W. *Letter to Charles Sumner with Statement of Outrages upon Freedmen in Georgia*. Washington: Chronicle Print, 1870.

Power, Tyrone. *Impressions of America; during the Years 1833, 1834, and 1835*. 2 vols. Philadelphia: Carey, Lea & Blanchard, 1836.

Powers, Stephen. *Afoot and Alone: A Walk from Sea to Sea*. Hartford: Columbian Book Co., 1872.

Proceedings of the Convention of the Equal Rights and Educational Association of Georgia, Assembled at Macon, October 29th, 1866. Augusta, Ga.: Loyal Georgian Publishing House, 1866.

Proceedings of the Council of the Georgia Equal Rights Association, Assembled at Augusta, Georgia, April 4th, 1866. Augusta, Ga.: Loyal Georgian Publishing House, 1866.

Proceedings of the Freedmen's Convention of Georgia, Assembled at Augusta, January 10th, 1866. Augusta, Ga.: Loyal Georgian Publishing House, 1866.

Proceedings of the Southern States Convention of Colored Men, Held in Columbia, S.C., Commencing October 18, Ending October 25, 1871. Columbia: Carolina Printing Co., 1871.

Rawick, George P., ed. *The American Slave: A Composite Autobiography*. Ser. 2, vols. 12–13, Georgia Narratives. Westport, Conn.: Greenwood Press, 1972.

Rawick, George P., Jan Hillegas, and Ken Lawrence, eds. *The American Slave: A Composite Autobiography*. Suppl. ser. 1, vols. 3–4, Georgia Narratives. Westport, Conn.: Greenwood Press, 1977.

Reid, Whitelaw. *After the War: A Southern Tour*. Cincinnati: Moore, 1866.

Ripley, C. Peter, Jeffery S. Rossback, Roy E. Finkenbine, Fiona E. Spiers, Paul A. Cimbala, Michael F. Hembree, and Donald Yacovone, eds. *The Black Abolitionist Papers*. 5 vols. Chapel Hill: University of North Carolina Press, 1985–92.

Rose, Willie Lee, ed. *A Documentary History of Slavery in North America*. New York: Oxford University Press, 1976.

Royall, Mrs. Anne. *Mrs. Royall's Southern Tour; or, Second Series of the Black Book*. 3 vols. Washington, D.C.: n.p., 1830–31.

Simmons, William J. *Men of Mark: Eminent, Progressive, and Rising*. 1887. Reprint. New York: Arno Press, 1968.

Somers, Robert. *Southern States since the War, 1870–71*. London: Macmillan, 1871.

Stearns, Charles. *The Black Man of the South and the Rebels; or, The Characteristics of the Former, and the Recent Outrages of the Latter*. 1872. Reprint. New York: Negro Universities Press, 1969.

————. *The Exodus and Its Causes: An Eventful Experience of Plantation and Cabin Life*. Philadelphia: Union Publishing Co., 1879.

Steward, Theophilus Gould. *Fifty Years in the Gospel Ministry*. Philadelphia: A.M.E. Book Concern, 1922.

Stirling, James. *Letters from the Slave States*. London: John W. Parker and Son, 1857.

Stone, Alfred Holt. *Studies in the American Race Problem*. New York: Doubleday, Page & Co., 1908.

Stuart, James. *Three Years in North America*. 2 vols. Edinburgh: Robert Cadell, 1833.

Trowbridge, John T. *A Picture of the Desolated States; and the Work of Restoration, 1865–1868*. Hartford: L. Stebbins, 1866.

————. *The South: A Tour of Its Battle Fields and Ruined Cities, a Journey through the Desolated States, and Talks with the People*. Hartford: L. Stebbins, 1866.

Van Epps, Howard. *Analytical Index-Digest of Georgia Reports; Embracing Volumes 1–100, Inclusive, of the Supreme Court Reports*. 3 vols. Nashville: Marshall & Bruce Co., 1899.

Wayman, Alexander W. *My Recollections of African M.E. Ministers*. Philadelphia: A.M.E. Book Rooms, 1881.

Wilson, James H. *Under the Old Flag*. 2 vols. New York: D. Appleton, 1912.

Wright, R. R., Jr. *The Bishops of the African Methodist Episcopal Church*. Nashville: A.M.E. Sunday School Union, 1963.

SECONDARY SOURCES

Adamson, Alan H. *Sugar without Slaves: The Political Economy of British Guiana, 1838–1904*. New Haven: Yale University Press, 1974.

Alexander, Adele Logan. *Ambiguous Lives: Free Women of Color in Rural Georgia, 1789–1879*. Fayetteville: University of Arkansas Press, 1991.

Allen, James. *Reconstruction: The Battle for Democracy*. New York: International Publishers, 1937.

Anderson, Eric. *Race and Politics in North Carolina, 1872–1901*. Baton Rouge: Louisiana State University Press, 1981.

Anderson, James D. *The Education of Blacks in the South, 1860–1935*. Chapel Hill: University of North Carolina Press, 1988.

Aptheker, Herbert. *American Negro Slave Revolts*. New York: Columbia University Press, 1943.

Armstrong, Thomas. "From Task Labor to Free Labor: The Transition along Georgia's Rice Coast, 1820–1880." *Georgia Historical Quarterly* 64 (Winter 1980): 432–47.

Aston, T. H., and C. H. E. Philpin, eds. *The Brenner Debate: Agrarian Class Structure and Economic Development in Pre-Industrial Europe*. Cambridge: Cambridge University Press, 1985.

Ayers, Edward L. *Vengeance and Justice: Crime and Punishment in the 19th-Century American South*. New York: Oxford University Press, 1984.

Bacote, Clarence A. "The Negro in Georgia Politics, 1880–1908." Ph.D. dissertation, University of Chicago, 1955.

Banks, Enoch Marvin. *The Economics of Land Tenure in Georgia.* New York: Columbia University Press, 1905.

Barney, William L. *The Secessionist Impulse: Alabama and Mississippi in 1860.* Princeton: Princeton University Press, 1974.

Barron, Hal S. *Those Who Stayed Behind: Rural Society in Nineteenth-Century New England.* Cambridge: Cambridge University Press, 1984.

Bateman, Fred, and Thomas Weiss. *A Deplorable Scarcity: The Failure of Industrialization in the Slave Economy.* Chapel Hill: University of North Carolina Press, 1981.

Bauer, Raymond A., and Alice H. Bauer. "Day to Day Resistance to Slavery." *Journal of Negro History* 27 (Oct. 1942): 388–419.

Beeman, Richard. *The Evolution of the Southern Backcountry: A Case Study of Lunenburg County, Virginia, 1746–1832.* Philadelphia: University of Pennsylvania Press, 1984.

Bellamy, Donnie D. "Macon, Georgia, 1823–1860: A Study in Urban Slavery." *Phylon* 45 (Dec. 1984): 298–310.

Belz, Herman. *Emancipation and Equal Rights: Politics and Constitutionalism in the Civil War Era.* New York: W. W. Norton & Co., 1978.

Benedict, Michael Les. *A Compromise of Principle: Congressional Republicans and Reconstruction, 1863–1869.* New York: W. W. Norton & Co., 1974.

Bensel, Richard Franklin. *Yankee Leviathan: The Origins of Central State Authority in America, 1859–1877.* Cambridge: Cambridge University Press, 1990.

Bentley, George R. *A History of the Freedmen's Bureau.* Philadelphia: University of Pennsylvania Press, 1955.

Berlin, Ira. *Slaves without Masters: The Free Negro in the Antebellum South.* New York: Pantheon, 1974.

———. "Time, Space, and the Evolution of Afro-American Society in British Mainland North America." *American Historical Review* 85 (Feb. 1980): 44–78.

Berlin, Ira, and Herbert G. Gutman. "Natives and Immigrants, Free Men and Slaves: Urban Workingmen in the Antebellum American South." *American Historical Review* 88 (Dec. 1983): 1175–1200.

Biehle, Reba Strickland. "Edward Oxford, Pioneer Farmer of Middle Georgia." *Georgia Historical Quarterly* 52 (June 1968): 187–98.

Billings, Dwight B., Jr. *Planters and the Making of a "New South": Class, Politics, and Development in North Carolina, 1865–1900.* Chapel Hill: University of North Carolina Press, 1979.

Blackett, R. J. M. *Beating against the Barriers: Biographical Essays in Nineteenth-Century Afro-American History.* Baton Rouge: Louisiana State University Press, 1986.

———. "Fugitive Slaves in Britain: The Odyssey of William and Ellen Craft." *Journal of American Studies* 12 (Apr. 1978): 41–62.

Blassingame, John W. "Before the Ghetto: The Making of the Black Community in Savannah, Georgia, 1865–1880." *Journal of Social History* 6 (Summer 1973): 463–88.

———. *The Slave Community: Plantation Life in the Antebellum South.* Rev. ed. New York: Oxford University Press, 1979.

————. "Using the Testimony of Ex-Slaves: Approaches and Problems." *Journal of Southern History* 41 (Nov. 1975): 473–92.

Bleser, Carol K. R. *The Promised Land: The History of the South Carolina Land Commission, 1869–1890*. Columbia: University of South Carolina Press, 1969.

Blum, Jerome. *The End of the Old Order in Rural Europe*. Princeton: Princeton University Press, 1978.

————. *Noble Landowners and Agriculture in Austria, 1815–1848: A Study in the Origins of the Peasant Emancipation of 1848*. Baltimore: Johns Hopkins University Press, 1948.

Bode, Frederick, and Donald Ginter. *Farm Tenancy and the Census in Antebellum Georgia*. Athens: University of Georgia Press, 1986.

Bogue, Allan G. *From Prairie to Corn Belt: Farming on the Illinois and Iowa Prairies in the Nineteenth Century*. Chicago: Quadrangle Books, 1968.

Bogue, Margaret B. *Patterns in the Sod: Land Use and Tenure in the Grand Prairie, 1850–1900*. Springfield: Illinois State Historical Library, 1959.

Boles, John B., ed. *Masters and Slaves in the House of the Lord: Race and Religion in the American South, 1740–1870*. Lexington: University Press of Kentucky, 1988.

Bolster, W. Jeffrey. " 'To Feel like a Man': Black Seamen in the Northern States, 1800–1860." *Journal of American History* 76 (Mar. 1990): 1173–99.

Bonner, James C. *A History of Georgia Agriculture, 1732–1860*. Athens: University of Georgia Press, 1964.

————. *Milledgeville: Georgia's Antebellum Capital*. Athens: University of Georgia Press, 1978.

————. "Profile of a Late Ante-Bellum Community [Hancock County, Georgia]." *American Historical Review* 49 (July 1944): 663–80.

Boyd, W. D. "Negro Colonization in the Reconstruction Era, 1865–1870." *Georgia Historical Quarterly* 40 (Dec. 1956): 360–82.

Bracey, John H., Jr., August Meier, and Elliot Rudwick, eds. *Black Nationalism in America*. Indianapolis: Bobbs-Merrill, 1970.

Bremner, Robert H. *The Public Good: Philanthropy and Welfare in the Civil War Era*. New York: Alfred A. Knopf, 1980.

Brewer, James H. *The Confederate Negro: Virginia's Craftsmen and Military Laborers, 1861–1865*. Durham: Duke University Press, 1969.

Bridenbaugh, Carl. *Myths and Realities: Societies of the Colonial South*. New York: Atheneum, 1976.

Brooks, Robert Preston. *The Agrarian Revolution in Georgia, 1865–1912*. Madison: University of Wisconsin, 1914.

Bryan, T. Conn. *Confederate Georgia*. Athens: University of Georgia Press, 1953.

Burton, Michael L., and Douglas R. White. "Sexual Division of Labor in Agriculture." *American Anthropologist* 86 (Sept. 1984): 568–83.

Burton, Orville Vernon. *In My Father's House Are Many Mansions: Family and Community in Edgefield, South Carolina*. Chapel Hill: University of North Carolina Press, 1985.

Burton, Orville Vernon, and Robert C. McMath, Jr., eds. *Class, Conflict, and Consensus: Antebellum Southern Community Studies*. Westport, Conn.: Greenwood Press, 1982.

————, eds. *Toward a New South? Studies in Post–Civil War Southern Communities.* Westport, Conn.: Greenwood Press, 1982.

Callaway, James E. *The Early Settlement of Georgia.* Athens: University of Georgia Press, 1948.

Campbell, John. "As 'A Kind of Freeman'?: Slaves' Market-Related Activities in the South Carolina Upcountry, 1800–1860." *Slavery and Abolition* 12 (May 1991): 131–69.

Carlton, David L. *Mill and Town in South Carolina, 1880–1920.* Baton Rouge: Louisiana State University Press, 1982.

Carter, Dan T. "The Anatomy of Fear: The Christmas Day Insurrection Scare of 1865." *Journal of Southern History* 42 (Aug. 1976): 345–64.

————. "From the Old South to the New: Another Look at the Theme of Change and Continuity." In *From the Old South to the New: Essays on the Transitional South*, edited by Walter J. Fraser, Jr., and Winfred B. Moore, Jr., pp. 23–32. Westport, Conn.: Greenwood Press, 1981.

————. *When the War Was Over: The Failure of Self-Reconstruction in the South, 1865–1867.* Baton Rouge: Louisiana State University Press, 1985.

Cason, Roberta F. "The Loyal League in Georgia." *Georgia Historical Quarterly* 20 (June 1936): 125–53.

Central Georgia Genealogical Society. *First Hundred and Ten Years of Houston County, Georgia (1822–1932).* Chelsea, Mich.: Bookcrafters, 1983.

Channing, Steven A. *Crisis of Fear: Secession in South Carolina.* New York: Simon and Schuster, 1970.

Chaplin, Joyce E. "Creating a Cotton South in Georgia and South Carolina, 1760–1815." *Journal of Southern History* 47 (May 1991): 171–200.

Chirot, Daniel. "The Growth of the Market and Service Labor Systems in Agriculture." *Journal of Social History* 8 (Winter 1975): 67–80.

Christler, Ethel Maude. "Participation of Negroes in the Government of Georgia, 1867–1870." Master's thesis, Atlanta University, 1932.

Christopher, Maurine. *Black Americans in Congress.* Rev. ed. New York: Thomas Y. Crowell, 1976.

Cimbala, Paul A. "The Freedmen's Bureau, the Freedmen, and Sherman's Grant in Reconstruction Georgia, 1865–1867." *Journal of Southern History* 55 (Nov. 1990): 597–632.

————. "'The Talisman Power': Davis Tillson, the Freedmen's Bureau, and Free Labor in Reconstruction Georgia, 1865–1866." *Civil War History* 28 (June 1982): 153–71.

Clark, Blanche H. *The Tennessee Yeoman, 1840–1860.* Nashville: Vanderbilt University Press, 1942.

Clark, Christopher. "Household Economy, Market Exchange and the Rise of Capitalism in the Connecticut Valley, 1800–1860." *Journal of Social History* 13 (Winter 1979): 169–89.

————. *The Roots of Rural Capitalism: Western Massachusetts, 1780–1869.* Ithaca: Cornell University Press, 1990.

Clemens, Paul G. E. *The Atlantic Economy and Colonial Maryland's Eastern Shore: From Tobacco to Grain.* Ithaca: Cornell University Press, 1980.

Clinton, Catherine. *The Plantation Mistress: Women's World in the Old South*. New York: Pantheon, 1982.

Cohen, David W., and Jack P. Greene, eds. *Neither Slave Nor Free: The Freedmen of African Descent in the Slave Societies of the New World*. Baltimore: Johns Hopkins University Press, 1972.

Cohen, William. *At Freedom's Edge: Black Mobility and the Southern White Quest for Racial Control, 1861–1915*. Baton Rouge: Louisiana State University Press, 1991.

———. "Negro Involuntary Servitude in the South, 1865–1940: A Preliminary Analysis." *Journal of Southern History* 42 (Feb. 1976): 31–60.

Conrad, Robert. *The Destruction of Brazilian Slavery, 1850–1888*. Berkeley: University of California Press, 1972.

Conway, Alan. *The Reconstruction of Georgia*. Minneapolis: University of Minnesota Press, 1966.

Cooper, William. *Liberty and Slavery: Southern Politics to 1860*. New York: Alfred A. Knopf, 1983.

———. *The South and the Politics of Slavery, 1828–1856*. Baton Rouge: Louisiana State University Press, 1978.

Coulter, E. Merton. *Negro Legislators in Georgia during the Reconstruction Period*. Athens: Georgia Historical Society, 1968.

———. *The South during Reconstruction, 1865–1877*. Baton Rouge: Louisiana State University Press, 1951.

Cox, LaWanda. *Lincoln and Black Freedom: A Study in Presidential Leadership*. Columbia: University of South Carolina Press, 1981.

Craton, Michael. *Searching for the Invisible Man: Slaves and Plantation Life in Jamaica*. Cambridge: Harvard University Press, 1978.

———. *Testing the Chains: Resistance to Slavery in the British West Indies*. Ithaca: Cornell University Press, 1982.

Craven, Avery. *Soil Exhaustion as a Factor in the Agricultural History of Virginia and Maryland, 1606–1860*. Urbana: University of Illinois Press, 1926.

Crosby, Alfred H. *Ecological Imperialism: The Biological Expansion of Europe, 900–1900*. Cambridge: Cambridge University Press, 1986.

Currie-McDaniel, Ruth. *Carpetbagger of Conscience: A Biography of John Emory Bryant*. Athens: University of Georgia Press, 1987.

Curtin, Philip. *The Atlantic Slave Trade: A Census*. Madison: University of Wisconsin Press, 1969.

———. *The Rise and Fall of the Plantation Complex: Essays in Atlantic History*. Cambridge: Cambridge University Press, 1990.

———. *Two Jamaicas: The Role of Ideas in a Tropical Colony, 1830–1865*. Cambridge: Harvard University Press, 1955.

Curtis, L. P. *Anglo-Saxons and Celts: A Study of Anti-Irish Prejudice in Victorian England*. Bridgeport, Conn.: New England Universities Press, 1968.

Danhof, Clarence. *Change in Agriculture: The Northern States, 1820–1870*. Cambridge: Harvard University Press, 1969.

Daniel, Pete. *The Shadow of Slavery: Peonage in the South, 1901–1969*. Urbana: University of Illinois Press, 1972.

Davis, David Brion. *The Problem of Slavery in the Age of Revolution, 1770–1823.* Ithaca: Cornell University Press, 1975.

———. *Slavery and Human Progress.* New York: Oxford University Press, 1984.

Davis, Ronald L. F. *Good and Faithful Labor: From Slavery to Sharecropping in the Natchez District, 1860–1890.* Westport, Conn.: Greenwood Press, 1982.

———. "Labor Dependency among Freedmen, 1865–1880." In *From the Old South to the New: Essays on the Transitional South,* edited by Walter J. Fraser, Jr., and Winfred B. Moore, Jr., pp. 155–65. Westport, Conn.: Greenwood Press, 1981.

Dawley, Alan. *Class and Community: The Industrial Revolution in Lynn.* Cambridge: Harvard University Press, 1976.

DeBats, Donald A. "An Uncertain Arena: The Georgia House of Representatives, 1808–1861." *Journal of Southern History* 46 (Aug. 1990): 423–56.

DeCanio, Stephen J. *Agriculture in the Postbellum South: The Economics of Production and Supply.* Cambridge: MIT Press, 1974.

DeCredico, Mary A. *Patriotism for Profit: Georgia's Urban Entrepreneurs and the Confederate War Effort.* Chapel Hill: University of North Carolina Press, 1990.

Desantis, Vincent P. *Republicans Face the Southern Question—The New Departure Years, 1877–1897.* Baltimore: Johns Hopkins University Press, 1959.

Destler, Chester McArthur. "David Dickson's 'System of Farming' and the Agricultural Revolution in the Deep South, 1850–1885." *Agricultural History* 31 (July 1957): 30–39.

Dew, Charles B. *Ironmaker to the Confederacy: Joseph R. Anderson and Tredegar Iron Works.* New Haven: Yale University Press, 1966.

Dittmer, John. *Black Georgia in the Progressive Era, 1900–1920.* Urbana: University of Illinois Press, 1977.

Dobb, Maurice. *Studies in the Development of Capitalism.* New York: International Publishers, 1949.

Drago, Edmund L. *Black Politicians and Reconstruction in Georgia: A Splendid Failure.* Baton Rouge: Louisiana State University Press, 1982.

———. "How Sherman's March through Georgia Affected Slaves." *Georgia Historical Quarterly* 57 (Fall 1973): 361–75.

Dublin, Thomas. *Women at Work: The Transformation of Work and Community in Lowell, Massachusetts, 1826–1860.* New York: Columbia University Press, 1979.

Du Bois, William Edward Burghardt. *Black Reconstruction: An Essay Toward a History of the Part Which Black Folk Played in the Attempt to Reconstruct Democracy in America, 1860–1880.* New York: Russell & Russell, 1935.

———. "The Negro Landholder of Georgia." U.S. Department of Labor, *Bulletin No. 35* (July 1901): 647–777.

———. *The Souls of Black Folk: Essays and Sketches.* Chicago: A. C. McClurg, 1903.

Duncan, Russell. *Freedom's Shore: Tunis Campbell and the Georgia Freedmen.* Athens: University of Georgia Press, 1986.

Dunn, Richard S. "'Dreadful Idlers' in the Cane Fields: The Slave Labor Pattern on a Jamaican Sugar Estate, 1762–1831." In *British Capitalism and Caribbean Slavery: The Legacy of Eric Williams,* edited by Barbara L. Solow and Stanley L. Engerman, pp. 163–90. Cambridge: Cambridge University Press, 1987.

Dupre, Daniel. "Ambivalent Capitalists on the Cotton Frontier: Settlement and Development in the Tennessee Valley of Alabama." *Journal of Southern History* 46 (May 1990): 215–40.

Eaton, Clement. *The Mind of the Old South.* Baton Rouge: Louisiana State University Press, 1964.

Edwards, Thomas J. "The Tenant System and Some Changes since Emancipation." *Annals of the American Academy of Political and Social Science* 49 (1913): 38–46.

Eisterhold, John A. "Commercial, Financial, and Industrial Macon, Georgia, during the 1840s." *Georgia Historical Quarterly* 53 (Dec. 1969): 425–38.

Engerman, Stanley L. "Economic Adjustments to Emancipation in the United States and British West Indies." *Journal of Interdisciplinary History* 12 (Autumn 1982): 191–220.

———. "Slavery and Emancipation in Comparative Perspective: A Look at Some Recent Debates." *Journal of Economic History* 46 (June 1986): 317–39.

Engerman, Stanley, and Eugene D. Genovese, eds. *Race and Slavery in the Western Hemisphere: Quantitative Studies.* Princeton: Princeton University Press, 1975.

Escott, Paul D. *After Secession: Jefferson Davis and the Failure of Confederate Nationalism.* Baton Rouge: Louisiana State University Press, 1978.

———. "The Context of Freedom: Georgia's Slaves during the Civil War." *Georgia Historical Quarterly* 58 (Spring 1974): 79–104.

———. *Slavery Remembered: A Record of Twentieth-Century Slave Narratives.* Chapel Hill: University of North Carolina Press, 1979.

Faragher, John Mack. *Sugar Creek: Life on the Illinois Prairie.* New Haven: Yale University Press, 1986.

Faulkner, William. *Go Down, Moses.* 1942. Reprint. New York: Vintage Books, 1973.

———. *The Mansion.* 1955. Reprint. New York: Vintage Books, 1965.

Faust, Drew Gilpin. *James Henry Hammond and the Old South: A Design for Mastery.* Baton Rouge: Louisiana State University Press, 1982.

———, ed. *The Ideology of Slavery: Proslavery Thought in the Antebellum South, 1830–1860.* Baton Rouge: Louisiana State University Press, 1981.

Ferleger, Lou, ed. *Agriculture and National Development: Views on the Nineteenth Century.* Ames: Iowa State University Press, 1990.

Fields, Barbara Jeanne. "The Advent of Capitalist Agriculture: The New South in a Bourgeois World." In *Essays on the Postbellum Southern Economy,* edited by Thavolia Glymph and John H. Kushma, pp. 73–94. College Station: Texas A&M University Press, 1985.

———. "Ideology and Race in American History." In *Region, Race, and Reconstruction: Essays in Honor of C. Vann Woodward,* edited by J. Morgan Kousser and James M. McPherson, pp. 143–77. New York: Oxford University Press, 1982.

———. "The Nineteenth-Century American South: History and Theory." *Plantation Society in the Americas* 2 (Apr. 1983): 7–27.

———. *Slavery and Freedom on the Middle Ground: Maryland during the Nineteenth Century.* New Haven: Yale University Press, 1985.

Fields, Barbara Jeanne, and Leslie S. Rowland. "Free Labor Ideology and Its Exponents in the South during the Civil War and Reconstruction." *Labor History* (forthcoming).

Finley, M. I. *Ancient Slavery and Modern Ideology*. New York: Penguin Books, 1980.

Fitzgerald, Michael W. "Radical Republicanism and the White Yeomanry during Alabama Reconstruction, 1865–1868." *Journal of Southern History* 54 (Nov. 1988): 565–96.

———. "'To Give Our Votes to the Party': Black Political Agitation and Agricultural Change in Alabama, 1865–1870." *Journal of American History* 76 (Sept. 1989): 489–505.

———. *The Union League Movement in the Deep South: Politics and Agricultural Change during Reconstruction*. Baton Rouge: Louisiana State University Press, 1989.

Flanagan, Daniel J. "Criminal Procedure in Slave Trials in the Antebellum South." *Journal of Southern History* 40 (Nov. 1974): 537–64.

Flanders, Ralph B. "The Free Negro in Ante-Bellum Georgia." *North Carolina Historical Review* 9 (July 1932): 250–72.

———. *Plantation Slavery in Georgia*. Chapel Hill: University of North Carolina Press, 1933.

———. "Two Plantations and a County of Ante-Bellum Georgia." *Georgia Historical Quarterly* 12 (March 1928): 1–37.

Flynn, Charles L., Jr. *White Land, Black Labor: Caste and Class in Late Nineteenth-Century Georgia*. Baton Rouge: Louisiana State University Press, 1983.

Fogel, Robert William. *Without Consent or Contract: The Rise and Fall of American Slavery*. New York: W. W. Norton & Co., 1989.

Fogel, Robert William, and Stanley L. Engerman. *Time on the Cross: The Economics of American Negro Slavery*. 2 vols. Boston: Little, Brown, 1974.

Foley, Albert S., S.J. *Bishop Healy: Beloved Outcaste, The Story of a Great Man Whose Life Has Become a Legend*. New York: Farrar, Straus and Young, 1954.

Foner, Eric. *Free Soil, Free Labor, Free Men: The Ideology of the Republican Party before the Civil War*. New York: Oxford University Press, 1970.

———. *Nothing But Freedom: Emancipation and Its Legacy*. Baton Rouge: Louisiana State University Press, 1983.

———. *Politics and Ideology in the Civil War Era*. New York: Oxford University Press, 1980.

———. *Reconstruction: America's Unfinished Revolution, 1863–1877*. New York: Harper & Row, 1988.

———. *Tom Paine and Revolutionary America*. New York: Oxford University Press, 1976.

Ford, Lacy K. *Origins of Southern Radicalism: The South Carolina Upcountry, 1800–1860*. New York: Oxford University Press, 1988.

———. "Rednecks and Merchants: Economic Development and Social Tensions in the South Carolina Upcountry, 1865–1900." *Journal of American History* 71 (Sept. 1984): 294–318.

———. "Republican Ideology in a Slave Society: The Political Economy of John C. Calhoun." *Journal of Southern History* 54 (Aug. 1988): 405–24.

Formwalt, Lee W. "Antebellum Planter Persistence: Southwest Georgia—A Case Study." *Plantation Society in the Americas* 1 (Oct. 1981): 410–29.

Fox-Genovese, Elizabeth. *Within the Plantation Household: Black and White Women of the Old South*. Chapel Hill: University of North Carolina Press, 1988.

Fox-Genovese, Elizabeth, and Eugene D. Genovese. *Fruits of Merchant Capital: Slavery and Bourgeois Property in the Rise and Expansion of Capitalism*. New York: Oxford University Press, 1983.

Franklin, John Hope. *The Emancipation Proclamation*. Garden City, N.Y.: Doubleday & Co., 1963.

Fredrickson, George M. *The Black Image in the White Mind: The Debate on Afro-American Character and Destiny, 1817–1914*. New York: Oxford University Press, 1972.

———. *White Supremacy: A Comparative Study in American and South African History*. New York: Oxford University Press, 1981.

Gallay, Alan. *The Formation of a Planter Elite: Jonathan Bryan and the Southern Colonial Frontier*. Athens: University of Georgia Press, 1989.

Gaspar, David Barry. "Slavery, Amelioration, and Sunday Markets in Antigua, 1823–1831." *Slavery and Abolition* 9 (May 1991): 1–28.

Gates, Paul W. *The Farmer's Age: Agriculture, 1815–1860*. New York: Holt, Rinehart and Winston, 1960.

———. *Landlords and Tenants on the Prairie Frontier: Studies in American Land Policy*. Ithaca: Cornell University Press, 1973.

Genovese, Eugene D. *From Rebellion to Revolution: Afro-American Slave Revolts in the Making of the Modern World*. Baton Rouge: Louisiana State University Press, 1979.

———. *The Political Economy of Slavery: Studies in the Economy and Society of the Slave South*. New York: Pantheon, 1966.

———. *Roll, Jordan, Roll: The World the Slaves Made*. New York: Pantheon, 1974.

———. *The World the Slaveholders Made: Two Essays in Interpretation*. New York: Pantheon, 1979.

———. "Yeomen Farmers in a Slaveholders' Democracy." *Agricultural History* 49 (Apr. 1973): 331–42.

Gerteis, Louis S. *From Contraband to Freedman: Federal Policy toward Southern Blacks, 1861–1865*. Westport, Conn.: Greenwood Press, 1974.

Gispen, Kees, ed. *What Made the South Different?* Jackson: University Press of Mississippi, 1990.

Glatthaar, Joseph T. *The March to the Sea and Beyond: Sherman's Troops in the Savannah and Carolina Campaigns*. New York: New York University Press, 1985.

Glymph, Thavolia. "Freedpeople and Ex-Masters: Shaping a New Order in the Postbellum South, 1865–1868." In *Essays on the Postbellum Southern Economy*, edited by Thavolia Glymph and John H. Kushma, pp. 48–72. College Station: Texas A&M University Press, 1985.

Glymph, Thavolia, and John H. Kushma, eds. *Essays on the Postbellum Southern Economy*. College Station: Texas A&M University Press, 1985.

Goldfield, David R. *Urban Growth in the Age of Sectionalism: Virginia, 1847–1861*. Baton Rouge: Louisiana State University Press, 1977.

Goldin, Claudia. *Urban Slavery in the American South, 1820–1860: A Quantitative History*. Chicago: University of Chicago Press, 1976.

Gottlieb, Manuel. "The Land Question in Georgia during Reconstruction." *Science and Society* 3 (Summer 1939): 356–88.

Gould, Stephen Jay. *The Flamingo's Smile: Reflections in Natural History*. New York: W. W. Norton & Co., 1985.

———. *The Mismeasure of Man*. New York: W. W. Norton & Co., 1981.

Govan, Thomas P. "Banking and the Credit System in Georgia, 1810–1860." *Journal of Southern History* 4 (May 1938): 164–84.

Governor Treutlen Chapter, Daughters of the American Revolution, comp. *History of Peach County, Georgia*. Atlanta: Cherokee Publishing Co., 1972.

Graham, Richard. "Economics or Culture? The Development of the U.S. South and Brazil in the Days of Slavery." In *What Made the South Different?*, edited by Kees Gispen, pp. 97–128. Jackson: University Press of Mississippi, 1990.

Gray, Lewis Cecil. *History of Agriculture in the Southern United States to 1860*. 2 vols. Washington: Carnegie Institution, 1933.

Green, William A. *British Slave Emancipation: The Sugar Colonies and the Great Experiment, 1830–1865*. Oxford: Oxford University Press, 1976.

Greenberg, Kenneth S. *Masters and Statesmen: The Political Culture of American Slavery*. Baltimore: Johns Hopkins University Press, 1985.

Gross, Robert. *The Minutemen and Their World*. New York: Hill & Wang, 1976.

Gutman, Herbert G. *The Black Family in Slavery and Freedom, 1750–1925*. New York: Pantheon, 1976.

Hahn, Steven. "Class and State in Postemancipation Societies: Southern Planters in Comparative Perspective." *American Historical Review* 95 (Feb. 1990): 75–98.

———. "Common Right and Commonwealth: The Stock-Law Struggle and the Roots of Southern Populism." In *Region, Race, and Reconstruction: Essays in Honor of C. Vann Woodward*, edited J. Morgan Kousser and James M. McPherson, pp. 51–88. New York: Oxford University Press, 1982.

———. "Emancipation and the Development of Capitalist Agriculture: The South in Comparative Perspective." In *What Made the South Different?*, edited by Kees Gispen, pp. 71–96. Jackson: University Press of Mississippi, 1990.

———. "Hunting, Fishing, and Foraging: Common Rights and Class Relations in the Postbellum South." *Radical History Review* 26 (1982): 37–64.

———. *The Roots of Southern Populism: Yeoman Farmers and the Transformation of the Georgia Upcountry, 1850–1890*. New York: Oxford University Press, 1983.

Hahn, Steven, and Jonathan Prude, eds. *The Countryside in the Age of Capitalist Transformation: Essays in the Social History of Rural America*. Chapel Hill: University of North Carolina Press, 1985.

Hammond, Matthew B. *The Cotton Industry: An Essay in American Economic History*. New York: Macmillan, 1897.

Harris, J. William. "The Organization of Work on a Yeoman Slaveholder's Farm." *Agricultural History* 64 (Winter 1990): 39–52.

———. *Plain Folk and Gentry in a Slave Society: White Liberty and Black Slavery in Augusta's Hinterlands*. Middleton, Conn.: Wesleyan University Press, 1985.

———. "Plantations and Power: Emancipation on the David Barrow Plantations." In *Toward a New South? Studies in Post–Civil War Southern Communities*, edited by Orville Vernon Burton and Robert C. McMath, Jr., pp. 246–64. Westport, Conn.: Greenwood Press, 1982.

———. "Portrait of a Small Slaveholder: The Journal of Benton Miller." *Georgia Historical Quarterly* 74 (Spring 1990): 1–19.

Heath, Milton Sydney. *Constructive Liberalism: The Role of the State in the Economic Development of Georgia to 1860*. Cambridge: Harvard University Press, 1954.

Henretta, James. "Families and Farms: *Mentalité* in Pre-Industrial America." *William and Mary Quarterly*, 3d ser., 35 (Jan. 1978): 3–32.

———. "The War for Independence and American Economic Development." In *The Economy of Early America: The Revolutionary Period, 1763–1790*, edited by Ronald Hoffman, John H. McCusker, Russell R. Menard, and Peter J. Albert, pp. 45–87. Charlottesville: University Press of Virginia, 1988.

Hickson, Bobbe Smith. *A Land So Dedicated: Houston County, Georgia*. N.p.: Houston County Library Board, 1976.

Higgs, Robert. *Competition and Coercion: Blacks in the American Economy, 1865–1914*. Cambridge: Cambridge University Press, 1977.

———. "Patterns of Farm Rental in the Georgia Cotton Belt." *Journal of Economic History* 34 (June 1974): 468–82.

Higman, B. W. *Slave Population and Economy in Jamaica, 1807–1834*. Cambridge: Cambridge University Press, 1976.

———. *Slave Populations of the British Caribbean, 1807–1834*. Baltimore: Johns Hopkins University Press, 1984.

Hilliard, Sam Bowers. *Atlas of Antebellum Southern Agriculture*. Baton Rouge: Louisiana State University Press, 1984.

———. *Hog Meat and Hoecake: Food Supply in the Old South, 1840–1860*. Carbondale: Southern Illinois University Press, 1972.

Hilton, Rodney, ed. *The Transition from Feudalism to Capitalism*. London: NLB, 1976.

Hindus, Michael S. "Black Justice under White Law: Criminal Prosecutions of Blacks in Antebellum South Carolina." *Journal of American History* 63 (Dec. 1976): 575–99.

———. *Prison and Plantation: Crime, Justice, and Authority in Massachusetts and South Carolina, 1767–1878*. Chapel Hill: University of North Carolina Press, 1980.

Hirshon, Stanley P. *Farewell to the Bloody Shirt: Northern Republicans and the Southern Negro, 1877–1893*. Bloomington: Indiana University Press, 1962.

Hobsbawm, Eric. *The Age of Capital, 1848–1875*. New York: Charles Scribner's Sons, 1975.

———. *The Age of Revolution, 1789–1848*. New York: World Publishing Co., 1962.

———. *Workers: Worlds of Labor*. New York: Pantheon, 1984.

Hoffman, Charles, and Tess Hoffman. "The Limits of Paternalism: Driver-Master Relations on a Bryan County Plantation." *Georgia Historical Quarterly* 68 (Fall 1983): 321–35.

Hoffman, Ronald, Thad W. Tate, and Peter J. Albert, eds. *An Uncivil War: The Southern Backcountry during the American Revolution*. Charlottesville: University Press of Virginia, 1985.

Hollingsworth, R. R. "Education and Reconstruction in Georgia." *Georgia Historical Quarterly* 19 (June 1935): 112–33 and (Sept. 1935): 229–50.

Holt, Thomas C. *Black over White: Negro Political Leadership in South Carolina during Reconstruction*. Urbana: University of Illinois Press, 1977.

———. "'An Empire Over the Mind': Emancipation, Race, and Ideology in the British West Indies and the American South." In *Region, Race, and Reconstruction: Essays in Honor of C. Vann Woodward*, edited by J. Morgan Kousser and James M. McPherson, pp. 283–312. New York: Oxford University Press, 1982.

———. *The Problem of Freedom: Race, Labor, and Politics in Jamaica, 1832–1938*. Baltimore: Johns Hopkins University Press, 1992.

Horsman, Reginald. *Race and Manifest Destiny: The Origins of American Racial Anglo-Saxonism*. Cambridge: Harvard University Press, 1981.

Horwitz, Morton J. *The Transformation of American Law, 1780–1860*. Cambridge: Harvard University Press, 1977.

Huffman, Frank J., Jr. "Old South, New South: Continuity and Change in a Georgia County, 1850–1880." Ph.D. dissertation, Yale University, 1974.

Hume, Richard L. "The Black and Tan Constitutional Conventions of the Ten Former Confederate States: A Study of the Memberships." Ph.D. dissertation, University of Washington, 1969.

———. "Negro Delegates to the State Constitutional Conventions of 1867–69." In *Southern Black Leaders of the Reconstruction Era*, edited by Howard N. Rabinowitz, pp. 129–53. Urbana: University of Illinois Press, 1982.

Hyman, Michael R. "Taxation, Public Policy, and Political Dissent: Yeoman Disaffection in the Post-Reconstruction Lower South." *Journal of Southern History* 55 (Feb. 1989): 49–76.

Innes, Stephen, ed. *Work and Labor in Early America*. Chapel Hill: University of North Carolina Press, 1988.

Inscoe, John C. *Mountain Masters, Slavery, and the Sectional Crisis in Western North Carolina*. Knoxville: University of Tennessee Press, 1989.

Isaac, Rhys. *The Transformation of Virginia, 1740–1790*. Chapel Hill: University of North Carolina Press, 1982.

Jaffee, David. "Peddlers of Progress and the Transformation of the Rural North, 1790–1860." *Journal of American History* 78 (Sept. 1991): 511–35.

Jaynes, Gerald David. *Branches without Roots: Genesis of the Black Working Class in the American South, 1862–1882*. New York: Oxford University Press, 1986.

Jenkins, William Sumner. *Pro-Slavery Thought in the Old South*. Chapel Hill: University of North Carolina Press, 1935.

Jensen, Joan M. *Loosening the Bonds: Mid-Atlantic Farm Women, 1750–1850*. New Haven: Yale University Press, 1986.

Johnson, Michael P. *Toward a Patriarchal Republic: The Secession of Georgia*. Baton Rouge: Louisiana State University Press, 1977.

Johnson, Michael P., and James L. Roark. *Black Masters: A Free Family of Color in the Old South*. New York: W. W. Norton & Co., 1984.

Johnson, Paul. *A Shopkeeper's Millennium: Society and Revivals in Rochester, New York, 1815–1837*. New York: Hill & Wang, 1978.

Johnston, James Hugo. *Race Relations in Virginia and Miscegenation in the South, 1776–1860*. Amherst: University of Massachusetts Press, 1970.

Jones, Jacqueline. *Labor of Love, Labor of Sorrow: Black Women, Work, and the Family from Slavery to the Present*. New York: Basic Books, 1985.

———. *Soldiers of Light and Love: Northern Teachers and Georgia Blacks, 1865–1873*. Chapel Hill: University of North Carolina Press, 1980.

Jordan, Weymouth T. *Hugh Davis and His Alabama Plantation*. University: University of Alabama Press, 1948.

Jordan, Winthrop. *White over Black: American Attitudes toward the Negro, 1550–1812*. Chapel Hill: University of North Carolina Press, 1968.

Joyner, Charles. *Down by the Riverside: A South Carolina Slave Community*. Urbana: University of Illinois Press, 1984.

Kaestle, Carl F. *Pillars of the Republic: Common Schools and American Society, 1780–1860*. New York: Hill & Wang, 1983.

Kerridge, Eric. *The Farmers of Old England*. Totowa: Roman and Littlefield, 1973.

Kilson, Marion D. de B. "Towards Freedom: An Analysis of Slave Revolts in the United States." *Phylon* 25 (Summer 1964): 175–87.

King, J. Crawford, Jr. "The Closing of the Southern Range: An Exploratory Study." *Journal of Southern History* 48 (Feb. 1982): 53–70.

Kiple, Kenneth F., and Virginia Himmelsteib King. *Another Dimension to the Black Diaspora: Diet, Disease, and Racism*. Cambridge: Cambridge University Press, 1981.

Klein, Rachel N. "Frontier Planters and the American Revolution: The South Carolina Backcountry, 1775–1782." In *An Uncivil War: The Southern Backcountry during the American Revolution*, edited by Ronald Hoffman, Thad W. Tate, and Peter J. Albert, pp. 37–69. Charlottesville: University Press of Virginia, 1985.

———. "Ordering the Back Country: The South Carolina Regulation." *William and Mary Quarterly*, 3d ser., 38 (Oct. 1981): 661–80.

———. *Unification of a Slave State: The Rise of the Planter Class in the South Carolina Backcountry, 1760–1808*. Chapel Hill: University of North Carolina Press, 1990.

Knight, Franklin W. *Slave Society in Cuba during the Nineteenth Century*. Madison: University of Wisconsin Press, 1970.

Kolchin, Peter. *First Freedom: The Responses of Alabama's Blacks to Emancipation and Reconstruction*. Westport, Conn.: Greenwood Press, 1972.

———. *Unfree Labor: American Slavery and Russian Serfdom*. Cambridge: Harvard University Press, 1987.

Kousser, J. Morgan. *The Shaping of Southern Politics: Suffrage Restriction and the Establishment of the One-Party South, 1880–1910*. New Haven: Yale University Press, 1974.

Kousser, J. Morgan, and James M. McPherson, eds. *Region, Race, and Reconstruction: Essays in Honor of C. Vann Woodward*. New York: Oxford University Press, 1982.

Kulik, Gary. "Dams, Fish, and Farmers: Defense of Public Rights in Eighteenth-Century Rhode Island." In *The Countryside in the Age of Capitalist Transformation: Essays in the Social History of Rural America*, edited by Steven Hahn and Jonathan Prude, pp. 25–50. Chapel Hill: University of North Carolina Press, 1985.

Kulikoff, Allan. *Tobacco and Slaves: The Development of Southern Cultures in the Chesapeake, 1680–1800*. Chapel Hill: University of North Carolina Press, 1986.

———. "The Transition to Capitalism in Rural America." *William and Mary Quarterly*, 3d ser., 46 (Jan. 1989): 120–44.

———. "Uprooted Peoples: Black Migrants in the Age of the American Revolution, 1790–1820." In *Slavery and Freedom in the Age of the American Revolution*, edited by Ira Berlin and Ronald Hoffman, pp. 143–71. Charlottesville: University Press of Virginia, 1983.

Laurie, Bruce. *Artisans into Workers: Labor in Nineteenth-Century America*. New York: Noonday Press, 1989.

Lebsock, Suzanne. *The Free Women of Petersburg: Status and Culture in a Southern Town, 1784–1860*. New York: W. W. Norton & Co., 1984.

Lee, Jean Butenhoff. "The Problem of Slave Community in the Eighteenth-Century Chesapeake." *William and Mary Quarterly*, 3d ser., 43 (July 1986): 333–61.

Lemon, James T. *The Best Poor Man's Country: A Geographical Study of Early Southeastern Pennsylvania*. Baltimore: Johns Hopkins University Press, 1972.

Levine, Lawrence. *Black Culture and Black Consciousness: Afro-American Folk Thought from Slavery to Freedom*. New York: Oxford University Press, 1977.

Lewis, Ronald L. *Coal, Iron, and Slaves: Industrial Slavery in Maryland and Virginia, 1715–1865*. Westport, Conn.: Greenwood Press, 1979.

Lichtenstein, Alex. " 'That Disposition to Theft, With Which They Have Been Branded': Moral Economy, Slave Management, and the Law." *Journal of Social History* 21 (Spring 1988): 413–40.

Linden, Fabian. "Economic Democracy in the Slave South: An Appraisal of Some Recent Views." *Journal of Negro History* 31 (Apr. 1946): 140–89.

Litwack, Leon. *Been in the Storm So Long: The Aftermath of Slavery*. New York: Alfred A. Knopf, 1979.

Lonn, Ella. *Foreigners in the Confederacy*. Chapel Hill: University of North Carolina Press, 1940.

Luraghi, Raimondo. *The Rise and Fall of the Planter Class*. New York, New Viewpoints, 1978.

Lynd, Staughton. "The Genesis of the Idea of a Community Right to Industrial Property in Youngstown and Pittsburgh, 1977–1987." *Journal of American History* 74 (Dec. 1987): 926–58.

McDonald, Forrest, and Grady McWhiney. "The Antebellum Southern Herdsman: A Reinterpretation." *Journal of Southern History* 41 (May 1975): 147–66.

———. "The South from Self-Sufficiency to Peonage: An Interpretation." *American Historical Review* 85 (Dec. 1980): 1095–118.

McDonnell, Lawrence D. "Money Knows No Master: Market Relations and the American Slave Community." In *Developing Dixie: Modernization in a Traditional Society*, edited by Winfred B. Moore, Jr., Joseph F. Tripp, and Lyon G. Tyler, Jr., pp. 31–44. Westport, Conn.: Greenwood Press, 1988.

McFeely, William S. *Yankee Stepfather: General O. O. Howard and the Freedmen*. New Haven: Yale University Press, 1968.

McPherson, James M. "Was West Indian Emancipation a Success?: The Abolitionist Argument during the American Civil War." *Caribbean Studies* 4 (July 1964): 28–34.

Maddox, Jack P., Jr. "Virginia: The Persistence of Centrist Hegemony." In *Reconstruction and Redemption in the South*, edited by Otto H. Olsen, pp. 113–55. Baton Rouge: Louisiana State University Press, 1980.

Magdol, Edward. "Local Black Leaders in the South, 1867–1875: An Essay toward the Reconstruction of Reconstruction History." *Societas—A Review of Social History* 4 (Spring 1974): 81–110.

———. *A Right to the Land: Essays on the Freedmen's Community*. Westport, Conn.: Greenwood Press, 1977.

Mandle, Jay R. *The Roots of Black Poverty: The Southern Plantation Economy after the Civil War*. Durham: Duke University Press, 1978.

Mangum, Charles S., Jr. *The Legal Status of the Tenant Farmer in the Southeast*. Chapel Hill: University of North Carolina Press, 1952.

Mann, Susan Archer. *Agrarian Capitalism in Theory and Practice*. Chapel Hill: University of North Carolina Press, 1990.

———. "Slavery, Sharecropping, and Sexual Inequality." *Signs* 14 (1989): 774–98.

Marx, Karl. *Capital*. 3 vols. New York: International Publishers, 1967.

Mathews, Donald G. *Religion in the Old South*. Chicago: University of Chicago Press, 1977.

———. *Slavery and Methodism: A Chapter in American Morality, 1780–1845*. Princeton: Princeton University Press, 1965.

Matthews, John M. "Jefferson Franklin Long: The Public Career of Georgia's First Black Congressman." *Phylon* 42 (June 1981): 145–56.

———. "The Negro in Georgia Politics, 1865–1880." Master's thesis, Duke University, 1967.

———. "Negro Republicans in the Reconstruction of Georgia." *Georgia Historical Quarterly* 60 (Summer 1976): 145–64.

Medick, Hans. "The Proto-industrial Family Economy: The Structural Function of Household and Family during the Transition from Peasant Society to Industrial Capitalism." *Social History* 3 (1976): 291–315.

Merrill, Michael. "Cash Is Good to Eat: Self-Sufficiency and Exchange in the Rural Economy of the United States." *Radical History Review* 4 (Winter 1977): 42–71.

Miller, Randall M. "The Enemy Within: Some Effects of Foreign Immigration on Antebellum Southern Cities." *Southern Studies* 24 (1985): 30–53.

———. "The Failure of the Colony of Georgia under the Trustees." *Georgia Historical Quarterly* 53 (Mar. 1969): 1–17.

Mintz, Sidney. *Caribbean Transformations*. Chicago: Aldine Publishing Co., 1974.

———. "The Question of Caribbean Peasantries: A Comment." *Caribbean Studies* 1 (Oct. 1961): 31–34.

———. "Slavery and the Rise of Peasantries." *Historical Reflections/Reflections Historique* 6 (Summer 1980): 213–42.

———. "Was the Plantation Slave a Proletarian?" *Review* 2 (Summer 1978): 81–98.

Mintz, Sidney, and Richard Price. *An Anthropological Approach to the Afro-American Past: A Caribbean Perspective*. Philadelphia: Institute for the Study of Human Issues, 1976.

Mohr, Clarence L. "Before Sherman: Georgia Blacks and the Union War Effort, 1861–1864." *Journal of Southern History* 45 (Aug. 1979): 331–52.

———. *On the Threshold of Freedom: Masters and Slaves in Civil War Georgia*. Athens: University of Georgia Press, 1986.

———. "Slavery in Oglethorpe County, Georgia, 1773–1865." *Phylon* 33 (Spring 1972): 4–21.

Montgomery, David. *Beyond Equality: Labor and the Radical Republicans, 1862–1872.* New York: Alfred A. Knopf, 1967.

———. *The Fall of the House of Labor: The Workplace, the State, and American Labor Activism, 1865–1925.* Cambridge: Cambridge University Press, 1987.

Moore, Albert Burton. *Conscription and Conflict in the Confederacy.* New York: Macmillan, 1924.

Moore, Barrington, Jr. *Social Origins of Dictatorship and Democracy: Lord and Peasant in the Making of the Modern World.* Boston: Beacon Press, 1966.

Moore, John Hebron. *The Emergence of the Cotton Kingdom in the Old Southwest: Mississippi, 1770–1860.* Baton Rouge: Louisiana State University Press, 1988.

Moreno Fraginals, Manuel, Frank Moya Pons, and Stanley L. Engerman, eds. *Between Slavery and Free Labor: The Spanish-Speaking Caribbean in the Nineteenth Century.* Baltimore: Johns Hopkins University Press, 1985.

Morgan, Edmund S. *American Slavery, American Freedom: The Ordeal of Colonial Virginia.* New York: W. W. Norton & Co., 1975.

Morgan, Philip D. "Black Society in the Lowcountry, 1760–1810." In *Slavery and Freedom in the Age of the American Revolution,* edited by Ira Berlin and Ronald Hoffman, pp. 83–141. Charlottesville: University Press of Virginia, 1983.

———. "Work and Culture: The Task System and the World of Lowcountry Blacks, 1700–1880." *William and Mary Quarterly,* 3d ser., 39 (Oct. 1982): 563–99.

Mullin, Gerald M. *Flight and Rebellion: Slave Resistance in Eighteenth-Century Virginia.* London: Oxford University Press, 1972.

Murdock, George P., and Caterina Provost. "Factors in the Division of Labor by Sex: A Cross-Cultural Analysis." *Ethnology* 12 (Apr. 1973): 203–25.

Murray, Paul. *The Whig Party in Georgia, 1825–1853.* Chapel Hill: University of North Carolina Press, 1948.

Nash, A. E. Keir. "Fairness and Formalism in the Trials of Blacks in the State Supreme Courts of the Old South." *Virginia Law Review* 56 (1970): 64–100.

———. "A More Equitable Past? Southern Supreme Courts and the Protection of the Antebellum Negro." *North Carolina Law Review* 48 (Feb. 1970): 197–242.

———. "Reason of Slavery: Understanding the Judicial Role in the Peculiar Institution." *Vanderbilt Law Review* 32 (1979): 8–218.

Nathans, Elizabeth Studley. *Losing the Peace: Georgia Republicans and Reconstruction, 1865–1871.* Baton Rouge: Louisiana State University Press, 1968.

Nieman, Donald G. *To Set the Law in Motion: The Freedmen's Bureau and the Legal Rights of Blacks, 1865–1868.* Millwood, N.Y.: KTO Press, 1979.

North, Douglass C. *The Economic Growth of the United States, 1790–1860.* Englewood Cliffs, N.J.: Prentice-Hall, 1961.

Northen, William J., ed. *Men of Mark in Georgia.* 6 vols. Atlanta: A. B. Caldwell, 1907–12.

Novak, Daniel A. *The Wheel of Servitude: Black Forced Labor after Slavery.* Lexington: University of Kentucky Press, 1978.

Oakes, James. *The Ruling Race: A History of American Slaveholders*. New York: Alfred A. Knopf, 1982.

————. *Slavery and Freedom: An Interpretation of the Old South*. New York: Alfred A. Knopf, 1990.

O'Brien, John T. "Factory, Church, and Community: Blacks in Antebellum Richmond." *Journal of Southern History* 44 (Nov. 1978): 509–36.

Olsen, Otto H. "Historians and the Extent of Slave Ownership in the Southern United States." *Civil War History* 18 (June 1972): 101–16.

————, ed. *Reconstruction and Redemption in the South*. Baton Rouge: Louisiana State University Press, 1980.

Orser, Charles E., Jr. *The Material Basis of the Postbellum Tenant Plantation: Historical Archeology in the South Carolina Piedmont*. Athens: University of Georgia Press, 1988.

Osthaus, Carl R. *Freedmen, Philanthropy, and Fraud: A History of the Freedman's Savings Bank*. Urbana: University of Illinois Press, 1976.

Oubre, Claude F. *Forty Acres and a Mule: The Freedmen's Bureau and Black Landownership*. Baton Rouge: Louisiana State University Press, 1978.

Owens, James L. "The Negro in Georgia during Reconstruction." Ph.D. dissertation, University of Georgia, 1972.

Owens, Leslie Howard. *This Species of Property: Slave Life and Culture in the Old South*. New York: Oxford University Press, 1976.

Owsley, Frank L. *Plain Folk of the Old South*. Baton Rouge: Louisiana State University Press, 1949.

Paige, Jeffery M. *Agrarian Revolution: Social Movements and Export Agriculture in the Underdeveloped World*. New York: Academic Press, 1975.

Parks, Joseph H. *Joseph E. Brown of Georgia*. Baton Rouge: Louisiana State University Press, 1977.

Patterson, Orlando. *Slavery and Social Death: A Comparative Study*. Cambridge: Harvard University Press, 1982.

Perkins, Elizabeth A. "The Consumer Frontier: Household Consumption in Early Kentucky." *Journal of American History* 78 (Sept. 1991): 486–510.

Phillips, Ulrich Bonnell. *American Negro Slavery: A Survey of the Supply, Employment, and Control of Negro Labor as Determined by the Plantation Regime*. 1918. Reprint. Baton Rouge: Louisiana State University Press, 1966.

————. *Georgia and State Rights: A Study of the Political History of Georgia from the Revolution to the Civil War, with Particular Regard to Federal Relations*. Washington: American Historical Association, 1902.

————. *A History of Transportation in the Eastern Cotton Belt to 1860*. 1908. Reprint. New York: Octo Press, 1968.

————. *Life and Labor in the Old South*. Boston: Little, Brown, 1929.

————. *The Life of Robert Toombs*. New York, 1913.

————. "The Origin and Growth of the Southern Black Belts." *American Historical Review* 11 (July 1906): 798–816.

Ponton, Mungo Melanchthon. *Life and Times of Henry M. Turner*. Atlanta: A. B. Caldwell Publishing Co., 1917.

Pope, Christie Farnham. "Southern Homesteads for Negroes." *Agricultural History* 44 (Apr. 1970): 201–12.

Powdermaker, Hortense. *After Freedom: A Cultural Study in the Deep South.* 1939. Reprint. New York: Atheneum, 1968.

Powell, Lawrence. *New Masters: Northern Planters during the Civil War and Reconstruction.* New Haven: Yale University Press, 1980.

——. "The Politics of Livelihood: Carpetbaggers in the Deep South." In *Region, Race, and Reconstruction: Essays in Honor of C. Vann Woodward*, edited by J. Morgan Kousser and James M. McPherson, pp. 315–47. New York: Oxford University Press, 1982.

——. "The Prussians Are Coming." *Georgia Historical Quarterly* 71 (Winter 1987): 638–67.

Proctor, William G., Jr. "Slavery in Southwest Georgia." *Georgia Historical Quarterly* 49 (Mar. 1965): 1–23.

Prude, Jonathan. *The Coming of Industrial Order: Town and Factory Life in Rural Massachusetts, 1810–1860.* Cambridge: Cambridge University Press, 1983.

——. "To Look Upon the 'Lower Sort': Runaway Ads and the Appearance of Unfree Laborers in America, 1750–1800." *Journal of American History* 78 (June 1991): 124–59.

Pruitt, Bettye Hobbs. "Self-Sufficiency and the Agricultural Economy of Eighteenth-Century Massachusetts." *William and Mary Quarterly*, 3d ser., 41 (July 1984): 333–64.

Quarles, Benjamin. *Black Abolitionists.* New York: Oxford University Press, 1969.

Rabinowitz, Howard N. "From Exclusion to Segregation: Southern Race Relations, 1865–1890." *Journal of American History* 63 (Sept. 1976): 325–50.

——. *Race Relations in the Urban South, 1865–1890.* New York: Oxford University Press, 1978.

Rable, George C. *But There Was No Peace: The Role of Violence in the Politics of Reconstruction.* Athens: University of Georgia Press, 1984.

Raboteau, Albert. *Slave Religion: The "Invisible Institution" in the Antebellum South.* New York: Oxford University Press, 1978.

Rachleff, Peter J. *Black Labor in the South: Richmond, Virginia, 1865–1890.* Philadelphia: Temple University Press, 1984.

Range, Willard. *A Century of Georgia Agriculture, 1850–1950.* Athens: University of Georgia Press, 1954.

Ransom, Roger L., and Richard Sutch. *One Kind of Freedom: The Economic Consequences of Emancipation.* Cambridge: Cambridge University Press, 1977.

Raper, Arthur F. *Preface to Peasantry: A Tale of Two Black Belt Counties.* Chapel Hill: University of North Carolina Press, 1936.

——. *Tenants of the Almighty.* New York: Alfred A. Knopf, 1943.

Rawick, George P. *From Sundown to Sunup: The Making of the Black Community.* Westport, Conn.: Greenwood Press, 1972.

Rediker, Marcus. *Between the Devil and the Deep Blue Sea: Merchant Seamen, Pirates, and the Anglo-American Maritime World, 1700–1750.* Cambridge: Cambridge University Press, 1987.

Redkey, Edwin S. *Black Exodus: Black Nationalist and Back-to-Africa Movements, 1890–1910*. New Haven: Yale University Press, 1969.

———, ed. *Respect Black!: The Writings and Speeches of Henry McNeal Turner*. New York: Arno Press, 1971.

Reid, Joseph D., Jr. "Sharecropping as an Understandable Market Response: The Post-Bellum South." *Journal of Economic History* 33 (Mar. 1973): 106–30.

———. "Sharecropping in History and Theory." *Agricultural History* 49 (Apr. 1975): 426–40.

———. "White Land, Black Labor, and Agricultural Stagnation: The Causes and Effects of Sharecropping in the Postbellum South." *Explorations in Economic History* 16 (Jan. 1979): 31–55.

Reidy, Joseph P. "Aaron A. Bradley: Voice of Black Labor in the Georgia Lowcountry." In *Southern Black Leaders of the Reconstruction Era*, edited by Howard N. Rabinowitz, pp. 281–308. Urbana: University of Illinois Press, 1982.

———. "Slavery, Emancipation, and the Capitalist Transformation of Southern Agriculture, 1850–1910." In *Agriculture and National Development: Views on the Nineteenth Century*, edited by Lou Ferleger, pp. 229–64. Ames: Iowa State University Press, 1990.

Reis, Jaime. "From *Banguê* to *Usina*: Social Aspects of Growth and Modernization in the Sugar Industry of Pernambuco, Brazil, 1850–1920." In *Land and Labour in Latin America: Essays on the Development of Agrarian Capitalism in the Nineteenth and Twentieth Centuries*, edited by Kenneth Duncan and Ian Rutledge, pp. 369–96. Cambridge: Cambridge University Press, 1977.

Richardson, David, ed. *Abolition and Its Aftermath: The Historical Context, 1790–1916*. London: F. Cass, 1985.

Roark, James L. *Masters without Slaves: Southern Planters in the Civil War and Reconstruction*. New York: W. W. Norton & Co., 1977.

Robinson, Armstead L. "Beyond the Realm of Social Consensus: New Meanings of Reconstruction for American History." *Journal of American History* 68 (Sept. 1981): 276–97.

———. "Bitter Fruits of Bondage: The Demise of Slavery and the Collapse of the Confederacy, 1861–1865." Forthcoming.

———. "Plans Dat Comed from God: Institution Building and the Emergence of Black Leadership in Reconstruction Memphis." In *Toward a New South? Studies in Post–Civil War Southern Communities*, edited by Orville Vernon Burton and Robert C. McMath, Jr., pp. 71–102. Westport, Conn.: Greenwood Press, 1982.

———. " 'Worser dan Jeff Davis': The Coming of Free Labor during the Civil War, 1861–1865." In *Essays on the Postbellum Southern Economy*, edited by Thavolia Glymph and John H. Kushma, pp. 11–47. College Station: Texas A&M University Press, 1985.

Rodney, Walter. *History of the Guyanese Working People*. Baltimore: Johns Hopkins University Press, 1983.

Rose, Willie Lee. *Rehearsal for Reconstruction: The Port Royal Experiment*. Indianapolis: Bobbs-Merrill, 1964.

———. *Slavery and Freedom*. Expanded ed., edited by William W. Freehling. Oxford: Oxford University Press, 1982.

Rosengarten, Theodore. *All God's Dangers: The Life of Nate Shaw*. New York: Alfred A. Knopf, 1974.

Rothenberg, Winifred B. "The Market and Massachusetts Farmers, 1750–1855." *Journal of Economic History* 41 (June 1981): 283–314.

Rothman, David J. *The Discovery of the Asylum: Social Order and Disorder in the New Republic*. Rev. ed. Boston: Little, Brown & Co., 1990.

Rothstein, Morton. "The Antebellum South as a Dual Economy: A Tentative Hypothesis." *Agricultural History* 41 (Oct. 1967): 373–82.

Russell, James Michael. *Atlanta, 1847–1890: City Building in the Old South and the New*. Baton Rouge: Louisiana State University Press, 1988.

Rutman, Darrett B., and Anita H. Rutman. *A Place in Time: Middlesex County, Virginia, 1650–1750*. New York: W. W. Norton & Co., 1984.

Ryan, Mary P. *Cradle of the Middle Class: The Family in Oneida County, New York, 1790–1865*. Cambridge: Cambridge University Press, 1981.

Saville, Julie. *The Work of Reconstruction*. Cambridge: Cambridge University Press, forthcoming.

Savitt, Todd L. *Medicine and Slavery: The Diseases and Health Care of Slaves in Antebellum Virginia*. Urbana: University of Illinois Press, 1978.

Scarborough, William K. *The Overseer: Plantation Management in the Old South*. Baton Rouge: Louisiana State University Press, 1966.

Schob, David E. *Hired Hands and Plowboys: Farm Labor in the Midwest, 1815–60*. Urbana: University of Illinois Press: 1975.

Schwarz, Philip. *Twice Condemned: Slaves and Criminal Laws of Virginia, 1705–1865*. Baton Rouge: Louisiana State University Press, 1988.

Scott, Anne Firor. *The Southern Lady from Pedestal to Politics*. Chicago: University of Chicago Press, 1970.

Scott, James C. *Domination and the Arts of Resistance: Hidden Transcripts*. New Haven: Yale University Press, 1990.

———. "Everyday Forms of Peasant Resistance." *Journal of Peasant Studies* 13 (Jan. 1986): 5–35.

———. *The Moral Economy of the Peasant: Rebellion and Subsistence in Southeast Asia*. New Haven: Yale University Press, 1976.

———. *Weapons of the Weak: Everyday Forms of Peasant Resistance*. New Haven: Yale University Press, 1985.

Scott, Rebecca. *Slave Emancipation in Cuba: The Transition to Free Labor, 1860–1899*. Princeton: Princeton University Press, 1985.

Seagrave, Charles E. *The Southern Negro Agricultural Worker: 1850–1870*. New York: Arno Press, 1975.

Sefton, James E. *The United States Army and Reconstruction, 1865–1877*. Baton Rouge: Louisiana State University Press, 1967.

Shadgett, Olive Hall. *The Republican Party in Georgia: From Reconstruction through 1900*. Athens: University of Georgia Press, 1964.

Sharkey, Robert P. *Money, Class, and Party: An Economic Study of Civil War and Reconstruction*. Baltimore: Johns Hopkins University Press, 1959.

Shaw, Barton C. *The Wool Hat Boys: Georgia's Populist Party*. Baton Rouge: Louisiana State University Press, 1984.

Shlomowitz, Ralph. "'Bound' or 'Free'? Black Labor in Cotton and Sugarcane Farming, 1865–1880." *Journal of Southern History* 50 (Nov. 1984): 569–96.

———. "The Origins of Southern Sharecropping." *Agricultural History* 53 (July 1979): 557–75.

———. "The Squad System on Postbellum Cotton Plantations." In *Toward a New South? Studies in Post–Civil War Southern Communities*, edited by Orville Vernon Burton and Robert C. McMath, Jr., pp. 265–80. Westport, Conn.: Greenwood Press, 1982.

Shore, Laurence. *Southern Capitalists: The Ideological Leadership of an Elite, 1832–1885*. Chapel Hill: University of North Carolina Press, 1986.

Siegel, Fred. "Artisans and Immigrants in the Politics of Late Antebellum Georgia." *Civil War History* 27 (Sept. 1981): 221–30.

Slaughter, Thomas P. *The Whiskey Rebellion: Frontier Epilogue to the American Revolution*. New York: Oxford University Press, 1986.

Smith, Julia Floyd. *Slavery and Rice Culture in Lowcountry Georgia, 1750–1860*. Knoxville: University of Tennessee Press, 1985.

Smith, S. D. *The Negro in Congress, 1870–1901*. Chapel Hill: University of North Carolina Press, 1940.

Snowden, Frank M., Jr. *Before Color Prejudice: The Ancient View of Blacks*. Cambridge: Harvard University Press, 1983.

Sobel, Mechal. *Trabelin' On: The Slave Journey to an Afro-Baptist Faith*. Westport, Conn.: Greenwood Press, 1979.

———. *The World They Made Together: Black and White Values in Eighteenth-Century Virginia*. Princeton: Princeton University Press, 1987.

Stampp, Kenneth M. *The Peculiar Institution: Slavery in the Antebellum South*. New York: Alfred A. Knopf, 1956.

Stansell, Christine. *City of Women: Sex and Class in New York, 1789–1860*. New York: Alfred A. Knopf, 1986.

Starobin, Robert S. *Industrial Slavery in the Old South*. New York: Oxford University Press, 1970.

Sweat, Edward F. "The Free Negro in Antebellum Georgia." Ph.D. dissertation, Indiana University, 1957.

Swint, Henry L. *The Northern Teacher in the South, 1862–1870*. Nashville: Vanderbilt University Press, 1941.

Sydnor, Charles S. *Gentlemen Freeholders*. Chapel Hill: University of North Carolina Press, 1952.

Tadman, Michael. *Speculators and Slaves: Masters, Traders, and Slaves in the Old South*. Madison: University of Wisconsin Press, 1989.

Takaki, Ronald T. *A Pro-Slavery Crusade: The Agitation to Reopen the African Slave Trade*. New York: Free Press, 1971.

Tannenbaum, Frank. *Slave and Citizen: The Negro in the Americas*. New York: Alfred A. Knopf, 1946.

Taylor, Alrutheus A. *The Negro in South Carolina during the Reconstruction*. Washington: Associated Publishers, 1924.

————. *The Negro in Tennessee, 1865–1880*. Washington, Associated Publishers, 1941.

————. *The Negro in the Reconstruction of Virginia*. Washington: Associated Publishers, 1926.

Taylor, George Rogers. *The Transportation Revolution, 1815–1860*. New York: Rinehart & Co., 1951.

Tebeau, C. W. "Visitors' Views of Georgia Politics and Life, 1865–1880." *Georgia Historical Quarterly* 26 (Mar. 1942): 1–15.

Thomas, Emory M. *The Confederacy as a Revolutionary Experience*. Englewood Cliffs, N.J.: Prentice-Hall, 1971.

Thompson, C. Mildred. "The Freedmen's Bureau in Georgia, 1865–6: An Instrument of Reconstruction." *Georgia Historical Quarterly* 5 (Mar. 1921): 40–49.

————. *Reconstruction in Georgia: Economic, Political, Social, 1865–1872*. 1915. Reprint. Savannah: Beehive Press, 1973.

Thompson, E. P. *The Making of the English Working Class*. New York: Pantheon, 1963.

————. *Whigs and Hunters: The Origin of the Black Act*. New York: Pantheon, 1975.

Thornton, J. Mills, III. *Politics and Power in a Slave Society: Alabama, 1800–1860*. Baton Rouge: Louisiana State University Press, 1978.

Tillson, Albert H., Jr. "The Southern Backcountry: A Survey of Current Research." *Virginia Magazine of History and Biography* 98 (July 1990): 387–422.

Tise, Larry E. *Proslavery: A History of the Defense of Slavery in America*. Athens: University of Georgia Press, 1987.

Tomich, Dale W. *Slavery in the Circuit of Sugar: Martinique and the World Economy, 1830–1848*. Baltimore: Johns Hopkins University Press, 1990.

Toplin, Robert Brent. *The Abolition of Slavery in Brazil*. New York: Athenuem, 1972.

Tushnet, Mark V. *The American Law of Slavery, 1810–1860: Considerations of Humanity and Interest*. Princeton: Princeton University Press, 1981.

Vandiver, Frank E. *Plowshares into Swords: Josiah Gorgas and Confederate Ordnance*. Austin: University of Texas Press, 1952.

Ver Steeg, Clarence L. *Origins of a Southern Mosaic: Studies of Early South Carolina and Georgia*. Athens: University of Georgia Press, 1975.

Wade, Richard C. *Slavery in the Cities: The South, 1820–1860*. London: Oxford University Press, 1964.

Walker, Clarence E. *A Rock in a Weary Land: The African Methodist Episcopal Church during the Civil War and Reconstruction*. Baton Rouge: Louisiana State University Press, 1982.

Wallace, Anthony F. C. *Rockdale: The Growth of an American Village in the Early Industrial Revolution*. New York: Alfred A. Knopf, 1978.

Wallenstein, Peter. *From Slave South to New South: Public Policy in Nineteenth-Century Georgia*. Chapel Hill: University of North Carolina Press, 1987.

Wallerstein, Immanuel. "American Slavery and the Capitalist World-Economy." *American Journal of Sociology* 81 (Mar. 1976): 1199–213.

————. *The Modern World-System III: The Second Great Expansion of the Capitalist World-Economy, 1730–1840s*. San Diego: Academic Press, 1989.

Watson, Harry L. "Conflict and Collaboration: Yeomen, Slaveholders, and Politics in the Antebellum South." *Social History* 10 (Oct. 1985): 273–98.

Wax, Darold D. "Georgia and the Negro before the American Revolution." *Georgia Historical Quarterly* 51 (Mar. 1967): 63–77.

Wayne, Michael. "An Old South Morality Play: Reconsidering the Social Underpinnings of Proslavery Ideology." *Journal of American History* 77 (Dec. 1990): 838–63.

———. *The Reshaping of Plantation Society: The Natchez District, 1860–1880.* Baton Rouge: Louisiana State University Press, 1983.

Weaver, Herbert. *Mississippi Farmers, 1850–1860.* Nashville: Vanderbilt University Press, 1945.

Webber, Thomas L. *Deep Like the Rivers: Education in the Slave Quarter Community, 1831–1865.* New York: W. W. Norton & Co., 1978.

Weiman, David F. "The Economic Emancipation of the Non-Slaveholding Class: Upcountry Farmers in the Georgia Cotton Economy." *Journal of Economic History* 45 (Mar. 1985): 71–93.

———. "Farmers and the Market in Antebellum America: A View from the Georgia Upcountry." *Journal of Economic History* 47 (Sept. 1987): 627–47.

White, Deborah Gray. *Ar'n't I a Woman: Female Slaves in the Plantation South.* New York: Oxford University Press, 1985.

Wiener, Jonathan M. "Class Structure and Economic Development in the American South, 1865–1955." *American Historical Review* 84 (Oct. 1979): 970–92.

———. "Planter-Merchant Conflict in Reconstruction Alabama." *Past and Present* 68 (Aug. 1975): 73–94.

———. "Planter Persistence and Social Change: Alabama, 1850–1870." *Journal of Interdisciplinary History* 7 (Autumn 1976): 235–60.

———. *Social Origins of the New South: Alabama, 1860–1880.* Baton Rouge: Louisiana State University Press, 1978.

Wilentz, Sean. *Chants Democratic: New York City and the Rise of the American Working Class, 1788–1850.* New York: Oxford University Press, 1984.

Williams, Carolyn White. *History of Jones County, Georgia: For One Hundred Years, Specifically 1807–1907.* Macon, Ga.: J. W. Burke Co., 1957.

Williams, Jack K. "Georgians as Seen by Ante-Bellum English Travelers." *Georgia Historical Quarterly* 32 (Sept. 1948): 158–74.

Williamson, Joel. *After Slavery: The Negro in South Carolina during Reconstruction, 1861–1877.* Chapel Hill: University of North Carolina Press, 1965.

Wilson, Theodore Brantner. *The Black Codes of the South.* University: University of Alabama Press, 1965.

Winters, Donald L. *Farmers without Farms: Agricultural Tenancy in Nineteenth-Century Iowa.* Westport, Conn.: Greenwood Press, 1978.

Wish, Harvey. "American Slave Insurrections before 1861." *Journal of Negro History* 22 (July 1937): 299–320.

Wolf, Eric. *Europe and the People without History.* Berkeley: University of California Press, 1982.

Wood, Betty. *Slavery in Colonial Georgia, 1730–1775.* Athens: University of Georgia Press, 1984.

Wood, Forrest G. *The Arrogance of Faith: Christianity and Race in America from the Colonial Era to the Twentieth Century*. New York: Alfred A. Knopf, 1990.

————. *Black Scare: The Racist Response to Emancipation and Reconstruction*. Berkeley: University of California Press, 1968.

Wood, Peter H. *Black Majority: Negroes in Colonial South Carolina from 1670 through the Stono Rebellion*. New York: Alfred A. Knopf, 1974.

Woodman, Harold D. "Economic Reconstruction and the Rise of the New South, 1865–1900." In *Interpreting Southern History: Historiographical Essays in Honor of Sanford W. Higginbotham*, edited by John B. Boles and Evelyn Thomas Nolan, pp. 254–307. Baton Rouge: Louisiana State University Press, 1987.

————. *King Cotton and His Retainers: Financing and Marketing the Cotton Crop of the South, 1800–1925*. Lexington: University of Kentucky Press, 1968.

————. "Post–Civil War Southern Agriculture and the Law." *Agricultural History* 53 (Jan. 1979): 319–37.

————. "The Reconstruction of the Cotton Plantation in the New South." In *Essays on the Postbellum Southern Economy*, edited by Thavolia Glymph and John H. Kushma, pp. 95–119. College Station: Texas A&M University Press, 1985.

————. "Sequel to Slavery: The New History Views the Postbellum South." *Journal of Southern History* 43 (Nov. 1977): 523–54.

Woodward, C. Vann. "Emancipations and Reconstructions: A Comparative Study." In *The Future of the Past*, pp. 145–64. New York: Oxford University Press, 1989.

————. *The Origins of the New South, 1877–1913*. Baton Rouge: Louisiana State University Press, 1951.

Woolfolk, George Ruble. *The Cotton Regency: Northern Merchants and Reconstruction, 1865–1880*. New York: Bookman Associates, 1958.

Wooster, Ralph A. *The People in Power: Courthouse and Statehouse in the Lower South, 1850–1860*. Knoxville: University of Tennessee Press, 1969.

Wright, Gavin. *Old South, New South: Revolutions in the Southern Economy since the Civil War*. New York: Basic Books, 1986.

————. *The Political Economy of the Cotton South: Households, Markets, and Wealth in the Nineteenth Century*. New York: W. W. Norton & Co., 1978.

Wynne, Lewis Nichols. *The Continuity of Cotton: Planter Politics in Georgia, 1865–1892*. Macon, Ga.: Mercer University Press, 1986.

Young, Ida, Julius Gholson, and Clara Nell Hargrove. *History of Macon, Georgia*. Macon: Lynn, Marshall & Brooks, 1950.

Zilversmit, Arthur. *The First Emancipation: The Abolition of Slavery in the North*. Chicago: University of Chicago Press, 1967.

INDEX

. . . .

Poll taxes. *See* Taxes: poll
Pope, John, 185, 191, 197, 305 (n. 68)
Populism, 240, 248
Powers (Irish thief), 105
Presbyterian church: in Macon, 77, 167;
    freedpeople desire separate congrega-
    tions, 168; Hopewell Presbytery, 168
Primus, Isaac L., 169, 172, 204–5, 297
    (n. 36)
Proslavery ideology, 44, 53–56, 67, 96,
    245
Provost marshal (U.S. Army), 144
"Prussian Road," 233

Quarters. *See* Slave quarters

Railroads, 49, 51–52, 85, 92, 192; facili-
    tate escape of slaves, 1, 103; hire slaves,
    103; hire freedmen, 144
Reconstruction, Congressional, 9, 11–12,
    165, 215, 241; and freedpeople's desire
    for land, 143; and African emigration-
    ism, 184; and Georgia politics, 186–214
    passim
Reconstruction, Presidential, 9, 11; proc-
    lamation of, 162; and Georgia politics,
    162–65
Reconstruction, third, of Georgia, 187,
    209
Reconstruction Acts (1867), 4, 186, 189
Relief: poor, 96–98, 144–45, 165, 288
    (n. 36); debtor, 164, 189; Freedmen's
    Bureau and, 165
Religion: slaves, 26, 28, 29, 66–67, 77;
    camp meetings, 26, 28, 47, 66–67, 220;
    church groups, 34; antebellum planters,
    34, 47; church disciplinary boards, 77,
    167; church buildings, 77–78, 168–69,
    170, 171; freedpeople, 166–70, 171–72,
    178, 179; ministers, 168–213 passim,
    297 (n. 36), 299–300 (n. 74). *See also*
    specific denominations
Renting. *See* Tenancy; Tenants
Republican ideology: among planters, 56;

among white artisans, 76; among slaves,
    76, 244; among freedpeople, 142,
    176–77, 182–84, 197, 213–14, 244, 301
    (n. 95). *See also* Free labor ideology
Republican party, 4, 10, 11, 166, 170,
    186–216 passim, 225, 231
Resistance party, 88
Revolutionary War, 111, 114; veterans of,
    and land lotteries, 17
Robinson, Ell, 129
Rogers, A. C., 124–25, 282 (n. 67)
Roman Catholic church, 79, 92, 275
    (n. 36)
Rome, Ga., 54
Rome, Italy, 53
Roundtree, Moses, 263 (n. 37)
Royals, John, 302
Rucker, E. B., 291 (n. 72)
Runaway slaves. *See* Fugitive slaves
Rushin, John, 33
Russia, 110, 186

Sarah (slave), 273 (n.91)
Savannah, Ga., 18, 74, 86, 104, 176, 178,
    181–82
Savannah River, 18
Savannah Tribune, 297 (n. 40), 308 (n. 18)
Scarborough, William S., 219–20, 229
Schofield Iron Works, 120
Secession, 110–11; growth in sentiment
    during 1850s, 87–89, 274 (nn. 14, 16)
Sharecropping, 225–26, 237
Share wages, 147, 148–49
Shelton, Cornelius, 196
Sherman, Lewis, 182–83, 300 (n. 86)
Sherman, William T., 9, 108, 128–33,
    142, 178, 223
Sibley, C. C., 289 (n. 44)
Singleton, G. W., 261 (n. 12)
Skilled laborers. *See* Artisans (freedpeo-
    ple); Artisans (white)
Slave code, 45–46, 101, 263 (n. 52), 268
    (n. 10)
Slaveholders, 21–23, 25–28, 35, 262

Wilkinson County, 203
Williams, Joseph, 196
Williams, W. D., 227
Wilmington, N.C., 1
Wilmot, David, 83, 87
Wilson, James H., 143–44, 288 (n. 40),
  290 (n. 51)
Womble, George, 129
Woodfolk, Silas, 139
Woodliff, Edward, 272 (n. 78), 308
  (n. 13)

Yeoman farmers: in black belt, 7, 14, 50,
  257 (nn. 17–18); and slaveholding
  planters, 7, 33, 50–51, 98, 101, 111;
  cotton cultivation, 19–20; subsistence
  agriculture with household production,
  19–20, 243; work with slaves, 25; grant

visiting privileges to slaves, 25–27; as
  slaveholders, 25–27, 62; and taxes, 48,
  52, 94, 98; in Houston County, 50; in
  Twiggs County, 50; in upper Piedmont, 83, 94; and secession, 110–11;
  and Confederate war effort, 111, 114;
  and postbellum planters, 136, 137–38,
  164, 184, 216, 222–24; favor debt relief,
  164; and freedpeople, 184, 189; homestead exemption, 189; and Republican
  party, 189, 194; oppose change in fence
  law, 224, 240; effects of game laws,
  226–27; Populist movement and, 240,
  247–48
YMCA, 229

Zettner, B. M., 227–30